# The Nature of Dreams

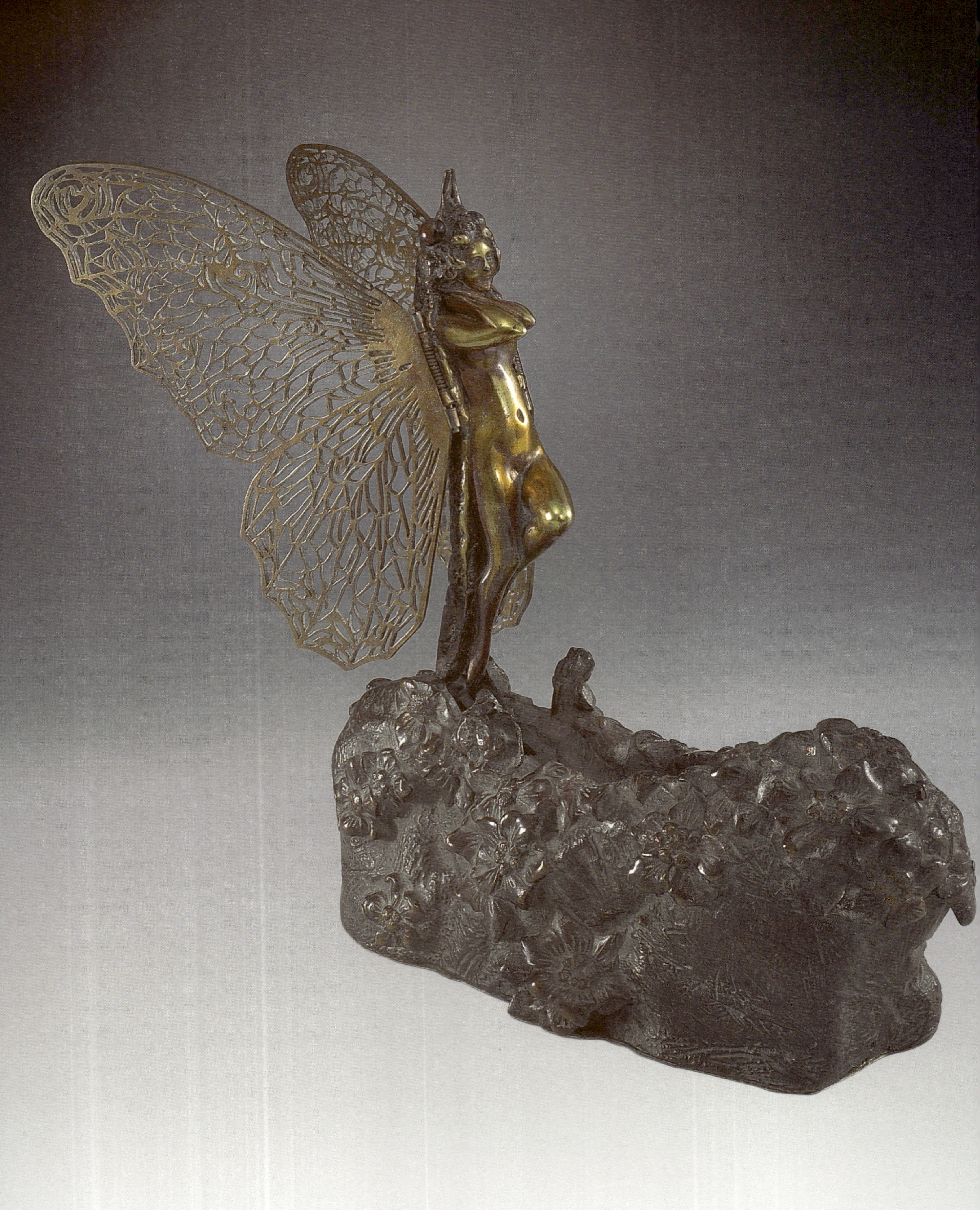

# The Nature of Dreams

## England and the formation of Art Nouveau

~Edited by Paul Greenhalgh~

This publication accompanies the exhibition:
*Art Nouveau: The Nature of Dreams*
Sainsbury Centre for Visual Arts

First published in Great Britain by
Sainsbury Centre for Visual Arts
Norwich Research Park
University of East Anglia
Norwich, NR4 7TJ
**sainsburycentre.ac.uk**



British Library Cataloguing-in-Publication Data.
A catalogue record is available from the British
Library.

ISBN 978-1-9161336-1-7

Exhibition Curator: Paul Greenhalgh
Book Design: Johnson Design
Copy Editor: Mandy Greenfield
Index: Brenda Stones
Project Curators: Tania Moore, Lisa Newby
Printed and bound in the UK by Swallowtail Print

First edition

10 9 8 7 6 5 4 3 2 1

# SAINSBURY CENTRE



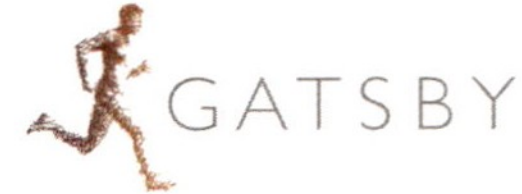
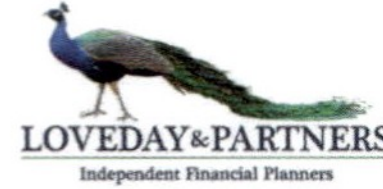
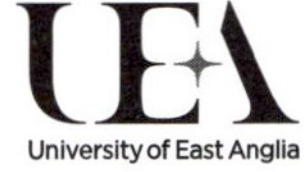

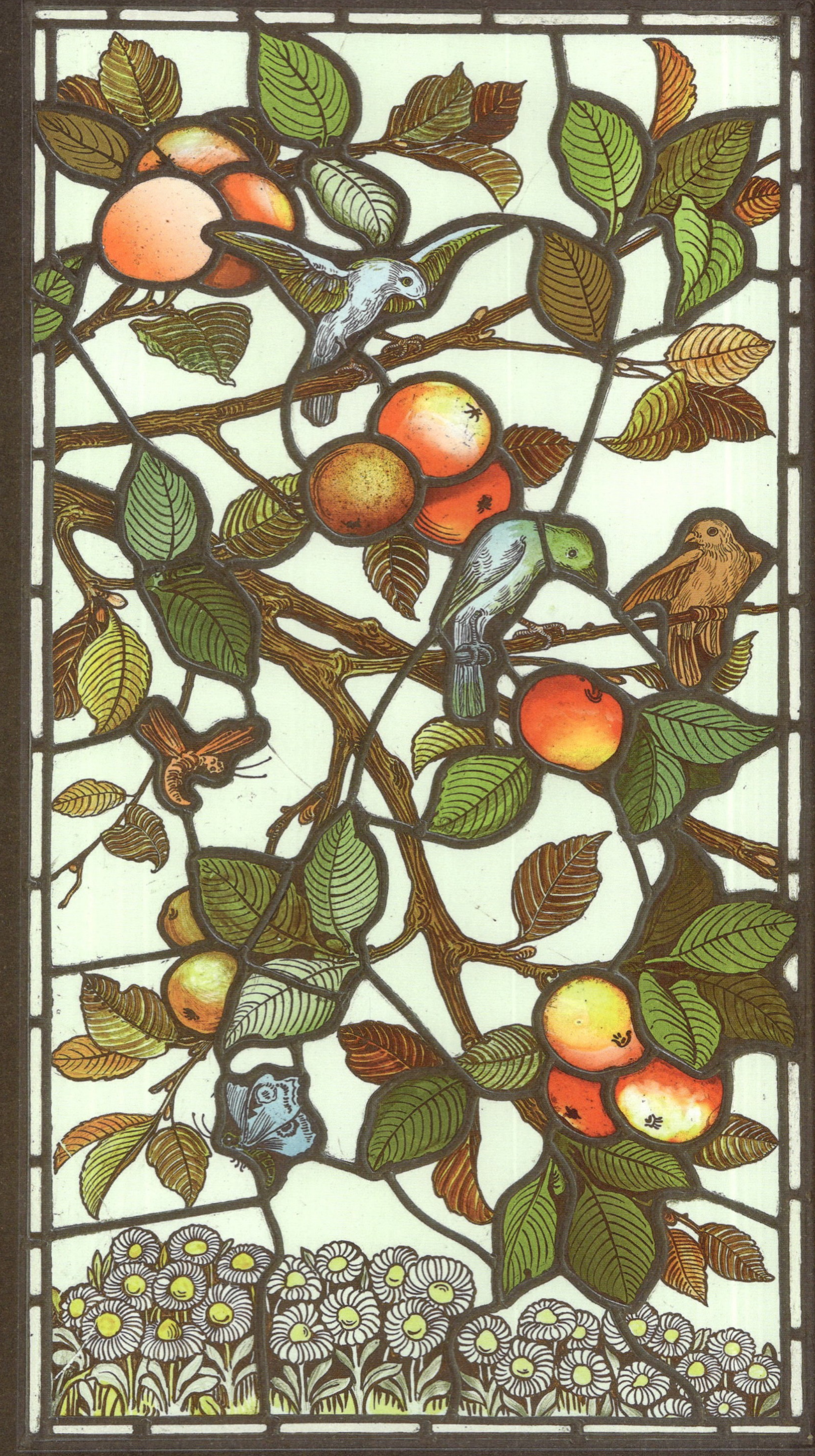

# ~Preface~

The Anderson Collection of Art Nouveau was donated to the Sainsbury Centre in 1978, the year it opened to the public. Since then there have been regular exhibitions featuring this nationally important collection. The gift was really a product of two things: the collecting skills of Sir Colin and Lady Anderson, who lovingly acquired these works over decades, and their friendship with Sir Robert and Lisa Sainsbury. As Robert and Lisa completed their own magnificent gift of the Centre to UEA, Sir Colin generously suggested that their holdings of Art Nouveau should become part of the Centre's holdings and so enter the public domain.

Over the last nine years the Anderson Collection has been used as the core component of a number of exhibitions about the fin de siècle and the Art Nouveau style. The view of the Centre's team is that Art Nouveau was the first stirring of the modern spirit in design, and these exhibitions have collectively explored that idea. The current exhibition, *Art Nouveau: The Nature of Dreams*, which this book accompanies, looks particularly at the role of English designers in the formation of the style. It is an interesting prospect, perhaps, as we finalise our arrangements with our European friends, that the Sainsbury Centre explores the cultural role of England in Europe.

Modern design has always been a research interest at the Sainsbury Centre, appropriate perhaps given our seminal building by Lord Norman Foster. After the Centre, the exhibition will tour to venues around the UK.

In conclusion, we are enormously grateful to all the lenders to this exhibition, and to the descendants of Sir Colin and Lady Anderson, the Carver family, who continue to support the Centre and to show us great friendship. I should also like to thank our Board and all of the Centre's patrons and supporters, and in particular the University of East Anglia, our owner and perpetual supporter. And, of course, the Centre remains a spectacular example of the generosity of the Sainsbury family. Our deepest thanks go to Lord David and the Gatsby Charitable Foundation, who make all these things possible.

~Dominic Christian~

Chair, Sainsbury Centre

*Opposite:* Unknown maker, panel, *c.*1915, stained glass. The Brian Clarke Collection of Stained Glass.

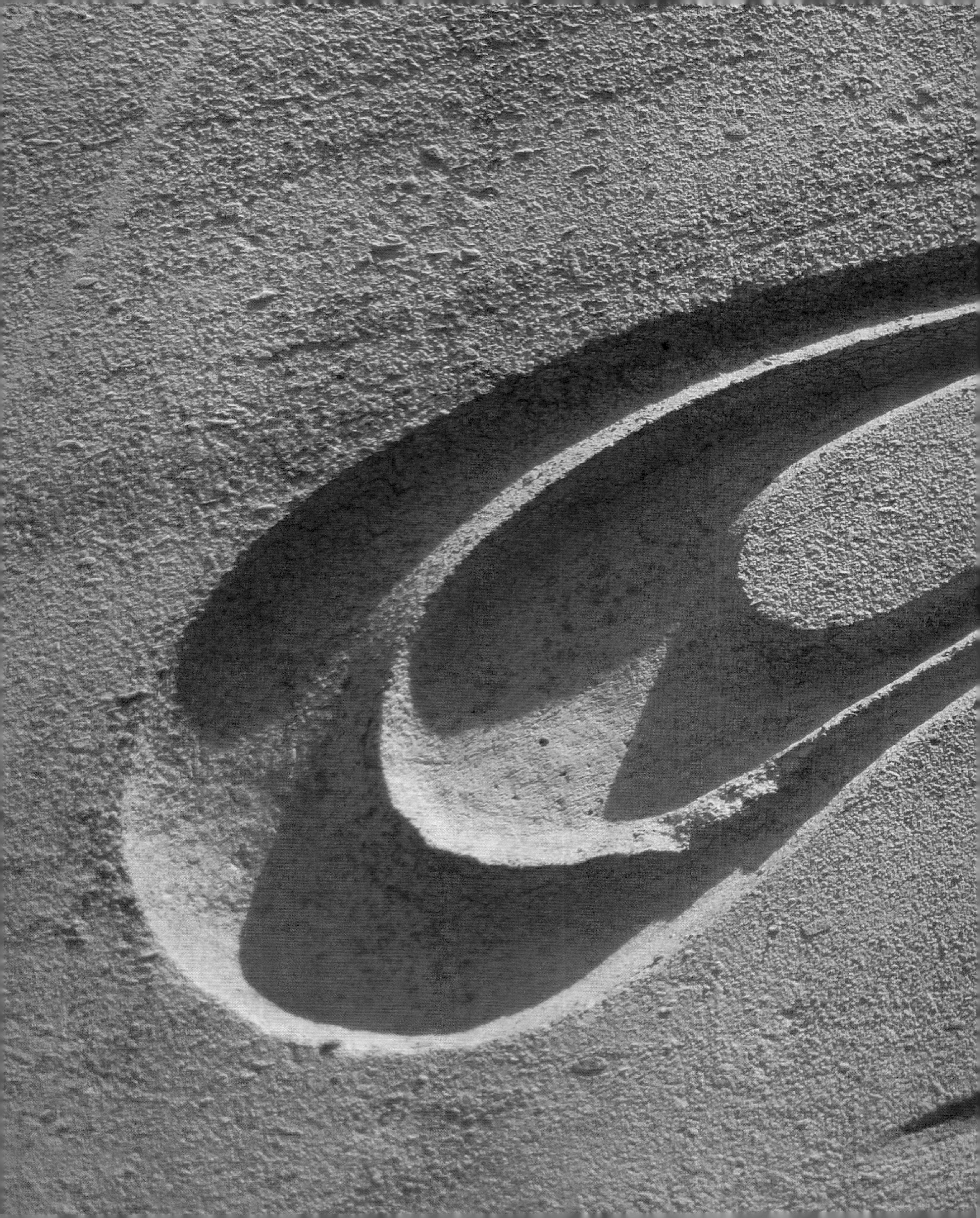

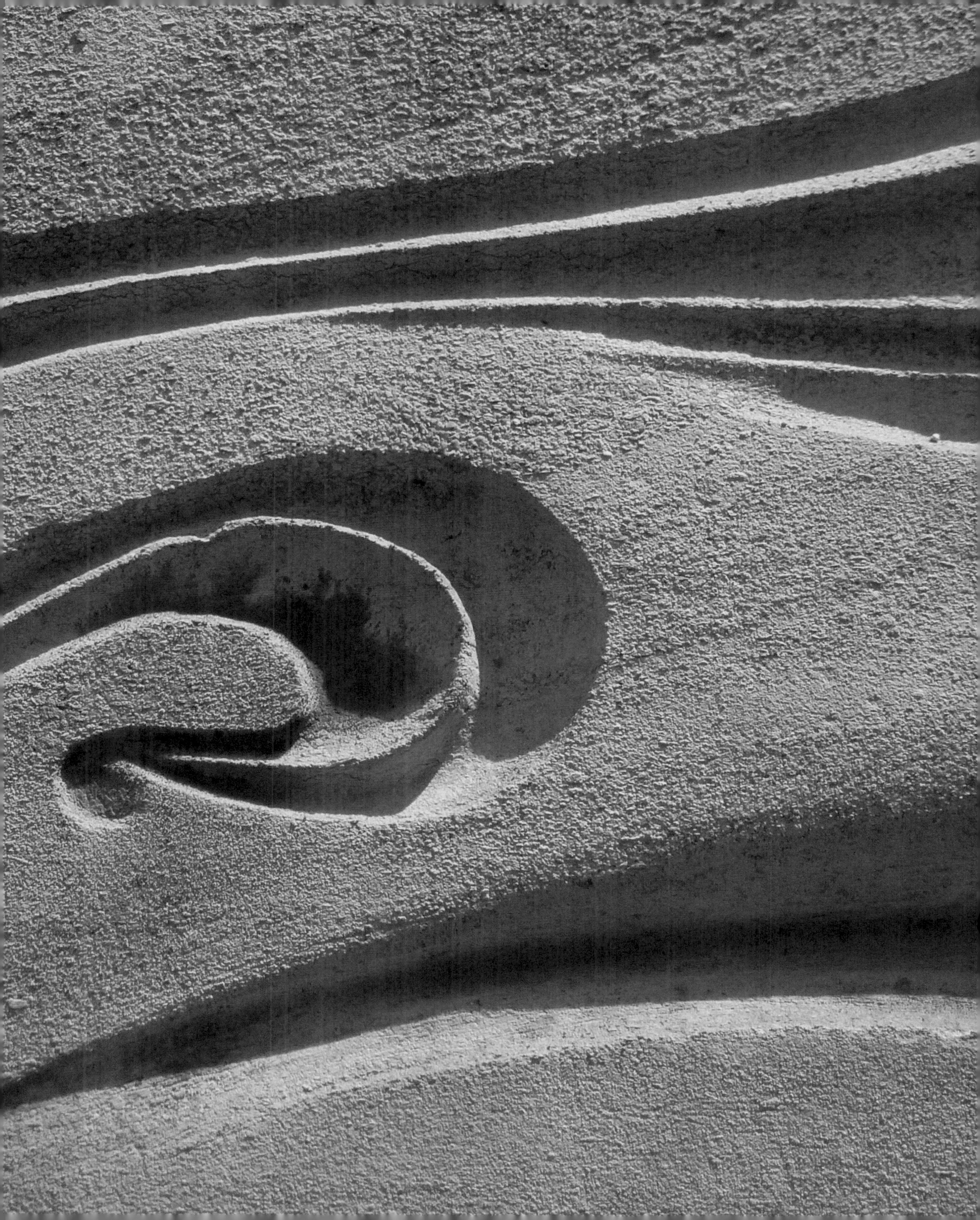

# ~The Nature of Dreams~

~Paul Greenhalgh~

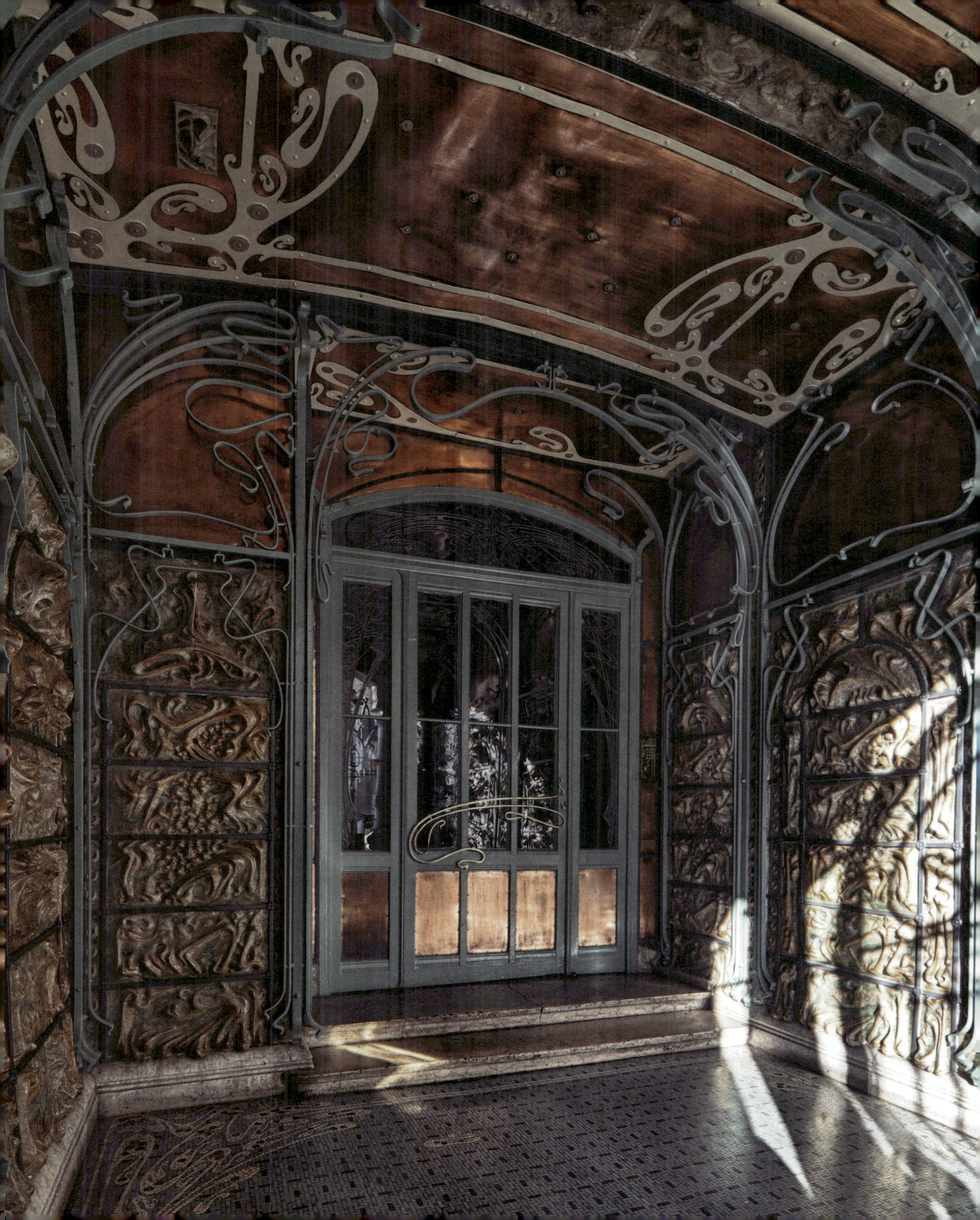

et's imagine Art Nouveau as a single landscape, as a rolling terrain made up of every type of art that the style touched. The first thing we notice, as we gaze at it from our observation platform, is that it had a strikingly variegated topography. It had regional differences and a good number of very distinct and occasionally unique features. It was a complicated terrain, full of peculiar, organic monuments. But at second glance, we can also see that it had considerable homogeneity. Despite its regional variance, the landscape flowed, with causally-connected hills, rivers, plains, and valleys that allow us to see it as a whole. We also detect underlying, ancient and slow-formed geological features, which shaped the whole landmass. It is on top of this bedrock that the variety of spectacular monuments nestles, these the product of recent disruptions and traumas. As important as the bedrock is, it is these younger events that gave Art Nouveau its ultimate character, the emotional intensity that arrests and impacts us. The style was ultimately a product of flux: it was constantly active and quick-moving: volcanic rather than glacial.

To use another natural image, the style crept across Europe like ivy up a wall. At first glance, it appears not to be moving, but then one realises that it has reached everywhere at surprising speed. In less than five years, in fact, the style twisted its way into dozens of urban centres. It gained a high level of legitimacy as it did this, as a style simultaneously representative of modern life and individual national cultures. It still plays that role in Barcelona, Brussels, Glasgow, Riga, and other cities, now repositioned as a dynamic and living heritage. When it originally established itself, it added economic value to luxury goods like jewellery, porcelain, and stained glass; it lent verve to less expensive things, like biscuit tins and tea caddies; it brought plumbing, fixtures and fittings into the cultural arena; it became an idiom of choice for

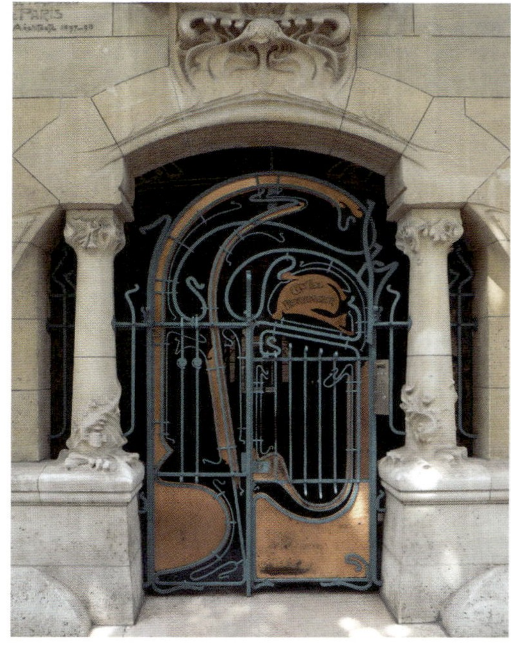

*Above:* Hector Guimard, Castel Béranger, Paris, 1895–1898.

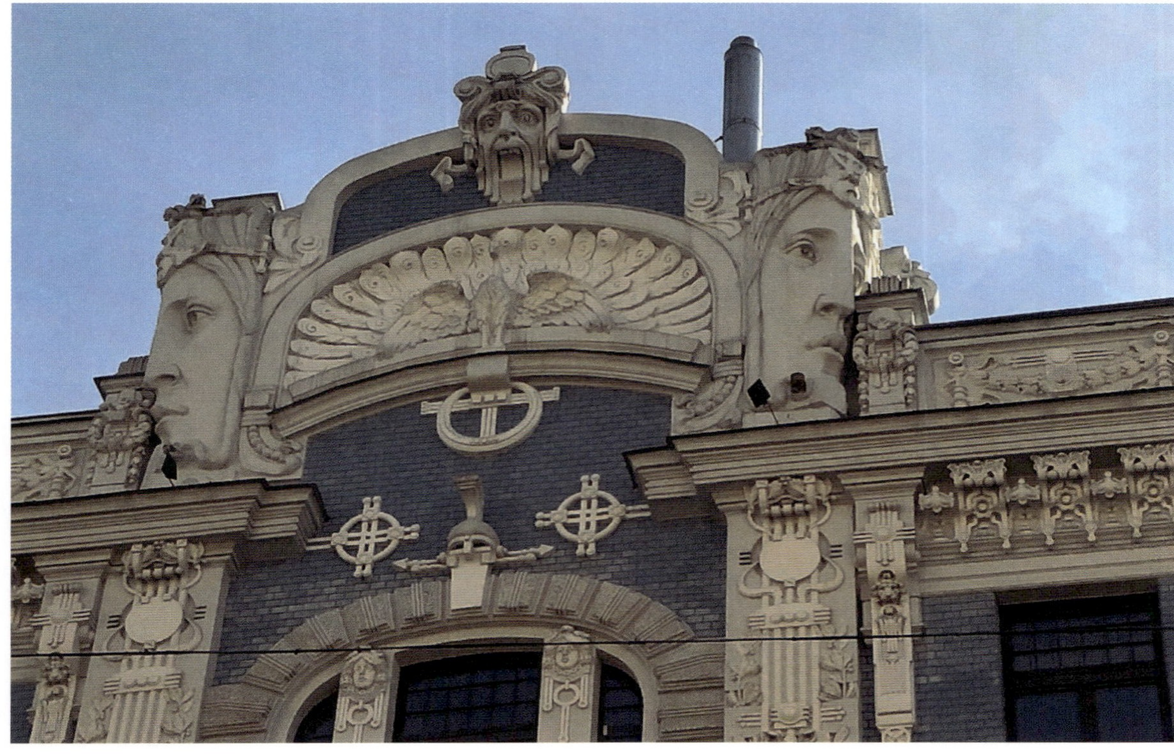

*Left:* Mikhail Eisenstein, Elizabetes ielá apartment block, Riga, Latvia, 1903.

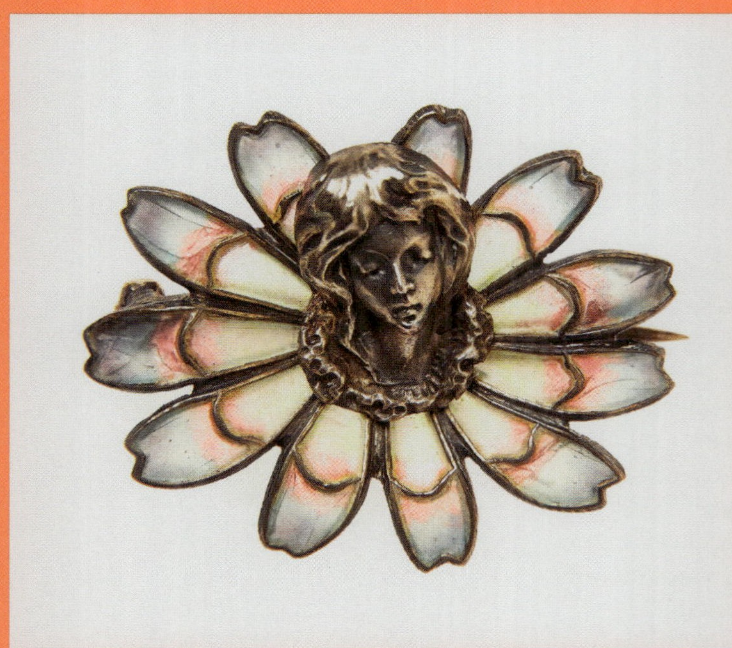

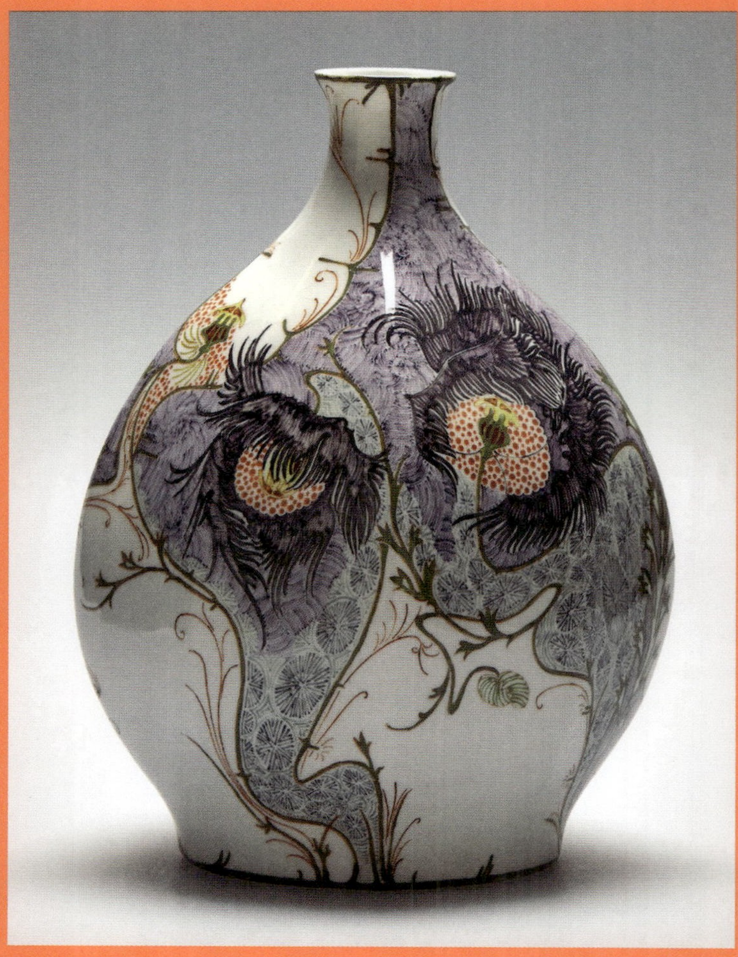

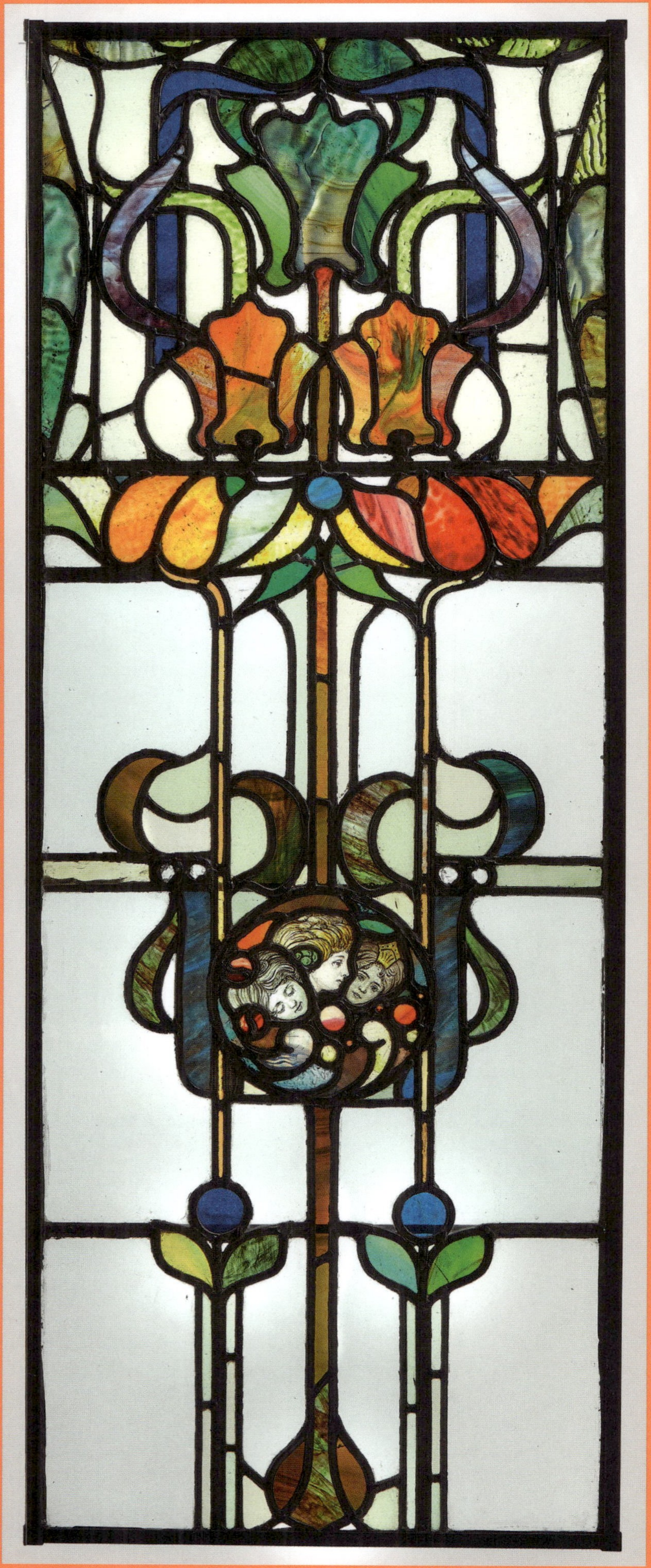

*Top:* Unknown maker, brooch, *c.*1900, silver and enamel. Sainsbury Centre.
*Above:* Juriaan Kok and W.P. Hartgring, vase, manufactured by Haagsche Plateelbakkerij Rozenburg, 1901, eggshell porcelain. Sainsbury Centre.
*Right:* T.W. Camm Studio, panel, 1888, stained glass. The Brian Clarke Collection of Stained Glass.

elite architects; and it was a positive signifier for political parties and religious sects, from the northernmost cultures to the southern shores of Europe. It was sensuous – and sensual – and it was popular.

How did this extraordinary and controversial style come about? Why did it happen in the way it did? Of course, there are many specific, local, and interconnected reasons why any style consolidates to become a public phenomenon. In the case of Art Nouveau, beyond the specifics of each city's movement, there were several large macro-developments during the last third of the 19th century that shaped the whole landscape. The title of this book and exhibition hint at these. 'Nature' and 'Dreams': these words identify both the physical world we live in and the inner life of the individual. The greatest of the Art Nouveau artists and designers were driven by the relationship of these two things, which were made into frenetic issues by the vicissitudes of the age.

The fin de siècle witnessed grand tensions that humanity had barely had to deal with before. The transformation of millions of lives through the rapid urbanisation of Europe brought people to see nature and the natural world differently, and to think differently about themselves. The fin de siècle period saw Brussels grow unprecedentedly, from 250,000 inhabitants to 800,000,[1] Barcelona also had 250,000 inhabitants in 1890, more than doubling this number by 1914, and Paris gained over a million souls between 1870 and 1910.[2] Such escalations were typical rather than exceptional across the Western world. Cities, and the issues affecting the mass-populations filling them, brought Art Nouveau into being. More than anything, it was a reaction to the transformation of the lived environment.

The leading Art Nouveau designers pondered constantly on the implications of the new urban context, and on the fate of individuality in this crowded morass. A constant mantra, repeated often by Siegfried Bing, one of the leaders of the style, was that the new generation shouldn't avoid the reality of the city, but rather, they needed to embrace the new conditions while resisting their worst aspects, in order to change the city for the better. This demanded a new art, one that recognised the situation they were in: the Art Nouveau generation were 'forced to subordinate the general character of our environment to all the conditions of modern life'.[3] Historical models, they believed, were of limited use.

The *New Art*. When we put it into English, the name of this extraordinary stylistic development acquires an unexpected directness for the English-speaking world. It gains a seriousness that signifies the aims and objectives of its proponents, and the vision they had for their work. It overtly implies modernity.

At the time some writers did use the English. But the majority of the Anglo-Saxon world used *Art Nouveau*, and after the decline of the style, invariably this has been the consistent nomenclature. In some ways, it's wholly logical: Art Nouveau is inconceivable in the absence of developments in Belgium and France, and many of the greatest masterpieces were made in those countries. For much of the 20th century, a number of noted historians limited it to being a Franco-Belgian phenomenon.[4]

But in England there was always something more complicated than the recognition of Gallic origins. A significant proportion of the cultural

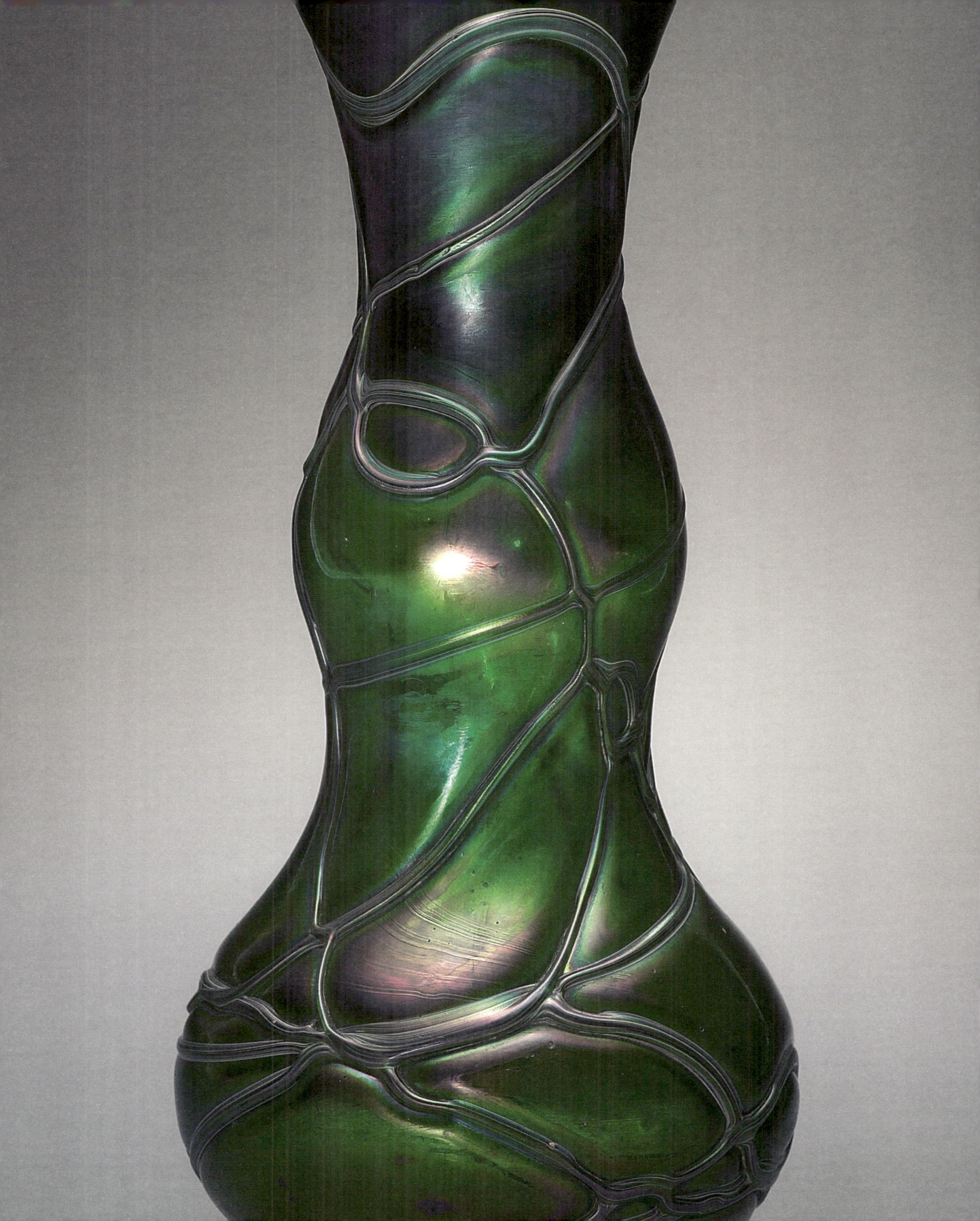

*Opposite:* Jan Toorop, poster for Delftsche Slaolie, 1896, colour lithograph. Private Collection.

intelligentsia, at the time and after, always *wanted* Art Nouveau to be foreign. They *wanted* to maintain a certain distance from it, and wished to deny it a place in the canon of art history. To many English ears, the French term gave comfort, that this thing wasn't part of the story of British art. It also suggested something pleasurable and light, and hence temporary and superficial.

To be fair, the English weren't the only ones to distance themselves from the style through the 20th century. There were notable exceptions, but in many countries, as the world crept towards 1914, it came to be understood as an adolescent aberration, and to be rejected even by some of its original creators. A number of the seminal Art Nouveau cities were demolishing their heritage even into the 1980s. The rejection mostly kicked-in after 1910, a number of prominent French writers seeing it as Austrian, English, German, or Japanese, but definitely not French. One exclaimed that 'I'd ignore all its faults if in future … it would achieve a French appearance.'[5] Another, while confidently telling us that 'Modern art is in its essence French', exonerated France from responsibility for Art Nouveau, believing it was 'hardly French' but had come 'from Austria under the name of "Secession"'.[6] Similar attitudes could be found in Belgium and Germany. Effectively, in the run-in to the Great War, Art Nouveau had shifted from being cosmopolitan and welcome, to being alien and scorned. Even so, the English had a very particular ambivalence right from the start.

This muse on names is intended to introduce three themes that run through this book and the exhibition it accompanies. The first is the role of England – as opposed to Britain – in the formation of European Art Nouveau. Scotland is a different story. The next chapter will focus on the English influence. Second, the book will concern itself with the notion of modern ornament, and the status of Art Nouveau as representative of modern life. It *was* the first style to declare, in manifesto style, its claims to modernity. Its supporters *did* embrace the notion of progress at a time when other utopians were busily rehabilitating the past. Yet after 1914, its claims to modernity were regularly denied, most vociferously by later Modernists.[7] Time has come to correct the historiography.

The third theme is understated but has a particular potency for our own times. The Art Nouveau style was self-consciously interdisciplinary. The idiom revealed itself capable of migrating from discipline to discipline. There was a powerful version of it in each visual art, to the extent that we can assert that a number of disciplines enjoyed a 'golden age'. The style is striking for the range of masterpieces in architecture, ceramic, furniture, graphic design, interior design, metalwork, print-making, textile, stained glass, and vessel glass. There was also an insistence among its supporters that the arts should relate closely to each other. The term *'gesamtkunstwerk'*, appropriated from the Wagnerian world of opera, became part of the vocabulary of architecture and design. It implied the orchestration of the various disciplines to create a 'total work of art'.

An interesting aspect of the erosion of the barriers between the disciplines was the relationship of painting, and to a lesser extent sculpture, to architecture and design. The migration of painters, and the painterly outlook, into the decorative arts is a particularly interesting feature of fin de siècle practice. A number of the key designers began as painters, including Jan Toorop, Henry Van de Velde, Johan Thorn Prikker, and Félix Bracquemond. Prominent painters were seriously active in other disciplines,

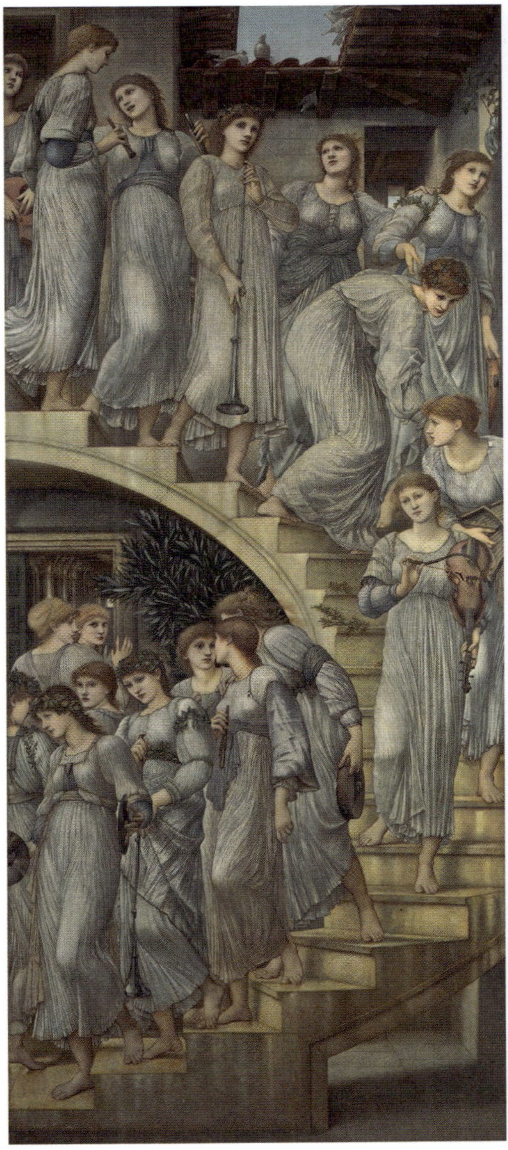

*Below:* Edward Burne-Jones, *The Golden Stairs*, 1880, oil on canvas. Tate, bequeathed by Lord Battersea 1924.

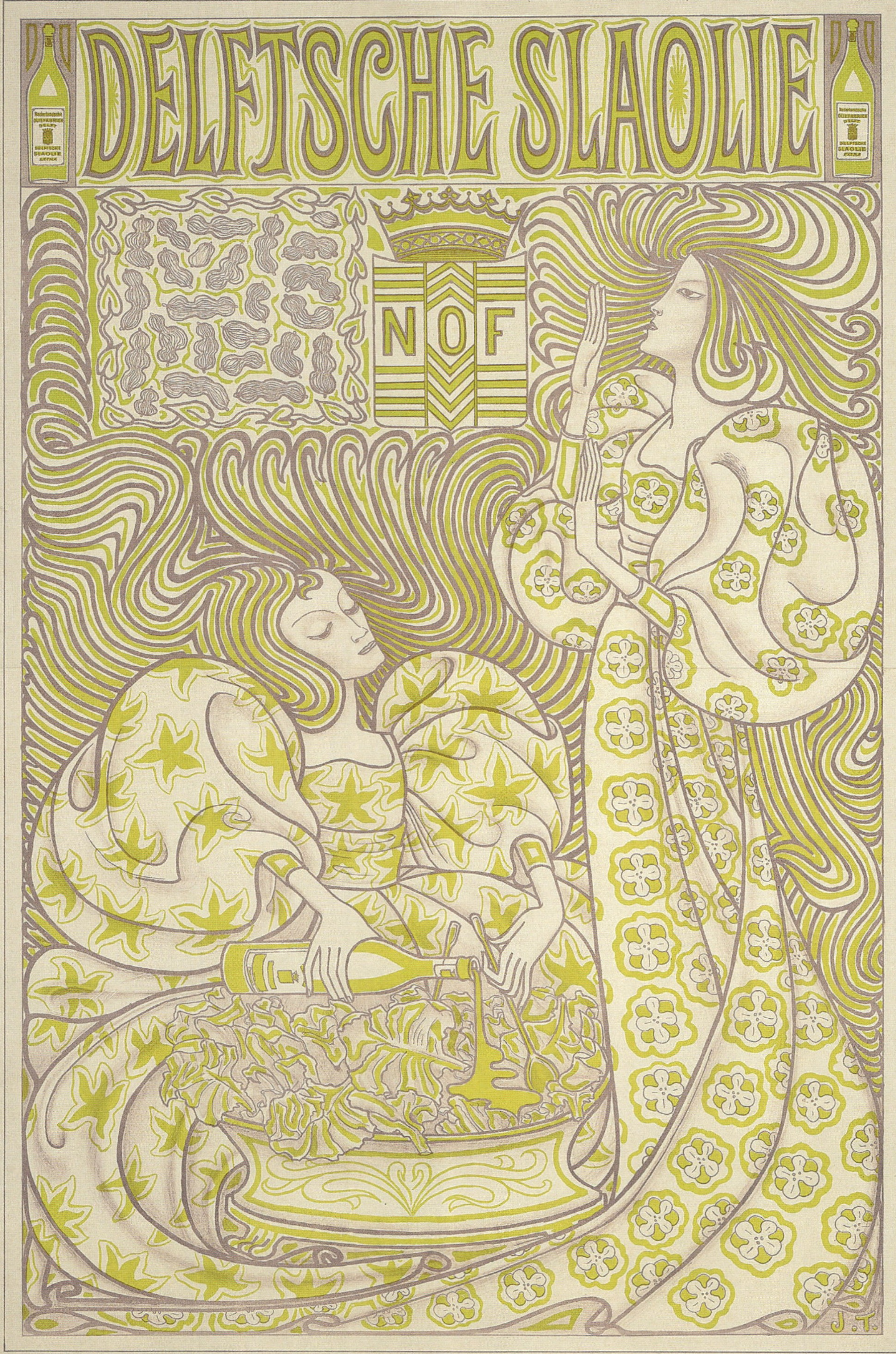

DELFTSCHE SLAOLIE
NOF
S. LANKHOUT & Cº
J.T.

led by luminaries like Paul Gauguin, Eduard Vuillard, Pierre Bonnard, Karl Larsson, and Jens Ferdinand Willumsen. In England, interdisciplinary approaches to practice effectively became a political creed under the leadership of William Morris, and Edward Coley Burne-Jones, the great Pre-Raphaelite painter, was intensely involved in stained glass, tapestry, and other disciplines. For many artists, the move out of painting was connected to a desire to connect with a larger audience, and to carry artistic practice into everyday life. It is hard to imagine the Art Nouveau sensibility in the absence of this interdisciplinary exchange.

Architecture is interesting in this regard. In some cities, it clearly drove the agenda, and was at the heart of the new style. This is very much the case with Barcelona, Brussels, and Riga, for example, where all the arts followed in the wake of a remarkable generation of architects. Elsewhere, however, we can see that it was the decorative and graphic arts that fronted-up and sustained local movements. Certainly this was largely the case with London and Paris, accepting the masterpieces of Hector Guimard. It was an idiom borne of dynamic draughtsmanship, of swirling, liberated line, and this manifested itself most dramatically in graphic design and metalwork. In short, Art Nouveau in most places – perhaps excepting Barcelona – was aggressively linear.

There is a certain irony in the fact that nature was the core source behind a style dedicated to urban renewal. Between 1840 and 1910, in fact, nature was continually the most important subject matter across all of the visual arts: Art Nouveau was one of the many beneficiaries of this activity. However, the style wasn't simply part of the ongoing naturalist continuum, but rather, it arrived as a result of the repositioning of nature within Western culture.

Through the period as a whole, France led the way. The development of Realism, under the leadership of Gustave Courbet, led to successive waves of naturalist art, culminating spectacularly in the 1870s with Impressionism. Painting *en plein air* – in the open air, in front of nature – put a primacy on directly experiencing the world, and placed un-idealised nature at the heart

*Left:* Hector Guimard, metalwork for the Paris Metro, 1900.
*Below:* Antoni Gaudí, metalwork fence, Güell Park, Barcelona, c.1903.

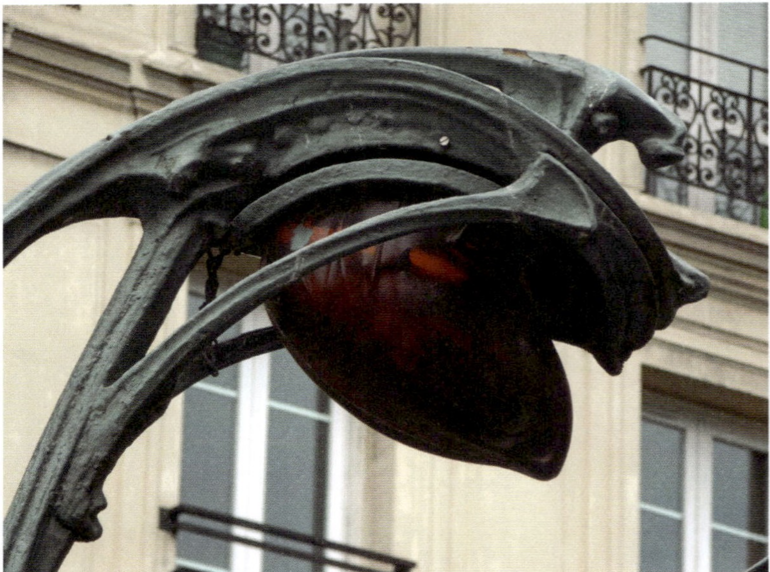

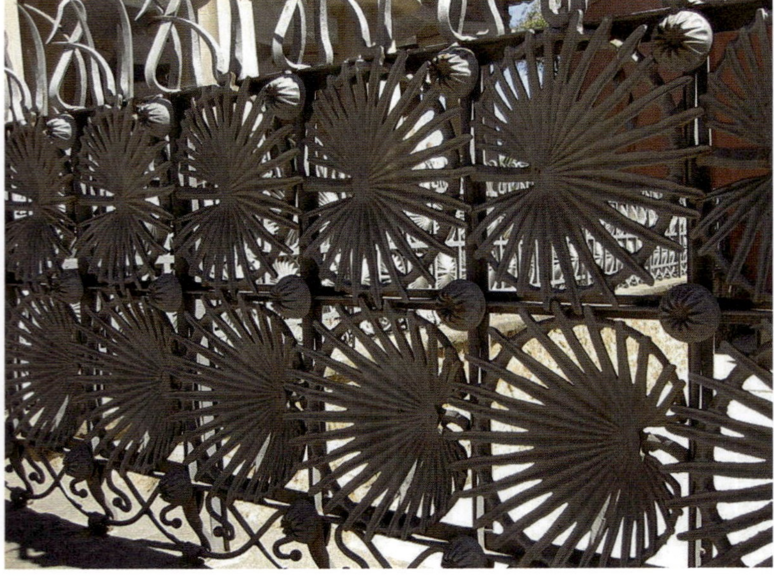

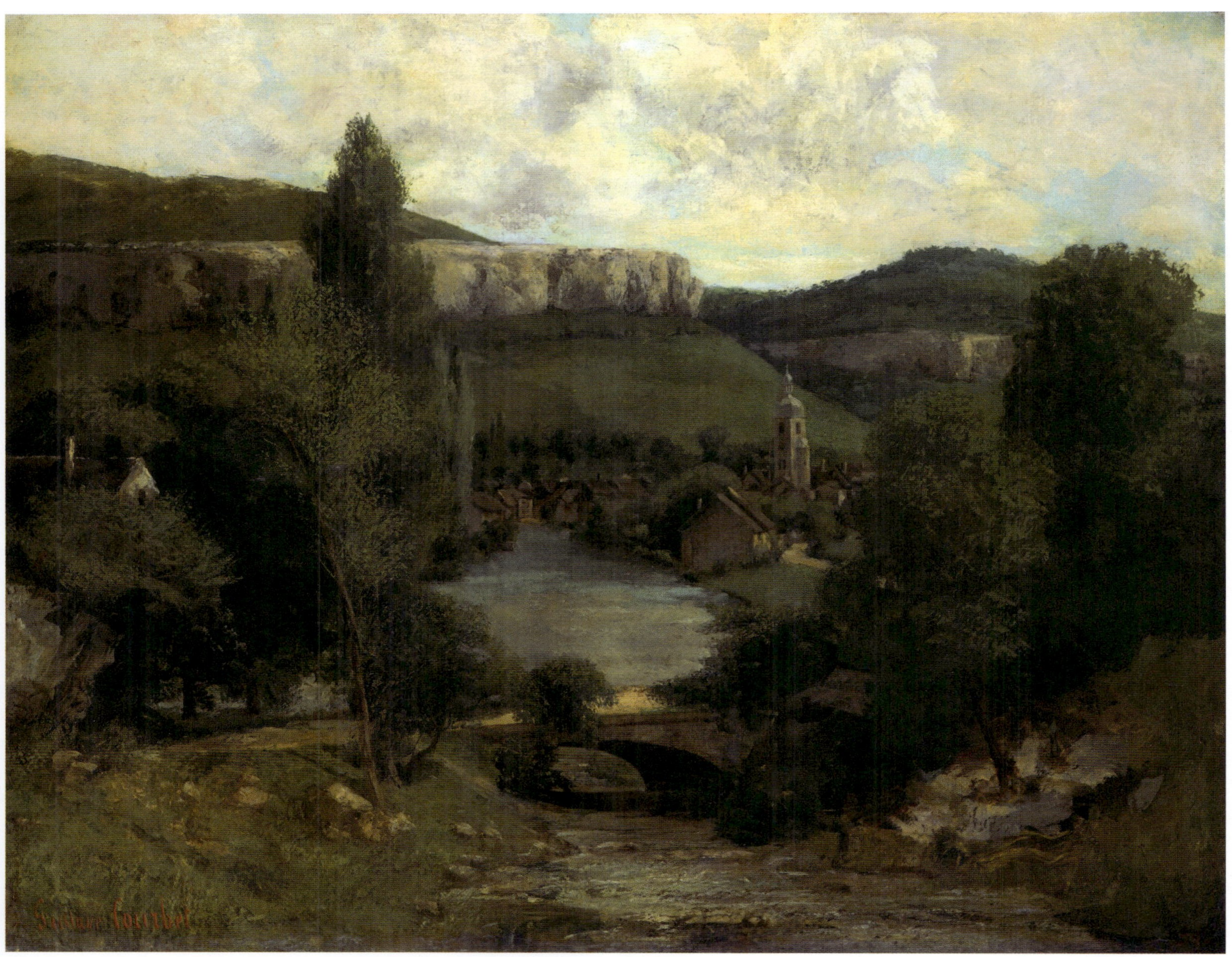

*Above:* Gustave Courbet, *View of Ornans*, *c.*1985, oil on canvas. The Metropolitan Museum of Art, bequest of Alice Tully.

of practice. The vision of nature given to us by Courbet, Jean-François Millet and others was often of a harsh reality, of the people's struggle against nature. As city life became more and more normalised for the majority, the idea of nature softened, and was increasingly understood to be a more benign, beautiful 'other', rather than the thing one grew up in and fought against to make a living. By the 1890s Impressionism was distinctly more contemplative and hedonist in spirit.

There is no doubt that the Impressionist palette and lyrical brush work had a powerful effect on many artists within the Art Nouveau camp. Monet's pinks and blues can be found everywhere. But during the last third of the century, the notion of 'the real' was increasingly rejected by various groups of artists who were interested in constructing their own vision of the world. Post-Impressionism is the retrospective name we use to collectivise those artists who didn't want to start with observation. Some, such as Georges Seurat and the Pointillist group, looked to complicate the realist agenda by subjecting it to optical scientific methods.[8] Alternatively, Paul Cézanne was interested not in the direct appearance of things but in their underlying, structural relationships. Van Gogh wanted to use colour and texture to generate empathy and expression.

Most important in this context, Paul Gauguin, Odilon Redon, and the Nabis wanted to develop a modern symbolism that began with nature, but

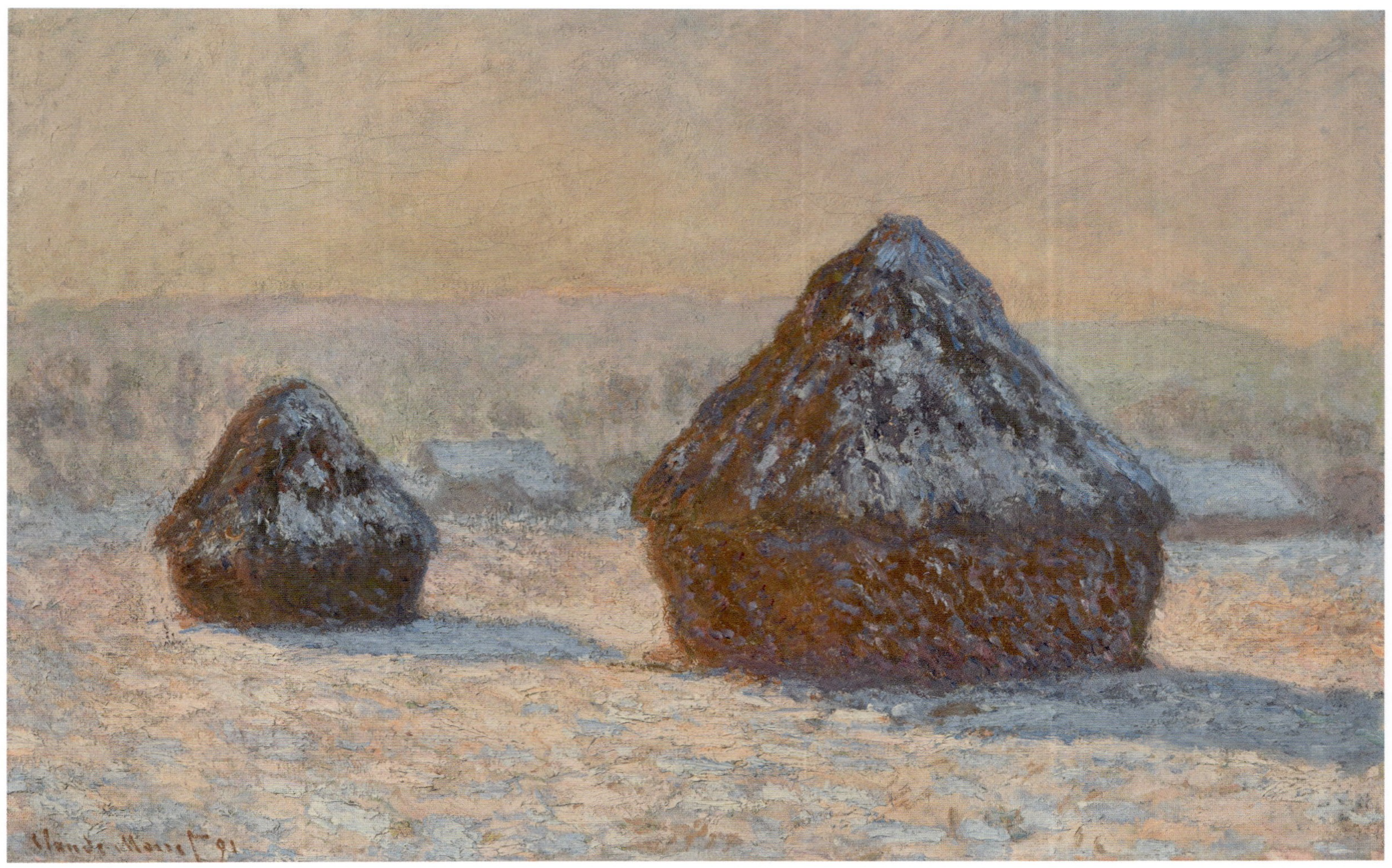

*Above:* Claude Monet, *Wheatstacks, Snow Effect, Morning*, 1891, oil on canvas. The J. Paul Getty Museum.

moved beyond it. For Gauguin, there was no point in attempting to copy nature direct: 'Will you ever have as much light as nature has, as much heat as the sun?'[9] At the same time, he believed, paint could do things that nature couldn't: 'A colour by itself has a raw quality that does not exist in nature.'[10] So nature had to be modified to take account both of the disinterested aesthetic power of colours and forms, and the subjectivity of the artist. In this sense, he understood art, logically enough, to be synthetic, to be an *artifice*. He went as far as naming this tendency *Synthétisme*.[11] The term 'abstraction' also emerged in the period, initially indicating the reduction of natural form to fundamental shapes and colours. Gauguin felt the need to help his fellow artists on the topic:

> Some advice: do not paint too much after nature. Art is an abstraction; derive this abstraction from nature while dreaming before it, and think more of the creation which will result than of nature. Creating like our Divine Master is the only way of rising toward God.[12]

In many respects he and Monet understood painting in the same way, as a physical – retinal – phenomenon that addresses the senses. They both sought to stimulate the emotions through the eye. However, they began from opposite poles: Monet in the *external* and objective, and Gauguin in the *internal* and subjective worlds. It was at this fascinating aesthetic crossroads that Art Nouveau came into being. It was the energetic – and ultimately unstable – progeny of Naturalism and Symbolism. It was the spawn of decades of experimentation for and against nature, which the new interdisciplinary outlook had placed in the middle of architecture and design.

The use of nature was intensified by two additional factors: the influx of exotic plants from all over the world, as a consequence largely of the British

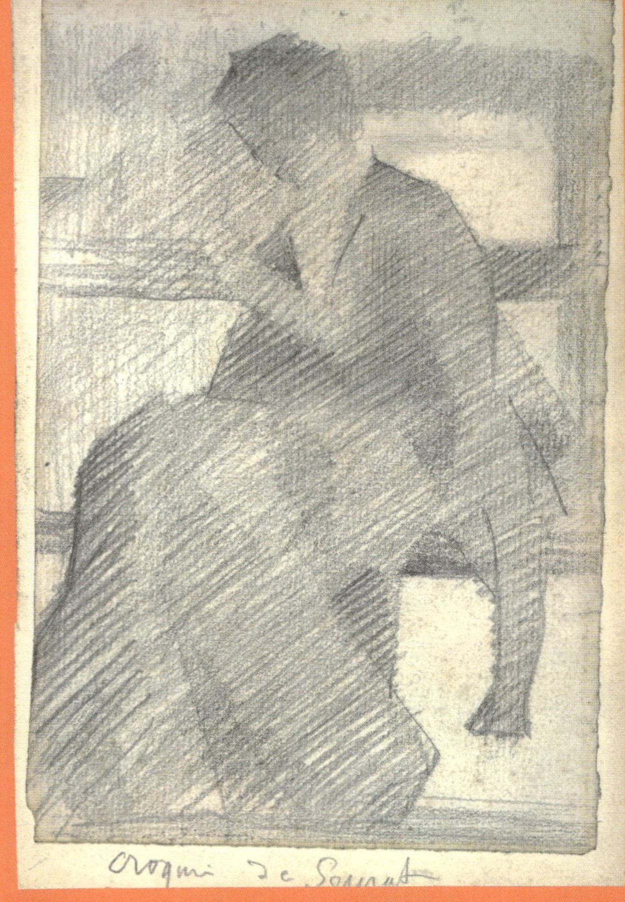

*Right:* George Seurat, *Repairing Her Cloak (Woman on a Bench)*, 1880–1881, graphite on paper. Sainsbury Centre.

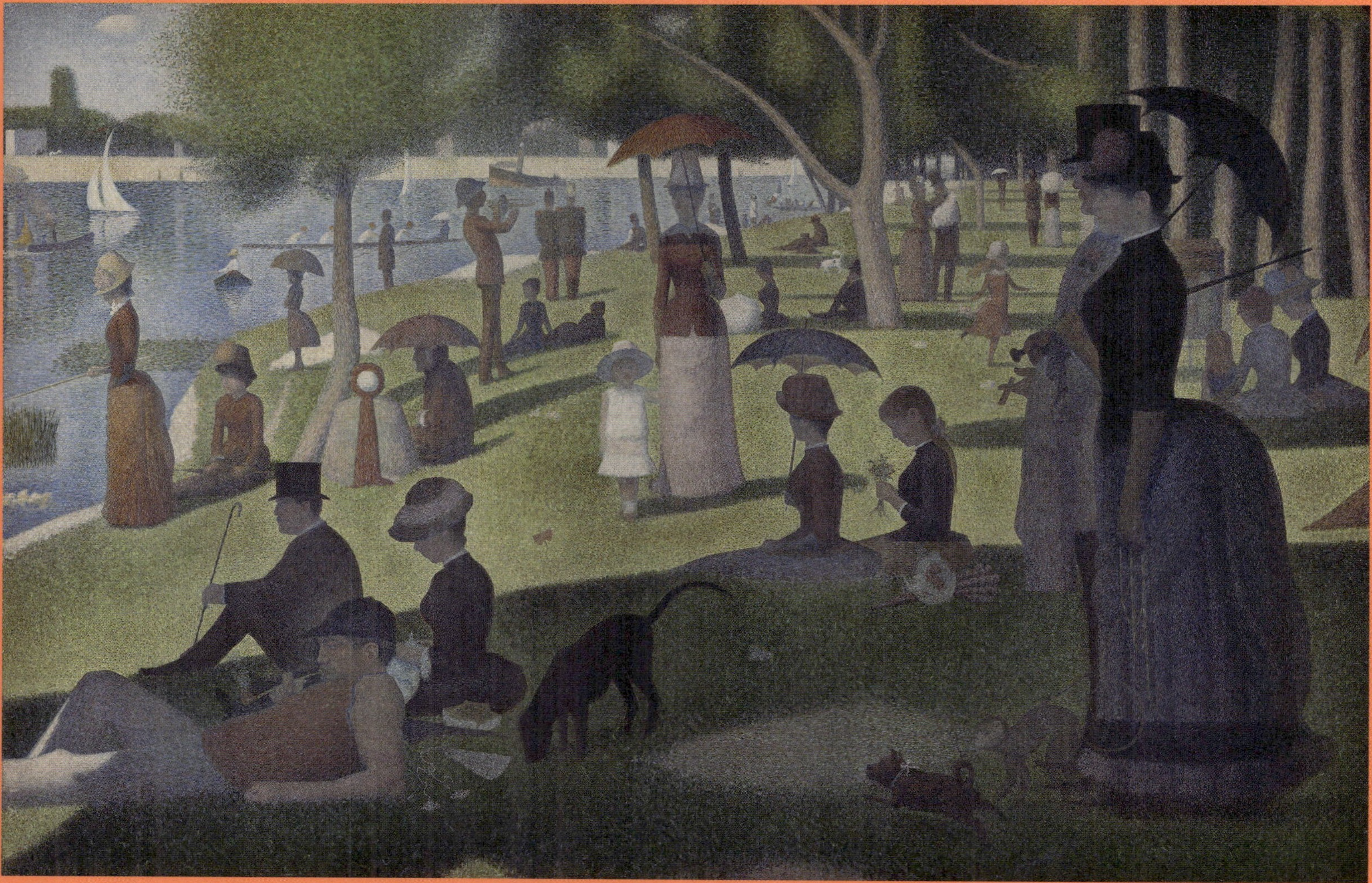

*Below:* Georges Seurat, *A Sunday on La Grande Jatte – 1884,* 1884–1886, oil on canvas. Art Institute of Chicago, Helen Birch Bartlett Memorial Collection.

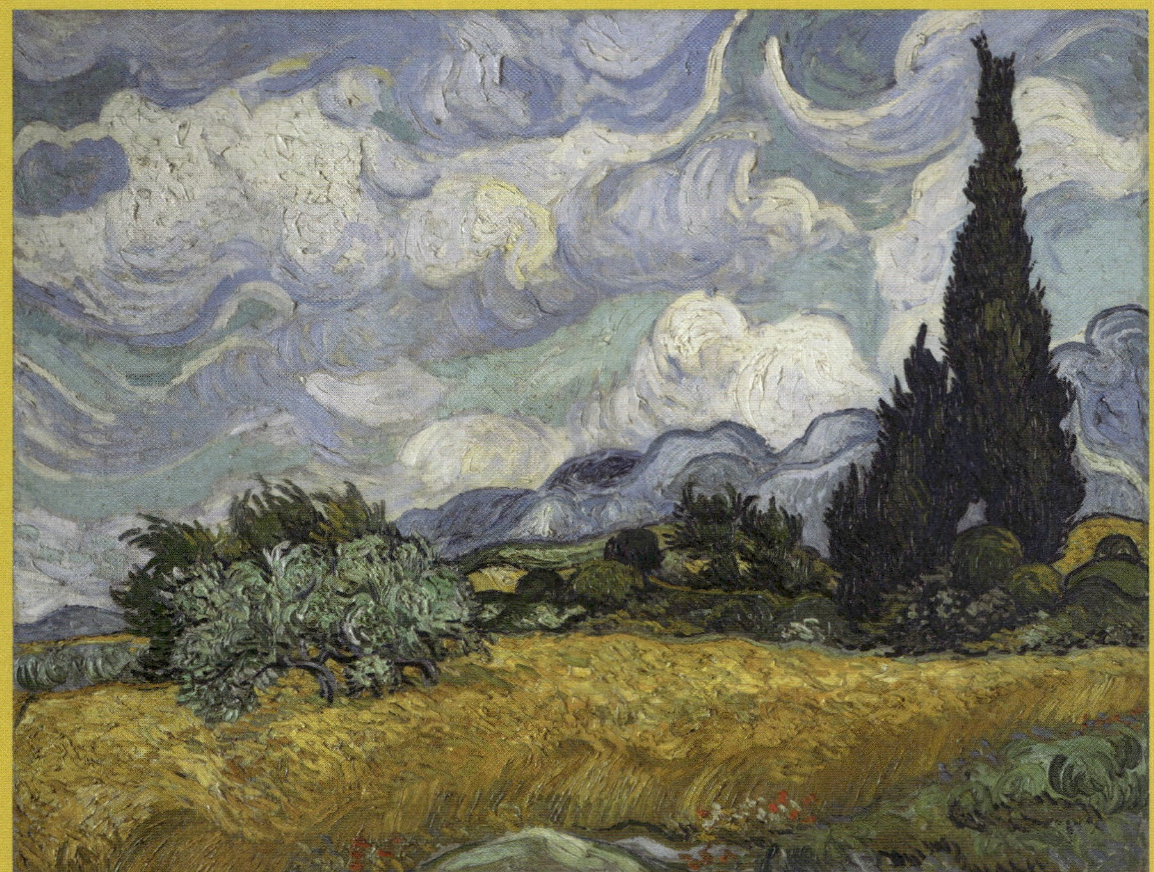

Left: Vincent van Gogh, *Wheat Field with Cypresses*, 1889, oil on canvas. The Metropolitan Museum of Art, The Annenberg Foundation Gift, 1993.
*Below:* Paul Gauguin, *Vision of the Sermon (Jacob Wrestling with the Angel)*, 1888, oil on canvas. National Galleries of Scotland.

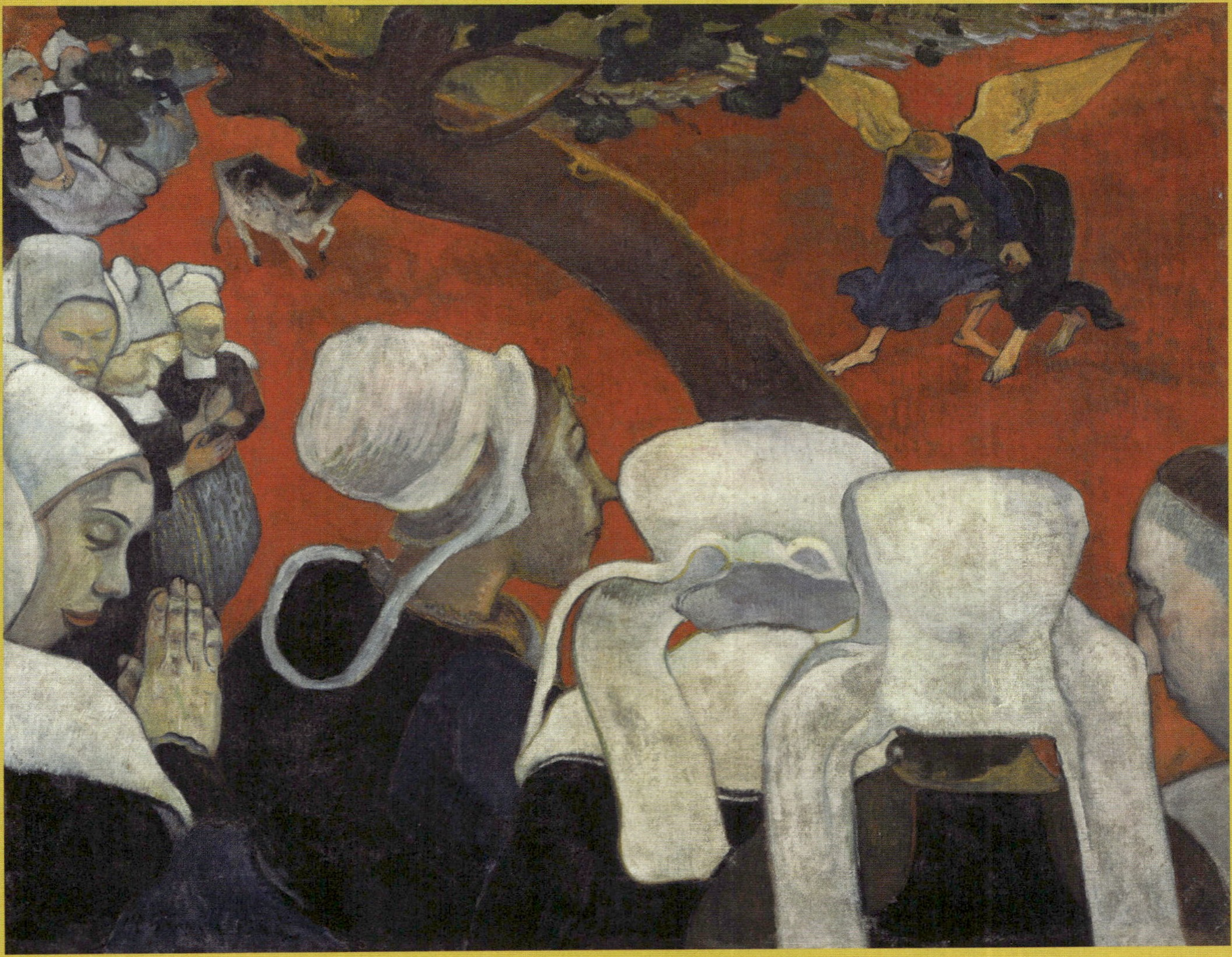

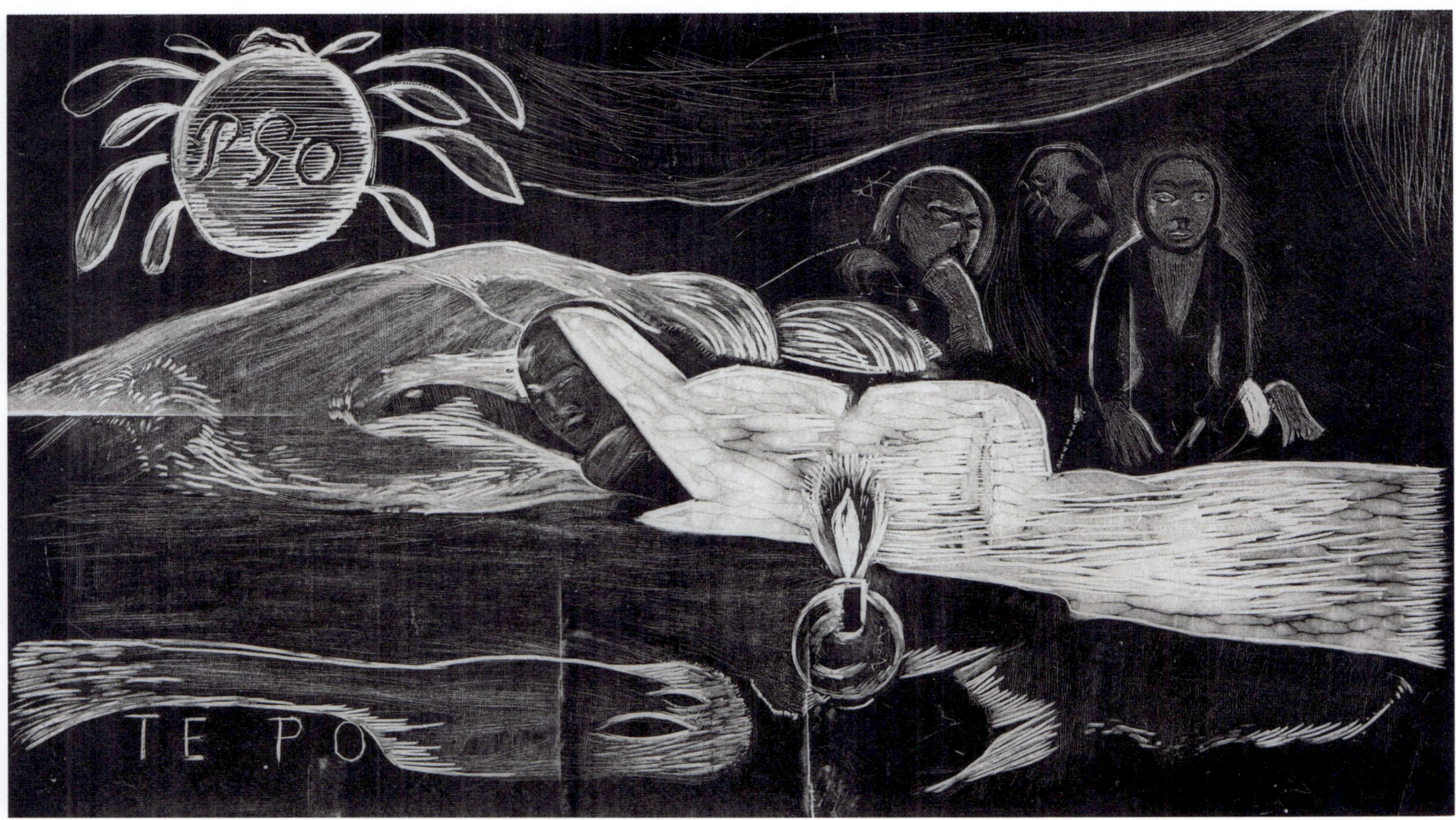

*Above:* Paul Gauguin, *Te Po (Eternal Night)* from *Noa Noa*, 1893–1894, woodcut on paper. Sainsbury Centre.

and French empires, and the new science of microscopy, which exposed the fundamental structure of natural forms. The move beyond native flora and fauna, and the embracing of cellular life, gave the style a cosmopolitan, universal demeanour.[13]

A vital aspect of the use of natural form, that essentially made the style possible, will be discussed in the next chapter. This is the innovative work of English pattern designers in the decades running up to the formation of Art Nouveau. In many respects, Art Nouveau can be understood as the coming-together of English style with European Post-Impressionist experimentation.

So there was another irony here. As with much Post-Impressionist practice, Art Nouveau, a style professing a logic in nature, *wasn't* actually natural in any meaningful sense. It was an artificial extrapolation from nature. Nature was the source, not the final aim. The organic, cellular, tensile, curving lines and forms and informal geometry that are the hallmark of the style are an equivalence to nature, and a celebration of artifice, designed to signify the complexity of the world the designers found themselves in. The style was a culmination of the decades-long dialogue about the meaning of the natural world, in the new urban context.

The basic Art Nouveau story has been told often, and it isn't an aim to repeat it here. Rather, the hope is to add dimensions to the established narratives, to show in some detail how exactly this explosion of creativity came about, and what it meant to participants in a small selection of countries. The focus will be on Belgium, England, France, and Spain. Contributing scholars Françoise Aubry, Barbara Bessac, and Lluís Bosch have the added, enviable advantage of having spent their lives and careers physically in the middle of the cities they focus on. Collectively, they will look at less-often discussed determinants that shaped the style, including theatre, literature, city planning, and political discourse. The authors also deal, in their various ways, with what we might term the emotional and intellectual disposition of the style. Art Nouveau has provided us with some of the most empathetically intense buildings, furnishings, accessories, and ornamentation in the history of art. This didn't happen by accident, it was an aim, and it raises fascinating issues about the motivations of the designers.

There is a final, important point that should be made in this Introduction. Recent research has demonstrated that Art Nouveau was a far more widespread phenomenon than is implied in the cities selected here. In fact, there was a version of it in over twenty countries, the last great flourishing being across middle and eastern Europe. Ljubljana, Riga, and St Petersburg, for example, have spectacular fin de siècle heritages, which only a handful of cities further west can begin to rival. The full reintegration of all these centres into the Art Nouveau narrative is under way, and a number of organisations are dedicated to this task.[14] There is still much empirical work to be done. Hopefully the reader will forgive the limitations of the current volume and exhibition, in the knowledge that we are aware of the issue, and are committed to supporting the new scholarship that is emerging. We all look forward to this extraordinary field of study expanding to reflect the complete breadth of European fin de siècle culture.

§

*Below:* Friedrich Sigmund, Galerija Emporium, Ljubljana, 1903.

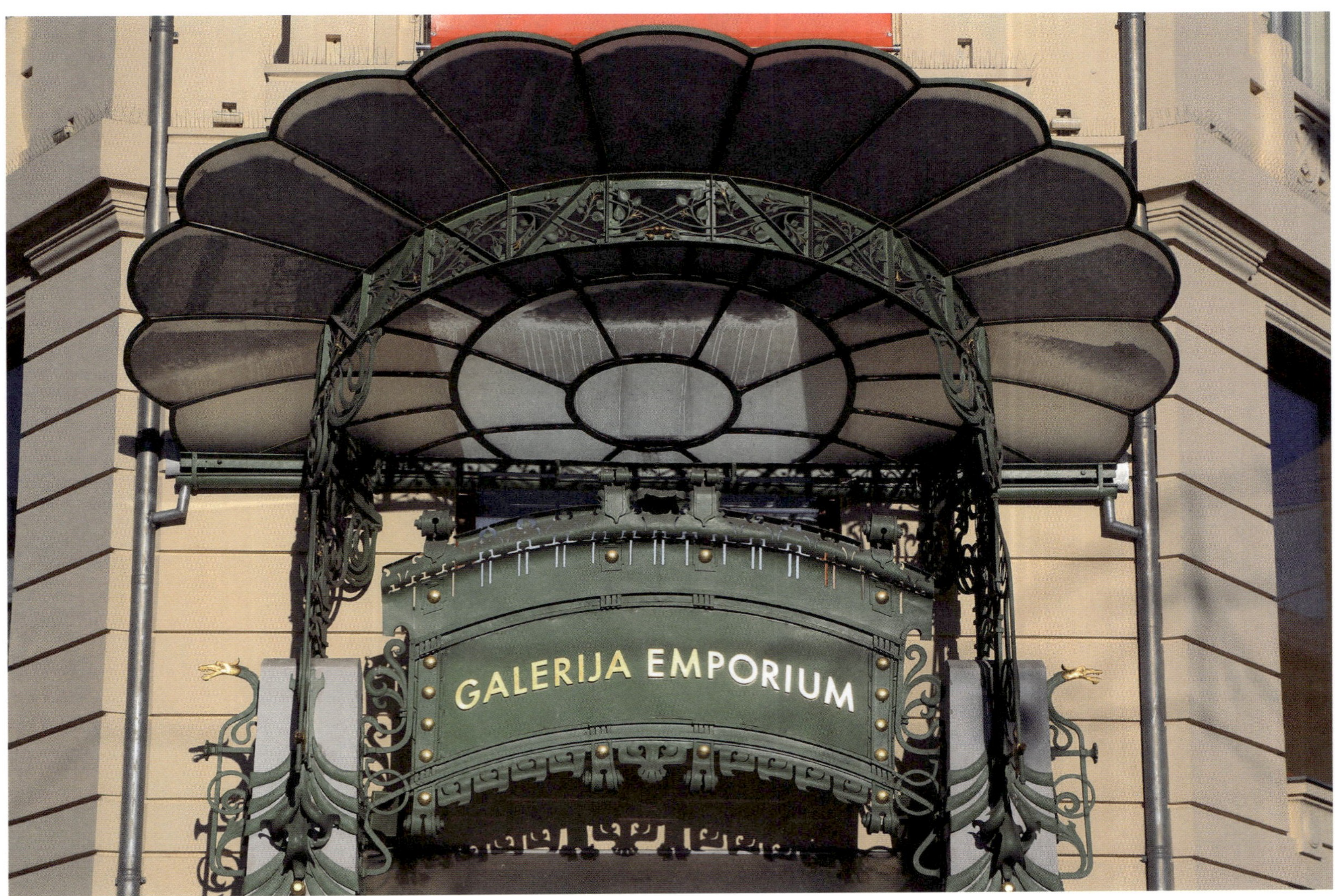

*Below:* François-Rupert Carabin,
container (woman with pepper),
*c.*1897, ceramic. Private Collection.

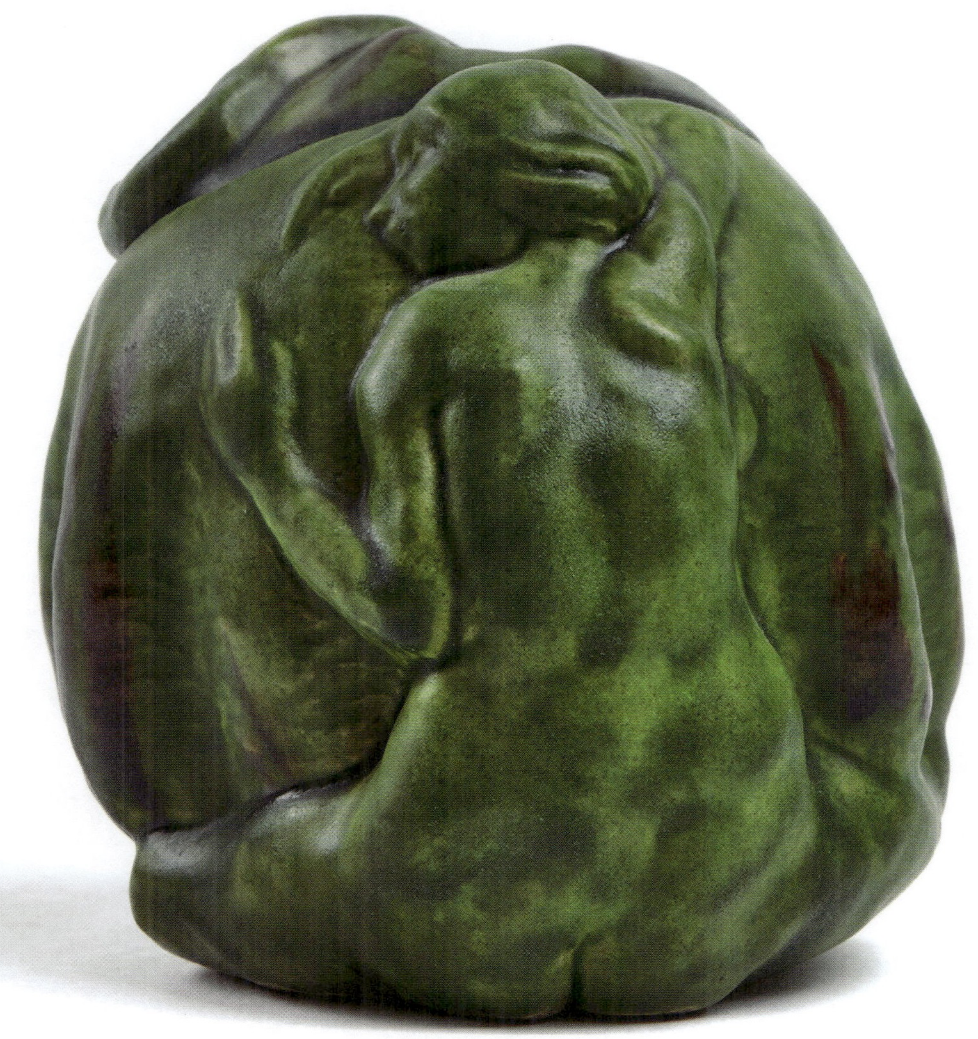

## ENDNOTES

1   See Maurice Culot, 'Belgium: red steel and blue aesthetic', in Frank Russell, *Art Nouveau Architecture* (London: Academy, 1983), pp.79–102.

2   See Demographia: 1.6 million in 1861, to 2.8 million in 1911.

3   Siegfried Bing, *The Craftsman*, October 1903, p.3.

4   See, for example, Yvonne Brunhammer, *Art Nouveau: Belgium and France*, catalogue of the exhibition of that title, Institute of the Arts, Rice University (Houston: Rice University, 1976).

5   Louis de Fourcauld, 'Le Bois', in *L'Art à l'Exposition Universelle de 1900* (Paris: 1900).

6   Emile Bayard, *Le Style Moderne* (Paris: 1919).

7   In a considerable part of the art-historical literature, where the style is depicted as a remnant of 19th-century historicism, as a 'bourgeois' response to the world, or as a short-term fad. The most vituperative criticism often came from the left, notably Le Corbusier, in *The Decorative Art of Today* (Paris: 1925), and Walter Benjamin. See Lieven de Cauter, 'The birth of pleinairism from the spirit of the interior: Walter Benjamin on Art Nouveau', in Françoise Aubry, Jos Vandenbreeden and Reiner Lautwein, *Horta: Art Nouveau to Modernism* (Ghent: Ludion Press, 1996), pp.13–26.

8   See, for example Gustave Kahn, 'Seurat', 1891, in Henri Dorra, *Symbolist Art Theories, a critical anthology* (Berkeley: University of California Press, 1994), pp.172–5.

9   Paul Gauguin, 'Notes Synthétiques', 1884–5, in Daniel Guérin (ed.), *Paul Gauguin: writings of a savage* (New York: De Capo, 1978), pp.8–11.

10  Ibid.

11  Ibid.

12  Paul Gauguin, Letter to Emile Schuffenecker, 14 August 1888, in H.B. Chipp, *Theories of Modern Art* (Los Angeles: University of California Press, 1968), p.60.

13  See Chapter 1.

14  The activities of the Réseau Art Nouveau in Brussels, and Coup de Fouet in Barcelona, have led the way in the re-drawing of the Art Nouveau map.

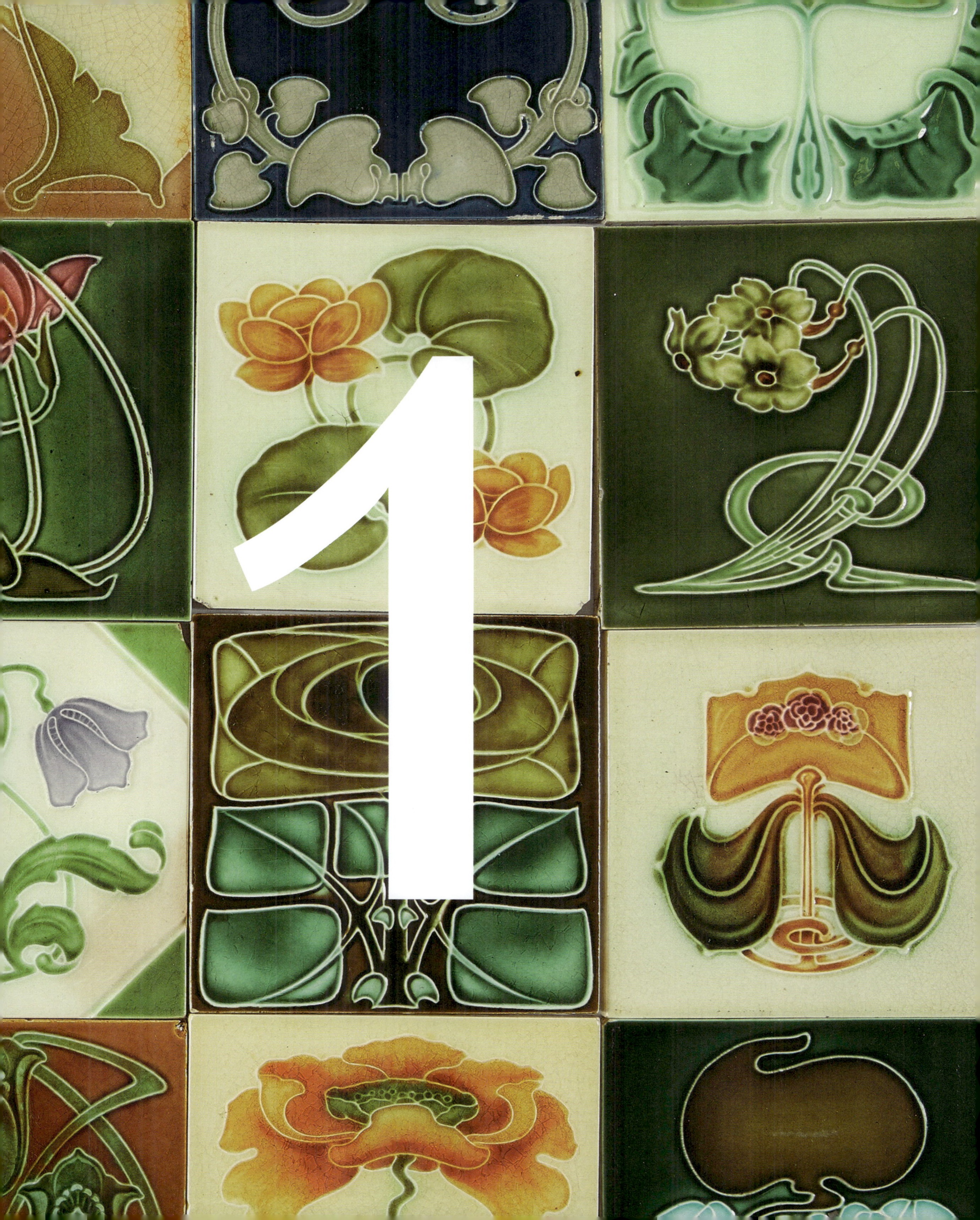

# ~England and the formation of Art Nouveau~

~Paul Greenhalgh~

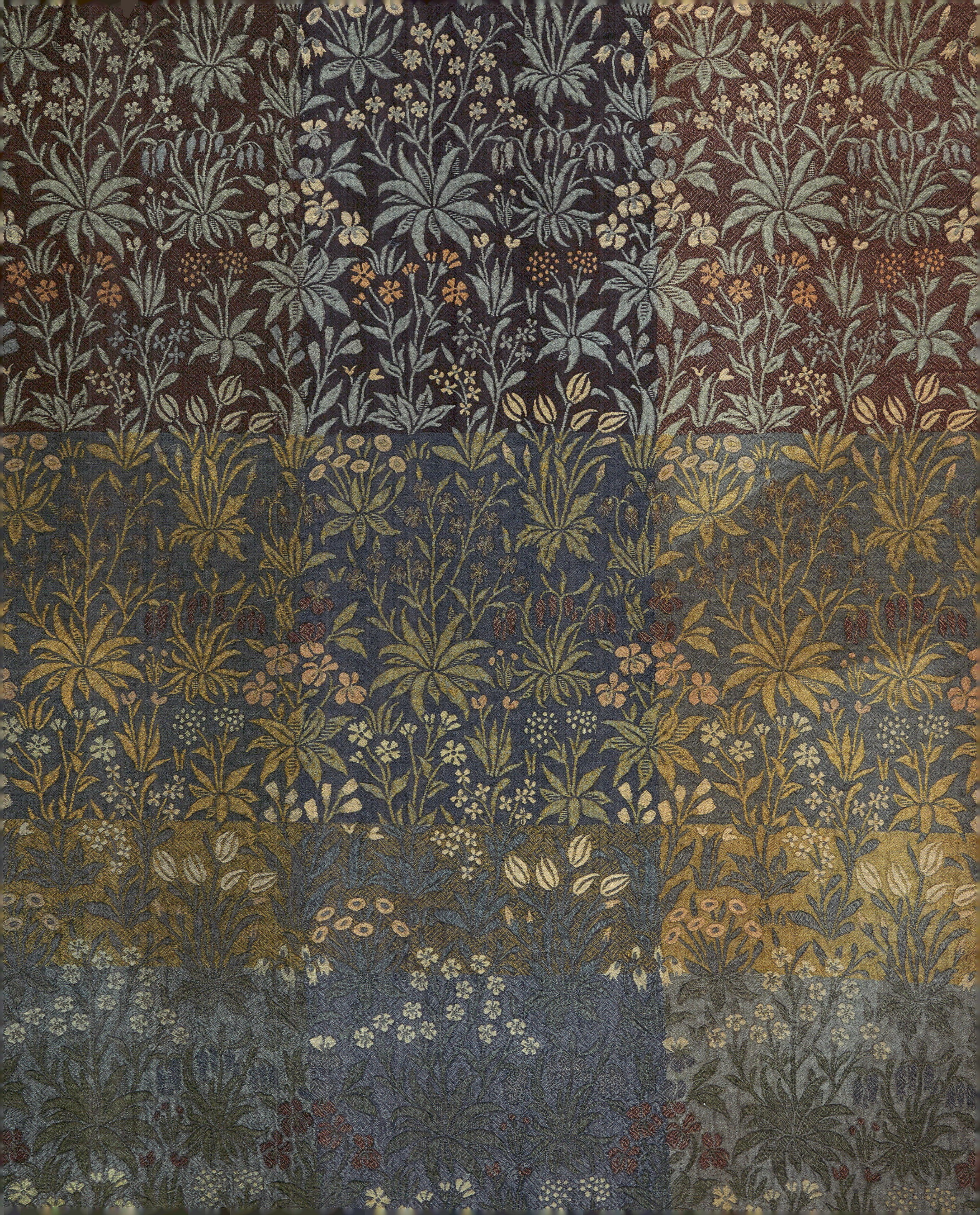

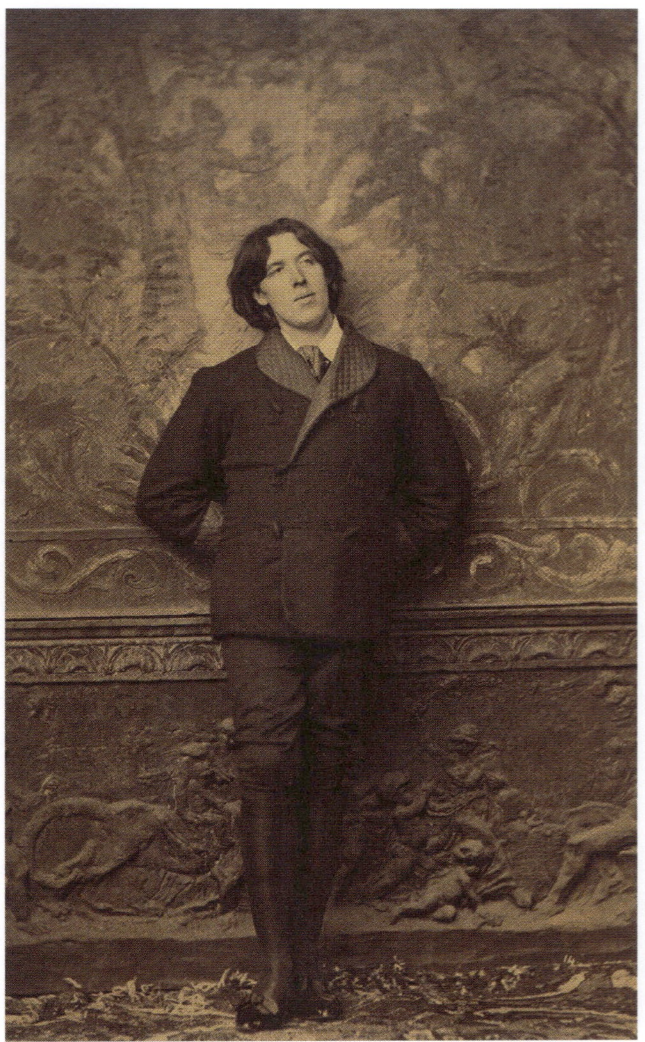

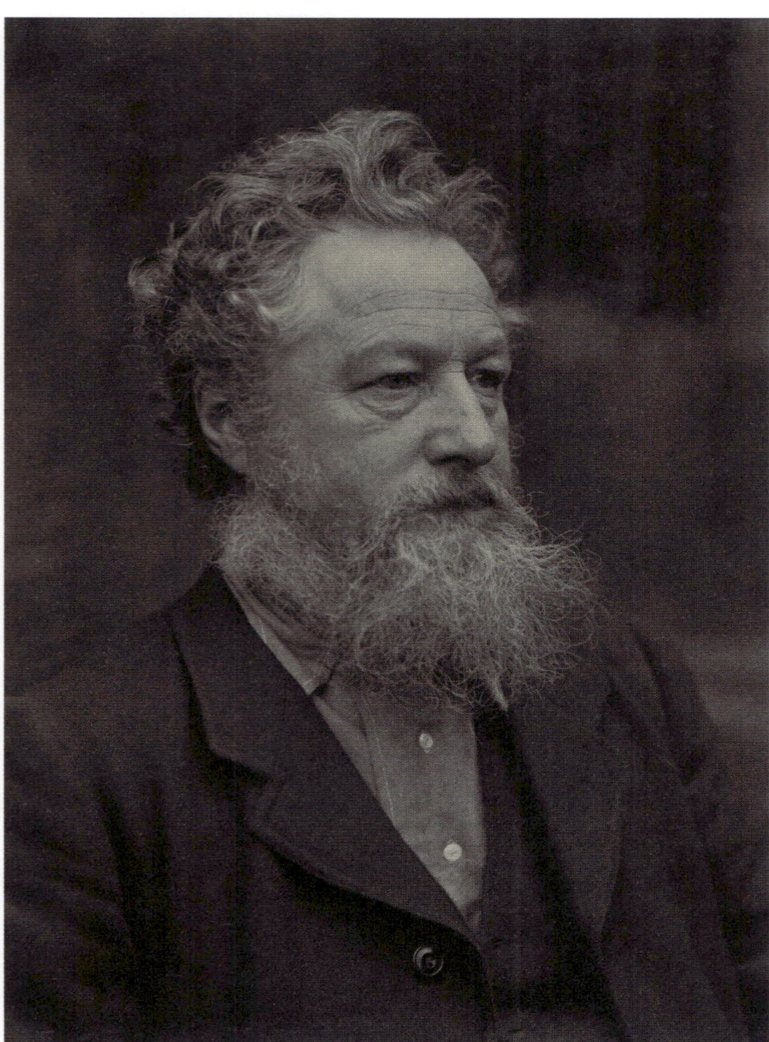



The relationship between the English visual arts and the Art Nouveau style has been pretty much universally recognised as being an important factor in the latter's formation, both at the time and consistently since. Yet during the fin de siècle, while there was a widely acknowledged marriage between the two, few thought at any point that it was one made in heaven. The most peculiar aspect of the relationship was that the majority of the English artists, designers, and thinkers that have been credited with impacting the style were often themselves unaware of it, or antipathetic about it, or in some cases, openly hostile towards it.

The picture is at the same time perplexing and fascinating. Among the luminaries associated with the formation of Art Nouveau, Oscar Wilde and William Morris had little personal engagement with it: when the style first appeared publicly and acquired its name, the former was incarcerated and the latter was dead. Gabriel Dante Rossetti and E.W. Godwin had both passed away more than a decade before, and the grand Pre-Raphaelite Edward Coley Burne-Jones was at best lukewarm towards it, insofar as he knew what it was. Walter Crane, Charles R. Ashbee, and Charles Voysey, and other leading figures of the Arts and Crafts Movement, knew what it was, and claimed to dislike it.[1] Sculptor Sir Alfred Gilbert, whose Neo-Baroque mannerisms, to the neutral observer, seemed to tip wholly into Art Nouveau terrain, fulminated against it.[2] One could go on.

After the Great War, after the style itself was finished, the story of its English connections that was told by historians was a reasonably consistent one virtually to the end of the century: after 1850, so it goes, London generated a number of movements that were conducive to modernity, namely Pre-Raphaelitism, the Design Reform Movement, the Aesthetic Movement, and the Arts and Crafts Movement. These impacted continental Europe, and were a factor in the formation of Art Nouveau in the early 1890s. So much so that some Europeans, including Siegfried Bing and Julius Meier-Graefe, leading supporters of the style, put forward the idea that it actually *began* in London. An exaggeration certainly, but one indicative of how the English school was regarded. Nevertheless, the narrative has been that, having accomplished this impressive early start, the English failed to generate a cohesive Art Nouveau movement of their own.[3] What they did create, led by some of their greatest artists and designers, was pretty much the opposite: a negative literature and institutional attitude that opposed Art Nouveau and everything it was perceived to stand for.[4] What adds to the peculiarity of the situation was that much of what was made in England, to the neutral observer, seemed to be in the Art Nouveau style.

I would like to revisit this picture, not particularly to question the core facts, as most of them are indisputable, but to complicate it perhaps, hopefully to better explain how England managed to produce modern design that impacted Europe, while rejecting what Europe did with it. It must be asserted at the outset, also, that this negative response cannot be dismissed simply as English anti-Europeanism, as fashionable as this might be at the present time. While jingoism was invented as a descriptor at the fin de siècle, and there was a steep rise in concern with national identity in England, much of the design community was stubbornly internationalist in outlook – including those who were against Art Nouveau – and many were openly indebted to the history of European art and design. So while there isn't any doubt that a relatively new 'Little Englander' mentality affected the cultural outlook, the politics of the situation were more complicated than that. Nationalism wasn't the only issue.

I'd like to deal with four areas concerning London and its relationship with European Art Nouveau centres that I believe were the most potent in helping shape the style. They can be summed up in four phrases, albeit crudely: use of nature in design; the incursion of literature and symbolism into design; the politics of individuality and communality in relation to design; and the pragmatic power of English industrialism. Each of these was a factor in the development of Art Nouveau as the first self-conscious attempt to create a modern style.

The first – nature – is the most important. The Introduction gives an indication of the role of nature in the European avant-garde. In many respects this was different from what happened in England. An intense, pantheistic love of nature had been at the heart of English Romantic painting from the late 18th century, but it was later, from the mid-century onwards, and especially after 1870, that designers developed a very different approach to the use of natural form in the decorative arts. The methodology for translating plants into patterns was as different from the Romantic vision of the natural world as it was possible to be. It was initially also at variance with Europe.

The method of creating pattern from natural form was generally referred to as conventionalisation. Essentially, one drew the plant, and then systemically broke this down into regular, geometric forms, which could be made into repeating patterns. This design naturalism was about *abstracting* the essentials from nature. As noted in the Introduction, the term entered

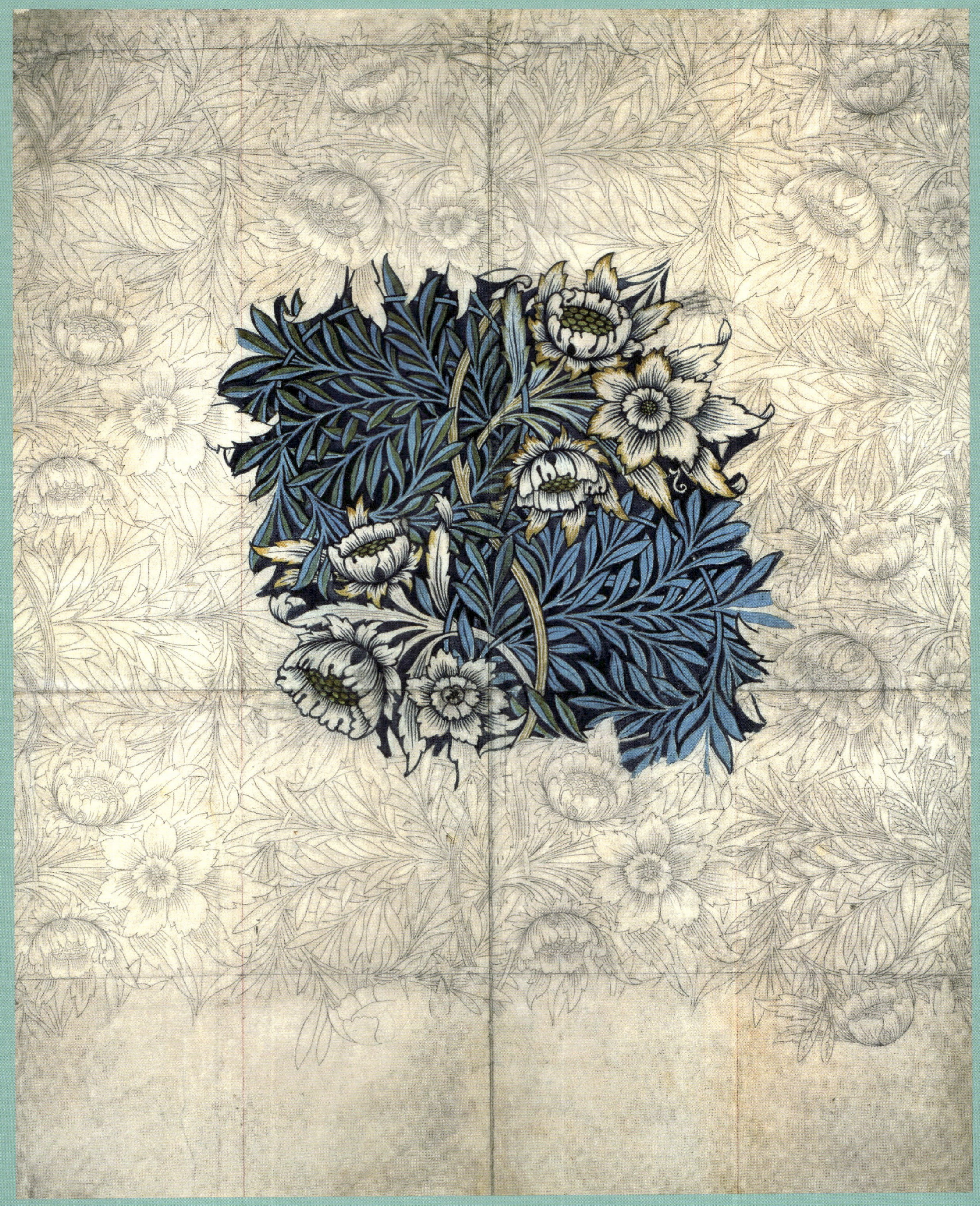

*Opposite:* William Morris, *Tulip and Willow* fabric design, 1873–1875, watercolour and pencil on paper. Birmingham Museums and Art Gallery.

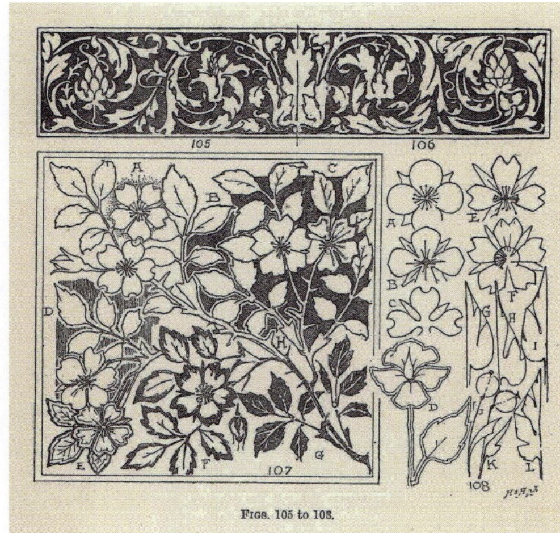

*Above:* Illustration for 'Method of Delineation', in Richard G. Hatton, *Elementary Design*, 1895.

*Below and right:* Illustrations for 'The Plant Form in Ornament', in James Ward, *The Principles of Ornament*, 1896.

into art vocabulary via discussion of decoration and ornament, for example, by thinkers in France like Eugène Emmanuel Viollet-le-Duc.[5] Paul Gauguin would also refer to abstraction as being a process in which nature was reduced to essentials, effectively making it into a formal synthetic pattern that the artist could control.[6] But the process of creating an abstracted pattern – conventionalisation – from nature was an English invention. It became a core methodology within the Art Nouveau style and synonymous with modernity in the broadest sense.

The ascent of nature in England was incremental rather than sudden, becoming a kind of liberal hegemony over decades, beginning with design reformers in the 1850s. All branches of advanced practice across the arts embraced it, and perhaps more significantly, at grass-roots level, it dominated the curriculum in the newly-formed and nationally-networked Schools of Design. Training manuals showed students how to conventionalise nature. While the process was hardly unique to the period – Islamic pattern designers had taken it to sublime heights a millennium before – in this context, it had a new relevance. Most emphatically, it allowed designers to avoid using standard historical styles, like the Rococo, Beaux Arts Classicism, and even the Gothic, the revival of which by 1890 had become highly formulaic. Natural pattern was indicative of permanence, stability, and authenticity. Symbolically, it not only replaced staid notions of history, but also implied the cycle of life. For many, it had universalist utopian connotations.

Students were particularly encouraged to draw plant forms, and to use these shapes in pattern design. The main task of their teachers was 'to suggest a line of work that may lead the student to seek in nature the ideas that may help him most in design',[7] because 'without the study of nature

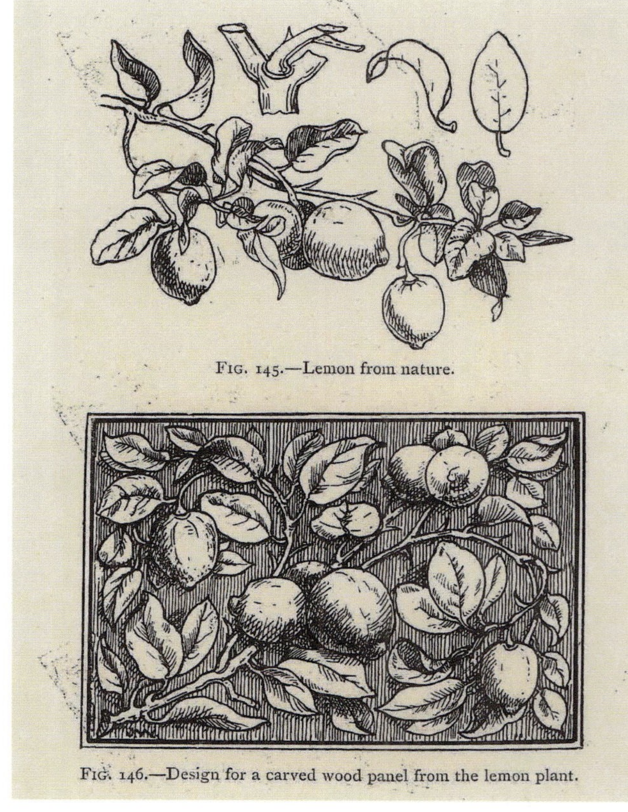

FIG. 145.—Lemon from nature.

FIG. 146.—Design for a carved wood panel from the lemon plant.

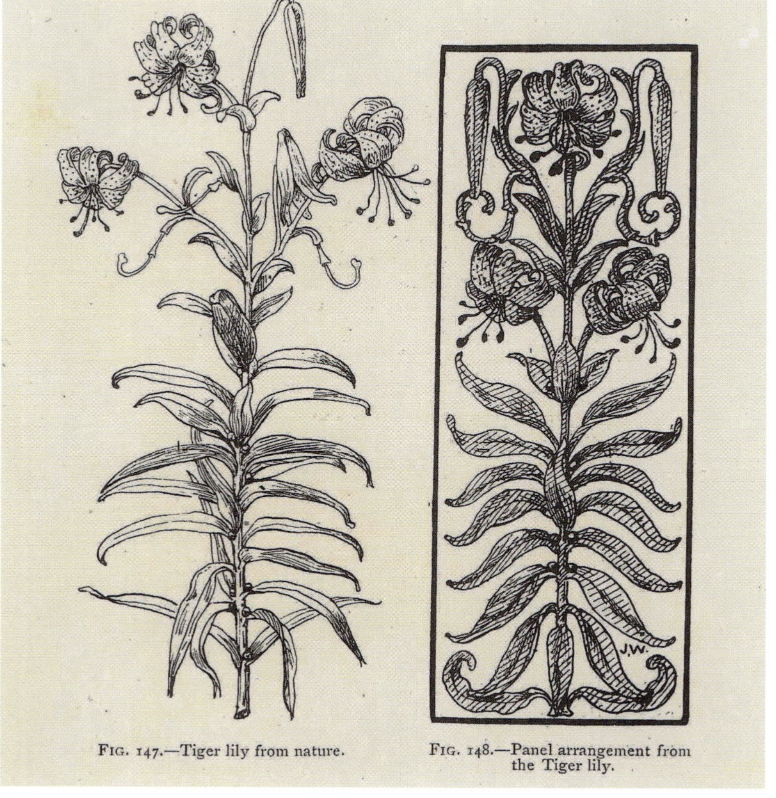

FIG. 147.—Tiger lily from nature.

FIG. 148.—Panel arrangement from the Tiger lily.

principles are useless'.[8] It wasn't the superficial copying of flora and fauna that was emphasised, but the structures that underpinned them: 'in nature, beauty and structure are interwoven: the two are inseparable. And so in design, the decoration must grow up with the structure.'[9]

It was accepted by virtually every major figure, regardless of ideological position, that it was the *scaffolding* and *processes* of nature that gave meaning to design. While major Europeans like Viollet-le-Duc proselytised in much the same way, by 1880 it was understood to be *Le style Anglais*. William Morris, for example, declared he was interested in the:

forms and intricacies, that do not necessarily imitate nature, but in which the hands of the craftsman are guided to work in the way that she does, till the web, the cup, or the knife, look as natural, nay as lovely, as the green field, the river bank, or the mountain flint.[10]

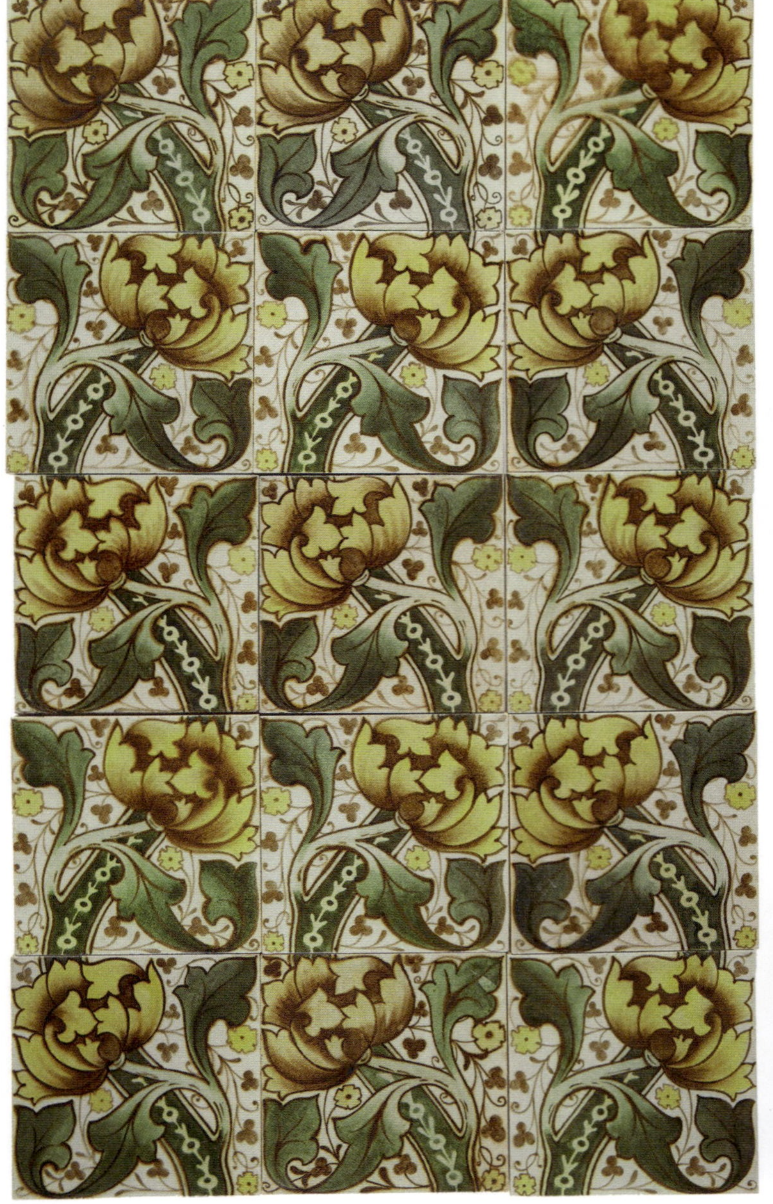

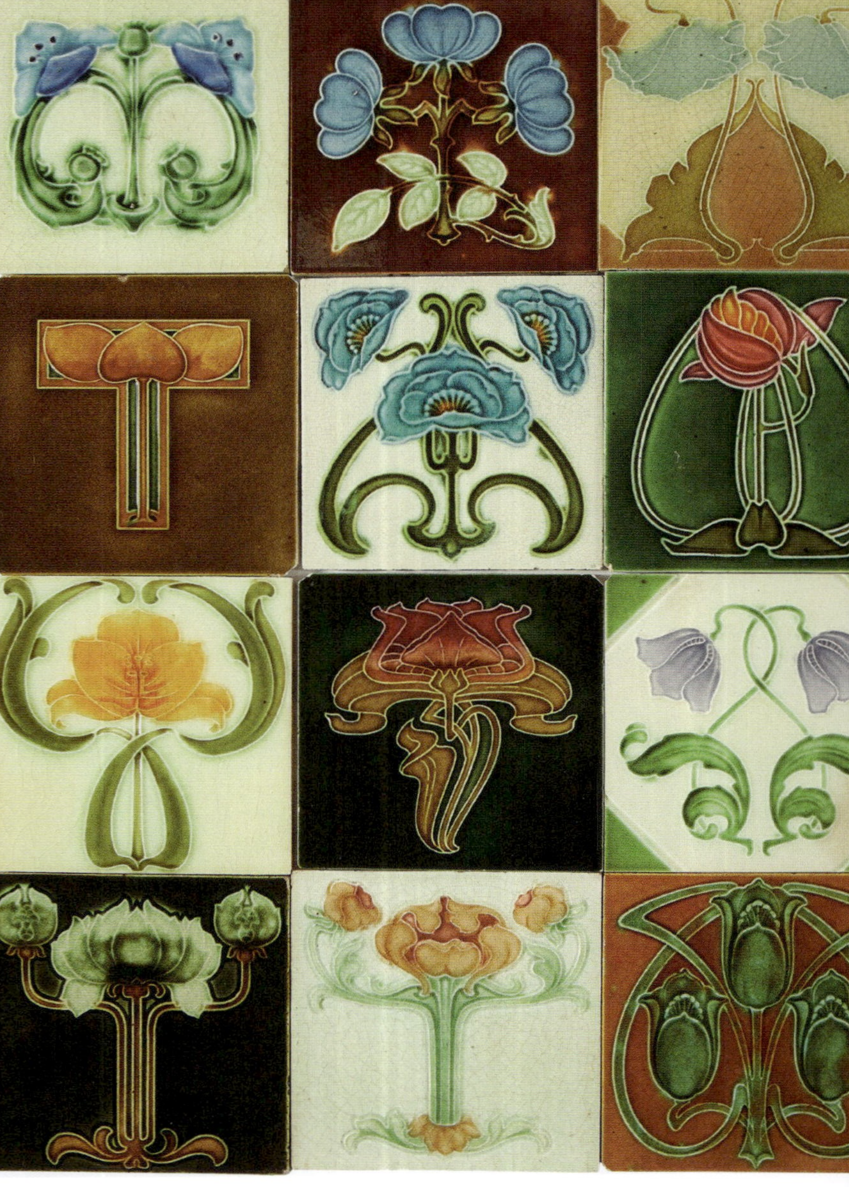

*Left:* Maw & Co., tile panel, *c.*1880, ceramic. Private Collection.

His designs for textile, ceramic, wallpaper, and stained glass fully present this thesis: his patterns don't replicate nature, they create superb equivalents of it. Much of the literature about Morris over the last century has drawn a sharp divide between his design work and his politics. While this is reasonable enough in some respects, it is important to acknowledge that the pattern work symbolises an outlook on the world. For Morris, in the spirit of the Islamic pattern he adored, it is to do with interconnectedness, interdependence, and the connectivity of life.

The methodology was transmitted across Europe, and by 1895 was embraced by the majority of intellectuals active in the design arena. In his seminal masterwork on style, *Stilfragen*, for example, Alois Riegl summed up the view of nature among contemporary avant-garde thinkers:

> All art, and that includes decorative art as well, is inextricably tied to nature. All art forms are based on models in nature. This is true not only when they actually resemble their natural prototypes but even when they have been drastically altered by the human beings who created them, either for practical purposes or simple pleasure.[11]

In other words, even when you couldn't directly witness nature in an object, if it had any sort of quality to it, it was there.

Morris and the Arts and Craft Movement designers after him were wholly committed to conventionalised nature. The Arts and Crafts Movement itself emerged and consolidated in the 1880s and was essentially comprised of a number of collaborating groups, or guilds. The Century Guild formed in 1882, The Art Workers' Guild in 1884, and the Guild of Handicraft in 1888. Vitally, also in 1888, The Arts and Crafts exhibition society was formed. More than anything else, these young utopians positioned nature at the heart of design. Typically, the flow of line is at once lyrical and redolent of stems, leaves, sepals, and petals, yet it has an underlying structure and discipline dependent on repetition and geometry. This was very much the case also in tile manufacture, where designers produced repeating ornamental compositions that tipped out of the more passive Art and Crafts compositions, into the more dynamic and extrovert idiom of Art Nouveau. Because of this, it is perhaps in tile design where the two styles are most difficult to tell apart.

In product design, a number of remarkable individuals came to the fore. W.A.S. Benson, for example, emerged from the heart of the Arts and Crafts Movement, but his metalwork had an innovative simplicity to it, an insistence on the development of bold, organic form, that separated him out from most of his contemporaries. More than any of the Arts and Crafts community, he engaged with the mechanics of his products, 'for seeing the chaos that has prevailed in such things, I have set myself to work steadily through the whole range of necessary furniture and fittings'.[12] He had a quiet confidence and humility in the way he achieved his forms, and in the way he talked about them. He wanted 'to improve these arts, and produce work consistent and original in style, of shapely form, and carefully designed for convenience of use'.[13] Herman Muthesius, perhaps the most influential European commentator on English design, thought Benson to be vital for the formation of the modern sensibility in fixtures and fittings. In his seminal work *Das englische haus* of 1904, he confirmed that:

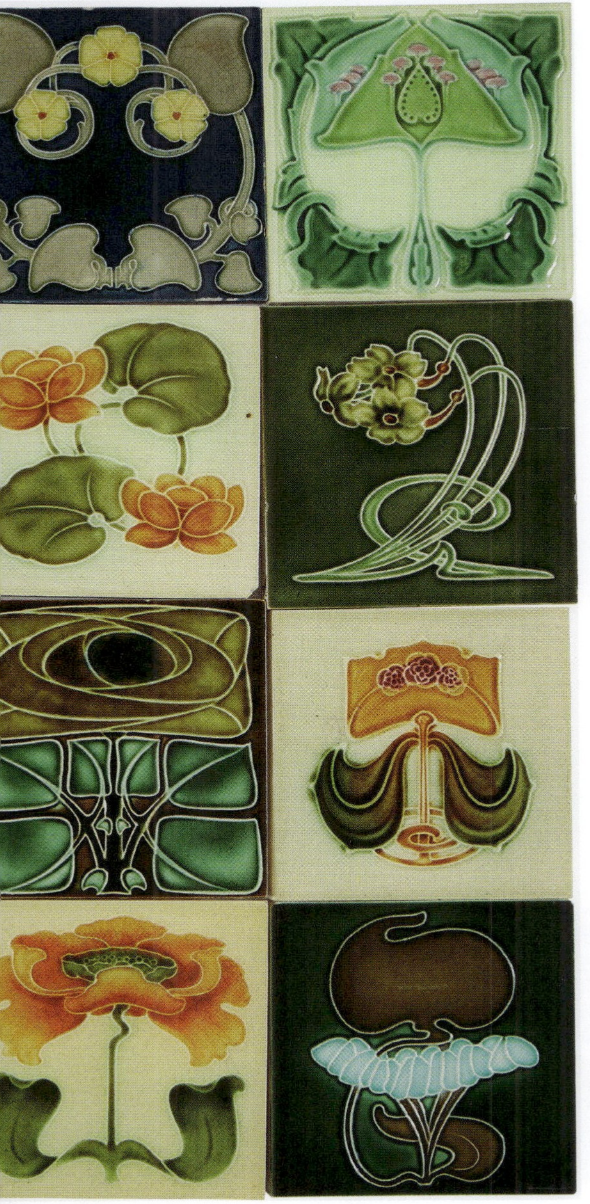

*Below:* Various English makers, tile panel, *c.*1905, ceramic. Private Collection.

*Below:* W.A.S Benson, glass by
James Powell & Sons, Whitefriars,
vase, *c.*1900, opalescent glass and
gilded copper.  Private Collection.

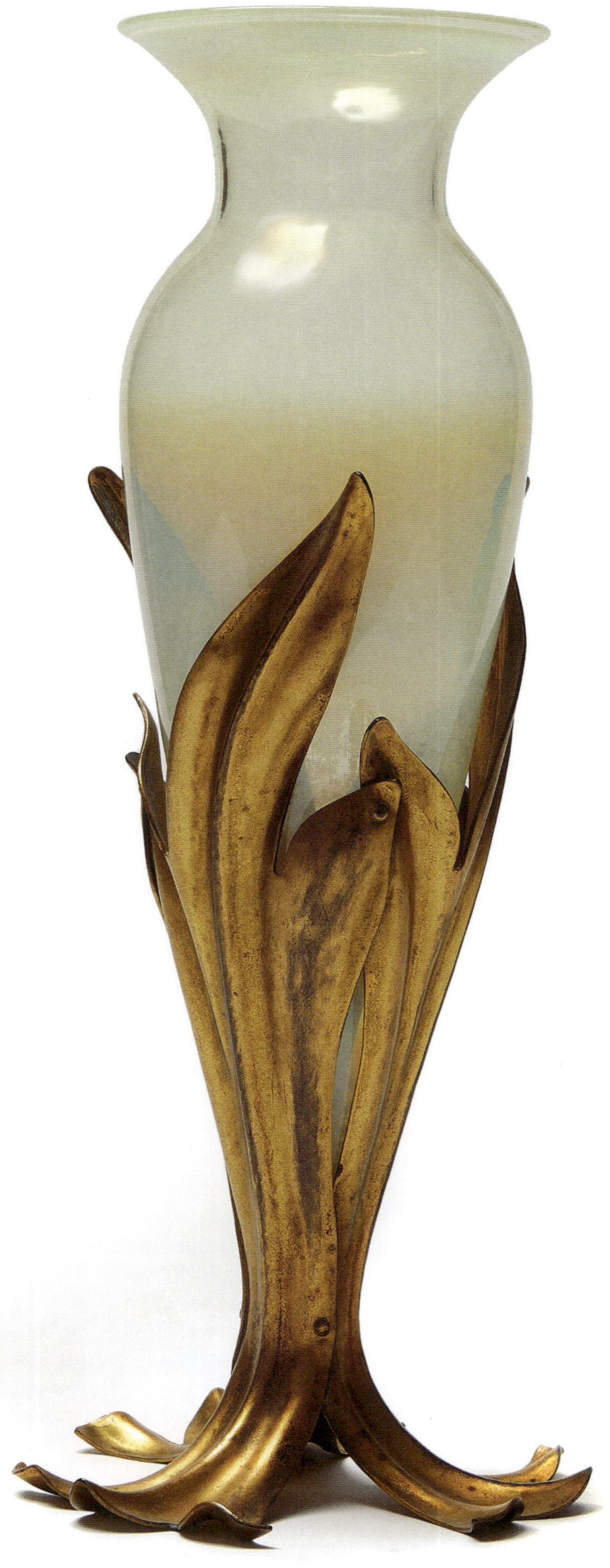

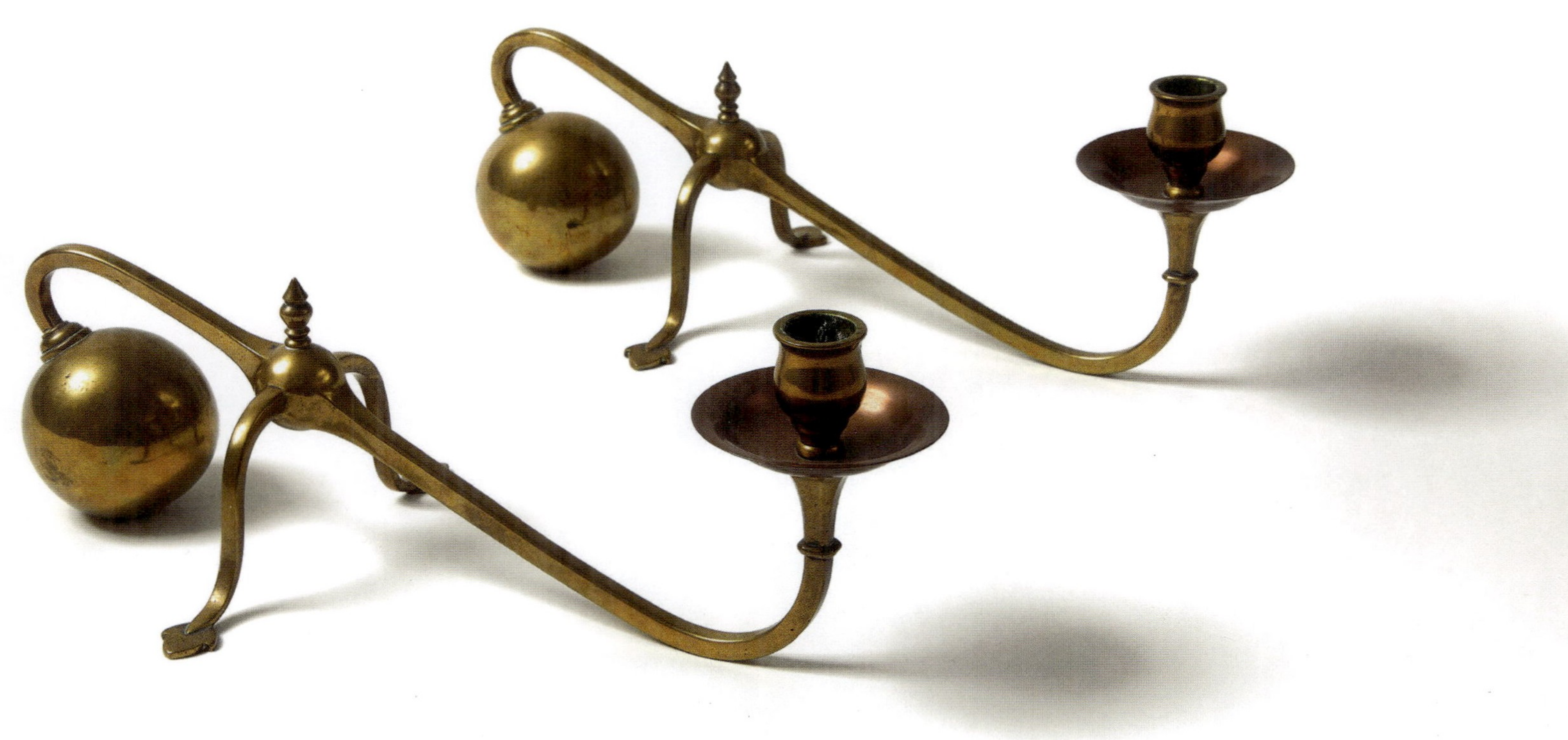

*Above:* W.A.S Benson, pair of candlesticks, *c.*1900, copper and brass.  Private Collection.

Benson was the first to solve the problem of design in metal in the modern spirit when he created the lamps that were to have a revolutionary effect on all our metalware ... Benson was the leading spirit in electric appliances in England, on the continent he was the fruitful instigator.[14]

Benson never left the tenets of the Arts and Crafts Movement behind. By contrast, Christopher Dresser, perhaps the single most important English designer of the Victorian period, never seriously embraced the moral imperatives of Ruskin and Morris. Too complex and energetic to be wholly attached to any one movement, we generally associate him as being part of the late flowering of the Design Reform Movement, and he is often positioned as part of Aestheticism.

Dresser was a product of the English Design Schools. Norwegian historian and curator Vidar Halen, in his seminal book on Dresser, tells us that he 'was one of the first professionally trained designers for machine production and may arguably be the first industrial designer in Europe'.[15] Dresser's use of nature, then, was tempered by his full embracing of technology, in a way that many of his contemporaries refused to contemplate. He was also very comfortable adapting himself to most media, and happily worked for a wide range of companies. He was an exemplary teacher and theoretician. As such, he not only provided endless visual examples for the Art Nouveau designers, but also a thoroughly modern vocabulary and model for practice. In many respects he anticipated the grand generation of Modernist designers of the 20th century.

As with Benson, perhaps the most striking thing about Dresser was his willingness to simplify-out his forms, to the point that his work could be described as a form of organic geometry. Both designers developed a flowing, lyrical, curvilinear approach to line and form that anticipated the mainstream, floral Art Nouveau style; and both also made use of repeated geometric forms and patterns that inspired the Glasgow School of designers, led by Charles Rennie Mackintosh, and the Secession movement in Vienna.

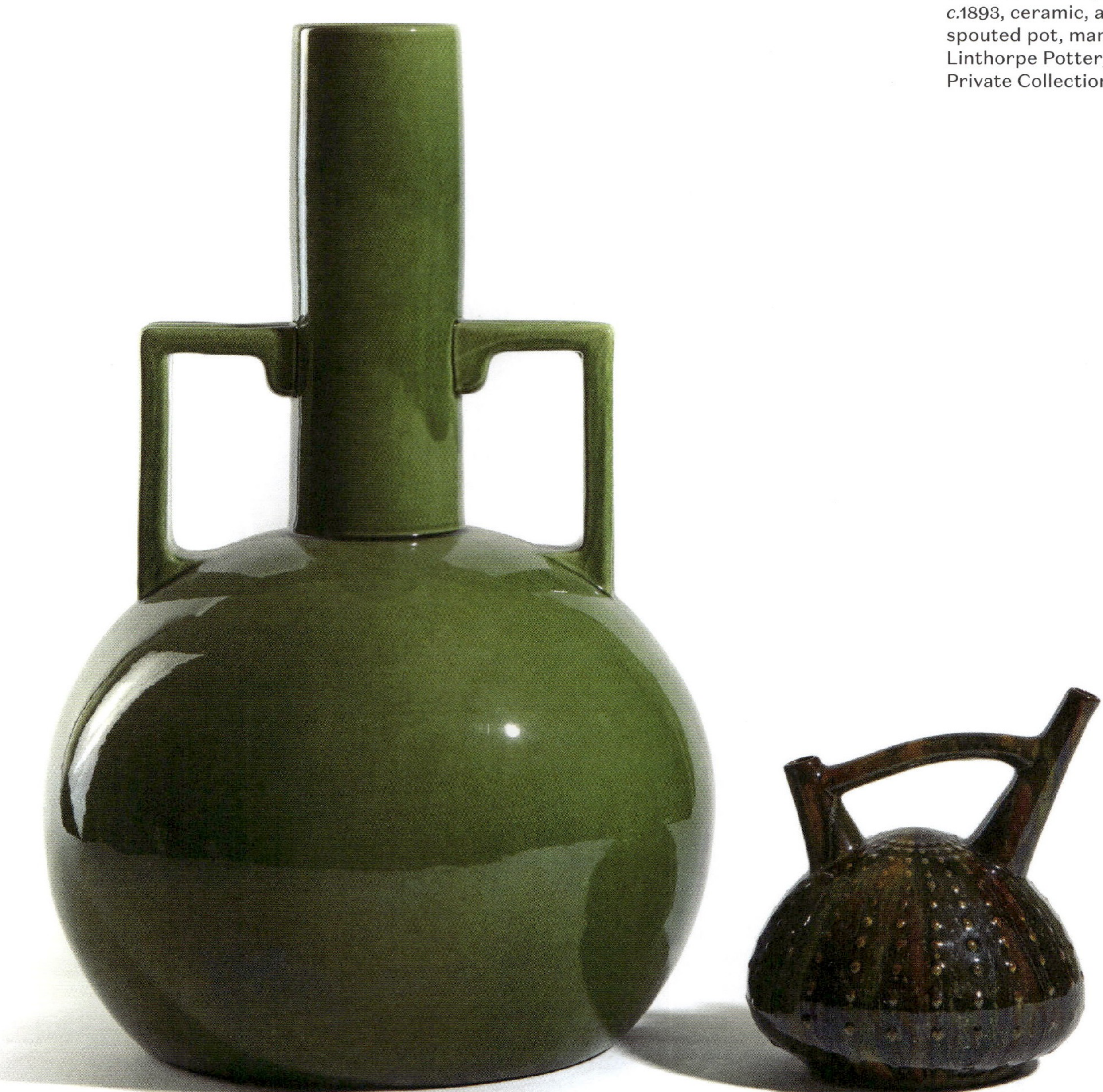



So why did most of these designers reject Art Nouveau? Why was that? Why would the English tile and stained-glass designers, for example, disown a style that the average observer couldn't tell apart from their own? Professional jealousy accepted, the reason is almost certainly bound-up in the ideas underlying conventionalisation. In essence, the clipping and controlling of nature was connected to the ethical vision of the role of design. Following Ruskin and Morris, Arts and Craft designers believed that art was fundamentally a moral activity: nature served humankind and, in domesticated form, it provided for humanity. Symbolically, conventionalisation allowed them to control nature, to coax it into the service of civilisation.

In this way, natural pattern forms related to the core political agenda: designers were committed to the struggle against rampant, unregulated industrialisation, and uncontrolled urbanisation, which reached an intense height in their own times. They embraced the idea that nature needed to be defended, and that a healthy life was dependent on the natural environment. Morris put into verse this early stirring of Green politics, in his dream of what London should be:

> Forget the six counties overhung with smoke,
> Forget the snorting steam and piston stroke,
> Forget the spreading of the hideous town,
> Think rather of the pack-horse on the down,
> And dream of London, small, and white, and clean,
> The clear Thames bordered by its gardens green ...[16]

It is noteworthy that he doesn't wish to return London to the feral, untamed wild, he wants to make it into a garden. The garden is the conceptual equivalent of conventionalisation, in that it was a means of harnessing nature, of ordering it for the common good. So for the English, conventionalisation wasn't simply an aesthetic formula, it was a process describing humankind's symbiotic relationship with nature. It had a spiritual dimension to it: nature was 'pure, simple, and holy'.[17]

This presented a problem with regard to Art Nouveau. While quite a few Belgian, French, and German designers dealt with nature entirely in the same way as the English, Art Nouveau generally had a heady, pantheistic, uncivilised side to it. It was less an ordered garden, more a hedonistic forest. More than this, in the work of many designers, there was an organic metamorphosis at work, in which human, animal, and plant forms were often fused together. Across Europe, but in French works especially, of Hector Guimard, Rupert Carabin, René Lalique, Georges Fouquet, and many others, the resulting forms could be highly sexualised. This was a double-hit for the English: it offended aesthetical *and* ethical sensibilities. Guimard's metro stations, or the furniture and ceramics of Carabin, or the jewellery of Lalique, Fouquet, and others, with their asymmetry, whiplash line, sensuous and sensual references to the body, and explosive movement, could never have been made in England. Likewise the flamboyant, swirling confidence of many Belgian buildings and furnishings. There is something beautifully ironic about one of Brussels' iconic works, the 'Old England' department store of 1899, designed by Paul Saintenoy.[18] The heady, frenetic metalwork that peels off the edges and corners of the structure had never been seen in any version of England, old or new.

There was another – radical and new – ingredient in play by 1895 that seemed to *modernise nature* itself. Charles Darwin's *On the Origin of Species* of 1859 had rocked Western civilisation, by transforming our view of the natural world, and his *The Descent of Man* of 1871 went on to fully immerse humankind in the processes of evolution. This scientific revolution had cultural, social, and political consequences that cannot be overestimated. Evolution in nature came to be distorted into being synonymous with progress in humankind. *The Descent of Man* affirmed the direct connection between society and evolution. Social Darwinism, as it later became known, acquired the status of scientific fact through the fin de siècle. The evolutionary process was no longer an arbitrary one, shaped by natural selection and environment, over millennia; it became a more determined phenomenon, which proved the advance of some human groups and the regression of others. It became a justification of imperial, political, and

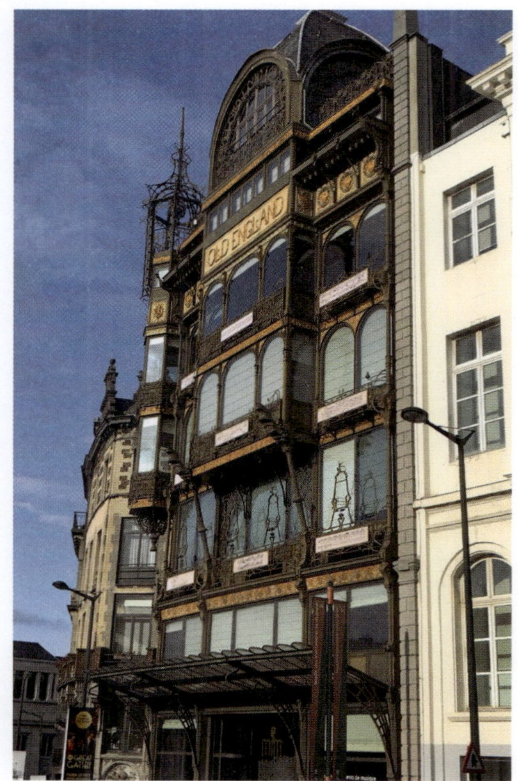

*Below:* Paul Saintenoy, Old England department store, Brussels, *c.*1899.

business life.[19] It demonstrated the inevitability of urban growth. Nature had been secularised, moved away from the spiritual realm, towards the material actuality of modernity. The symbolic association of nature with progress added to the vibrance and energy of the first generation of avant-garde thinkers in the visual arts, and it lent fire to the Art Nouveau style in a number of countries. For the Belgians, French, and Germans, for example, nature was a signifier of progress, and an essential part of modern, urban life.

This couldn't have been further from the outlook of most English Arts and Crafts aficionados. For the English, conventionalised nature symbolically represented utopian conservativism, because English socialism was itself conservative: its supporters embraced models from the Mediaeval past, and combined these with the well-tended garden, preferably walled. As with a wide swathe of the English left, it was a preservationist credo. Many of the leading Art Nouveau designers, on the other hand, expressed their socialism through dynamic, flowing movement, through progress, technology, and unfettered, youthful energy. They had taken the new naturalism, and used it to imagine the future, rather than to fantasise about the past. Designers like Henry Van de Velde – a greater rationalist than most of his fellow travellers – while fully embracing the moral outlook of Ruskin and Morris, openly rejected their Mediaevalism. He wanted to embrace the modern world:

> I am trying to find a new basis, on which we intend to create a new style; as a germ of this style I see before me one thing for which I must strive: to create nothing that has no reasonable grounds for existing. I also see a powerful means of realising this: heavy industry, with its massive engineering plants, and their consequences.[20]

It was as well that Morris was dead before the essay was published, and that no translation was available to Ruskin. Like Van de Velde, in their various ways, Hector Guimard, Victor Horta, Alphonse Mucha, and others, embraced conventionalisation, but they used it to push towards radical new ends. They had appropriated the system to another cause: and it would be an understatement to say that the Arts and Crafts Movement wasn't in tune with it.

The second English influence on Art Nouveau came from the confluence of literature, art, and design. It is an interesting proposition to suggest that literature – use of language – underpins every aspect of post-Renaissance English culture, but in the very least, it is an empirically observable phenomenon through the key Modernist period, of 1880 to 1940. At the fin de siècle, a number of the relevant practitioners and theorists were respected poets, including Morris, Oscar Wilde, and Dante Gabriel Rossetti. This encouraged a broad but very particular approach to narrative and symbolism across the face of practice. It came out especially in the most significant movement to emerge in England in the second half of the century: the Pre-Raphaelite Brotherhood.

The original movement had been formed in 1848. Triggered in part by the dominant role that the Gothic Revival was coming to play across British culture, the Brotherhood had ambitions to transform painting through analogous aesthetic and intellectual means. It was a rejection of the Beaux Arts classical heritage that had come overwhelmingly into the ascendant.

The initial group included John Everett Millais, Dante Gabriel Rossetti, and William Holman Hunt; these were joined by William Michael Rossetti, James Collinson, Frederic George Stephens, and Thomas Woolner. While Burne-Jones and Morris weren't formally part of the original group, they came to be closely connected with it. The first iteration of the Brotherhood didn't last long. It was disbanded by 1853. But the wider phenomenon ran on through the century, and a second generation of painters guaranteed its prominence at the fin de siècle. In the run-up to the new millennium, a number of artists, but especially Burne-Jones, enjoyed international popularity. The intense, serious, dark, and mythic treatment of grand themes was important for Belgian, French, Italian, and Scandinavian symbolists.

Vitally, Pre-Raphaelitism impacted the decorative arts. Most famously, it was out of this environment that Morris, Marshall and Faulkner and Company, William Morris's first business venture, emerged in 1862.[21] This was reorganised and renamed Morris and Company in 1875, becoming iconic through the last quarter of the century. Siegfried Bing, one of the seminal leaders of Art Nouveau, and the person who gave the style its name when he opened his *Maison de l'Art Nouveau* in Paris in 1895, unequivocally recognised this English thread as initiating the style:

> The initial movement ... began in England, under the influence of the Pre-Raphaelites and the ideas of John Ruskin, and was carried into practical affairs by the admirable genius of William Morris.[22]

Morris engaged with every aspect of the domestic interior, designing, producing, and selling furniture, wallpapers, textiles, and ceramic. The company also distributed a range of products by like-minded companies. William De Morgan's ceramic vessels and tiles, for example, are closely associated with Morris and Company.

However, it was the company's production of stained glass and tapestry that is rightly viewed as part of the mainstream Pre-Raphaelite story. Recent scholarship has shown us, in fact, that stained glass, and particularly the British contribution, is one of the great stories of fin de siècle culture. The interface of Pre-Raphaelitism and the Arts and Crafts Movement led to a Golden Age for the medium.[23]

Burne-Jones is the greatest of the Pre-Raphaelite painters to move into the wider universe of the ornamental arts in a fully committed manner. Often working directly with Morris, he engaged at various points with most disciplines: his enamel work, for example, has a beguiling intensity to it, that places him intriguingly close, on the one hand, to his great forebear William Blake, and on the other, to French symbolists such as Gustave Moreau and Odilon Redon. But it was his work in tapestry and stained glass that constitute a contribution to European art that is scarcely less important than his painting.

Burne-Jones' draughtsmanship underpinned his entire method. His mature oeuvre has a stark, intense linearity to it, which makes the deliberately shallow space in his paintings into a symbolic scaffolding. His drawings are among the great contributions to English fin de siècle culture, and it is that extraordinary use of line that lends his stained glass its power. By the time he died in 1898, he had followers all over Europe, not least among those still committed to various forms of symbolism. Fernand Khnopff and Gustave

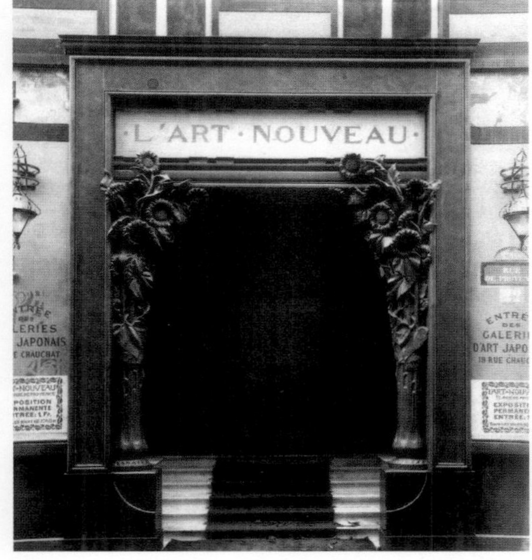


*Below:* The Maison de l'Art Nouveau, Paris, 1895.

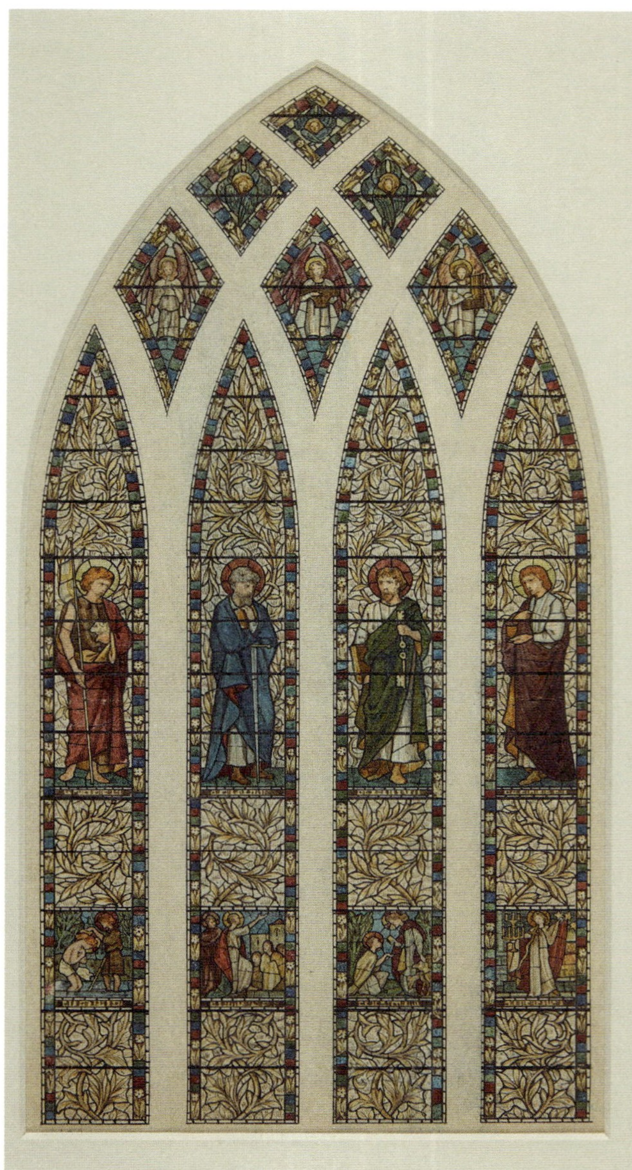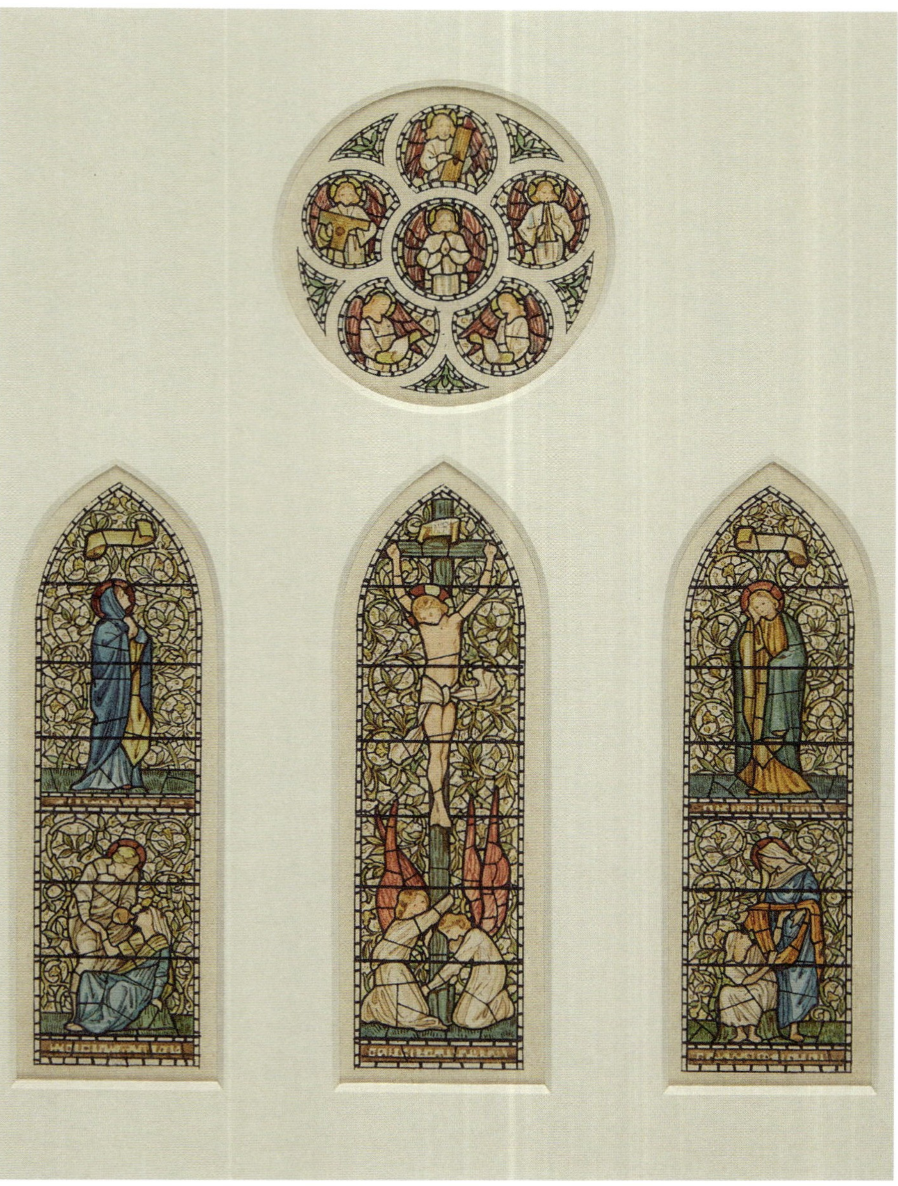

Klimt owed him a debt, for example, as did the young Picasso, as he moved out of his Impressionist phase, into the Blue Period. Art Nouveau – and especially the French and Belgian manifestations – is essentially a linear style, and the flow of its lines owes something to Edward Coley Burne-Jones.

Alongside the languid mysticism of the specific painters, but ultimately probably more significant, was what might be termed the Pre-Raphaelite spirit. This was exemplified by Dante Gabriel Rossetti, whose life and work were the absolute embodiment of fin de siècle melancholia. His personal – sexual – life was perceivable as a dark succession of incident-studded relationships that could have been created by Bram Stoker. *Dracula* is a product of the same age. Apart from an intense affair with Jane Morris, wife of his friend and business partner, his traumatic relationship and marriage to artist Elizabeth Siddall only reached a final conclusion after her death, when he exhumed her grave in order to retrieve a folder of his poems he had buried with her. Not surprisingly, much of his art was dedicated to trying to explain his idea of the female psyche. His depictions of women fed directly into the vocabulary of the Art Nouveau designers.

The Pre-Raphaelite spirit fed the Art Nouveau environment in a more generic way, in the form of a powerful archaism. This wasn't historicist in the sense of simply imitating art. Rather, it was about rehabilitating the past to generate a contemporary symbolism. Legend, myth, and ornament from pre-Classical cultures became central to the meaning of much contemporary

*Above:* William Morris, stained-glass designs for Paisley Abbey *(left)* and for Gordon Chapel, Fochabers, Scotland *(right)*, 1876, watercolour on paper. The Brian Clarke Collection of Stained Glass.

*Right:* Edward Burne-Jones, *Love in a Mist, c.*1880, enamel. Private Collection.

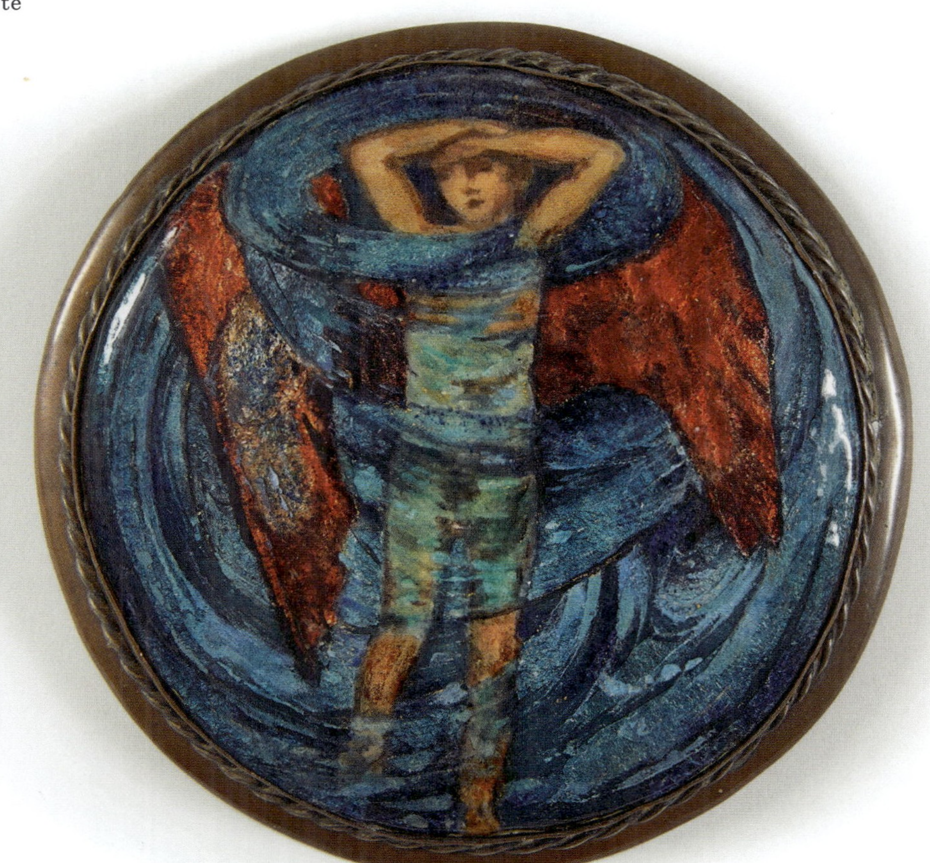

*Below:* Edward Burne-Jones, mermaid plaque, *c.*1880, bronze. Private Collection.

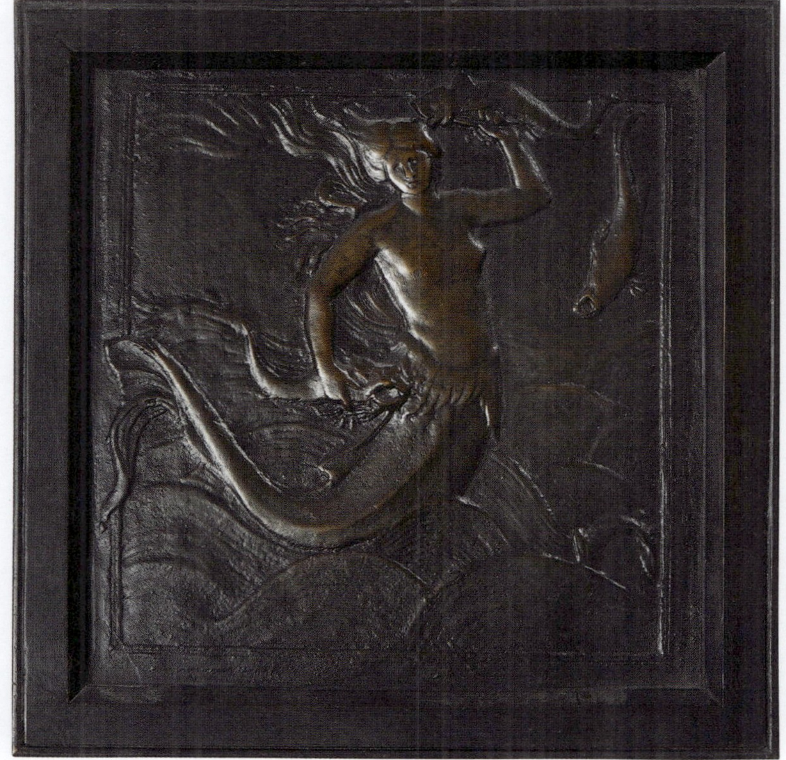

*Right:* Edward Burne-Jones, *The Magi Led by a Star,* 1880, pencil on paper. The Brian Clarke Collection of Stained Glass.

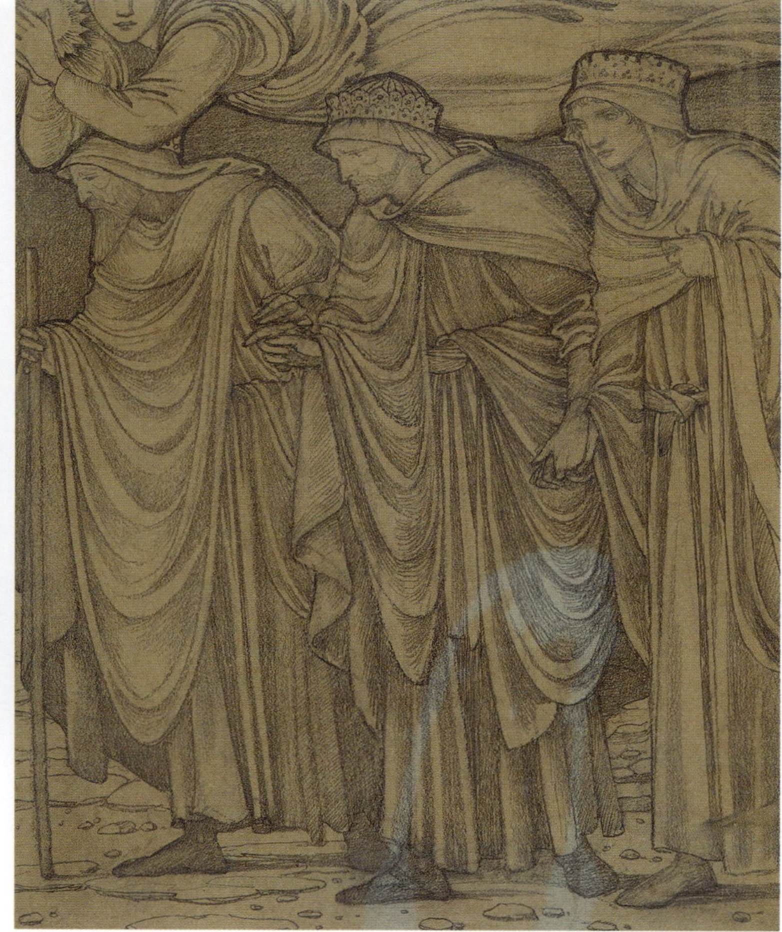

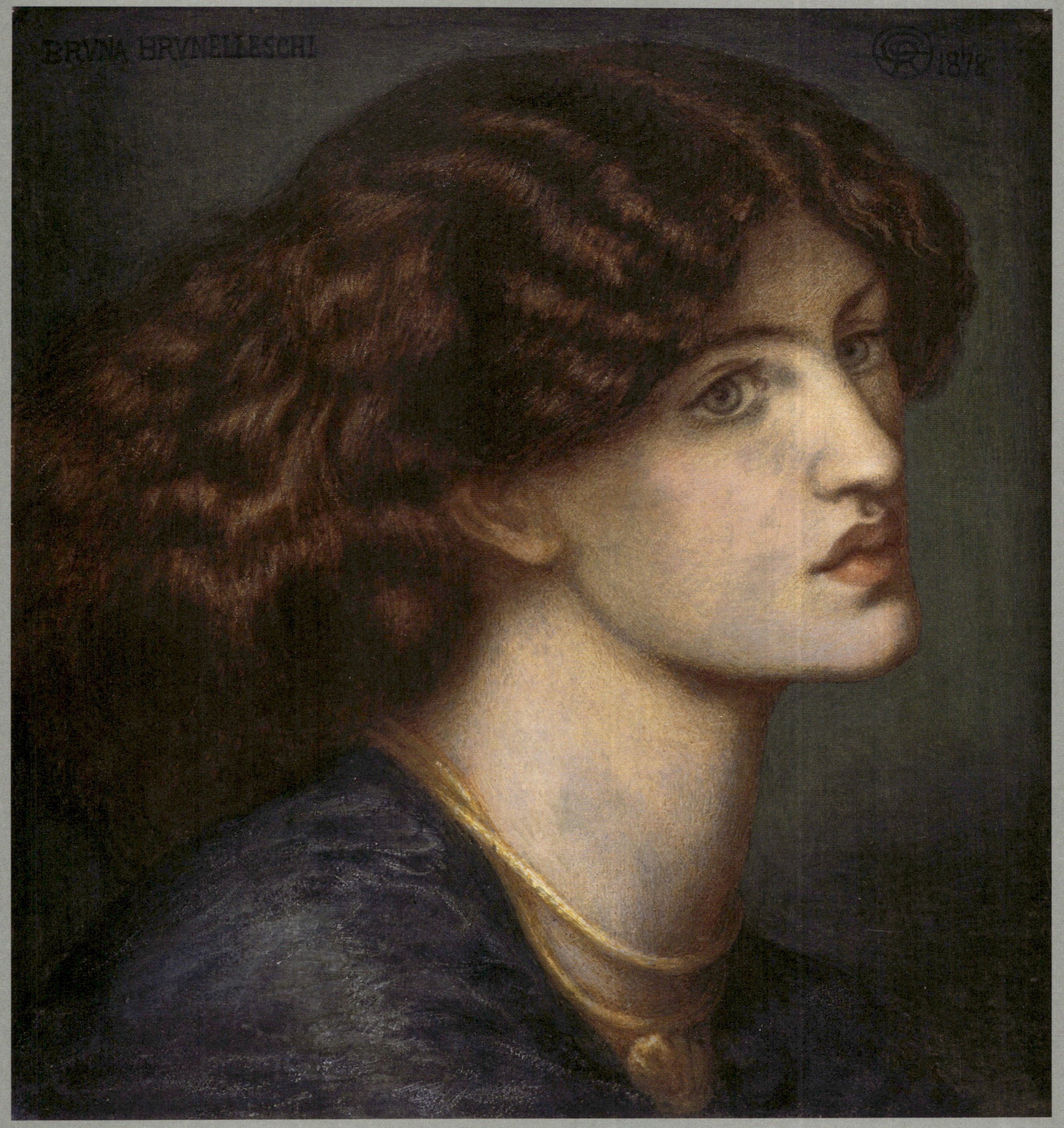

practice. Most famously, the Gaelic and Celtic revivals, and interpretations of Mediaeval and Romanesque art, underpinned advanced fin de siècle English design. The various Arts and Crafts guilds generated a fantasised antiquarianism around them. Barely understood at the time, these were perceived to be peripheral, and even 'outsider' cultures, and so were embraced for their alternative nature. Such archaism continued to impact the arts well into the 20th century. In jewellery and metal-smithing, for example, the work of designers like Omar Ramsden, William James Neatby, Alexander Fisher, Archibald Knox, and Mary Seton Watts cannot be understood in the absence of these ancient idioms. And it later came to inspire literary epics such J.R.R. Tolkien's *The Lord of the Rings*.

Interestingly, Knox and Watts both designed for Liberty of London – the department store internationally associated with Art Nouveau – and, more than most, both have been retrospectively described as Art Nouveau designers. While in itself, the application of the label in this way is of questionable usefulness, the oeuvres of both had a significant connection to, and importance for, much European practice. Knox was a Manx man – an inhabitant of the Isle of Man – who made the tense, curling structures of Gaelic pattern into a modern international idiom. Via Liberty, his work in pewter and silver had a European-wide following by 1900. These works were probably the most important international disseminators of neo-Celtic pattern through the period.[24]



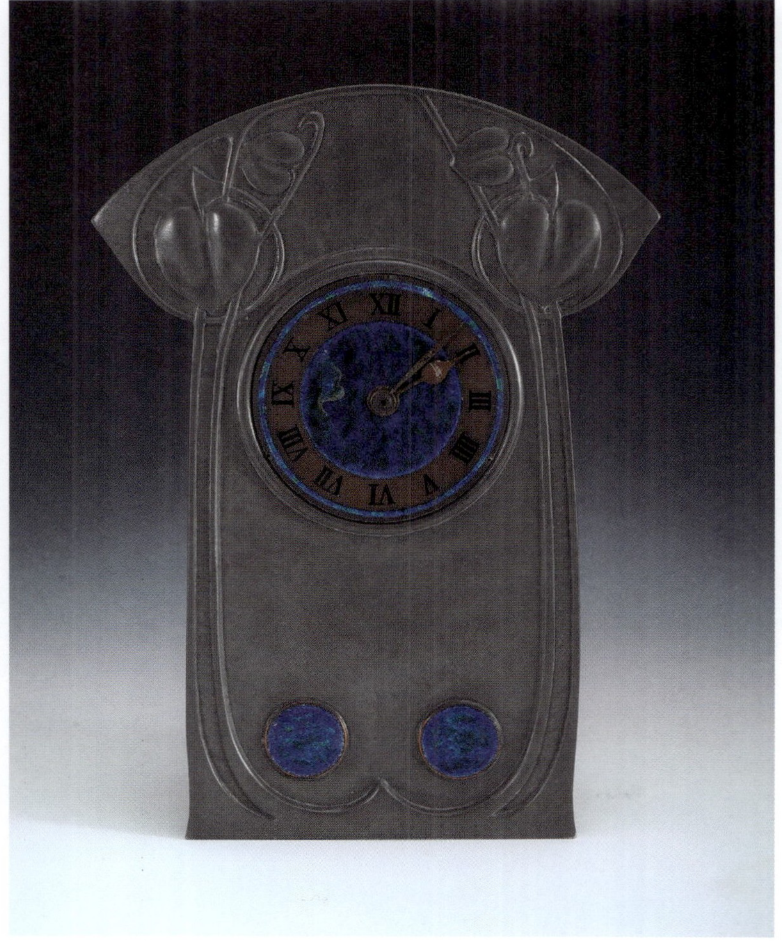

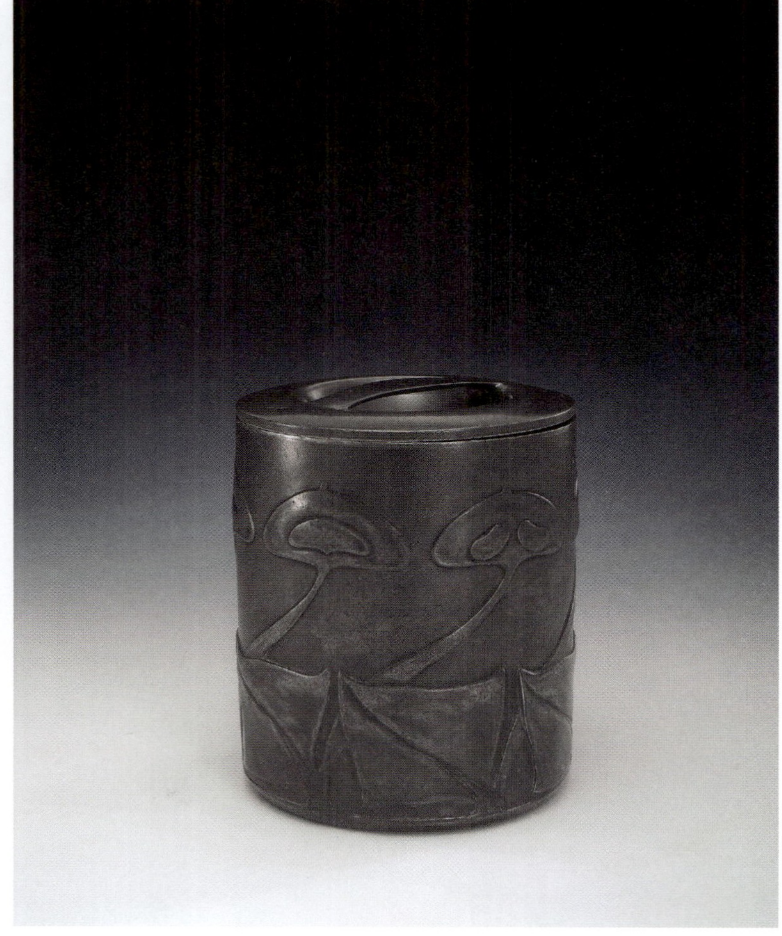

Mary Seton Watts was a fascinating character. Trained as a painter, before moving to work across a range of materials, she developed a very individual visual language, which emerged from her fusion of Celtic ornament with Pre-Raphaelitism. While superficially conforming to the Mediaevalism of the time, her ceramic figurines had a strange, melancholic feel to them that set them apart from her contemporaries using the same idiom. She reached her highest level of expression in her architectural relief work: her masterpiece is the Watts Cemetery Chapel, one of the most extraordinary buildings created in England in the period. She was also a leading organiser in the Arts and Crafts Movement. Her empirical vision led to her founding the Compton Pottery, and she employed in it a wide swathe of the – previously untrained – local population. Her Scottish background put her ideologically close to Knox, and together, they positioned Gaelic imagery at the heart of the Liberty business.[25]

There is an easily overlooked irony, of course, in the most powerful, modern, industrialised nation so far in history premising its art on archaic pre-industrial art; and fascinating that most of the great Pre-Raphaelite

*Below:* Mary Seton Watts, four figures, manufactured by the Compton Pottery, *c.*1900–1910, earthenware. Private Collection.

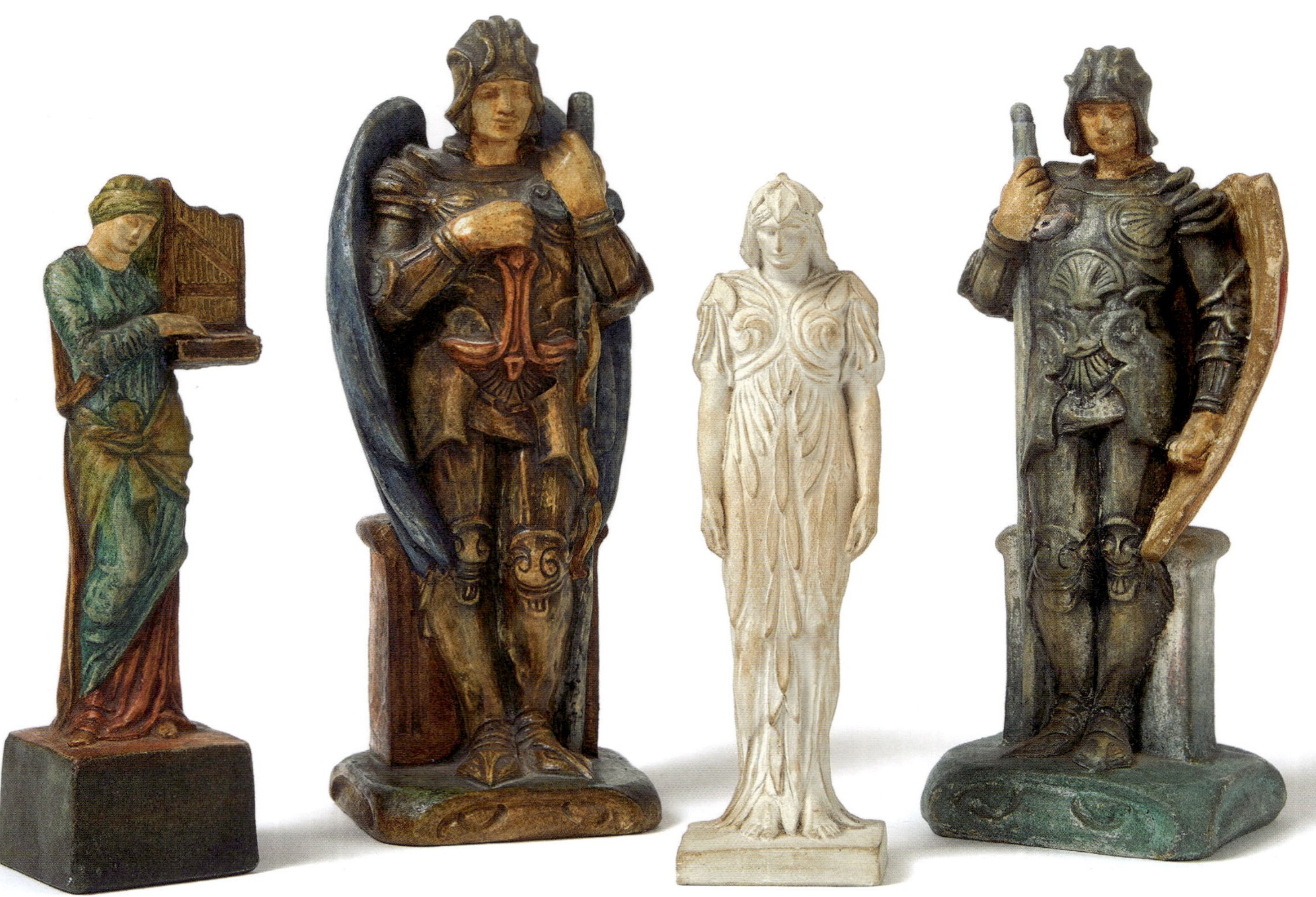

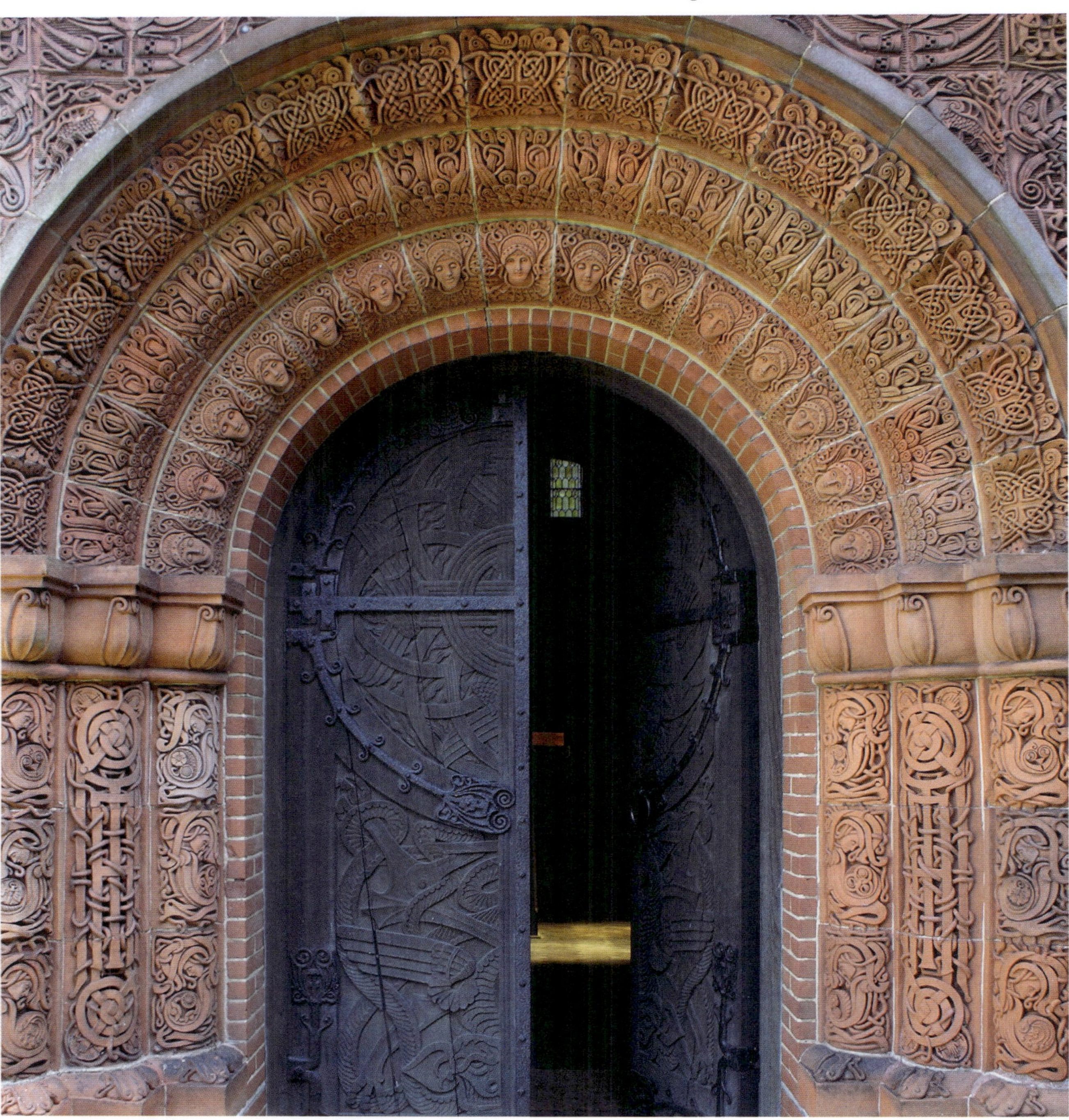

*Above:* Mary Seton Watts, Watts Cemetery Chapel, Compton, 1898.

patrons were based in the industrial heartlands of the nation, which is why many of the greatest examples are in museums in Birmingham, Manchester, and Liverpool. It would imply that the barons of industry were in denial about the world they had brought into being. This might well account for the discomfort with Art Nouveau among the elite of English art: it flagged up the contradictions – and perhaps hypocrisy – of a culture changing the planet through modernisation, while burying its collective head in the past. By openly embracing the 'massive engineering plants, and their consequences', to use Van de Velde's words, the Art Nouveau designers recognised the contradictions inherent in Mediaevalism, and embraced the idea that nature and industry could – and should – work together to create the city of the future. Famously, in the first years of the 20th century, the need to embrace technology was put forward by a number of the American Arts and Crafts groups, and was subject of a famous exchange between English Arts and Crafts designer C.R. Ashbee, on tour in America, and the young architect Frank Lloyd Wright. While Ashbee wasn't nearly as anti-technology as many followers of Ruskin, Wright's position made the Englishman uneasy:

*Opposite:* Aubrey Beardsley, *The Climax*, illustration for *Salome* by Oscar Wilde, 1893 (printed 1907), line block print. Arwas Archive.

He threw down the glove to me in characteristic Chicagoan manner in the matter of Arts and Crafts and the creations of the machine. 'My God' said he 'is machinery and the art of the future will be the expression of the individual artist through the thousand powers of the machine …'[26]

While Wright was never centrally involved with the style, his outlook tallied closely with most of the Art Nouveau architects: for him, in the houses he built in the first magical years of his output, nature had to sit alongside technology in order to create modern art.

This wasn't what the literary eclecticism of those influenced by the Pre-Raphaelites was about. They were after an alternative to the rationalism of modernisation, and to the tired and formulaic academicism they found all around them. Notably, as Barbara Bessac explores further into this volume, much design activity pulled art and design close to the theatre.[27] The dramatic, heady atmosphere of archaism pulled literature, theatre, and all forms of design into proximity. Sarah Bernhardt, the great actress and impresario, combined in her persona Pre-Raphaelitism, archaism, and exoticism, and in this way generated her own version of modernity. For a fascinating few years, Stoker's *Dracula* sat comfortably alongside Archibald Knox's pewter and silver wares. This mystical mélange penetrated deep into the Art Nouveau psyche.

And it was in London, in this mélange, that perhaps the very first Art Nouveau artist emerged: Aubrey Beardsley. His illustrations for Oscar Wilde's play *Salome*, published in 1893, had a swirling tensile line, asymmetric composition, and a heady, dark, decadence to it that anticipated the entire Art Nouveau style. One of the most remarkable figures in British art, Beardsley's entire mature oeuvre was concentrated into less than five years. He died in 1898 at the age of twenty-five.[28] In this time, he developed a radical approach to illustration that exploded onto the British and European scene. In many respects, his oeuvre is explained as being the application of his draughtsmanship and compositional flair to the visual languages that were available on the ground: the Arts and Crafts Movement, Design Reform, Aestheticism, and Pre-Raphaelitism. The core of his genius can be located in his ability to fuse together these often contrary aesthetic forces. For example, he was at the same time influenced by Burne-Jones and by Whistler, artists who were ideologically and aesthetically opposed. He was inspired by Japanese art, which was omnipresent in London by 1890, and his use of the arabesque revealed his predilection for Islamic design. Alongside these, he never quite lost his taste for the Mediaeval aesthetic.

The opposing forces at work in Beardsley went further. His friend, associate, and sometime publisher, Arthur Symons, suggested, just after the artist's death, that Beardsley's eclecticism was connected to an emotional contrariness that played-out in his art. Symons saw a dark side in the young artist, exacerbated by his awareness of mortality:

Here then, we have a sort abstract spiritual corruption, revealed in beautiful form; sin transfigured by beauty. And here, if we go no further, is an art intensely spiritual, an art in which evil purifies itself by its own intensity, and by the beauty which transfigures it.[29]

*Below:* Cover design for *Dracula* by Bram Stoker, 1897–1901, British Library.

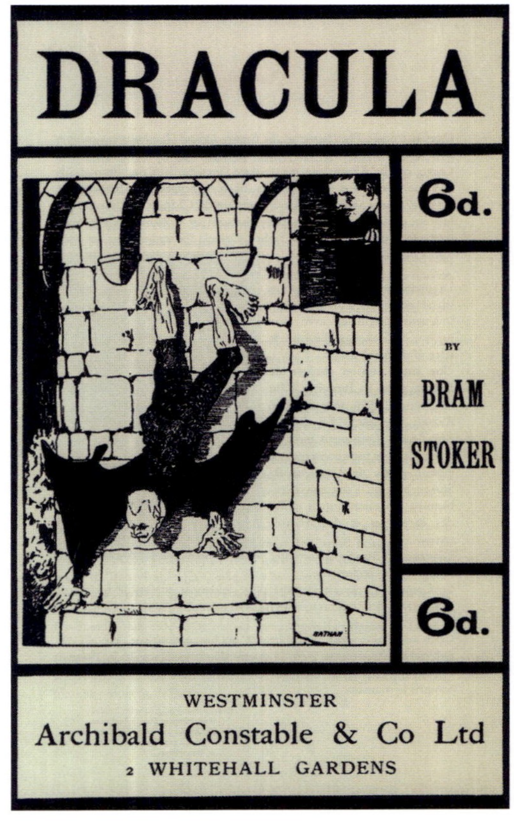

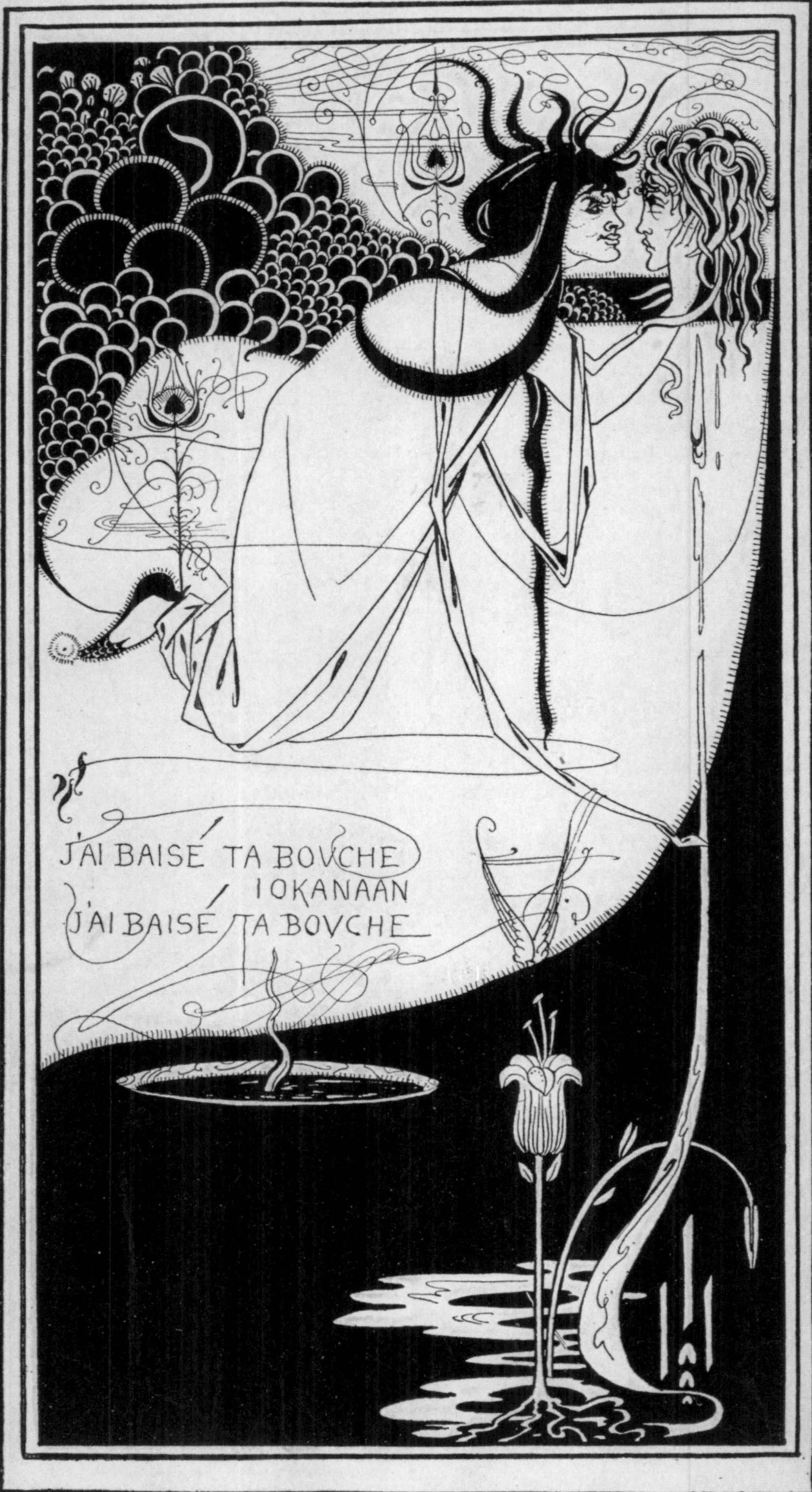
J'AI BAISÉ TA BOVCHE
IOKANAAN
J'AI BAISÉ TA BOVCHE

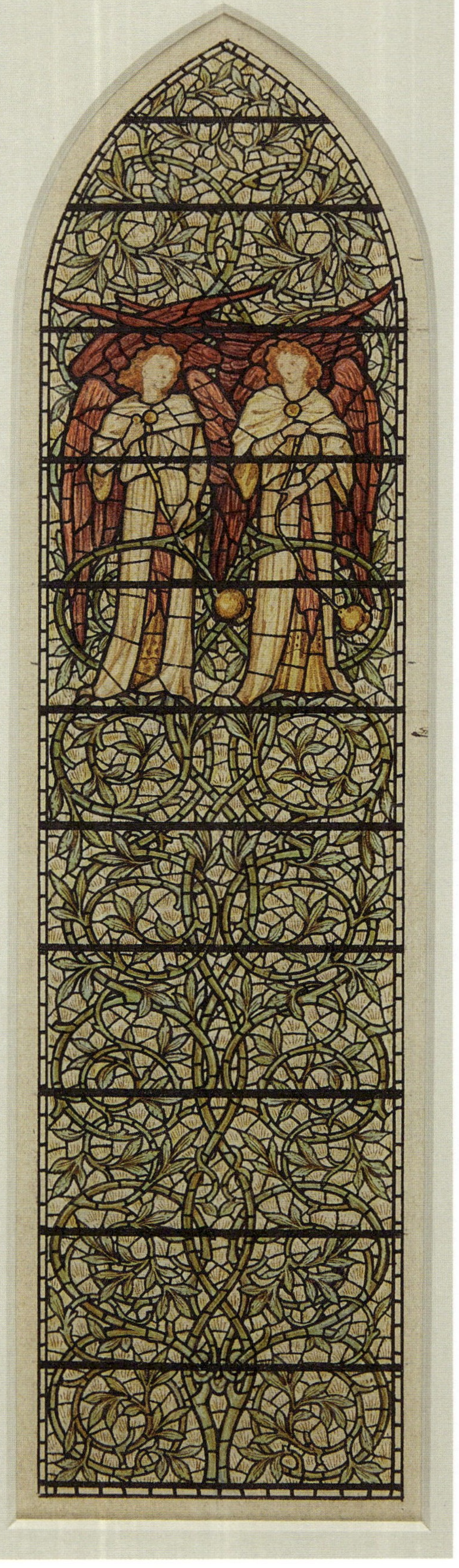

*Below:* William Morris, stained-glass design for Salisbury Cathedral, 1879, watercolour on paper. The Brian Clarke Collection of Stained Glass.

His dark eclecticism lent Beardsley's work a heady cosmopolitanism. The same could be said of Wilde, whose career was intertwined with his by virtue of *Salome*. One commentator noted that 'Wilde lived in a historical period in which the spirit of cosmopolitanism was beginning to flourish'.[30] It was true, and the same spirit flowed into every corner of Art Nouveau. The style was cosmopolitan by virtue of the fact that it brought together, in the modern urban context, cultural phenomena that hadn't previously corresponded with one another. This was enormously to the advantage of the style around 1900, when Europe was still fired by a laissez-faire internationalism. It was to become a far less useful feature as the continent drifted towards the First World War, under a cloud of frenetic nationalism.

The third English influence on Art Nouveau was more nebulous, but nevertheless vital for what might be termed the emotional make-up of the style. Reference has already been made to an intellectual tension that rose in the London art community in the last quarter of the century, between individualist and communal visions of art. That is, there were those who believed that the well-spring of art was in individual genius, that individuality was key to the making of art. And in opposition to this view, there were those who considered art to be the product of a community, to be socially generated. The implication, on the one hand, was that society was irrelevant to the making of art, and on the other, that art was the result of social activity. Interestingly, the political nature of the debate carried it beyond the confines of the art world: it played out in the pages of *The Times* and *Punch* magazine, and on the benches of the British Parliament. It even impacted the legal profession, with celebrated court cases that were a result of tensions between the two lobbies. Whistler vs Ruskin (1878) and Wilde vs Queensberry (1895) most famously carried cultural theory into the strident terrain of the law.

Oscar Wilde was the great individualist, and individualism didn't simply shape his idea of art. It was at the heart of his political credo, and underpinned his very particular idea of civilisation. A thinker on the left, but at odds with much of the British left-wing ethos, his fullest exposition of his ideas came in his seminal essay of 1891, *The soul of man under socialism*:

... for the full development of life to its highest mode of perfection ... What is needed is individualism ... At present, in consequence of the existence of private property, a great many people are enabled to develop a certain very limited amount of individualism. They are either under no necessity to work for their living, or are enabled to choose the sphere of activity that is really congenial to them and gives them pleasure. These are the poets, the philosophers, the men of science, the men of culture – in a word, the real men, the men who have realised themselves, and in whom all humanity gains a partial realisation. Upon the other hand, there are a great many people who, having no private property of their own, and being always on the brink of starvation, are compelled to do the work of beasts of burden ... These are the poor; and amongst them there is no grace of manner, of charm of speech, or civilisation or culture, or refinement in pleasures or joy of life.[31]

Having begun his career as a follower of Ruskin, and a supporter of the notion of art as a moral discourse, he came to the view that art cannot be expected to carry the concerns of society, but rather, is a disinterested phenomenon:

> this love of art for art's sake, is the point in which we of the younger school have made a departure from the teaching of Mr Ruskin – departure definite and different and decisive ... in his art criticism, his estimate of the joyous element of art, we are no longer with him; for the keystone to his ethical system is ethical always. He would judge of a picture by the amount of noble moral ideas it expresses ... But to us the rule of art is not the rule of morals ...[32]

This rejection of Ruskin put him at odds also with Morris and the Arts and Crafts thinkers. He was essentially taking to an aggressive conclusion the concept of *l'art pour l'art*, developed decades before by Baudelaire, Théophile Gautier and others in France, but in this context, it carried considerably greater controversy. For Wilde, art was wholly the product of individual genius, a truth he believed was evident in every work of art:

> It is not enough that a work of art conform to the aesthetic demands of the age: there should also be about it, if it is to give us any permanent delight, the impress of a distinct individuality. Whatever work we have in the 19th century must rest on the two poles of personality and perfection.[33]

He was, alongside Whistler, the champion of the Aesthetic Movement, and as such, his socio-cultural vision coloured the entire phenomenon. His coupling of amorality to the idea of individual genius ran full-scale against Morris, who was scathing about it:

> You will find clever and gifted men at the present day, who are prepared to sustain as a theory, that art has no function but the display of clever executive qualities ... No wonder that this theory should lead them into the practice of producing pictures which we might pronounce to be clever if we could understand what they meant.[34]

In the same spirit, Walter Crane commented on 'the ill-fated Oscar Wilde' that 'he was a notable figure in society at that time ... He led the so-called Aesthetic Movement of the early "eighties" ... If he ever fooled people, he was also befooled. He squandered the most brilliant talents on trifles.'[35] Burne-Jones was called as a witness at the Ruskin vs Whistler trial in 1878, in support of Ruskin, and he confirmed his discomfort with everything the Aesthetic Movement stood for.[36] At Wilde's trial in 1895, the prosecutor, William Carson, QC, made a direct connection between his amoral view of art and his moral conduct:

> Am I right in saying that you do not consider the effect of creating morality or immorality? ... So far as your works are concerned, you pose as not being concerned about morality or immorality?[37]

*Overleaf:* Daniel Cottier, Spring *(left)* and Autumn *(right)*, 1875, stained glass. The Brian Clarke Collection of Stained Glass.

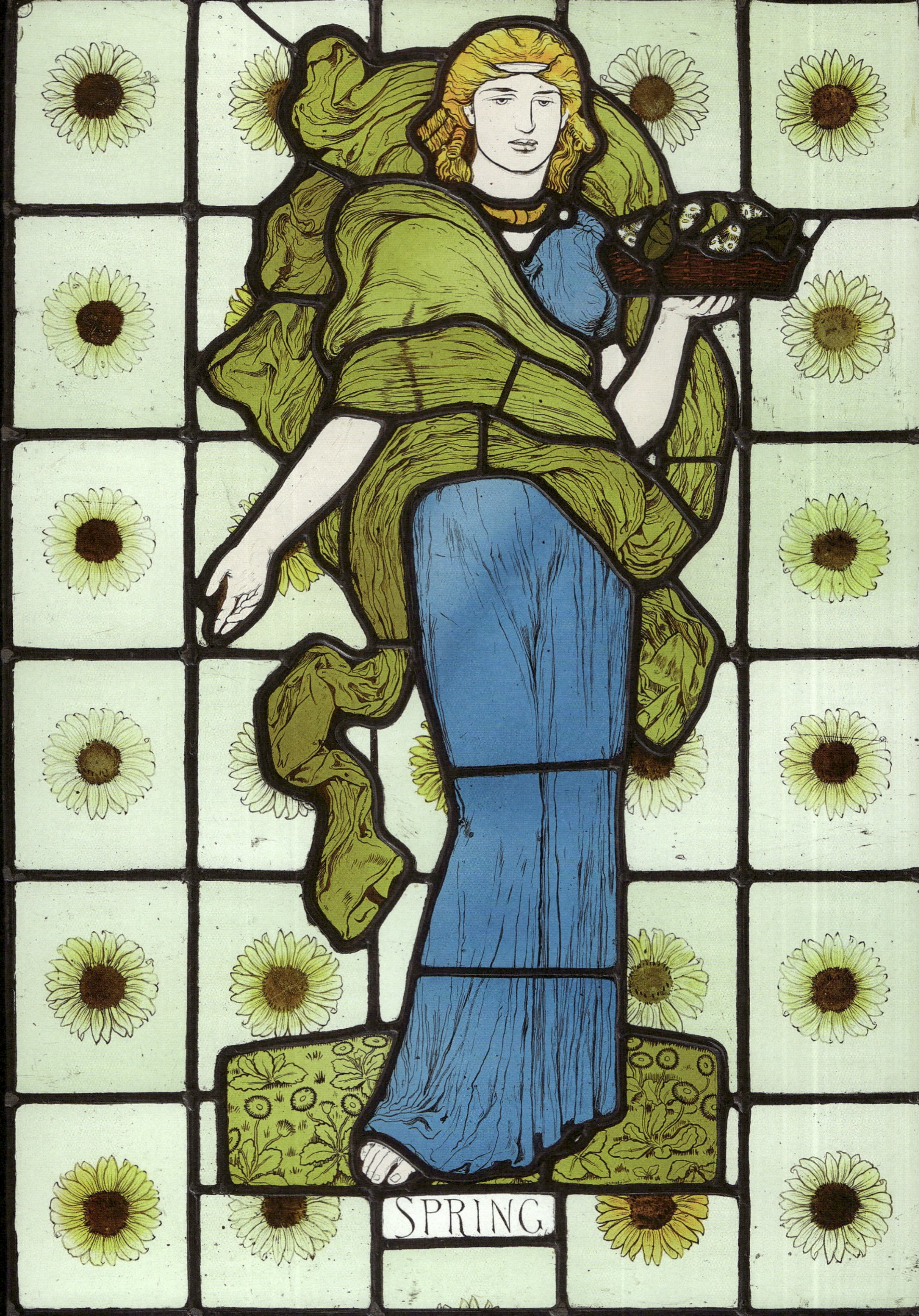

SPRING

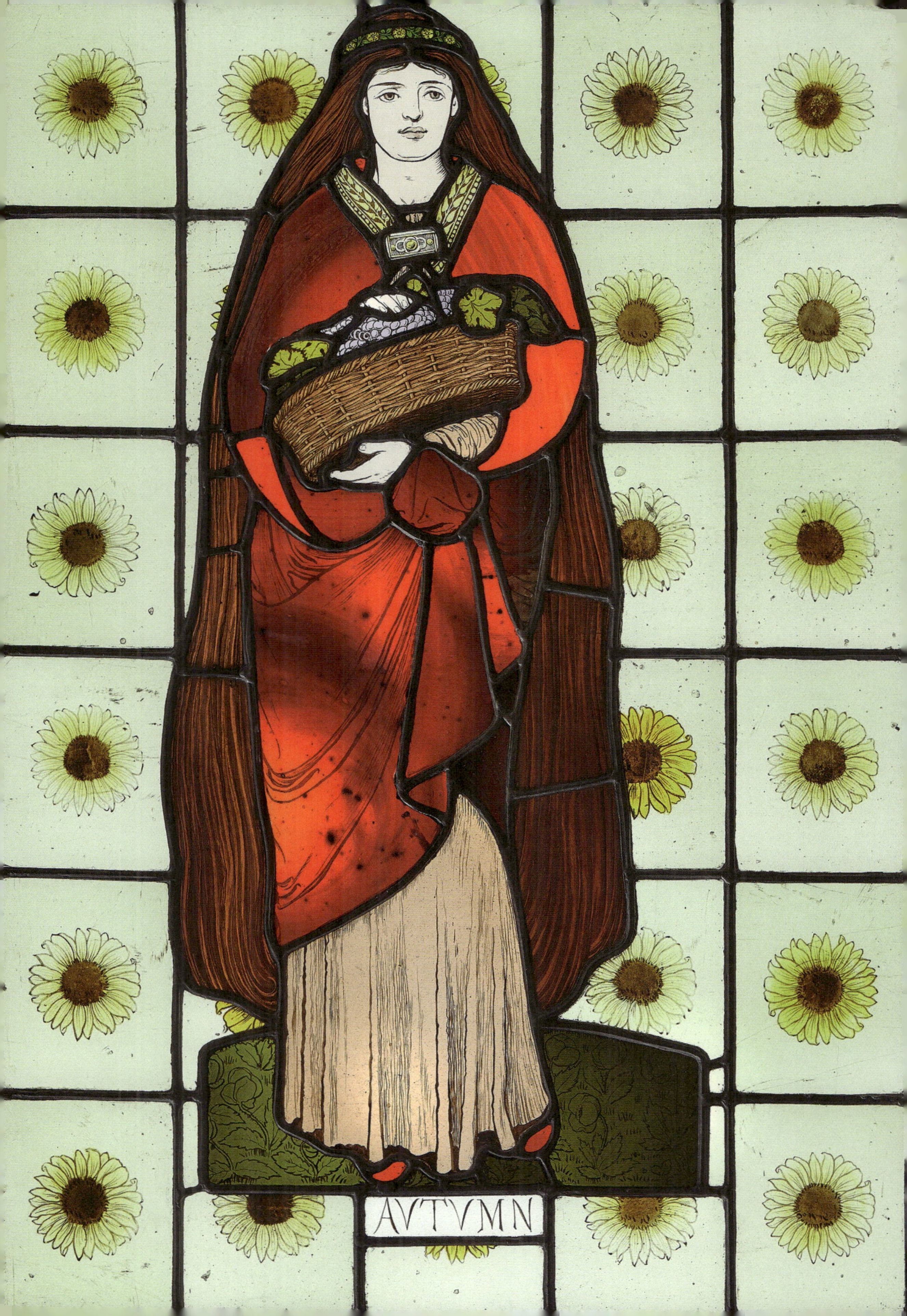
AVTVMN

Without doubt, and tragically, Aestheticism contributed to Wilde's going to prison.

The individual/social opposition was a major one through the whole modern period. It underlay much of the debate within the various Modern Movements in design. But before then, it was a presence in most of the schools of thought within Art Nouveau. It contributed to the emotional, frenetic energy of its rise, and also to its loss of shape and decline. It led to rifts between designers, and to rejection of the style by others. For Gustave Serrurier-Bovy and Henry Van de Velde, for example, the social meaning and role of design was an absolute given before it could be considered modern. This was far less a factor for Victor Horta, and many of the other leading Belgians. It was a tension at large in Barcelona, where Antoni Gaudí, fired by a deep-seated, religious communality, was sceptical of much *Modernista* practice he saw around him.[38] In short, the debate that raged in London became a part of the discourse in Art Nouveau circles.

But arguments between designers weren't the most important aspect of this tension. There was something else going on inside the swirling, contorting twists of Art Nouveau, and what it sought to represent. The dialectical struggle between universal, collective values, and individualism, played-out in works and oeuvres. In a lot of the great masterpieces, we are able to witness the fact that the style aspired to represent the collectivity of modern society, and the foibles of the individual mind, *at the same time.*

It was certainly a presence in Oscar Wilde's short stories and critical writings. We can feel in him the need to embrace at once the universal optimism of utopia, and the foibles of the human personality, as explored in the new discipline of psychology. One writer has observed that this psychological complexity struggled in England, and was always likely to receive greater appreciation among the French avant-garde: '. . . not only did the French appreciate Wilde before the English did, but it took the French reception to enlighten them'.[39] Perhaps this was also true in architecture and design.

At its strident height, around 1900, Art Nouveau was emotionally and intellectually driven by three things: the natural world, the individual psyche, and symbolic representations: the first two are held in proximity by the third, which is at once collective and subjective. It is this cognitive structure at the heart of the style that was so attractive twenty-five years later to the Surrealists: it implied the possibility of a subjective universality. Salvador Dalí and André Breton could see the 'self' in the explosive harmony of Hector Guimard's Paris metro stations: they were simultaneously natural, individual, and mythic. Street furniture had never been like this before, and arguably it never would be again. The simultaneity is a feature of Guimard's early masterpiece, the Castel Béranger. Designed from 1895, the year Siegfried Bing opened his gallery, Guimard's building was a compendium of everything that was going on in advanced design circles in northern Europe. Most interestingly, the architect embraced the increasing presence of engineering rationalism. He left raw iron beams showing on the main facades. The building is very visibly underpinned by a modern frame construction, and its overall plan is overtly shaped by functional need. On top of this, the organic flow of his linear patterns, carved into the stonework, show his pioneering grasp of the new vision of nature. Technology and nature: both have a universal feel to them, and celebrate

*Below:* Hector Guimard, metalwork for the Paris Metro, *c.*1900.
*Bottom:* Hector Guimard, ceramic relief, Castel Béranger, Paris, 1895–1898.

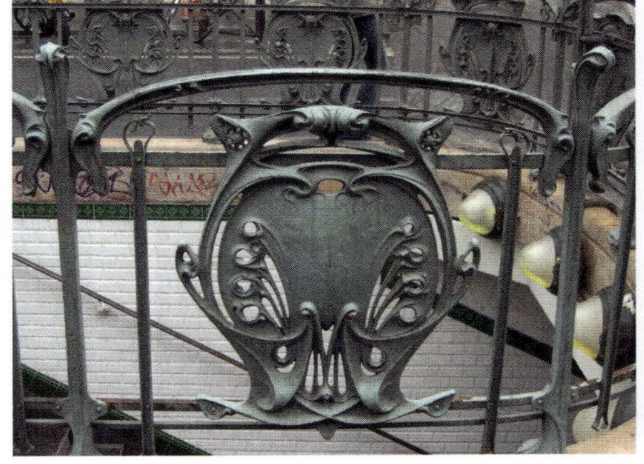

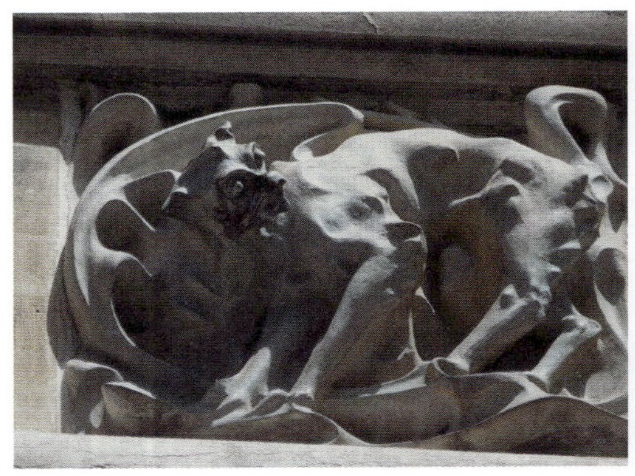

*Right:* Hector Guimard, Castel Béranger, Paris, 1895–1898, colour lithograph. Bibliothèque Des Arts Décoratifs.

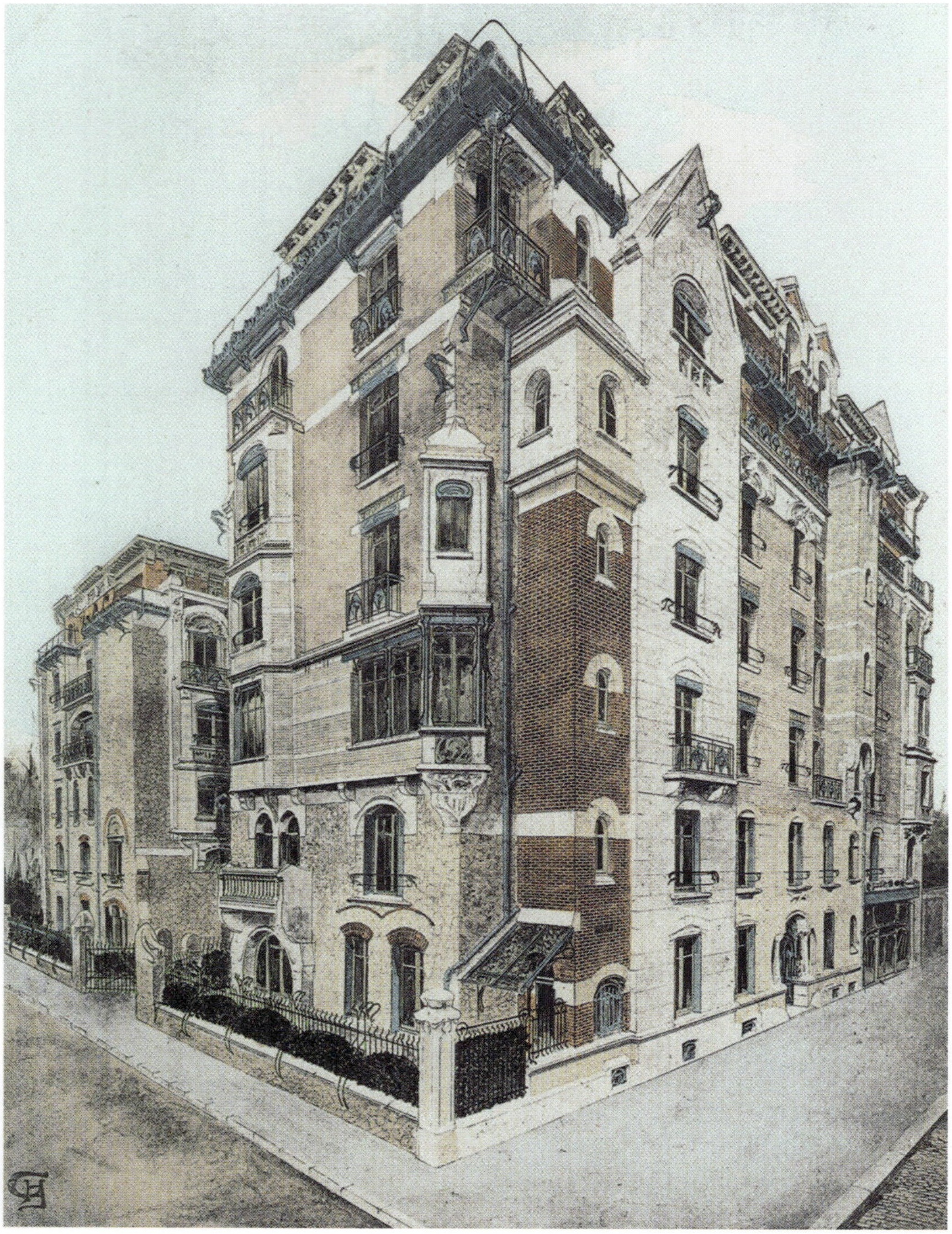

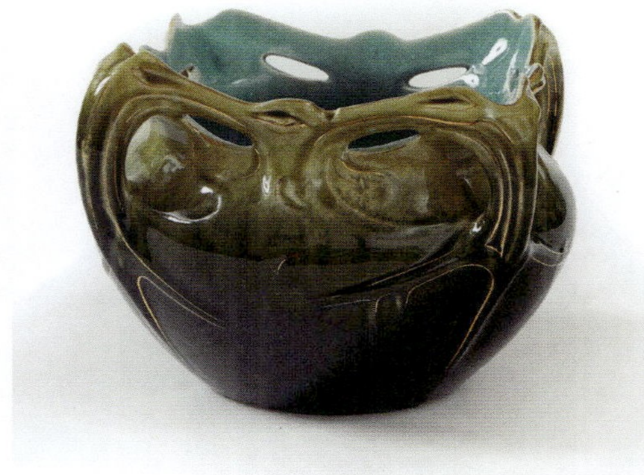

*Above:* Hector Guimard, *Jardinière,* *c.*1900, ceramic. Private Collection.
*Below and bottom:* Hector Guimard, Castel Béranger, Paris, 1895–1898.

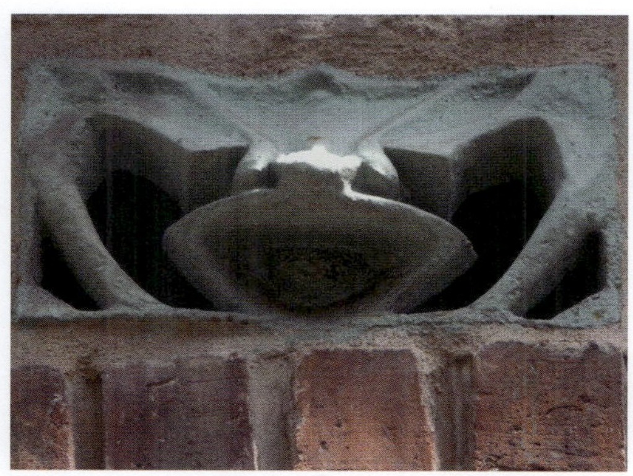

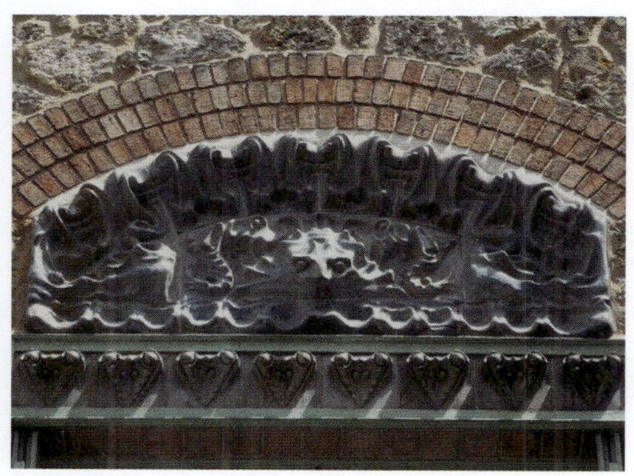

the arrival of modern life. Yet the facades are also covered in ceramic and metal imagery that is the stuff of fantastical dreams, if not nightmares. Cats, dragons, and screaming, contorted faces hiss and howl at us in ways that would have satisfied Poe or Stoker. The communal objectivity of nature and geometry is made to sit with the subjectivity of invented myths and nightmares. All this played-out on the facades of a well-to-do apartment block.

he fourth component of the English impact on Art Nouveau was the sheer power, scale, and pragmatism of English industry. English manufacturing was wholly driven by the need to export goods, and companies across the arts were more than happy to make use of the style to sell goods. The wallpaper, textile, ceramic, glass, and metalwork companies of the United Kingdom were happy to make what they understood to be Art Nouveau products, as long as people were prepared to buy them. And between 1895 and 1912, people did buy, on a large scale, across Europe. Additionally, the style had a definite commercial

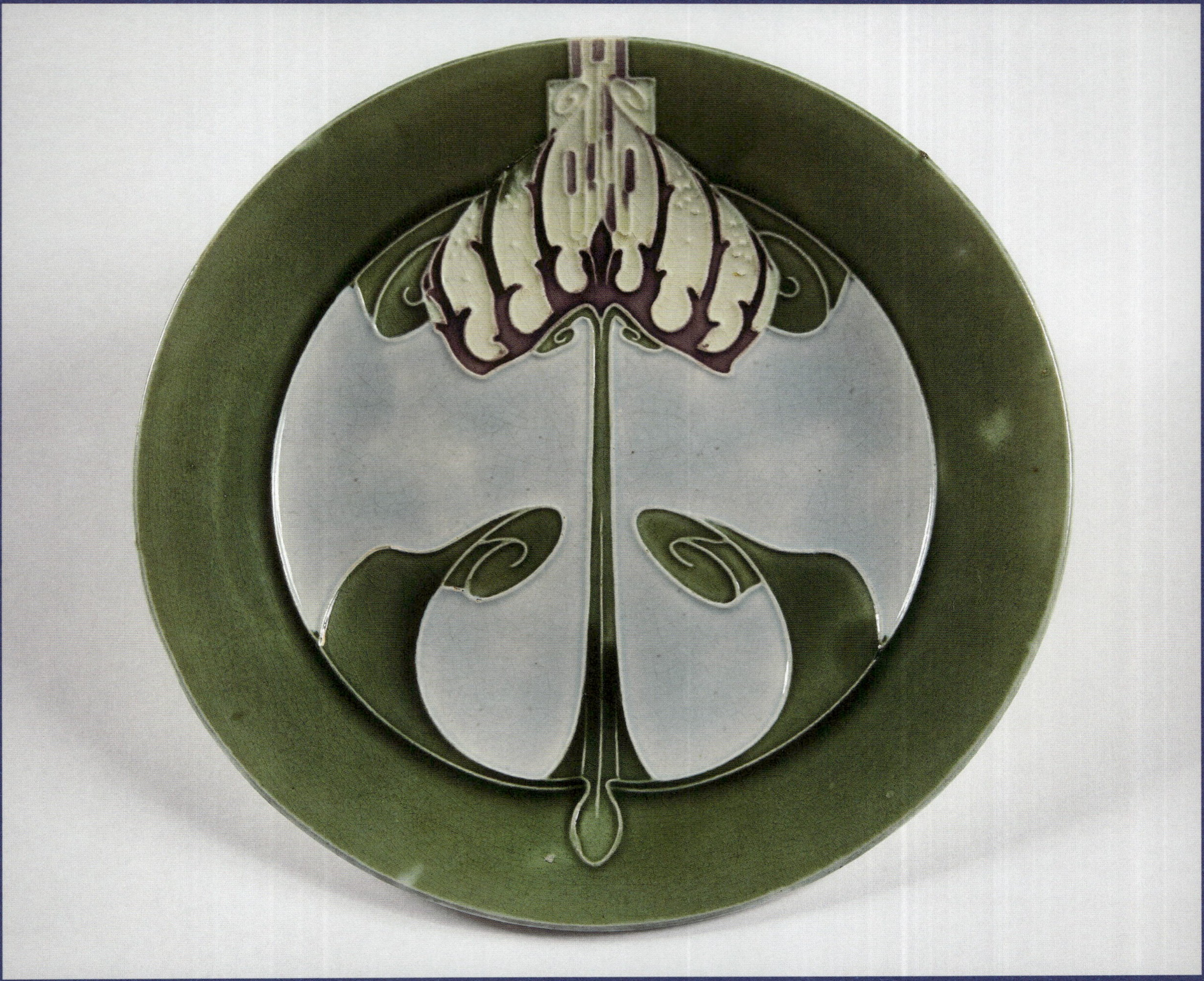

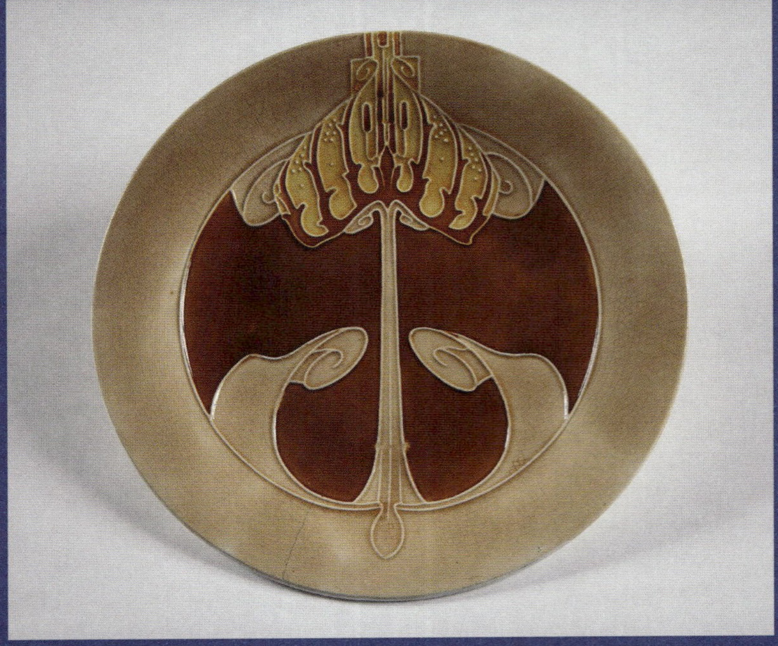

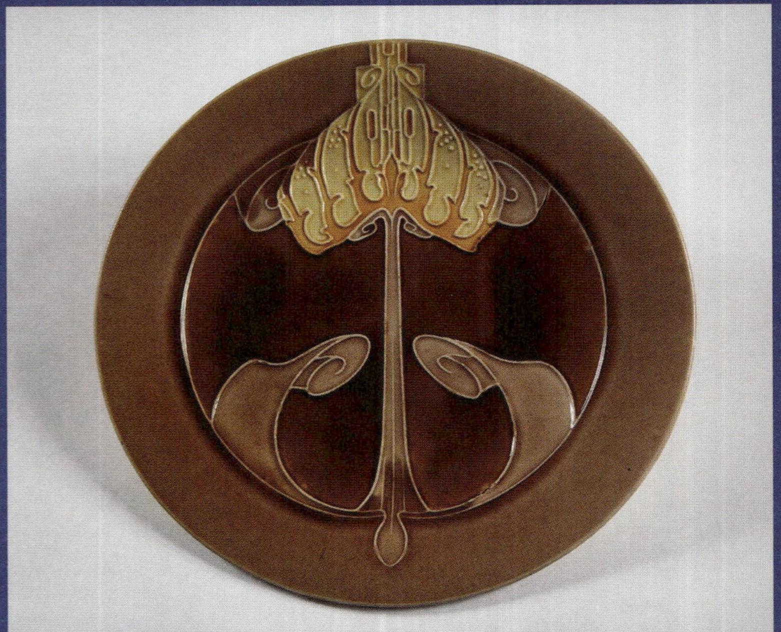

*Opposite:* Léon Victor Solon and John Wadsworth, set of three Secessionist Ware plates, manufactured by Minton & Co., 1904, earthenware. Sainsbury Centre.

viability in Britain, as witnessed by the millions of glass and ceramic vases, tiles, brooches, biscuit tins, tea caddies, and magazines that made use of the swirls, curls, and typography of the style. In that sense, there was a lot of English Art Nouveau, a combination of works produced by committed individuals going against the national grain, and pragmatic manufacturers concerned solely with the search for lucrative sales.

In fact, there is more than anecdotal evidence to show that the broader English public very much enjoyed having Art Nouveau on their products and furnishings. Antagonism towards it from then until now was virtually always led by the established art world itself. Through the 20th century, much of the institutionalised elite – university academics, art-school professors, museum curators, city planners – have attempted to brand it as lamentable kitsch. Ornament has been consistently denied a space within the canon of modernity. In this sense, little has changed since 1895.

*Below:* Metalwork by W.H. Hutton & Sons, glass by James Powell & Sons, Whitefriars, decanter, 1903, glass, silver and mother of pearl. Sainsbury Centre.

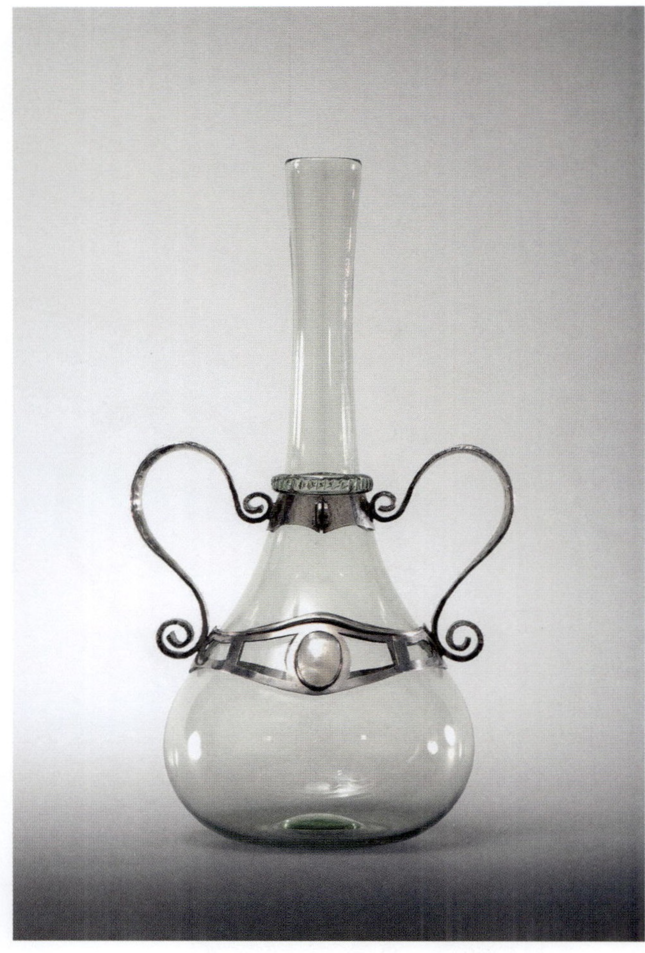

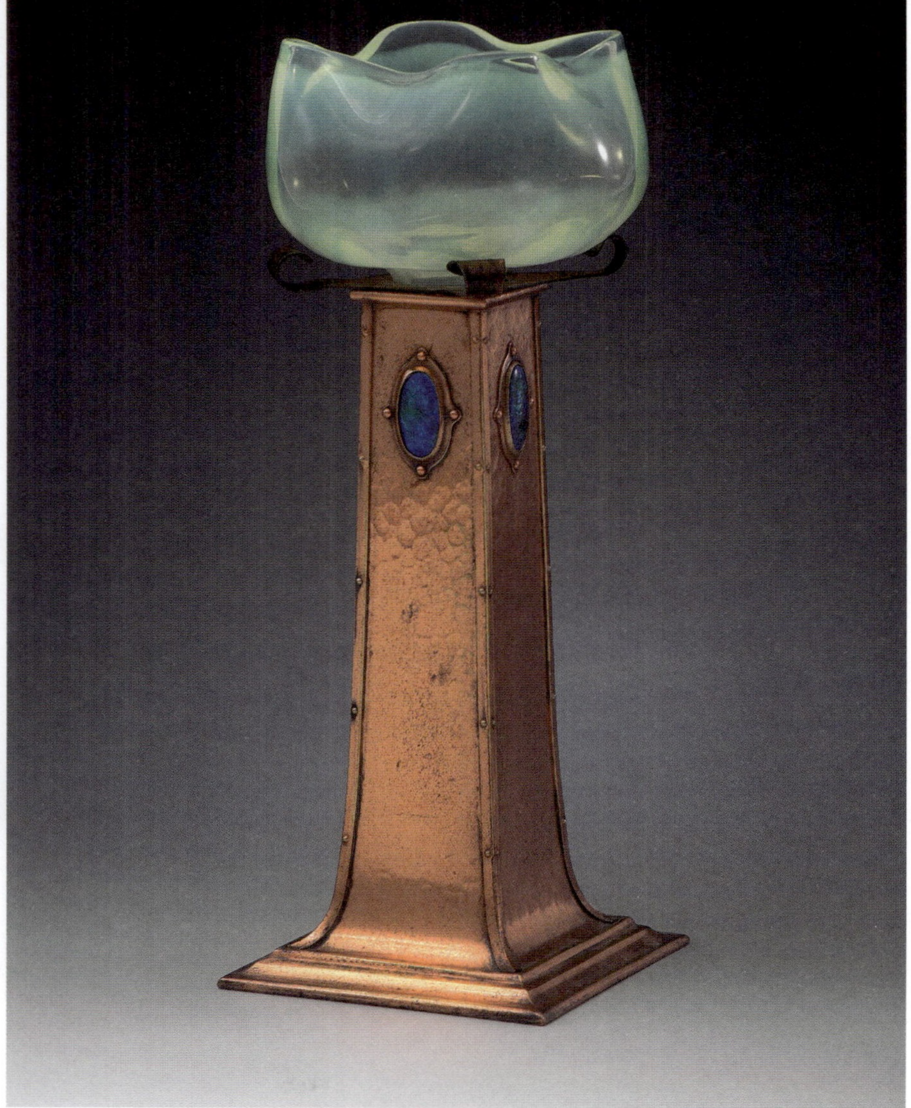

*Right:* Liberty & Co., Cambray Ware vase, *c.*1900, copper, enamel and glass. Sainsbury Centre.

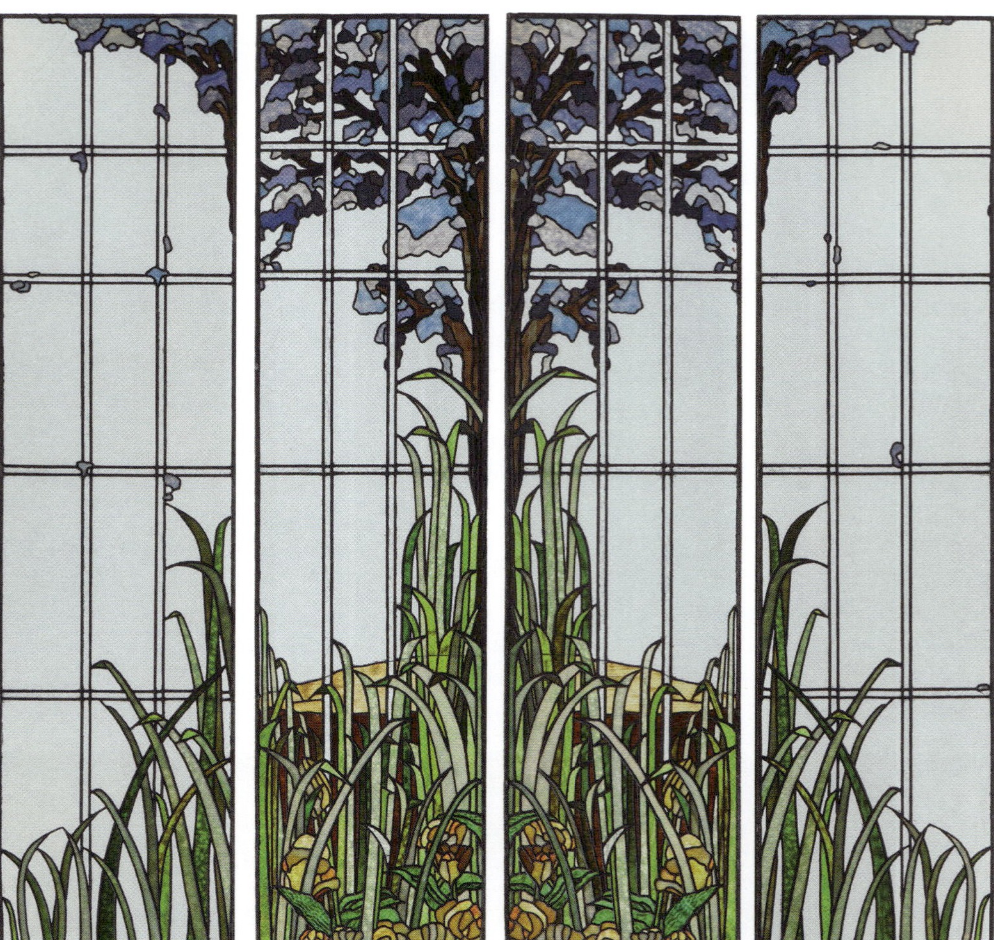

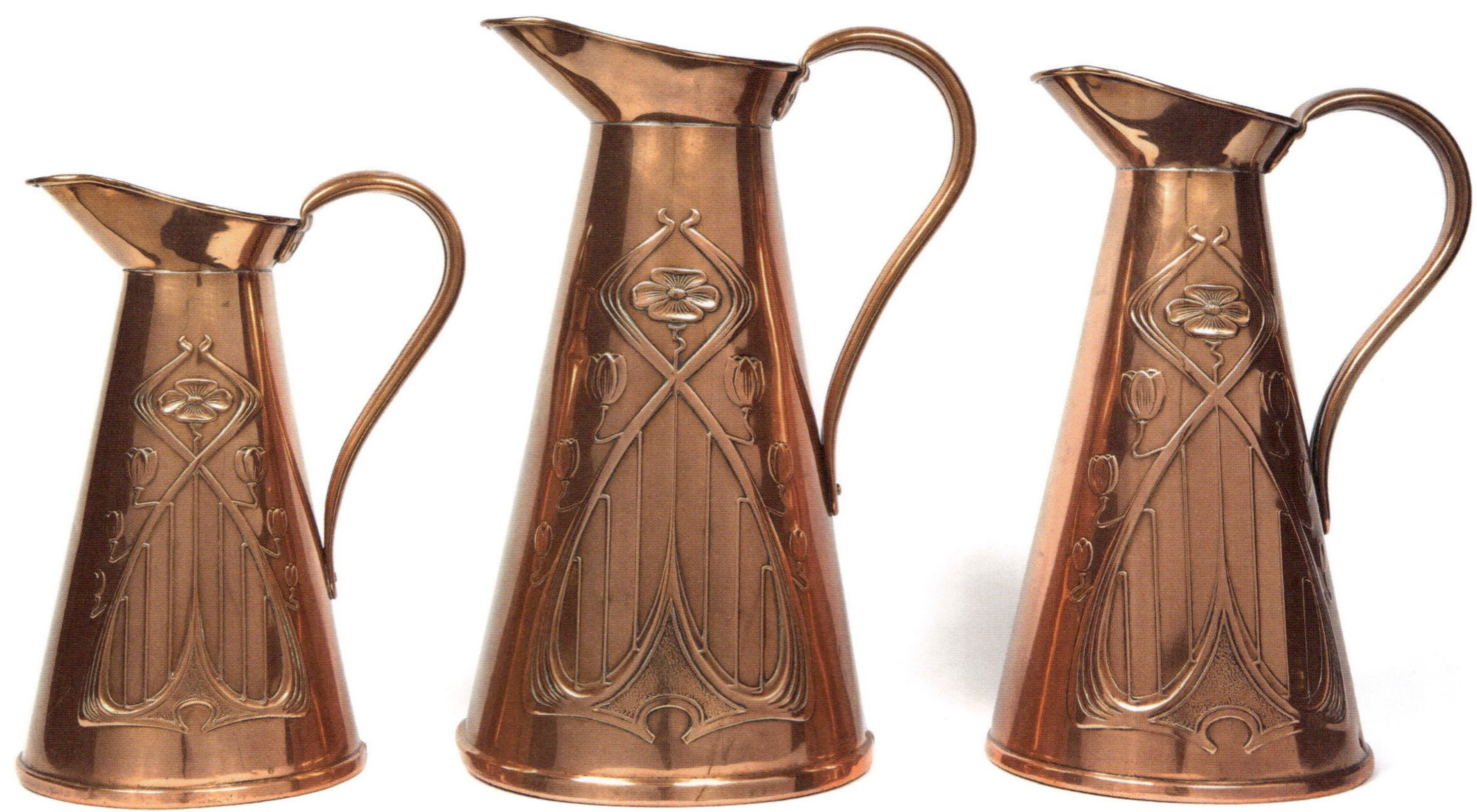

*Left:* Unknown maker, panels, *c.*1890, stained glass. The Brian Clarke Collection of Stained Glass.
*Below:* Joseph Sankey & Sons Ltd, set of three jugs, *c.*1900, copper. Sainsbury Centre.

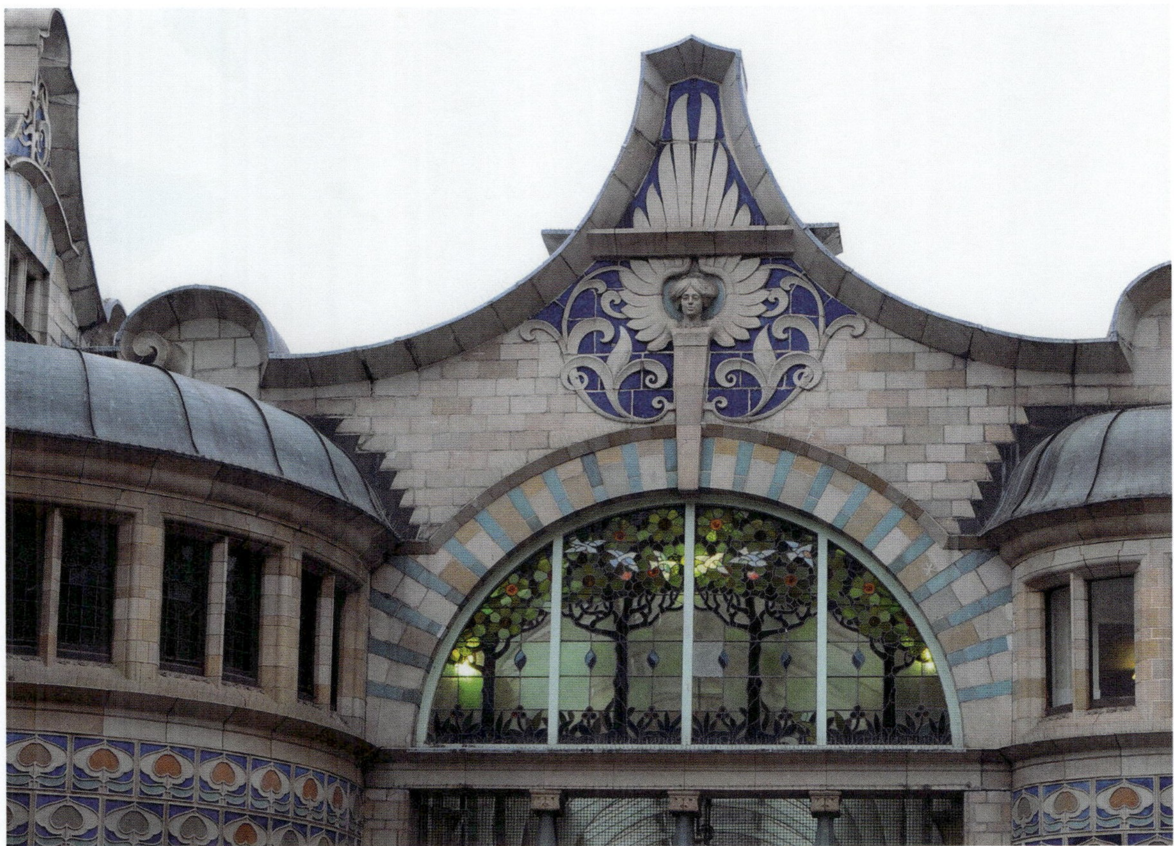

So, English Art Nouveau: a complex phenomenon, and one that has evaded identification and definition for much of the last 120 years. If we understand Art Nouveau to be a number of movements, based almost entirely in cities, which embraced the common visual language while developing their own particular take on the style, we can affirm that this didn't happen in England. No English city nurtured an Art Nouveau movement. There were fragmented moments: smatterings of it in London, and buildings in various other cities and counties, like the Royal Arcade in Norwich, and the Watts Cemetery Chapel in Surrey. Across the other arts, there were individuals who worked for a time with the style, and manufacturers who generated wares that absolutely looked the part. But there was never a core of artists, designers, companies, and writers in common cause, no specialist magazines or galleries championing the style, and no critical mass anywhere that could be meaningfully defined as Art Nouveau.

Style isn't just a matter of what things look like. It is also about what they mean. There were many objects manufactured in England that looked the part; but the emotional and intellectual direction of English art and design in the last part of the century wasn't in tune with the outlook Art Nouveau represented. Ideologically, the English had drifted elsewhere. There were also extraneous factors causing the move away from the hedonistic ideals of the new style: the depression of 1893 and its aftermath impacted America and the United Kingdom more directly than Europe, slowing adventurous consumerism; the Oscar Wilde trials in 1895 drastically reduced public support for anything that contained any form of sensual content, and fuelled suspicion of adventurous, exotic art-forms; and the outbreak of the Second Boer War in 1899 severely impacted English self-confidence, and fed anti-internationalist sentiment.

But Art Nouveau wouldn't have developed and triumphed in the way it did without the English art scene. The English were important for Art Nouveau, but, ultimately, they weren't part of it.

§

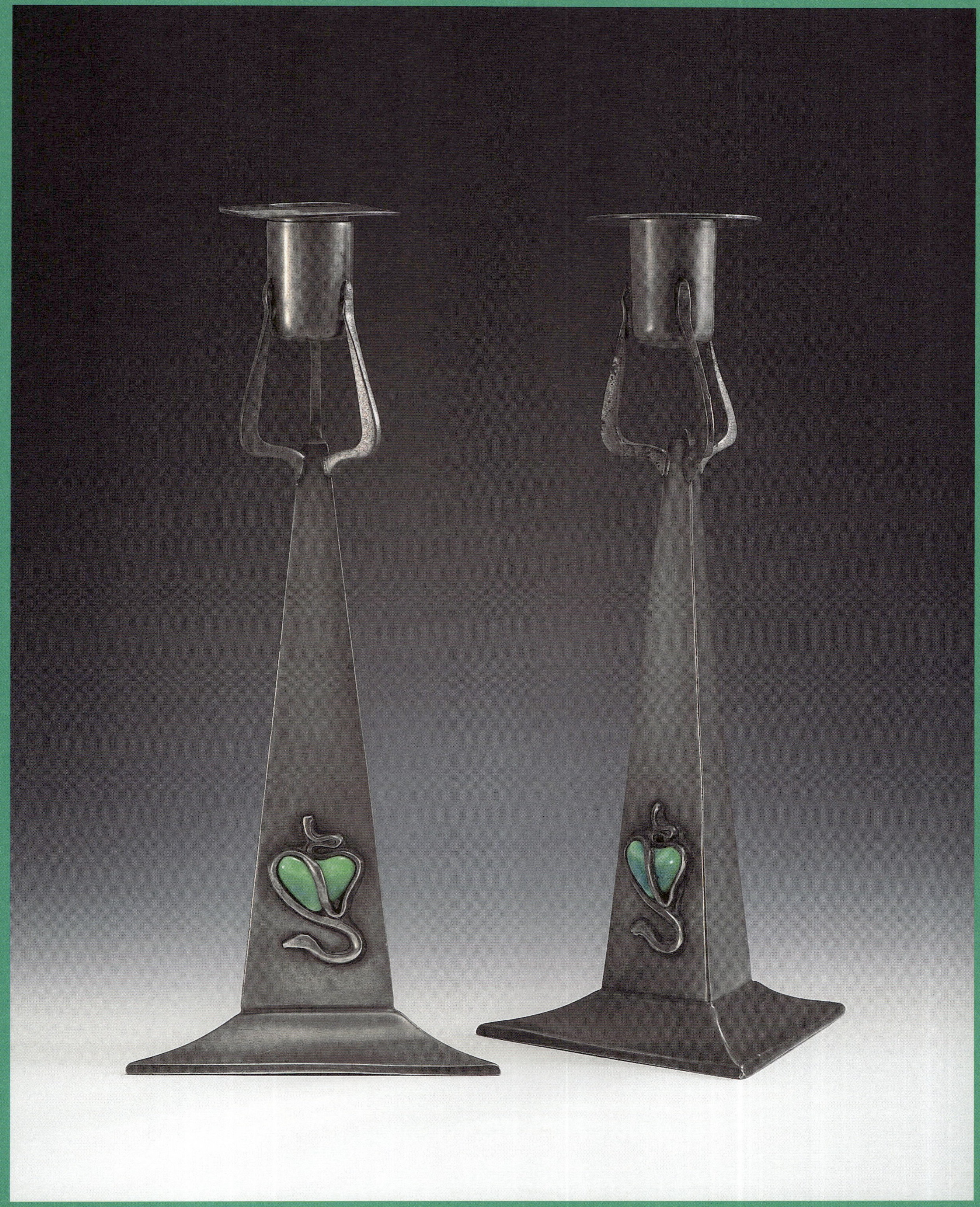

*Opposite:* Connell & Co., pair of candlesticks, *c.*1909, pewter and earthenware. Sainsbury Centre.
*Right:* Unknown maker, Arts and Crafts cabinet doors, *c.*1920, stained glass and wood. The Brian Clarke Collection of Stained Glass.

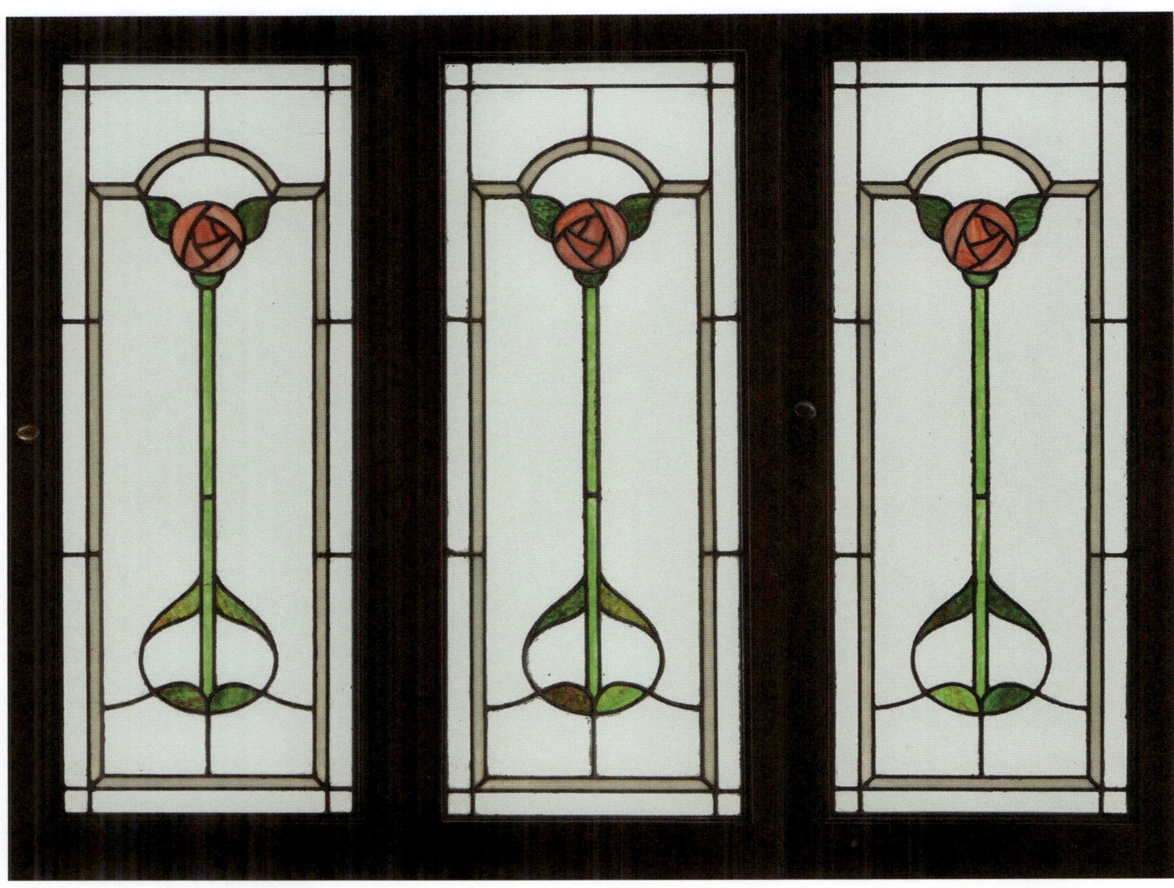

## ENDNOTES


1   See Paul Greenhalgh, 'Le Style Anglais: English Roots of the New Art', in Greenhalgh (ed.), *Art Nouveau 1890–1914* (London and New York: V&A Museum and Abrams, 2000), pp.127–45.

2   See Richard Dormant, *Albert Gilbert* (London: Mellon Centre, 1985).

3   Ibid.

4   See, for example, Ghislaine Wood, 'Art Nouveau at the V&A', in *Art Nouveau, an architectural indulgence* (London: Andrea Papadakis, 2000), pp.26–33.

5   See, for example, Viollet-Le-Duc, quoted in Prisse d'Avennes, *The Decorative Art of Arabia* (London: Studio Editions, 1873, reprinted 1989), p.10.

6   See Introduction.

7   Ernest Batchelder, *The principles of design* (Chicago: Inland Printer Company, 1911), p.144.

8   A.E. Lilley and W. Midgley, *A book of studies in plant form* (London: Richard Clay and Sons, 1902), p.1.

9   R.G. Hatton, quoted from Ernest Batchelder, *The principles of design* (Chicago: Inland Printer Company, 1911), p.142.

10   William Morris, from *The lesser arts*, in Asa Briggs (ed.), *William Morris, selected writings and designs* (London: Pelican, 1962), p.85.

11   Alois Riegl, *Problems of Style, foundations for a history of ornament* (Berlin: 1893), p.14.

12   W.A.S. Benson, *Notes on some of the minor arts* (London: 1883).

13   Ibid.

14   Ian Hamerton, *W.A.S. Benson: Arts and Crafts luminary and pioneer of modern design* (Woodbridge: Antique Collectors' Club, 2005), p.17.

15   Widar Halen, *Christopher Dresser* (London: 1990).

16   William Morris, *The Earthly Paradise, a poem* (London: Longmans, Green and Company, 1896), p.3.

17   F.E. Hulme, *Art Studies from Nature, as applied to design, for the use of architects, designers, and manufacturers* (London: Chapman and Hall, 1872, 1902).

18   Now the Musical Instrument Museum.

19   See Rebecca Stott, *Darwin's Ghosts, the secret history of evolution* (London: Bloomsbury, 2012).

20   Henry Van de Velde, 'Ein Kapitel über Entwurf und Bau moderner Möbel', 1897, from Klaus-Jurgen Sembach, *Henry Van De Velde* (London: Thames and Hudson, 1989), p.11.

21   Fiona McCarthy, *William Morris, a life for our times* (London: Faber, 1994); Charles Harvey and Jon Press, *William Morris, design and enterprise in Victorian Britain* (Manchester: Manchester University Press, 1991); Linda Parry (ed.), *William Morris* (London: Philip Wilson, 1996).

22   Siegfried Bing, 'L'Art Nouveau', *The Craftsman*, Vol. 5, No. 1, October 1903, p.7.

23   Peter Cormack, *Arts and Crafts stained glass* (New Haven, CT, and London: Paul Mellon Centre for the Study of British Art and Yale University Press, 2015).

24   A.J. Tilbrook, *The designs of Archibald Knox for Liberty and Co.* (Somerset: Richard Dennis, 1995).

25   See Veronica Franklin Gould, *Mary Seton Watts: unsung heroine of Art Nouveau* (London: The Watts Gallery, 1998).

26   Alan Crawford, *C.R. Ashbee, architect, designer, and Romantic socialist* (London and New Haven, CN: Yale University Press, 1985), p.98.

27   See Barbara Bessac, Chapter 2.

28   See, for example, Stephen Calloway, *Aubrey Beardsley* (London: V&A Publications, 1998).

29   Arthur Symons, *Aubrey Beardsley* (London: John Baker, 1898; this edition 1966), p.23.

30   Julia Prewitt Brown, *Cosmopolitan Criticism: Oscar Wilde's Philosophy of Art* (Charlottesville: University of Virginia Press, 1997), p.29.

31   Oscar Wilde, *The soul of man under socialism*, 1891, in *The collected works of Oscar Wilde* (London: Wordsworth Editions, 1997), p.898.

32   Oscar Wilde, *L'Envoi* (Philadelphia: J.M. Stoddart and Co., 1882), pp.121–2.

33   Ibid, p.123.

34   William Morris, *Transactions of the National Association of the Advancement of Art and its Applications to Industry*, Edinburgh Meeting (London: 1890), p.199.

35   Walter Crane, *Reminiscences of Oscar Wilde*, in E.H. Mikhail, *Oscar Wilde, interviews and recollections* (London: Macmillan, 1979), pp.150–1.

36   Linda Merrill, *A pot of paint: aesthetics on trial in Whistler v Ruskin* (London: 1991).

37   H. Montgomery Hyde (ed.), *The Trials of Oscar Wilde* (London: William Hodge, 1948), p.122.

38   *Modernista* was the Catalonian term for Art Nouveau. See Lluis Bosch, Chapter 4.

39   Stephan Evengelista (ed.), *The reception of Oscar Wilde in Europe* (London: Continuum, 2010), p.68.

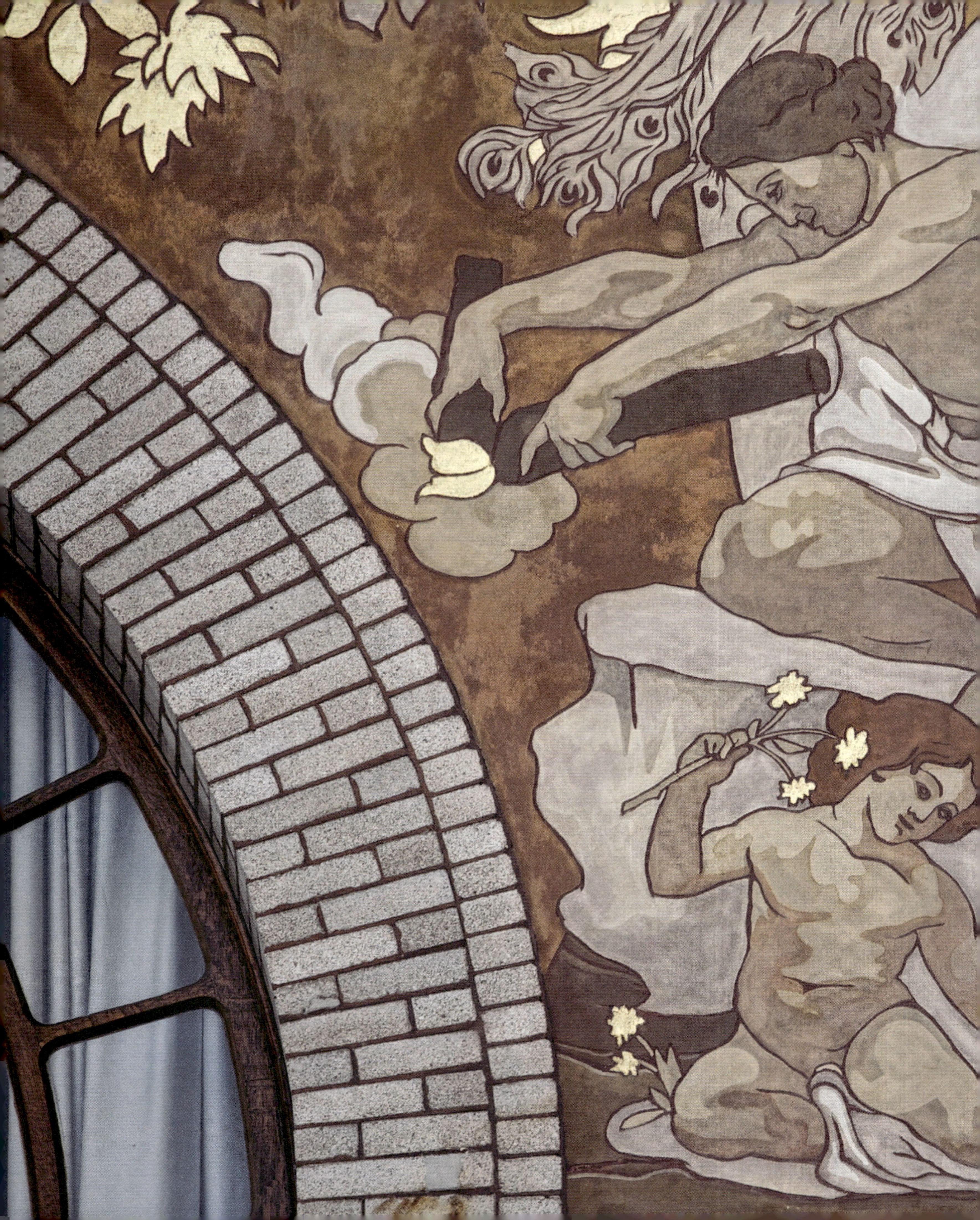

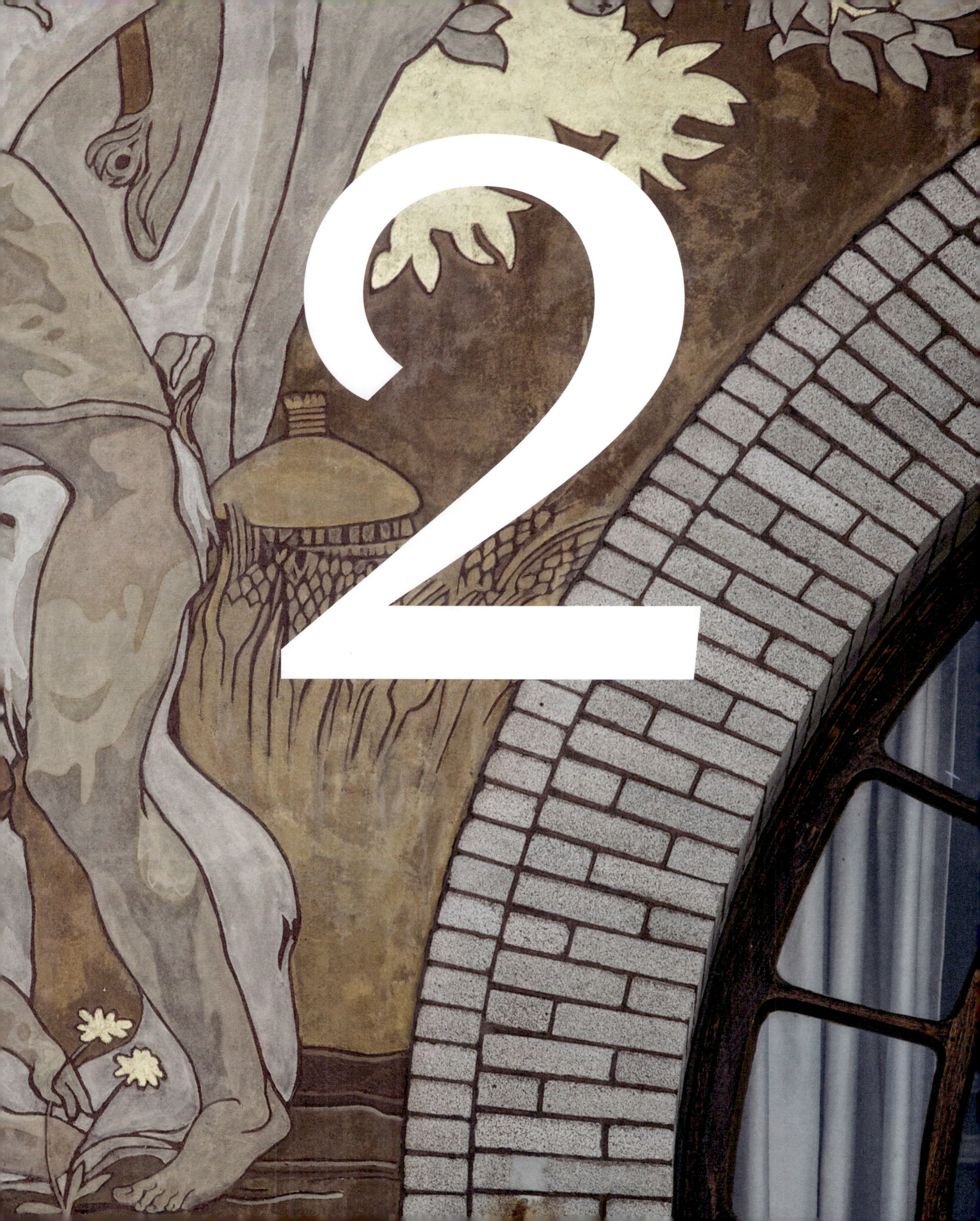

*Opposite:* Victor Horta, Hôtel Tassel, 1893.

# ~Belgian Art Nouveau~

~Françoise Aubry~

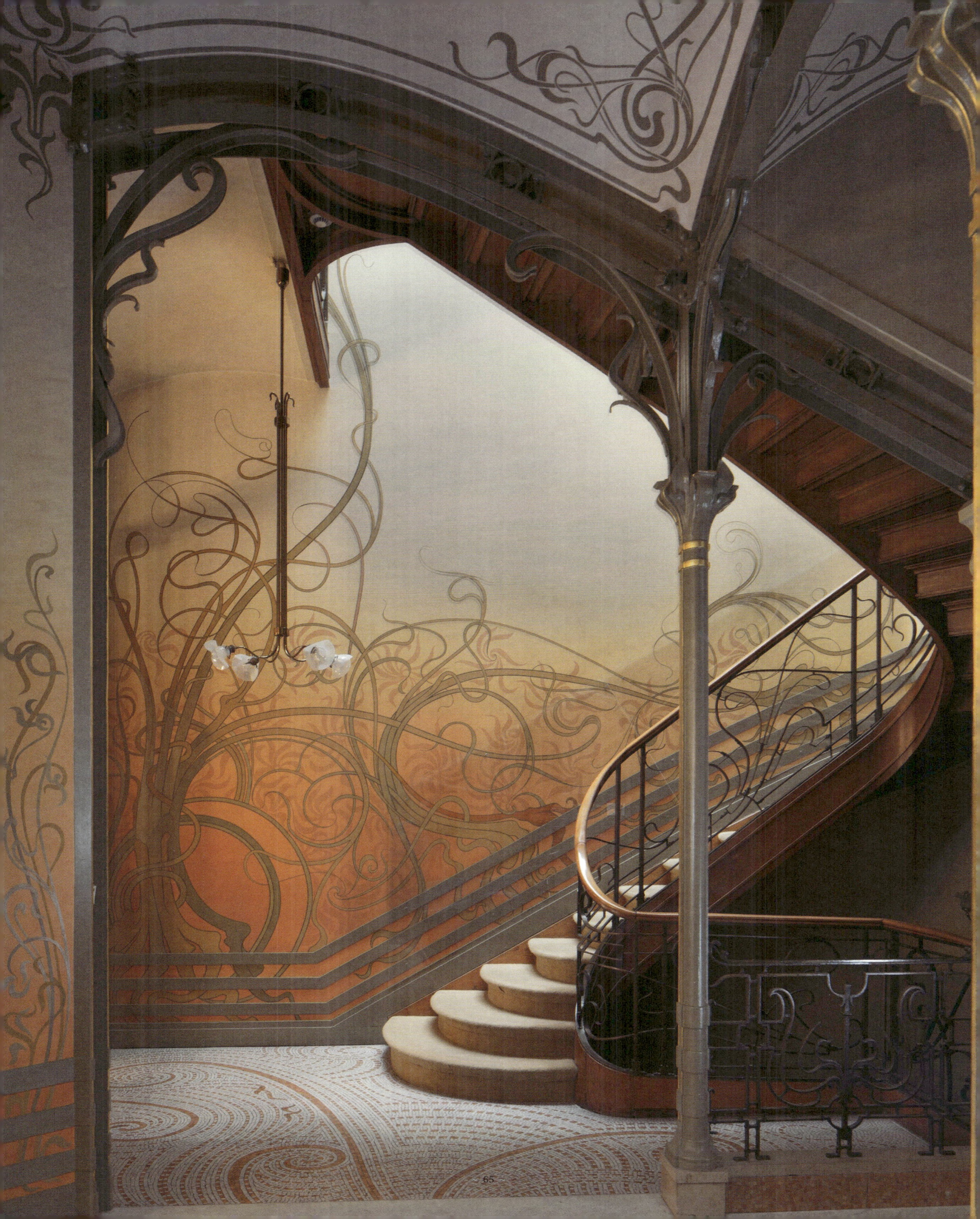

There's the asymmetry or dissymmetry of the furniture, similar in style to Japanese furniture, and straight lines always obstinately interrupted by curves, and flimsy supports with a nodular quality, arching like tree limbs, and then there's the 'vermicelli' – all that is Belgian, or Anglo-Belgian or Anglo-Japano-Belgian.[1]

The forms of expression that distinguish Belgian Art Nouveau derive from its ambition to realise the dreams of diverse social classes that aspired to a way of life no longer weighed down by tradition. The task was to build private mansions for the new bourgeoisie who had grown rich in industry and commerce; houses for cultured intellectuals (lawyers and university professors); modern premises for shopkeepers; studios for artists; and clean, decent accommodation for workers. In short, to construct new spaces for an evolving society whose prosperity went hand-in-hand with social and political advancements.

In 1894 Victor Horta (1861–1947) became architect to the Solvay family, and the following year he was commissioned to design the community centre for the Belgian Workers' Party, which had just achieved parliamentary representation for the first time.[2] Paul Hankar (1859–1901) designed studios for his artist friends and created shops in which every detail of both the frontage and the interior was conceived in minute, harmonious detail. In 1894 Gustave Serrurier-Bovy (1858–1910) approached the avant-garde artistic society La Libre Esthétique to offer them an exhibit for their annual *salon*: a *cabinet de travail* or workspace. This was the first example of a fully furnished room featuring in an art exhibition. At this same *salon* Henry Van de Velde (1863–1957),[3] who had just abandoned his career as a painter, delivered a lecture on the renaissance of arts and craft in England. His paper was called 'Future Art', and it claimed that the English 'were aiming less for style and more for something fresh, candid and joyful'.[4]

From the start of the 1890s a good many Belgian artists had shown a keen interest in the products of the English Arts and Crafts Movement and its attempts to rehabilitate the status of craftsmen and hand-made objects in a society overrun with factory-made goods. William Morris and John Ruskin – whom Van de Velde discovered in 1892, thanks to the Anglo-Belgian painter Willy Finch – became the prophets of a new era that would witness a renaissance among the creative professions. Ruskin's *The Seven Lamps of Architecture* and Morris's *News from Nowhere* reassured Van de Velde in his role as 'disciple': promoting beauty that was accessible to all and rejecting the primacy of the fine arts in favour of all the arts collectively. The decorative arts could no longer be referred to as 'minor'. Van de Velde was given a teaching post at the Anvers Academy in 1893 and could base his demonstrations on English samples that he had asked his wife, Maria Sèthe, to collect: wallpapers by Essex & Co., chromolithographs from the Fitzroy Picture Society, and so on.[5] He also used his new-found knowledge to write three articles about English wallpapers in the avant-garde review *L'Art Moderne* (in 1893 and 1894), praising the work of Walter Crane and Charles A. Voysey.[6] At the time these wallpapers were displayed at art exhibitions such as the 1892 *Art* fair at Anvers or the 1895 *L'œuvre artistique* fair at Liège, where their predecessors had been illustrated books by Walter Crane (sixteen albums at the 1891 *Salon des XX*) and Kate Greenaway. At the *Salon des XX* Crane's albums, which were owned by the painter Georges Lemmen, were

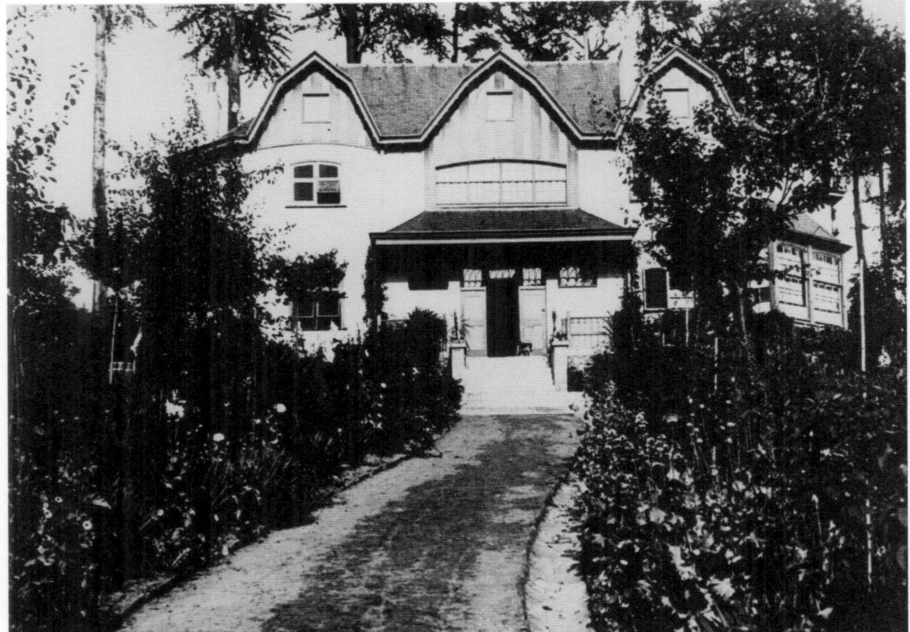

exhibited alongside paintings and sculptures by the likes of James Ensor, Fernand Khnopff, Auguste Rodin and Jan Toorop.

Van de Velde was very taken with the model of the English cottage that was celebrated in the review *The Studio* (featuring, amongst others, the creations of Mackay Hugh Baillie Scott and Charles A. Voysey): he liked its simplicity and comfort, and its relationship to the garden around it. So much so that he used it as a template when, in 1895, he built his own house, the 'Bloemenwerf',[7] at Uccle on the outskirts of Brussels. The art critic Julius Meier-Graefe dedicated the first edition of his review *L'Art Décoratif* (1898) to Van de Velde, and clearly indicates this inspiration because he describes the house as a 'cottage'. In his own memoir, Van de Velde expressed his amusement at the scandal produced by his home, which so eschewed all the architectural ornamentation that was usual in a country house. In about 1894 he designed his first pieces of furniture in a style inspired by the Arts and Crafts Movement: composite pieces such as a 'bench-trunk-bookcase', corner cupboards, tables and sofas with strong, angular lines. Having designed his house using self-taught concepts, he did the same with his furniture. He was exceptionally gifted in the field of typographical ornamentation, and effortlessly transferred this skill to book covers, stained-glass windows and embroidery, but he was more challenged when it came to three-dimensional objects. In 1896 a critic commented, quite justifiably, that 'Mr Van de Velde does not conceive his furniture in three dimensions, the way he draws his pieces means they are diminished when viewed in three-quarter profile or from the side.'[8]

Van de Velde may have been inspired by the Sussex chair sold by Morris, when he designed the chairs for his own dining room, with flat slats inset up the backs and rush seats, like simple country seating. When the furniture that he exhibited at the opening of the 'Art Nouveau' Bing Gallery in Paris in 1895 came in for fierce criticism, he explained his two guiding principles: 'rational concept and functional form'. In 1898 he followed William Morris's example and founded his own 'Workshops for industrial and ornamental art' in Ixelles; he deemed this essential to preserve the intimate relationship between the design and the execution of an object. He also promoted English wallpapers and fabrics, mostly from Liberty's, and supplied Victor Horta with Voysey wallpapers for the Hôtel Tassel and Hôtel Solvay (the 'Elaine', 'Astolat', 'Tokyo' and 'Savaric' patterns). He himself embarked on designing wallpapers and broke away from English examples by creating designs with abstract shapes and dynamic calligraphy, thereby accomplishing his dream of

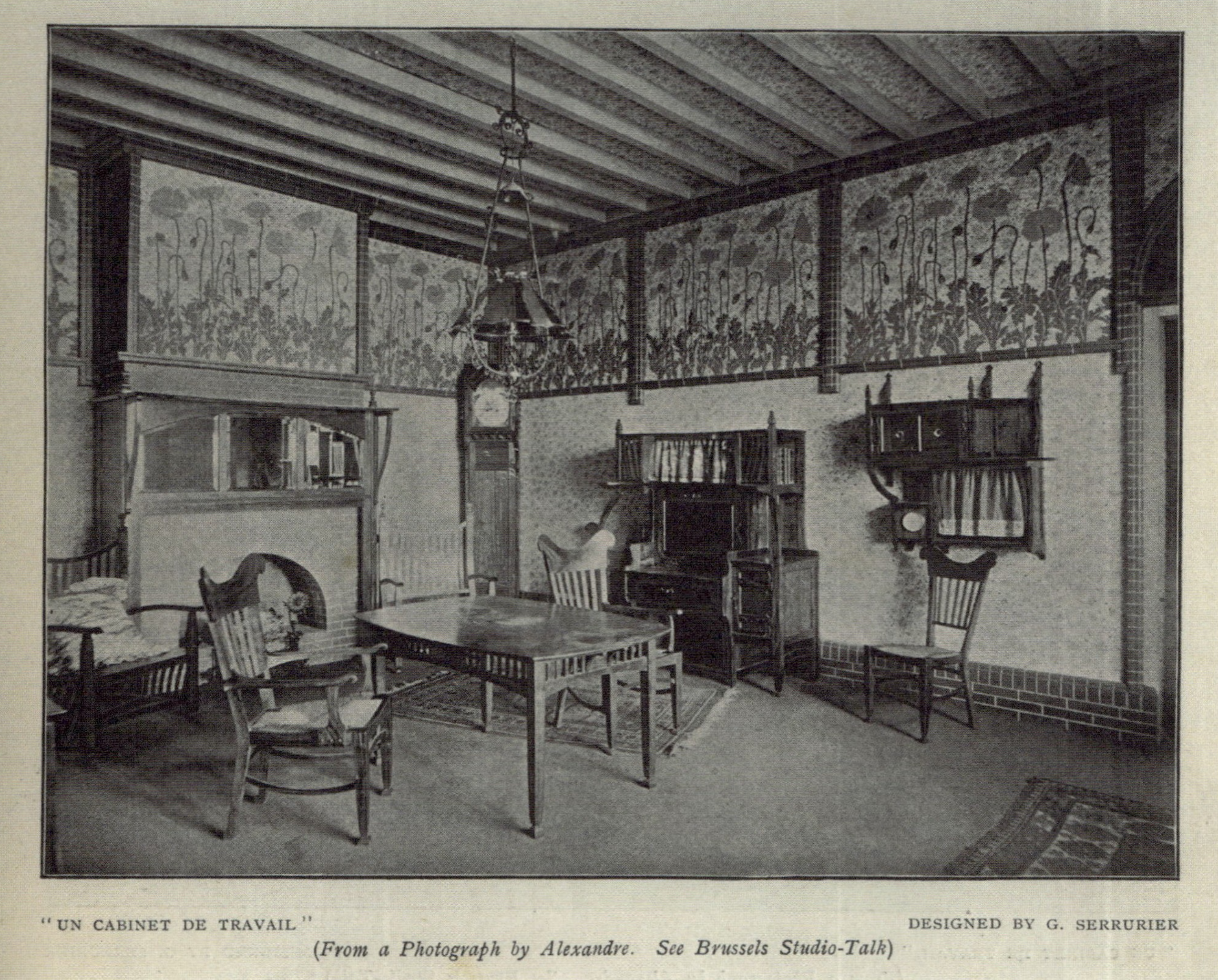



transcribing the 'fleeting, shifting, refined abstract shapes that the wind left lying on the sand',[9] which he saw when he walked along the Belgian coast. These shapes could be found embroidered onto the dresses that his wife wore at Bloemenwerf: Van de Velde designed loose-fitting styles for her, often made of English fabrics, freeing her waist of corsets, and being reminiscent of women's clothes in Pre-Raphaelite paintings.

He also contributed to the 1897 *Dresden Exhibition* under Bing's banner, and to the 1899 *Secession of Munich Exhibition* under his own name. After this, the majority of his customers were German, and this persuaded Van de Velde to leave Brussels in 1900 to move first to Berlin and then, in 1902, to Weimar. During this period he reviewed the last few years and wondered who precisely had launched Art Nouveau in Belgium. He refused to attribute this initiative to Horta, favouring instead Serrurier-Bovy,[10] an artist and cabinetmaker from Liège who had been the first to exhibit an arrangement of furniture simulating a habitable room at the 1894 *Salon de la Libre Esthétique*. This *cabinet de travail*, with its brightly coloured frieze of poppies along the tops of the walls, comprised an unusual combination of neo-Gothic and Arts and Crafts styles.

Serrurier-Bovy and his wife, Maria Bovy, had set up a shop in Liège that offered 'artistic furnishings', fabrics (mostly from Liberty's), carpets and exotic objects from India, China and Japan. One of the shop's advertisements mentioned that it sold English furniture in Queen Anne, Jacobean, Adam and Chippendale style. It has not been definitively established when Serrurier-Bovy first travelled to England, but his bookshelves included works by Lewis F. Day, Charles R. Ashbee and John D. Sedding, along with illustrated works by Walter Crane, Kate Greenaway and Randolph Caldecott. His first known trip to England was in 1893, when he visited an exhibition of the Arts and Crafts

*Above:* Gustave Serrurier-Bovy, *Un cabinet de travail*, from the Salon de la Libre Esthétique, 1894.

Exhibition Society. It must have been a recognised fact that Serrurier-Bovy was very familiar with English crafts, which explains this review of his *cabinet de travail* that appeared in *L'Art Moderne*: 'A modest, restrained, intimate model apartment. It is inspired by English designers without being a servile copy of their work.'[11] In 1895 Serrurier-Bovy exhibited a *Chambre d'artisan* (craftsman's bedroom) at the Libre Esthétique, and provided an accompanying booklet that defended the right of the most lowly people to enjoy art, explaining that simplicity did not preclude the right to live in an environment that bore the stamp of good taste. He felt that the popularisation of aesthetic sensibilities should be absolutely essential, and pointed out that 'the furniture is designed on a simple, practical basis, requiring as little labour as possible, but executed in keeping with the true principles of furniture construction.[12] The wrought ironwork for hinges, handles, rings and escutcheons constitutes about the only ornamentation in the furniture.'

Also in 1895 Serrurier-Bovy, who had founded a society for 'artistic work', organised an exhibition of applied arts, which featured work by Charles R. Ashbee, Robert Anning Bell, Lindsay P. Butterfield, Walter Crane, the Glasgow School of Art, William Morris, James Powell and Heywood Sumner. Fernand Khnopff was then appointed as Brussels correspondent for *The Studio* and, at the same time as this exhibition, he gave a talk on Walter Crane, probably delivering the same paper that he had given at the Brussels Cercle Artistique in December 1894. In his 'Studio Talks', published in 1896, he featured both of Serrurier-Bovy's interiors exhibited at La Libre Esthétique.[13] While Henry Van de Velde was developing his customer base in Germany, Serrurier-Bovy battled to conquer the French public: he exhibited a dining room at Bing in 1896;

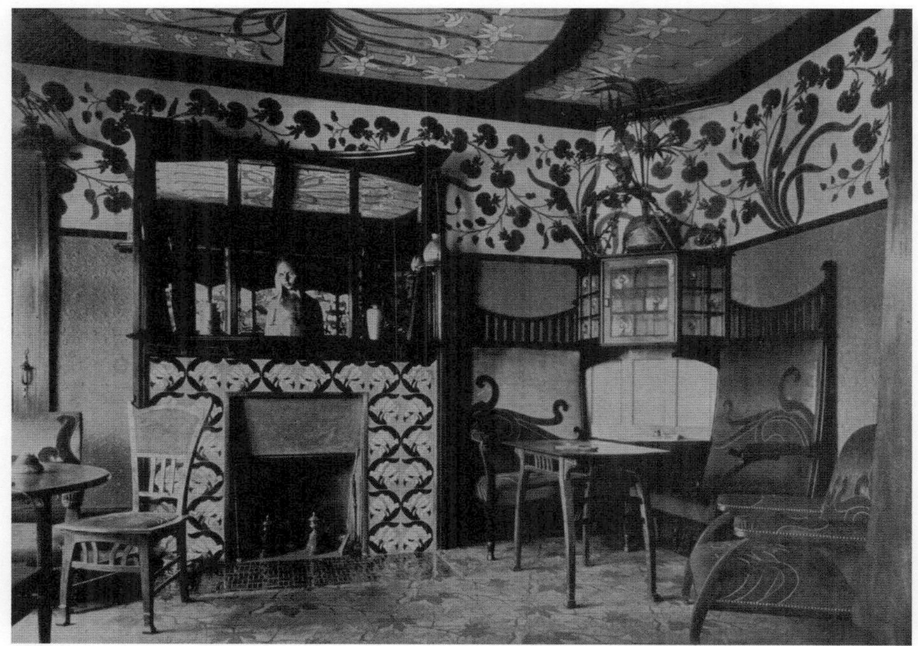

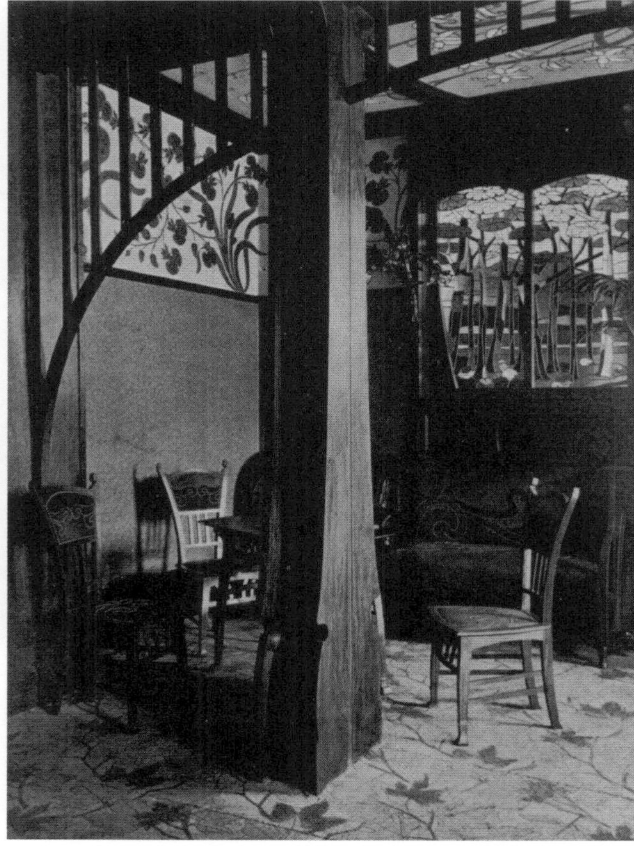

*Above and right:* Gustave Serrurier-Bovy, Hôtel Chatham, 1898.

decorated the smoking room at the Hôtel Chatham in Paris in 1898; and sent major contributions to the 1899 *Salon National des Beaux-Arts*, having moved his outlets and workshops from Liège to larger premises at the beginning of the year. He is known to have had sixty workers in 1903. Still in 1899, he collaborated with the French architect René Dulong, and together they created a temporary restaurant, the Pavillon Bleu, at the Paris World Fair. Serrurier-Bovy's contribution to this was something of an exception, because Belgian designers enjoyed little success in Paris. Horta was meant to build an imposing 'Congo Pavilion' for the exhibition, but King Leopold swiftly abandoned the project.

Serrurier-Bovy also differed from Van de Velde in his commercial ambition, because he opened *L'Art dans l'Habitation* shops in Brussels, Paris and Nice to sell his diverse creations: furniture, metal lamps, embroidered wall hangings, stained-glass panels and stencilled friezes. His first items of furniture were muscular-looking pieces in waxed wood, made using European resources (oak and pine) with metalwork in black iron, but he also adapted to satisfy the more luxurious tastes of some of his customers, working with mahogany and brass, and using arch-shapes to structure his furniture, briefly adopting the trend driven by Horta and Hankar. He was, however, still

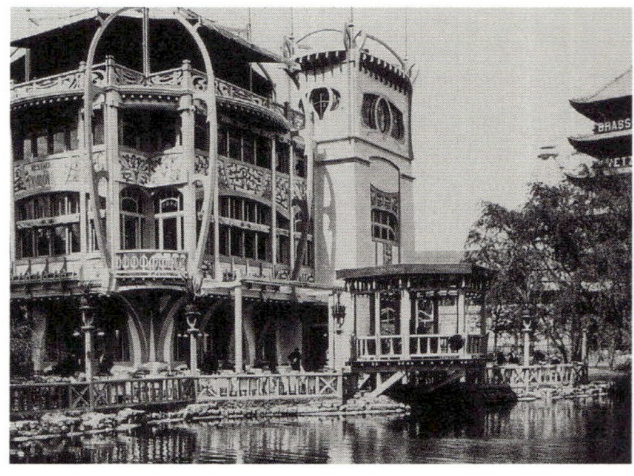

*Above:* Gustave Serrurier-Bovy and René Dulong, the Pavillon Bleu restaurant at the Paris World Fair, 1900.
*Below:* Gustave Serrurier-Bovy, dining-room design, 1904, published in L'Art Décoratif, November 1904.

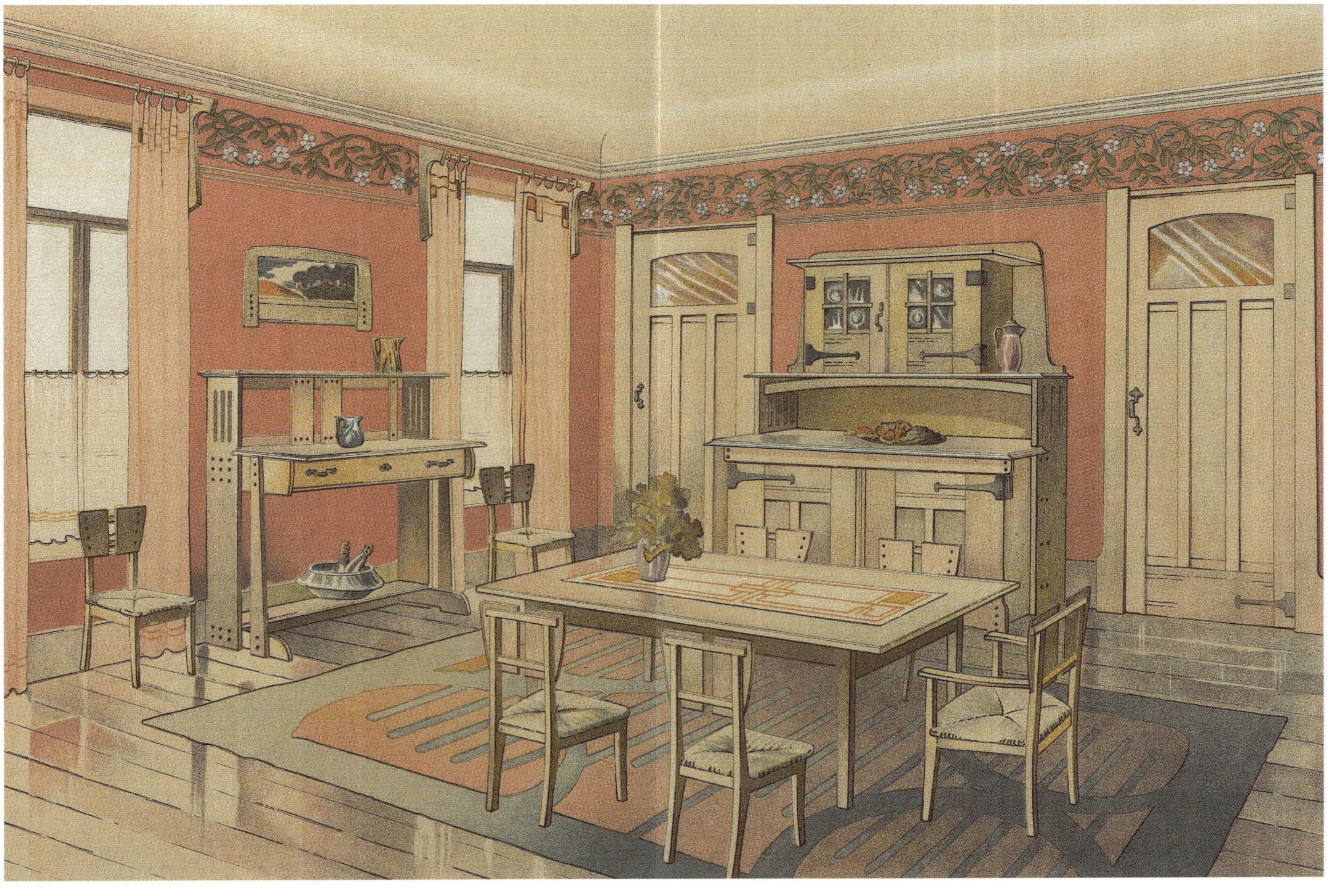

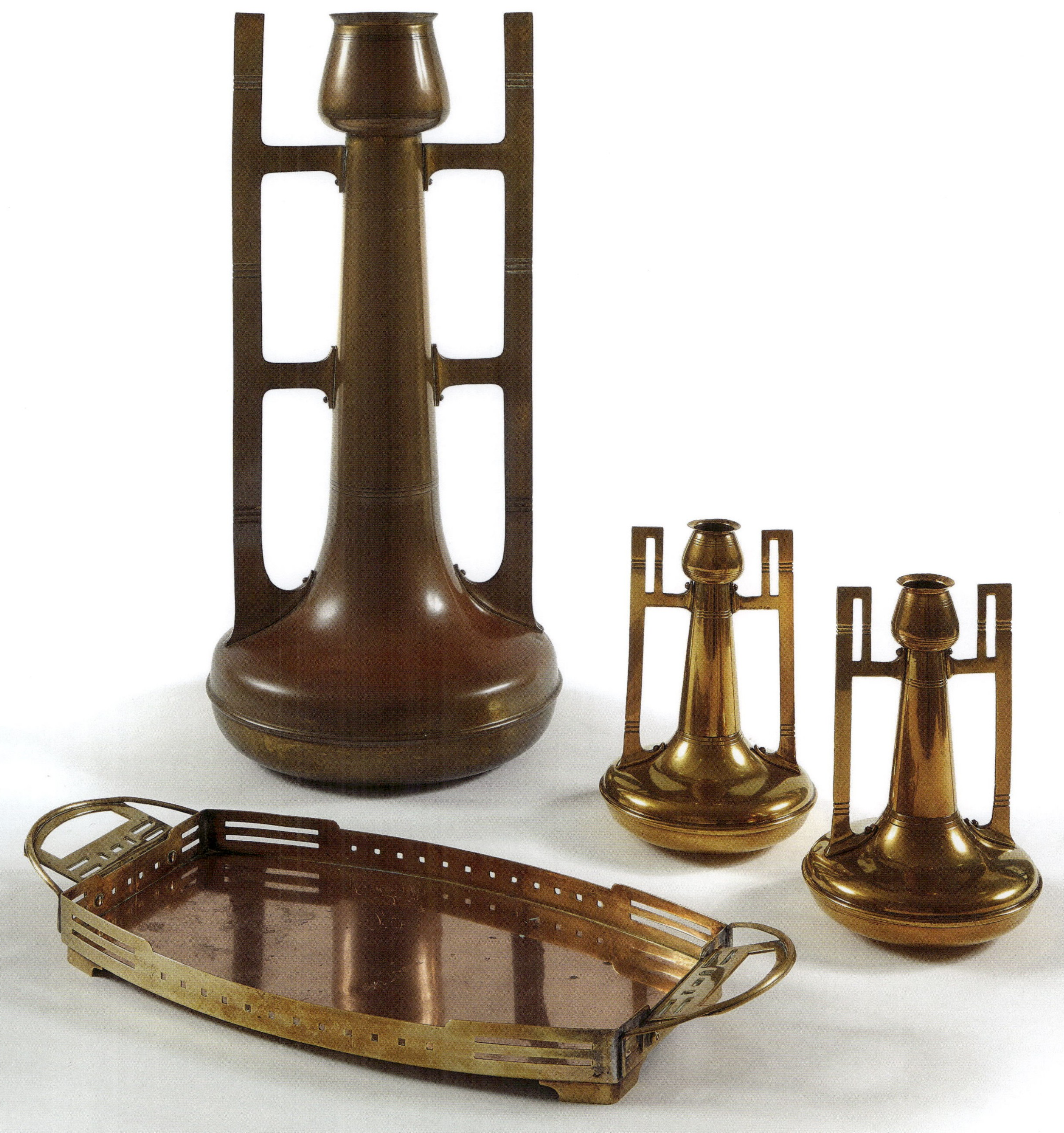

*Above:* Gustave Serrurier-Bovy,
large vase and tray, *c.*1906, brass
and copper. Private collection and
pair of smaller vases, *c.*1906, brass.
Sainsbury Centre.

keen to produce furniture that was accessible to the least well-off sector of the population, and strove to create simple yet beautiful pieces, starting with planks of bare wood with no carving or turning, so that the screws used in their assembly – and sometimes a stencilled design – constituted the only decorative element standing out against the cheap, light wood, such as poplar or beech. At the 1905 Liège World Fair, Serrurier-Bovy exhibited an *Ameublement d'intérieur ouvrier* (workman's interior) that he hoped was genuinely affordable for the working classes. He may well have been the only designer of his day to realise the ideal of 'art in everything for everyone'.

There may be similarities in Henry Van de Velde's and Gustave Serrurier-Bovy's trajectories (repeated contributions to exhibitions in Belgium and abroad; creations in every field of interior design; and the decision to have their own production workshops), but the story is very different for the two other major protagonists of Belgian Art Nouveau, Victor Horta and Paul Hankar, whose decorative-arts creations were intimately linked to their architecture. In Horta's case, his innovative architectural designs could not accommodate furniture unless it, too, was conceived by him. Hankar, meanwhile, gave his customers more freedom, and it was not unusual to see Renaissance or Louis XV furniture alongside his tailor-made pieces.

When in 1893 Victor Horta designed a small private mansion in Brussels at 6 rue Paul-Emile Janson for the engineer Emile Tassel,[14] he probably did not imagine it would usher in a style that would spread all across Europe. He had solid academic training, complemented by many hours spent working for the architect Alphonse Balat ('the purest classicist', according to Horta),[15] and he was immersed in the theories of Eugène Viollet-le-Duc, having read and reread his *Entretiens sur l'Architecture*. He adopted several traits from Viollet-le-Duc's 'Gothic rationalism': using contemporary, industrially produced materials (iron, cast iron and glass); adapting plans specifically for the project in question (the house must suit its owner like a made-to-measure suit); and devising ornamentation that did not obscure the basic structure. He was also convinced that natural light was an important factor in making urban interiors more pleasant spaces: the dimensions of street blocks in Brussels meant that the centres of houses were dark. Thanks to the metal structures that he left visible, both on the facade and internally, Horta opened up his buildings to let in the light. His facades are punctuated by huge windows, and many internal walls are replaced by metal posts. He used stairways as light-wells in the heart of homes, and looked for different ways to integrate conservatories, not merely grafting them onto the back of houses, but making them integral to living rooms.

Horta worked on giving metal an appropriate contemporary form, refusing to copy ancient and Gothic styles. The metal columns on the raised ground-floor landing at the Hôtel Tassel are palm trees made of iron and cast iron, and their reflections mingle with those of real palms in the mirrors in the conservatory. His metal corner-mouldings are enhanced with sinuous designs that are echoed on the banisters with a succession of scrolling lines, like the tendrils of a climbing plant. They have all the vitality of germinating seeds, and their stems unfurl in natural light. Horta's collusion with nature owes a great deal to his interest in Japanese art, an interest that was almost certainly

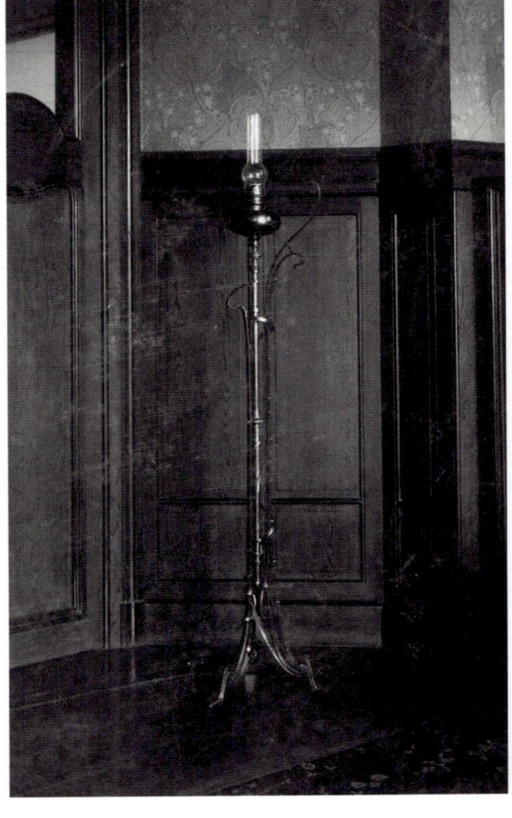

*Below:* Victor Horta, Bureau d'Emile Tassel with lampstand, 1893.

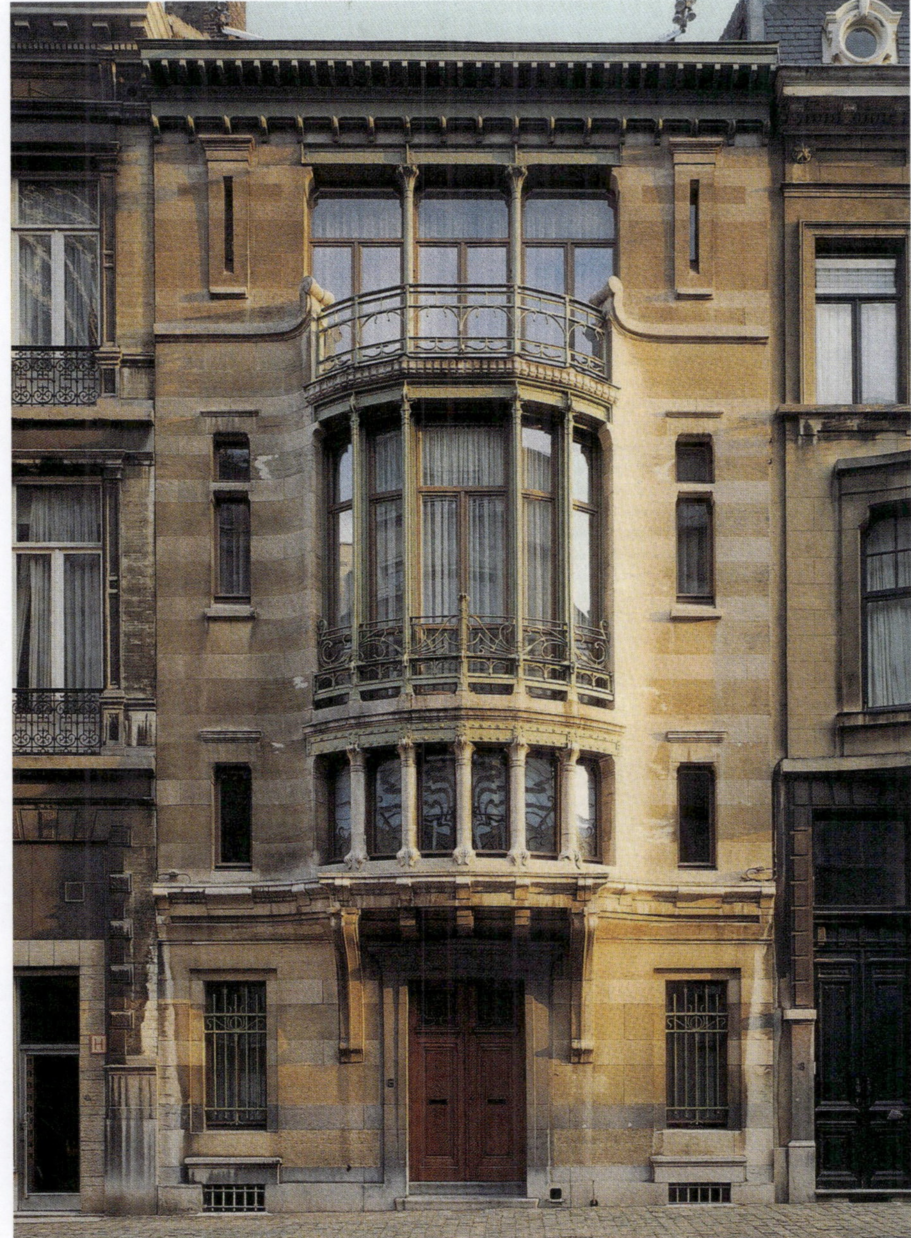

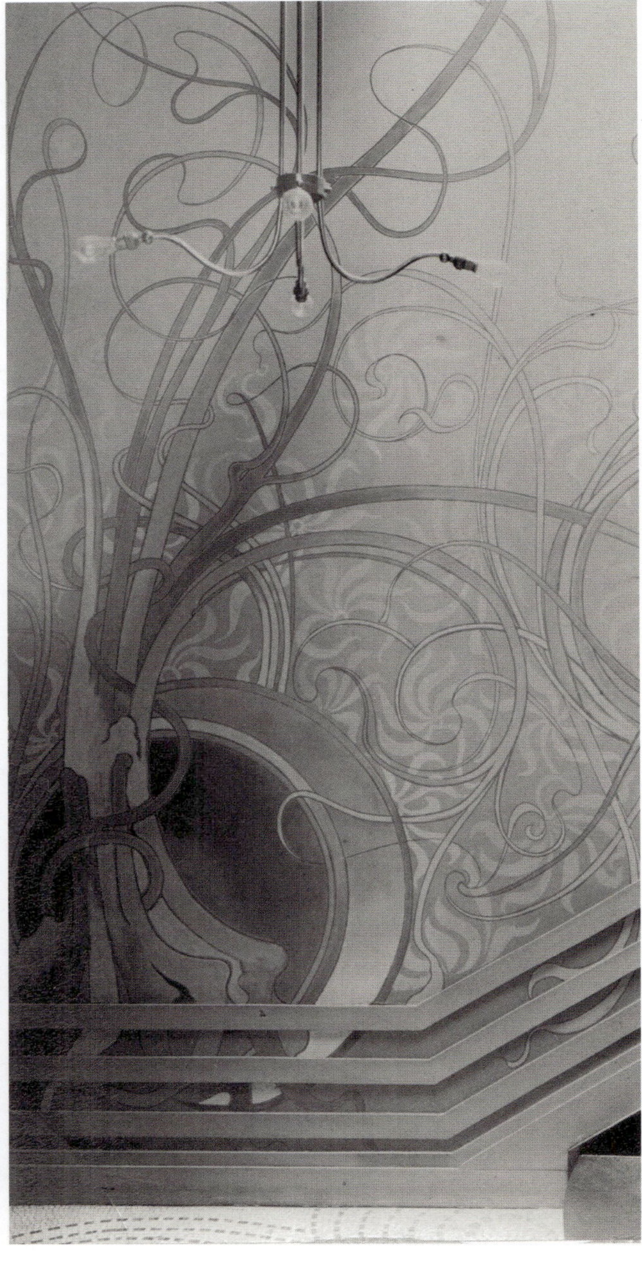

*Above and right:* Victor Horta, Hôtel Tassel, 1893.

fuelled by Emile Tassel, who was a fervent collector of the genre. In the first major article devoted to Horta, which appeared in the inaugural edition of *Art et Décoration* in 1897,[16] the author referred to Horta's concept of ornamentation – a concept that he very probably heard about from the architect himself:

> The starting point for this research is observing nature; but even when looking at nature, there are adjustments, for one reason or another, to the indications it gives. By appropriating the secrets of a plant's delicate undulations or the graceful curves of its stems, the artist's intention was to leave nothing that directly referenced nature. When devising the vagaries of a design, he might follow the hidden law that plants obey by adhering to immutable and consistently harmonious shapes, but he refrains just as rigorously from drawing any pattern or describing a single curve that could be identified as a pastiche of nature.[17]

The design of the staircase at the Hôtel Tassel, comprising arabesques against a background of fading colours with flowers floating through them, is reminiscent of the tree trunks with knotty roots and asymmetrical canopies featured in Japanese screens. This same profusion appears again

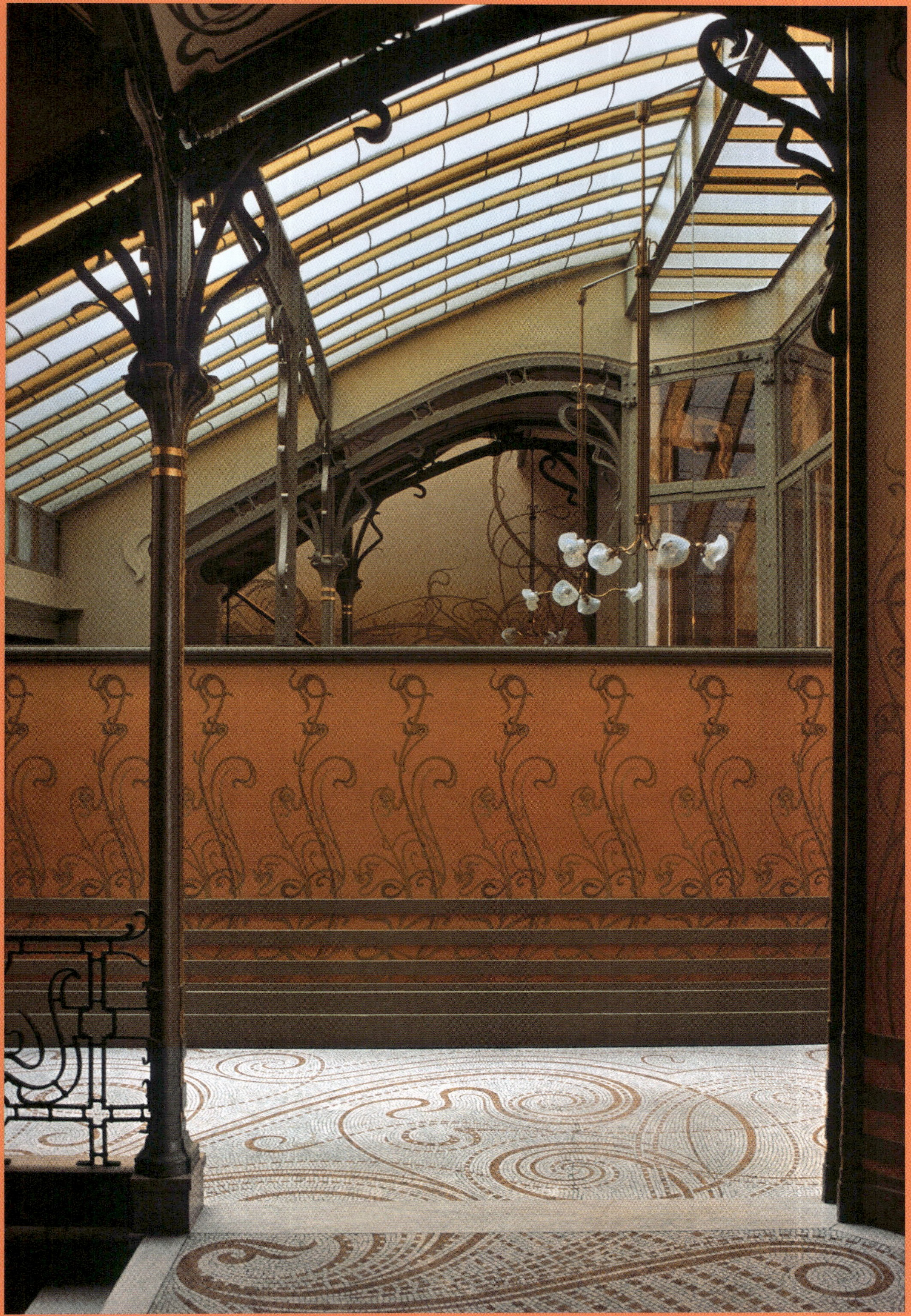

in the staircase design at the Hôtel Frison, the Winssinger, the Solvay and the
Van Eetvelde, but the lines grow less flamboyant in Horta's own home (1898–
1901, 23–5 rue Américaine, Brussels) and in the Hôtel Aubecq. Horta also
paid particular attention to the design of reception rooms: when decorating
the walls of the dining room at the Hôtel Van Eetvelde, built for the
Secretary-General of the Congo Free State, he drew inspiration from Africa,
putting orchids and elephant heads among the arabesques (although his
very stylised motifs are barely identifiable at first glance). In the sitting room
on the same floor, with its dado of onyx panelling, Horta contrasted the
freshness of a northern spring with the warm colours that dominated the
dining room. He covered the walls with Lindsay P. Butterfield's 'Daffodil'
fabric made by Morton.[18]

Horta's pursuit of this coherence between architecture and interior design
steered him towards designing furniture for his customers. Those with new
fortunes were mostly unencumbered with inherited furniture, and were
inclined to trust the design of all their furnishings to Horta, who proved
particularly gifted in creating lamps: he was able to invent a new type of
device, thanks to the supply of electricity that proliferated across Brussels
at the end of the nineteenth century. One of his first designs, for the raised
ground-floor landing at the Hôtel Tassel, consists of simple brass tubes
ending in an Edison-style bulb, a version of a flower stem and bud. Each
building would have its own different style of lamp, always highlighting a
detail from the architecture or the decor, and positioned so that no corner
was left in shadow; whether hanging from metallic structures, attached to
the corners of chimney breasts or the newel post at the foot of a staircase, or
hanging from the ceiling, they displayed the same mastery of design as the
architectural ironwork.

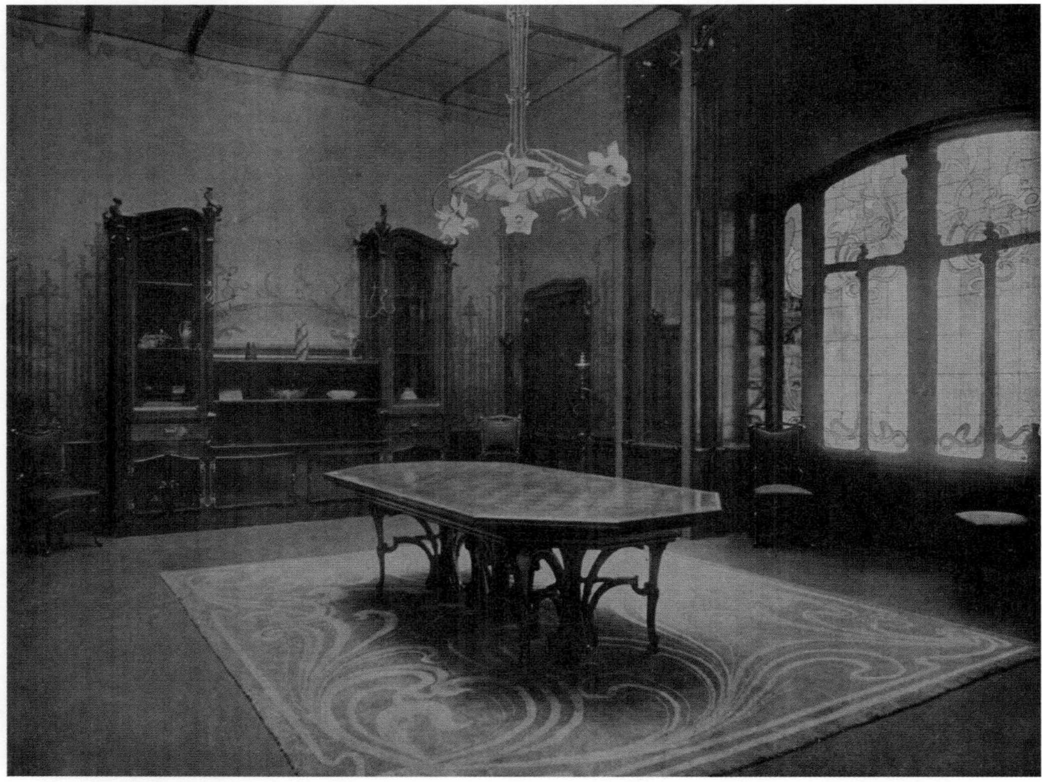

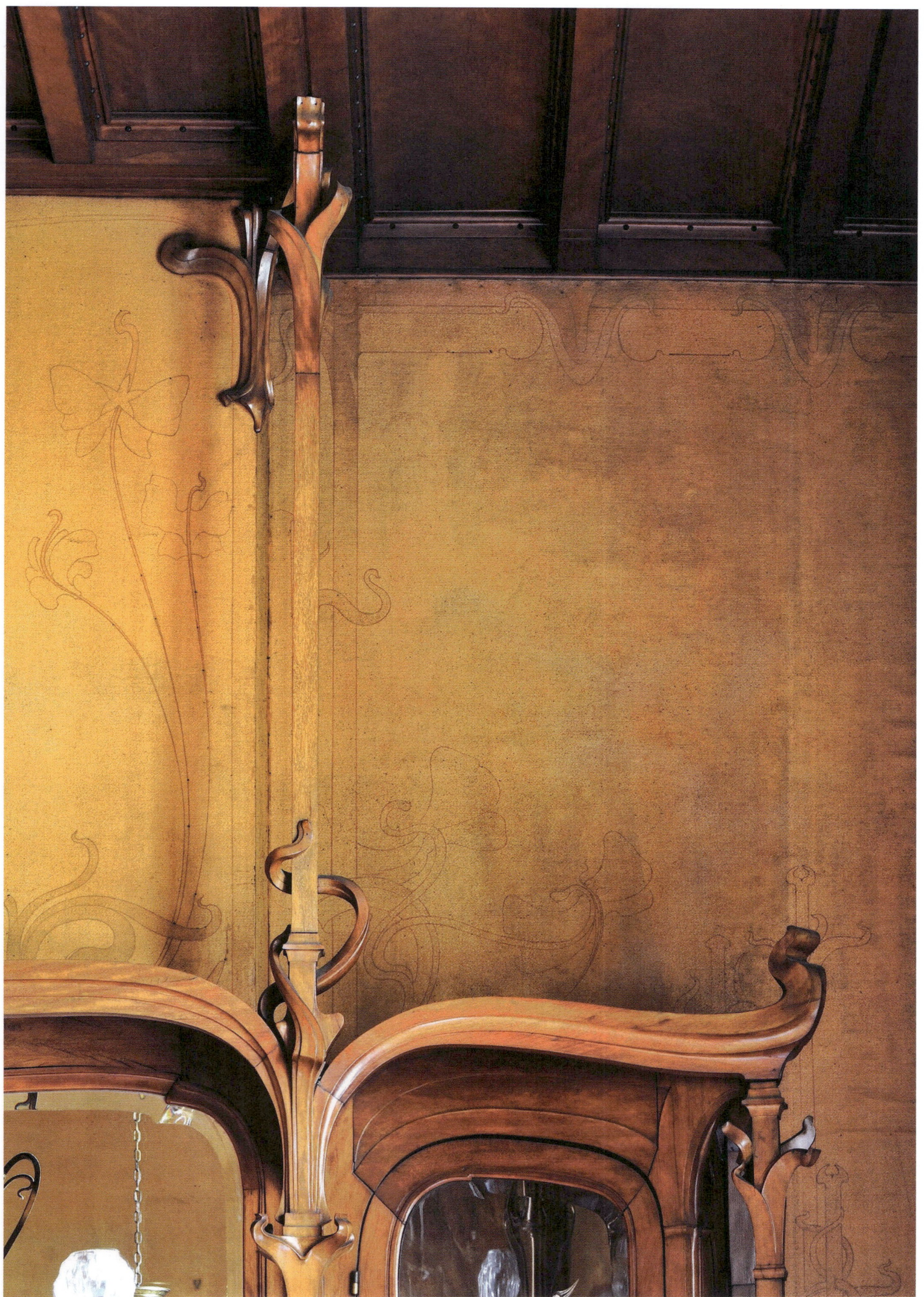

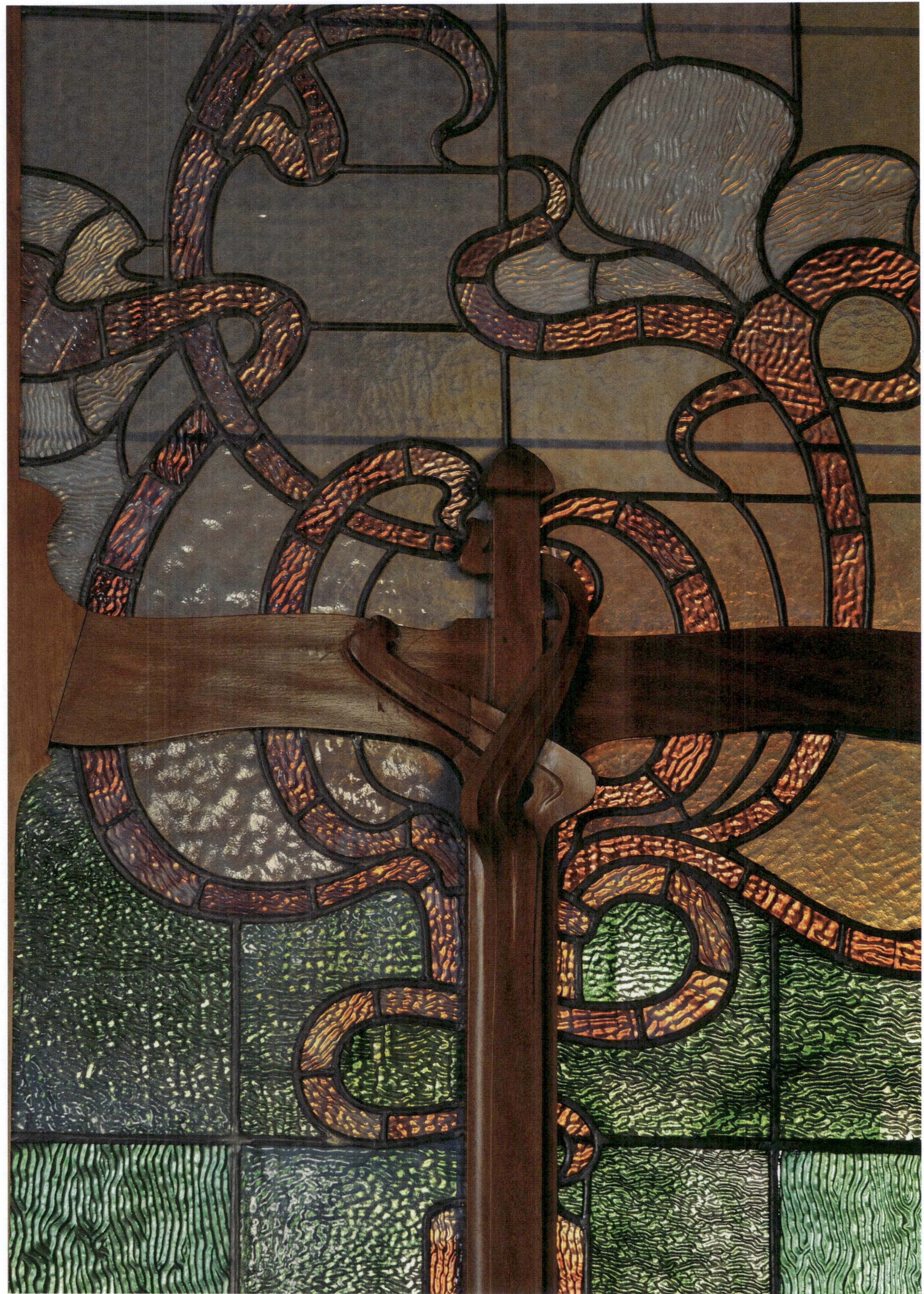

Horta's early work in furniture was less assured. As with his facades, he tried to avoid sharp angles, liked to smooth the joins between the different parts of each piece and made frequent use of curved lines. In his *Mémoires*[19] he explains that he designed furniture in the same way as he did buildings: his table legs comprised complex designs sculpted in very high-quality wood, constituting a new way of demonstrating their owners' wealth. This focus on asymmetrical sculptural details led Horta to work repeatedly with sculptors, who made plaster models that could be given to the different craftsmen. Almost every item was unique, conceived in relation to a specific building. Horta never aspired to work on a more industrial scale than these individual commissions. Many of his pieces of furniture are integral to the buildings, and there are a number of ingeniously positioned fitted cupboards. The novelty of his architecture was recognised immediately, but it was not until 1897 and the display of an impressive furnishings collection at the *Salon de la Libre Esthétique* that Horta also emerged as a furniture designer and decorator. He triumphed in this field at the 1902 Turin Exhibition, which was also his swansong: he was awarded a diploma of honour, but already looked dated in comparison to new trends from Scotland and Vienna. In *Art et Décoration* that year, Maurice Pillard Verneuil referred to Horta's 'slightly gaudy sumptuousness'.[20]

The commissions from private homes had grown scarce. When he built the Maison du Peuple (1895–1899) in Brussels, Horta had demonstrated his competence over a large project. He had measured up to the programme's complex requirements by bringing together shops, a large café, offices, a dispensary and a library in his great vessel of iron and glass, topped with a performance hall. This 'palace for the people', to use his own words, was demolished between 1965 and 1966.[21] At the start of the twentieth century Horta was commissioned to design several department stores – the Innovation and the Grand Bazar Anspach, in Brussels and Frankfurt respectively – and this made his style popular with a wide public. Perhaps this is one explanation for the disenchantment of his private clientele, who may have been squeamish about the popularisation of a style that had initially demonstrated the daring and the appetite for modernity of Horta's first clients.

n 1893 Paul Hankar[22] built his own private home at 71 rue Defacqz, not far from the Hôtel Tassel. A fellow student of Horta at the Brussels Royal Academy of Fine Arts, he trained with a different master: he was taken on by the workshops of Henri Beyaert, who designed remarkable buildings in the Flemish neo-Renaissance style – picturesque and very colourful structures with a wealth of ornamentation on their facades. From his first commissions, Hankar showed a predilection for using many colours and for juxtaposing different-textured materials with wrought iron. As early as 1888 he designed railings for the Hôtel Zegers-Regnard, which anticipated Art Nouveau: his preliminary drawings show trials of stylised floral patterns like the work of Christopher Dresser, along with studies of plant tendrils. He was not trying, as Horta did, to transpose natural shapes into abstract patterns. On the facade of his own home he left spaces for *sgraffitto* panels that were effectively small paintings in their own right, Japanese-inspired images produced by his friend Adolphe Crespin, whom Hankar would go on to use many times. He reworked the traditional bow window, replacing its wooden framework with fine metal profiles encased in solid stone uprights

*Opposite:* Paul Hankar, 71 rue Defacqz, 1893.

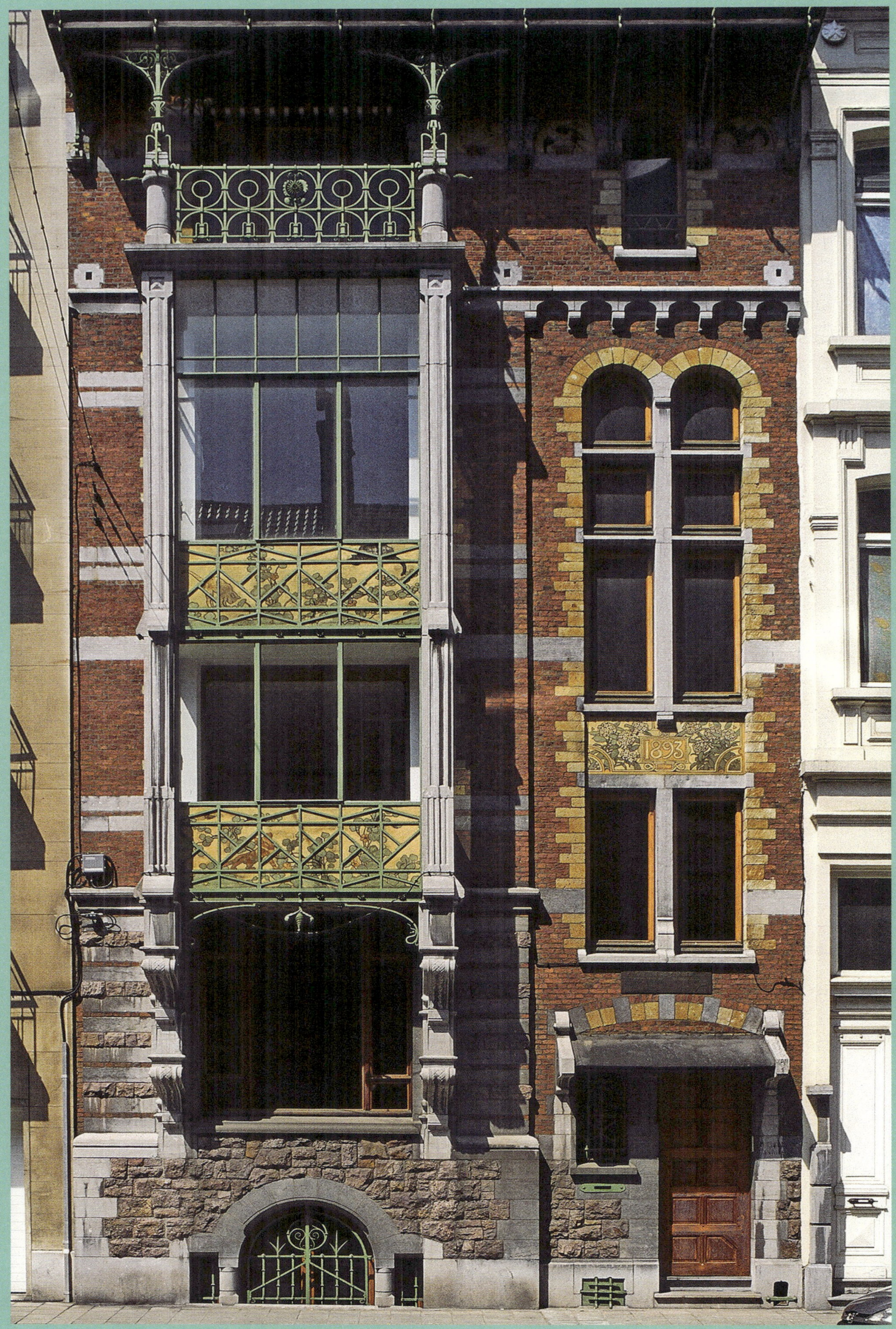

that covered two storeys. The facade also betrays Hankar's partiality to geometric shapes and broken lines reminiscent of Chinese woodwork. He used fewer metal structures in facades than Horta, but Hankar's balconies were incomparably diverse and imaginative. When he built the Hôtel Ciamberlani in 1897, he started a fashion for circular windows and subtly combined asymmetrical window spacing on the ground floor with the regular arrangement on the two upper floors.

Hankar's style appealed to many retailers, who commissioned shops that were instantly recognisable for the skeleton-like complexity of their fine woodwork. His aptitude in meeting the needs of commercial architecture (he designed all the interior furnishings down to the last detail) earnt him the role of coordinator for the 1897 Tervueren *Colonial Exhibition*.[23] King Leopold II wanted the exhibition to be a part of the International Fair in Brussels, to showcase the richness of the Congo to the Belgian public, who were somewhat reticent about the King's ambitions to carve himself an empire in central

*Below:* Paul Hankar, Hôtel Ciamberlani, 1897.

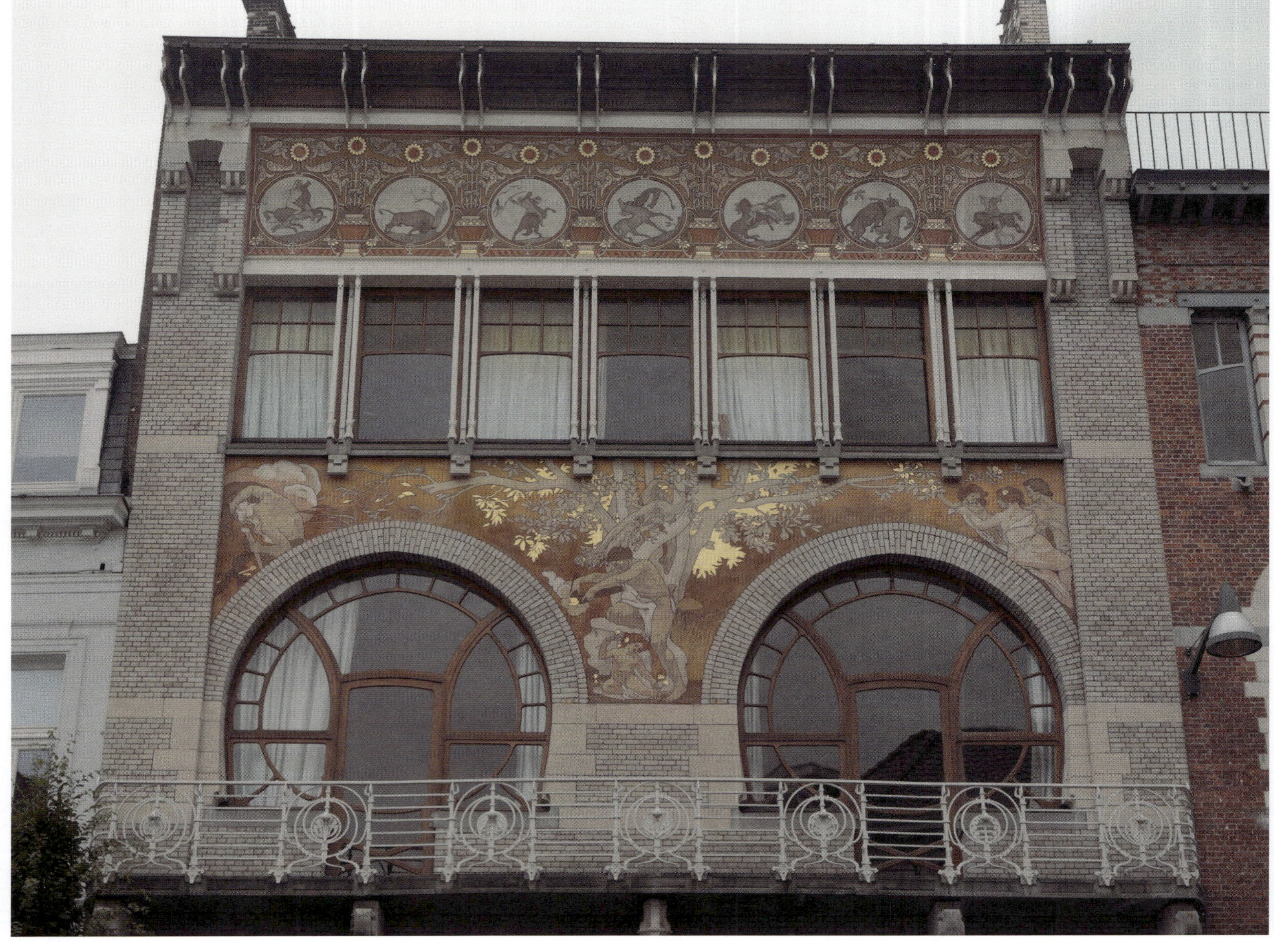

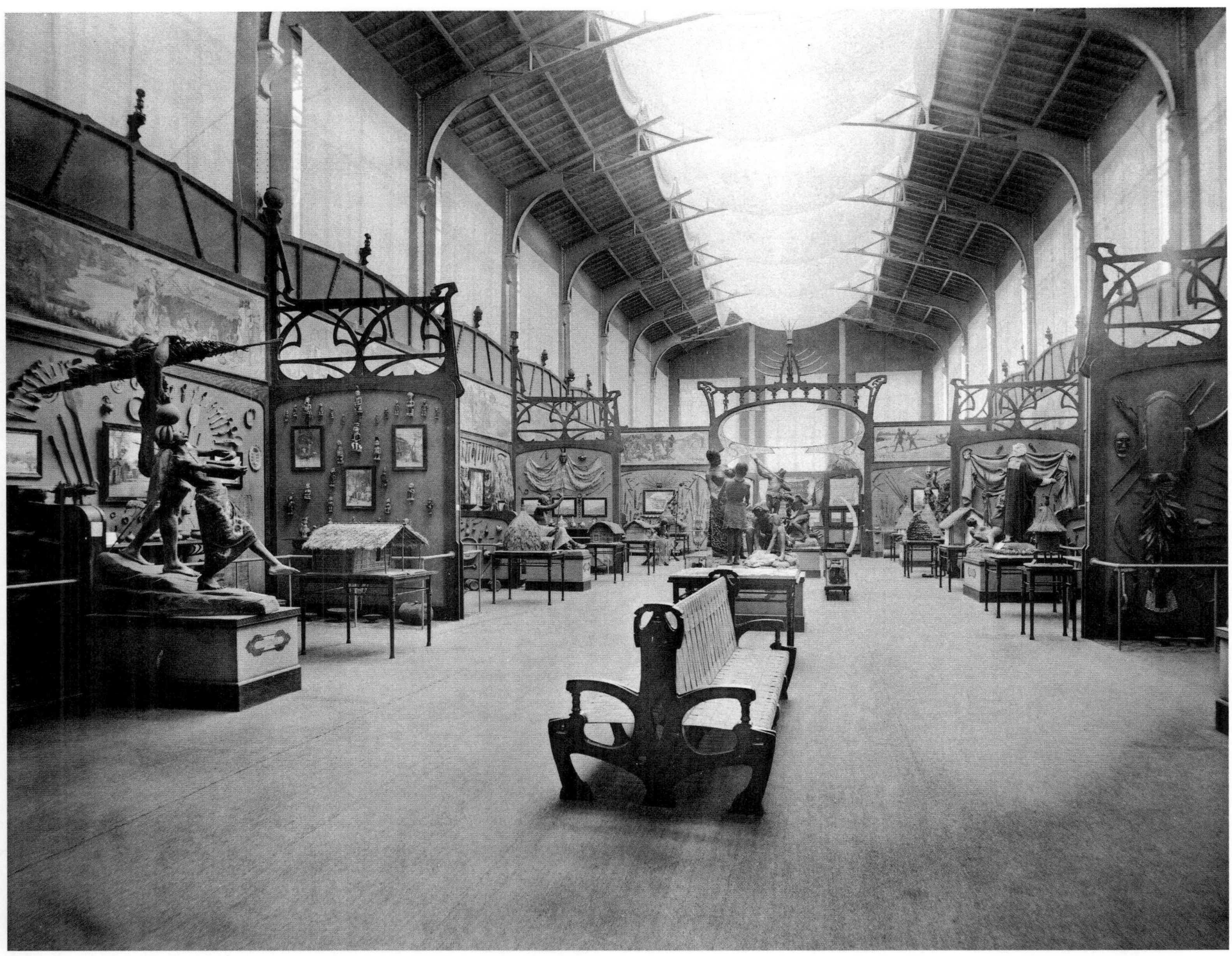

*Above:* Paul Hankar, Ethnographic Hall at the Tervueren *Colonial Exhibition*, 1897.

*Overleaf:* Georges Hobé and Antoine Pompe, study-room design, 1902, ink on paper.

Africa. Three other budding stars of the design world were involved in the project: Georges Hobé, Gustave Serrurier-Bovy and Henry Van de Velde. They were commissioned to devise attractive displays for an extraordinary diversity of products within the banal architecture of the exhibition space. They produced a multitude of pedestals, shelf units, tables, glass cases, benches and lightweight dividing walls, each true to his own style, but collectively dubbed 'Congo style' by the general public. Hankar's complex lines and their vigorous twists, punctuated with spurs, evoked a 'wilded' Gothic style in the Ethnography Hall, for which he was given responsibility.

Hankar's style is less coherent than Horta's, perhaps because he gave more freedom to his collaborators, particularly Léon Sneyers and Paul Hamesse, who went on to pursue independent careers after their mentor died in 1901. In Turin the following year Sneyers and Adolphe Crespin created a *cabinet de travail* as a homage to Hankar.[24] Crespin designed the wide frieze under the ceiling; its theme was 'The Arts' and it included variations on a heady pattern of stylised flower heads featured on the woodwork, carpets and cushions. Sneyer's furniture was restrained, with relatively straight lines. Taken together they testified to a distancing from Paul Hankar's inventiveness and decorative verve, to which they had formerly adhered so closely. Two other displays exhibited in Turin, by Georges Hobé and Antoine Pompe, adopted the same restraint, but not without some fine detailing:

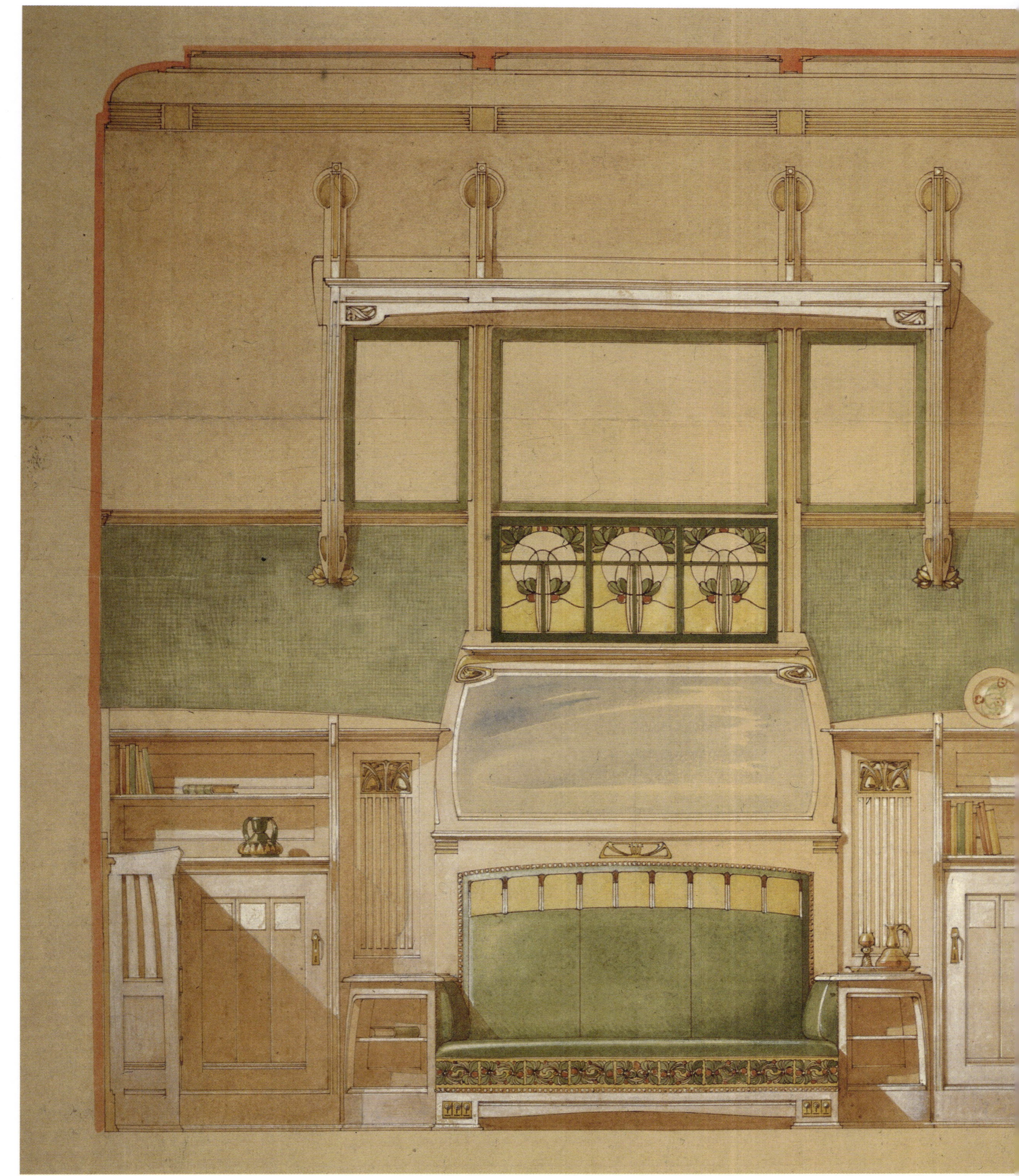

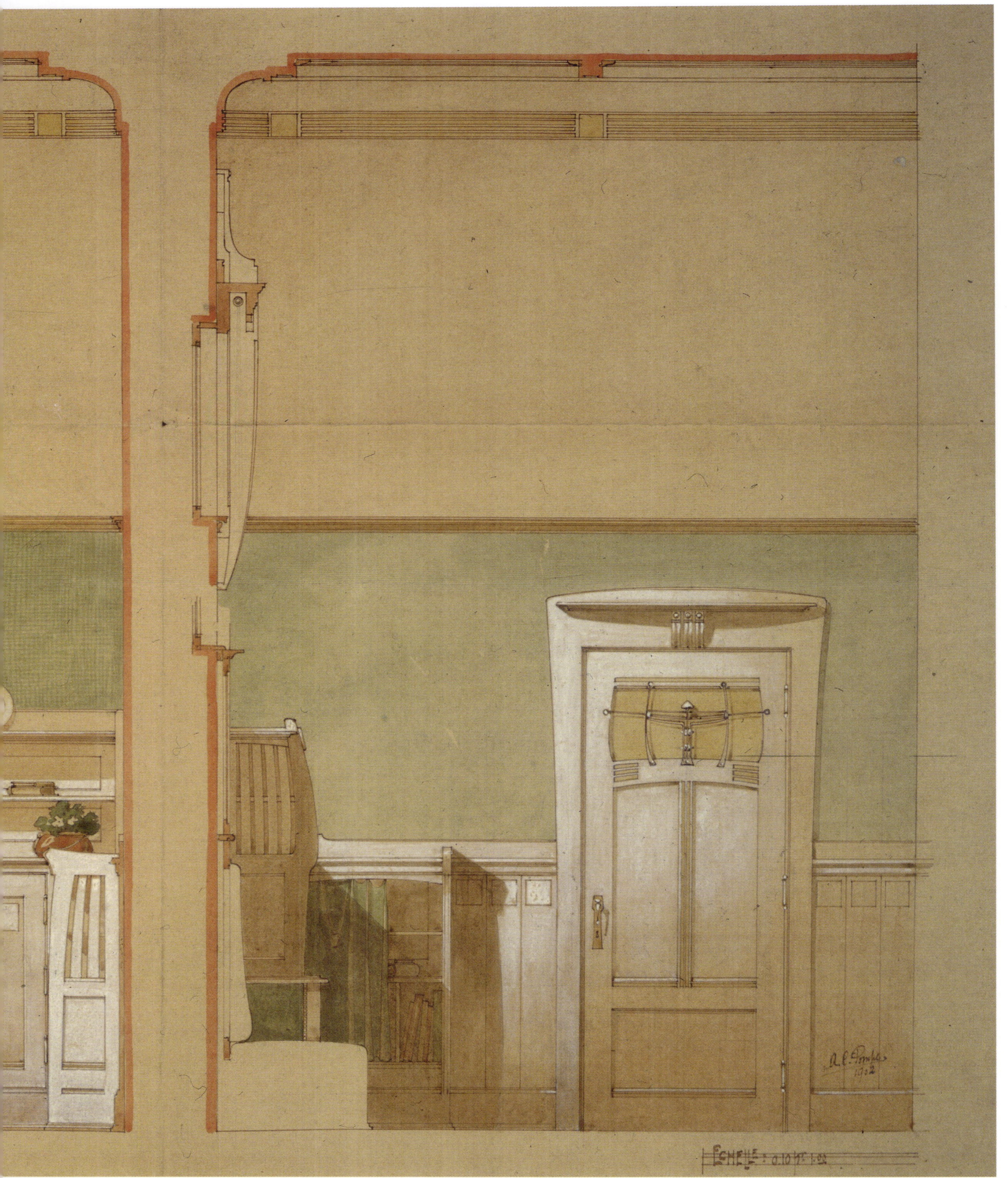

*Opposite:* Philippe Wolfers, *La Caresse du Cygne* (The Swan's Embrace), 1897, ivory, bronze and marble. Art & History Museum, Brussels.

stained glass, small sculpted designs and discreetly curved edges (on door frames, panelling and fitted furniture). The Belgians were no longer launching new trends, but learning to integrate the legacy of the Arts and Crafts Movement with the new language of form developed by artists of the Viennese Secession. The Stoclet Palace in Brussels, designed by Josef Hoffmann with the participation of the Wiener Werkstätte (a cooperative of artisans in Vienna, producing a wide range of artistic objects from 1903 to 1932), embodied the triumph of Viennese Art Nouveau.

Charles Rennie and Margaret Mackintosh's exhibit, the 'Rose Boudoir', at Turin was probably the inspiration for the painter-cum-decorator Paul Cauchie[25] when, in 1904, he began construction on his own house at 5 rue des Francs, Brussels. The large *sgraffitto* on the facade and the one that graces the dining-room walls were certainly indebted to Margaret Mackintosh's two gesso panels: 'The White Rose and the Red Rose' and 'Heart of the Rose'. The furniture, which was also designed by Cauchie, bears similarities to Mackintosh's, and Cauchie draws maximum effect from repeated motifs: they are painted using stencils or cut into the woodwork, and are offset by a series of matching decorative objects. The overall effect is spectacular, though not expensive – the element of luxury deriving, as it does, from the perfect cohesion of the whole design. Cauchie worked extensively as a *sgraffitist*: his work can be found all over Belgium. This method of decorating facades enjoyed a resurgence in Belgium in the 1880s and was very much in vogue during the Art Nouveau period, before disappearing after the First World War.

In the field of decorative arts, Belgian Art Nouveau stands out for its extensive use of ivory. Edmond van Eetvelde, Secretary-General of the Congo Free State, wanted to promote this material which was being shipped by the ton to Anvers; perhaps he hoped to rekindle the school of sculpture that had had its moment of glory in the seventeenth and eighteenth centuries. The first ivory pieces of Philippe Wolfers, who came from a family of goldsmiths and jewellers, were displayed at the Anvers World Fair in 1894. They are vases made from sections of elephant tusk, carved with scrupulously accurate botanical designs (such as orchids and poppies) and set in silver, bronze or tin bases. At the Tervueren Exhibition a special room was set aside for ivory-carving: an impressive number of Belgian sculptors contributed, sending pieces that were effectively fine art, but also some that were everyday objects: a mirror decorated with peacocks by Charles Samuel and Adolphe Crespin; fans, paper knives, a brooch and wedding gift box by Fernand Dubois; and a monumental vase – *'La caresse du cygnet'* (the swan's caress) – by Philippe Wolfers, who created it using an ivory tusk entwined with a bronze swan.

Wolfers often represented these birds, and they also feature in a strange object called *'Civilisation et Barbarie'*[26] (civilisation and barbarity), which was offered to Baron Van Eetvelde the same year. On either side of an ivory cylinder intended to contain a scroll with a text paying homage to the statesman, a silver swan and dragon confront each other, symbolising the struggle between light (shed by civilisation) and darkness (in the wild world). Wolfers drew his inspiration from nature and depicted it with powerfully expressed precision, which can also be seen in the jewellery he started designing towards 1897. Like other designers of his day – including Lalique, to whom Wolfers is often compared – he frequently used orchids, peacock feathers, butterflies, dragonflies and the female form in his designs, but did not shy away from depicting more peculiar creatures, such as bats and crabs.

*Below:* Philippe Wolfers, *La Caresse du Cygne* (The Swan's Embrace) (detail), 1897, ivory, bronze and marble. Art & History Museum, Brussels.

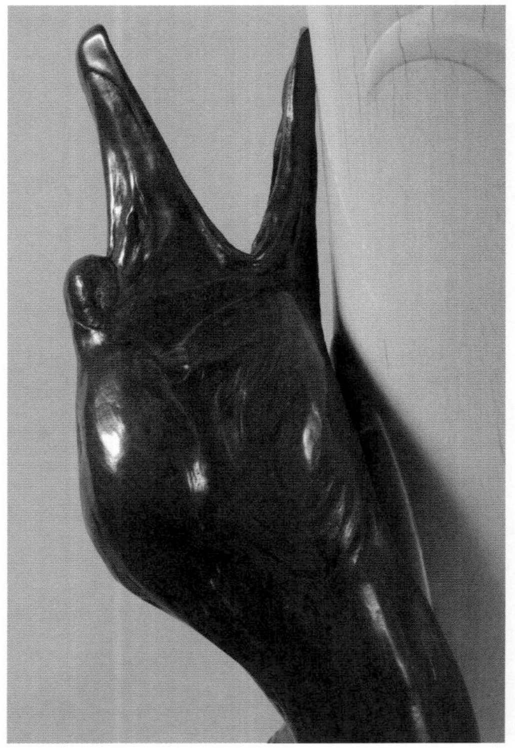

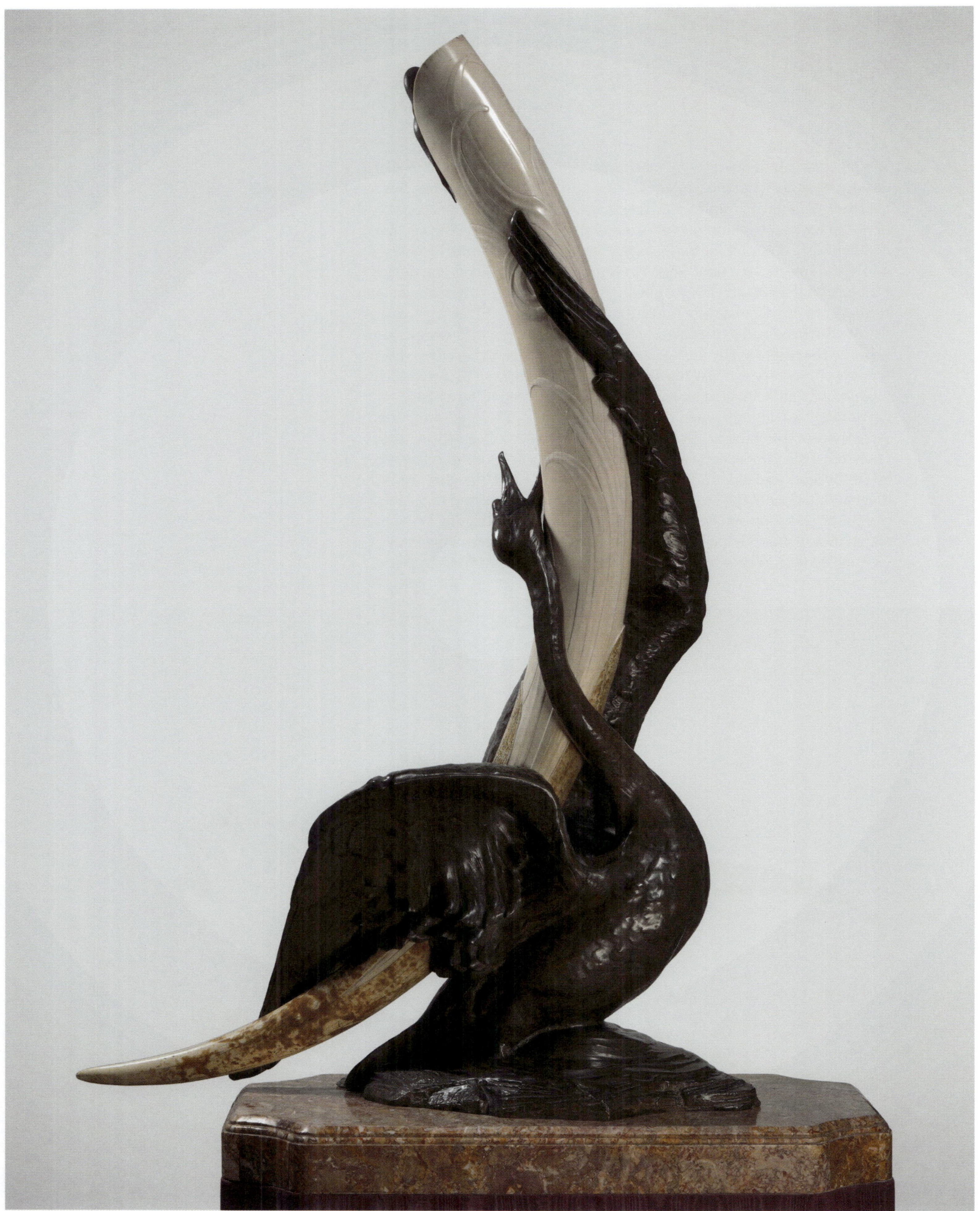

His 'Medusa' pendant – an oval mask with opal eyes – gives a glimpse of a darker, slightly menacing tendency that features in many symbolist works of the time. Wolfers also applied his talent as a sculptor to cutting crystal vases blown to his specifications at Val Saint-Lambert in Liège. Having mastered enamelling techniques for his jewellery, he used them to embellish vases and silver goblets. At a time when Art Nouveau was having its last hurrah, Philippe Wolfers turned away from almost all his activities associated with the decorative arts, to devote himself to sculpting graceful female figures.[27]

Art Nouveau had a brief blaze of glory in Belgium, but it surprised and inspired the whole of Europe. In this kingdom, which had been in existence for only sixty years and was one of the most industrialised in the world, the prosperous and cultivated bourgeoisie bankrolled a budding artistic movement that demonstrated the country's spirit of enterprise and its receptivity to the wider world. Brussels was no longer a sleepy provincial town, but a place for every kind of exchange, and a hub for the avant-garde: artists, writers and poets all agreed with Henry Van de Velde that 'art is the decoration of life'.[28] The buzz surrounding the movement could not last, and the public was soon saturated by the ornamental vocabulary of Art Nouveau, which now featured in posters, shop displays and everyday items; they wanted change – a new fashion. The time had come for Art Deco.

§



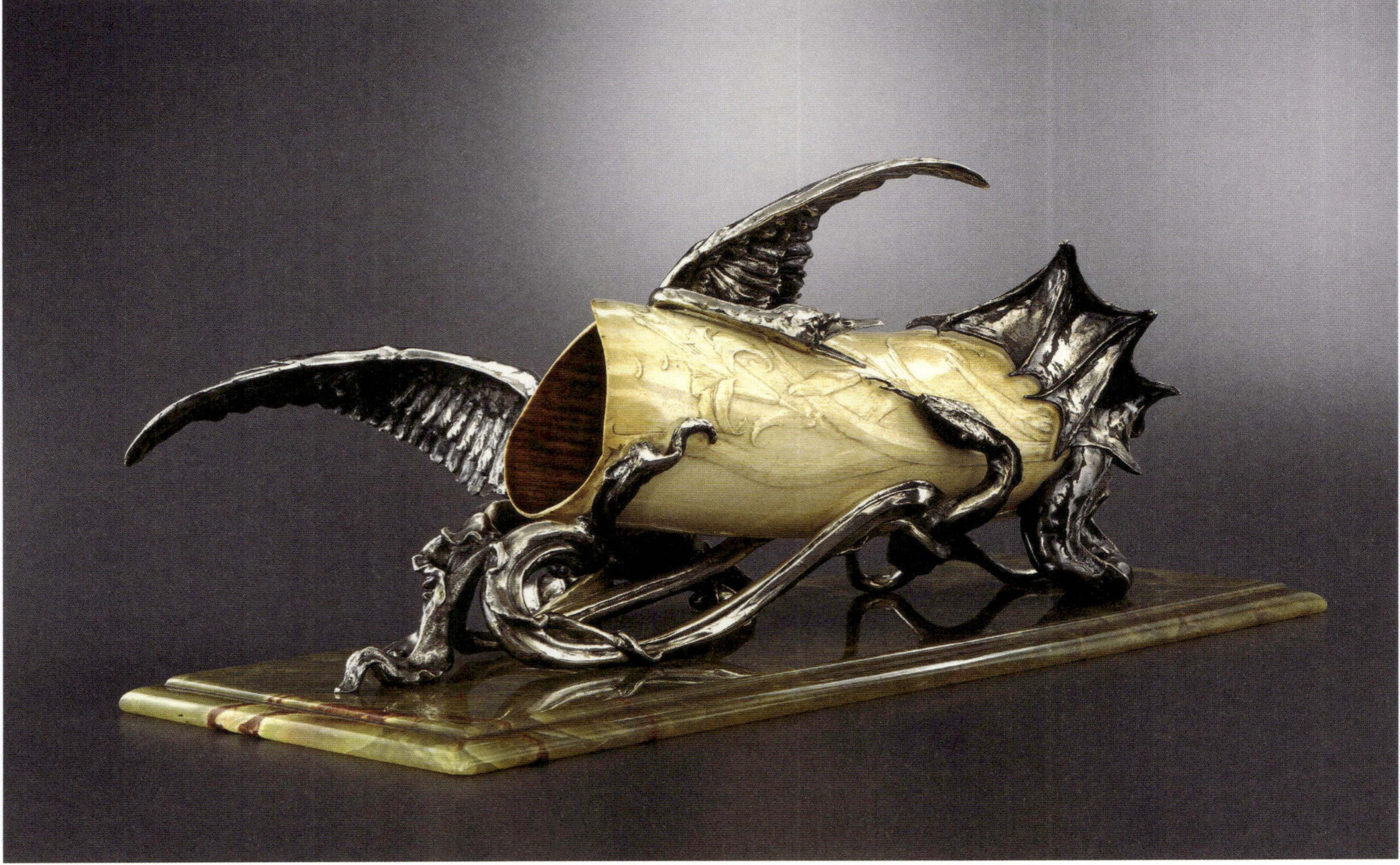

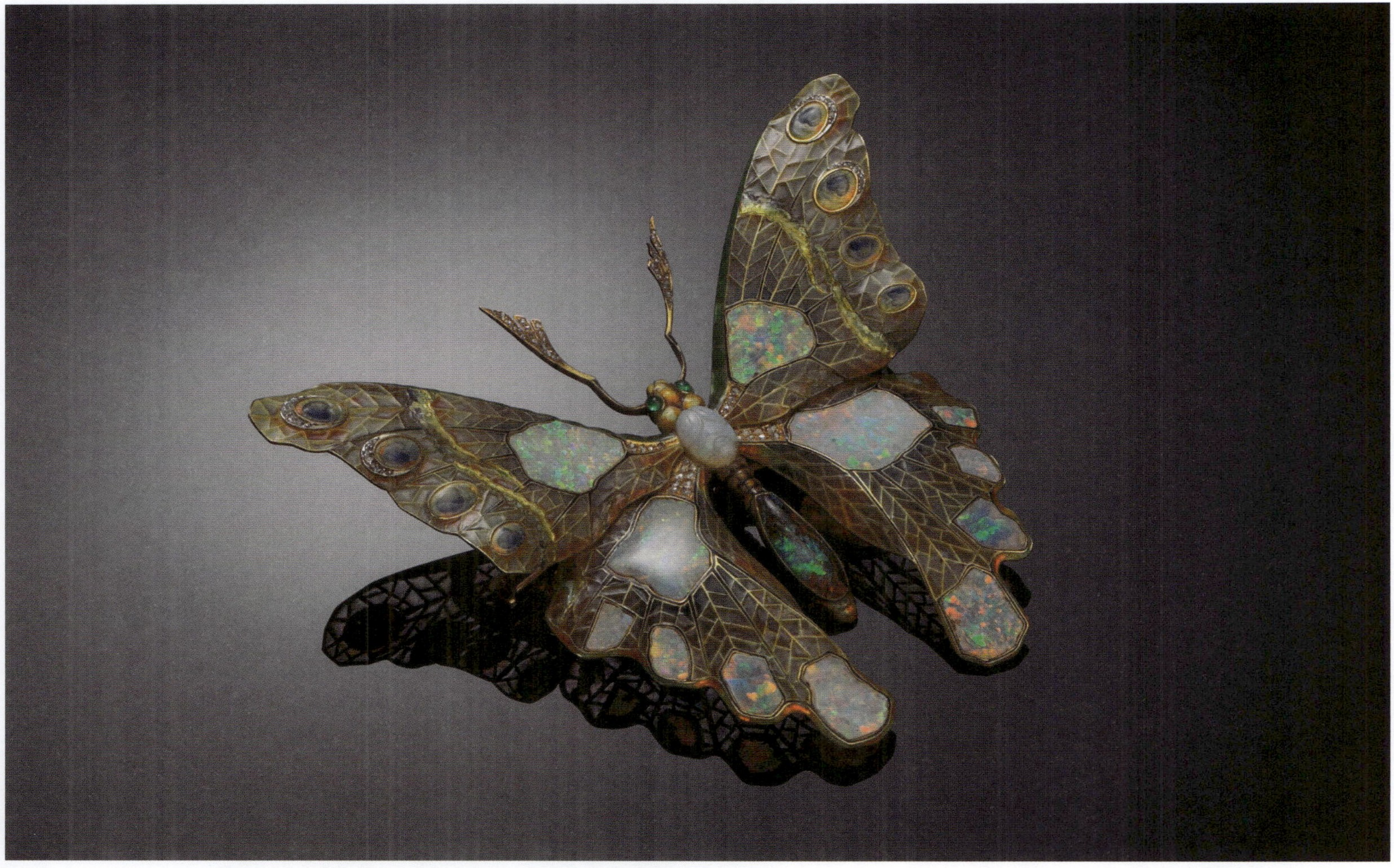


## ENDNOTES

1   Jean Lahor, *L'Art Nouveau: Son histoire, L'Art nouveau étranger à l'exposition, L'Art nouveau au point de vue social* (Paris: Lemerre, 1901), p.15.

2   Michèle Goslar, *Victor Horta 1861–1947* (Brussels: Fondation Pierre Lahaut et Fonds Mercator, 2012); David Dernie and Alastair Carew-Cox, *Victor Horta: The architect of Art Nouveau* (London: Thames & Hudson, 2018).

3   Katherine M. Kuenzli, *Henry Van de Velde: Designing Modernism* (New Haven, CT, and London: Yale University Press, 2019).

4   *Henry Van de Velde: Récit de ma vie. Anvers-Bruxelles-Paris-Berlin. I. 1863–1900*, with a commentary by Anne Van Loo (Brussels: Flammarion / Versa, 1992), p.230.

5   Letter from Henry Van de Velde to Maria Sèthe sent from Kalmthout, Belgium, n.d. (May 1893). Van de Velde's letters are preserved in the Henry Van de Velde Collection in the Literature Museum and Archives at the Albert I Royal Library in Brussels, dossier FSX 784.

6   'Artistic Wallpapers', *L'Art Moderne*, 1893, No. 25, pp.193–5; No. 26, pp.202–4; 'Essex and Co. Westminster wallpapers', *L'Art Moderne*, 1894, No. 32, pp.254–5.

7   Anne Van Loo, 'Le Bloemenwerf d'Henry Van de Velde: Enquête sur une construction mythique', *Bruxelles-Patrimoine*, December 2018, No. 29, pp.40–51.

8   Henry Nocq, 'L'exposition de la Libre Esthétique', *Revue des Arts Décoratifs*, 1896, pp.141–8, on p.145.

9   Henry Van de Velde: *Récit de ma vie*, p.339.

10   Françoise Bigot du Mesnil du Buisson and Etienne du Mesnil du Buisson, *Serrurier-Bovy, un créateur précurseur 1858–1910* (Dijon: Editions Faton, 2008).

11   'Le Salon de la libre Esthétique, l'Art appliqué', *L'Art Moderne*, 1894, pp.84–6, on p.86.

12   This fourteen-page booklet, published by Bénard in Liège in 1895, is reproduced in its entirety in Françoise Bigot du Mesnil du Buisson, *Gustave Serrurier-Bovy (1858–1910). Parcours d'un architect à l'aube du XXe sickle: Rationalisme, Art Social, symbolisation*, a doctoral thesis on the history of architecture presented to the University of Versailles Saint-Quentin-en-Yvelines (Atelier National de reproduction des thèses, 2004), pp.49–52, on pp.51–2.

13   *The Studio*, Vol. VIII, July 1896, pp.118, 119.

14   François Loyer and Jean Delhaye, *Victor Horta: Hôtel Tassel 1893–1895* (Brussels: AAM, 1986).

15   These words feature in Horta's will, written towards the end of his life on 7 February 1944, in which he reiterates one last time his debt to his master.

16   François Thiebault-Sisson, 'L'Art Décoratif en Belgique, Un novateur: Victor Horta', *Art et Décoration*, 1897, pp.11–18.

17   Ibid., pp.16–17.

18   Françoise Aubry, 'L'hôtel Van Eetvelde: restauration de décor intérieur du salon', *Restauration(s) et Conservation* (Brussels: Service des Monuments et Sites de la Région de Bruxelles-Capitale, 2011), pp.148–57.

19   *Victor Horta: Mémoires*, edited by Cécile Duliere (Brussels: Ministry of the French Community of Belgium, 1985).

20   Maurice Pillard Verneuil, 'L'exposition d'art décoratif moderne à Turin', *Art et Décoration*, 1902, pp.65–112, on p.75.

21   Jean Delhaye and Françoise Dierkens-Aubry, *La Maison du Peuple de Victor Horta* (Brussels: Atelier Vokaer, 1987).

22   François Loyer, *Paul Hankar: La naissance de l'Art Nouveau* (Brussels: Archives d'Architecture Moderne, 1986).

23   M. Luwel and M. Bruneel-Hye de Crom, *Tervueren 1897* (Tervueren: Musée Royal de l'Afrique Centrale, 1967).

24   Enrico Thovez, 'The Turin Exhibition: The Belgian Section', *The Studio XXVI*, January 1903, pp.279–83; Georg Fuchs, 'La section belge à l'exposition de Turin', *L'exposition internationale des Arts Décoratifs modernes à Turin* (Darmstadt, 1902), pp.242–56.

25   Paul Cauchie, *Architecte, peintre, décorateur* (Brussels: Edition Maison Cauchie, 1994).

26   Werner Adriaenssens and Françoise Aubry, *Philippe Wolfers: Civilisation et Barbarie* (Brussels: Fondation Roi Baudouin, 2002).

27   Werner Adriaenssens and Raf Steel, *La dynastie Wolfers: De l'Art Nouveau à l'Art déco* (Anvers: Pandora, 2006).

28   Henry Van de Velde, *Aperçus en vue d'une synthèse d'art* (Brussels: Veuve Monnom, 1895), p.20.

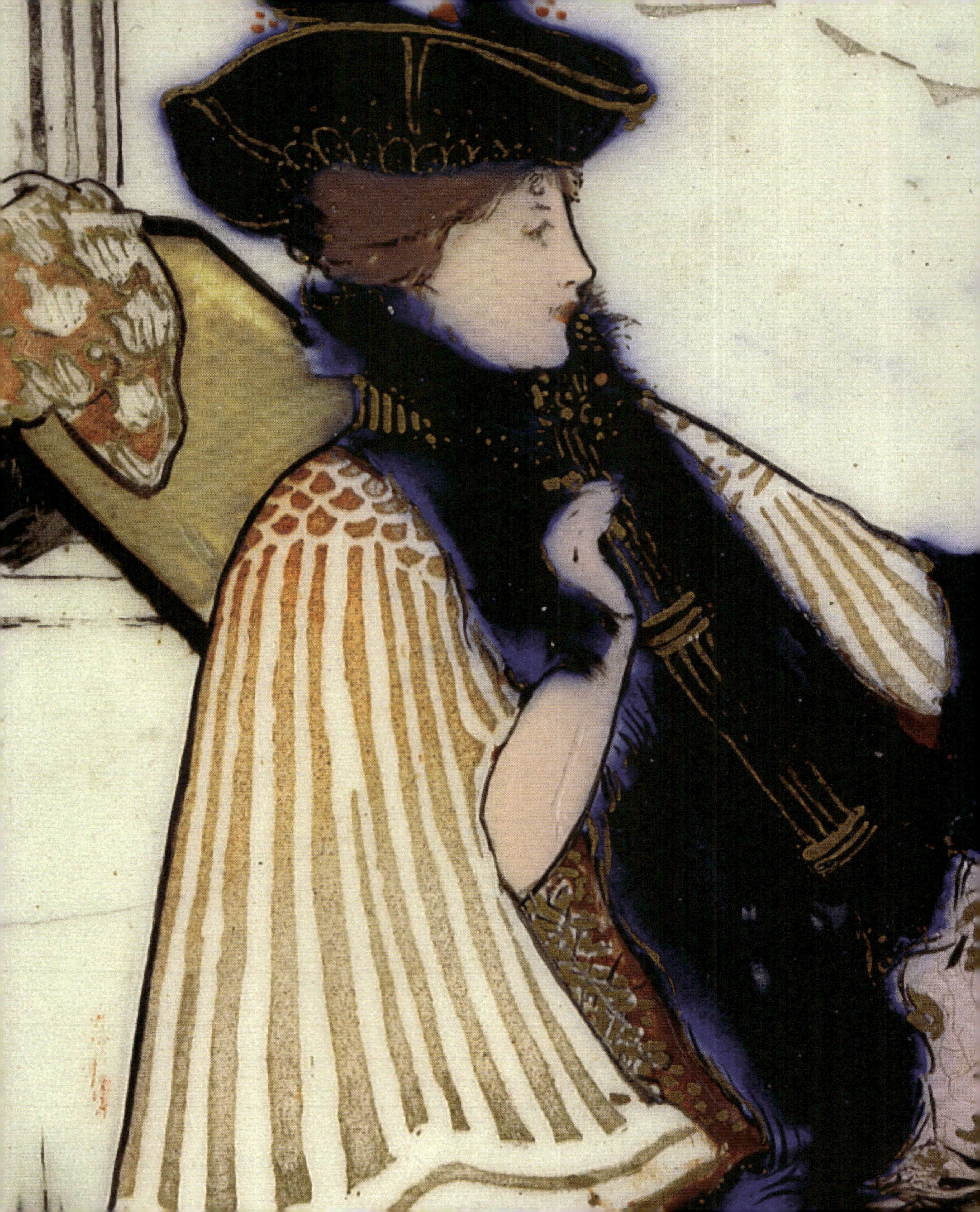

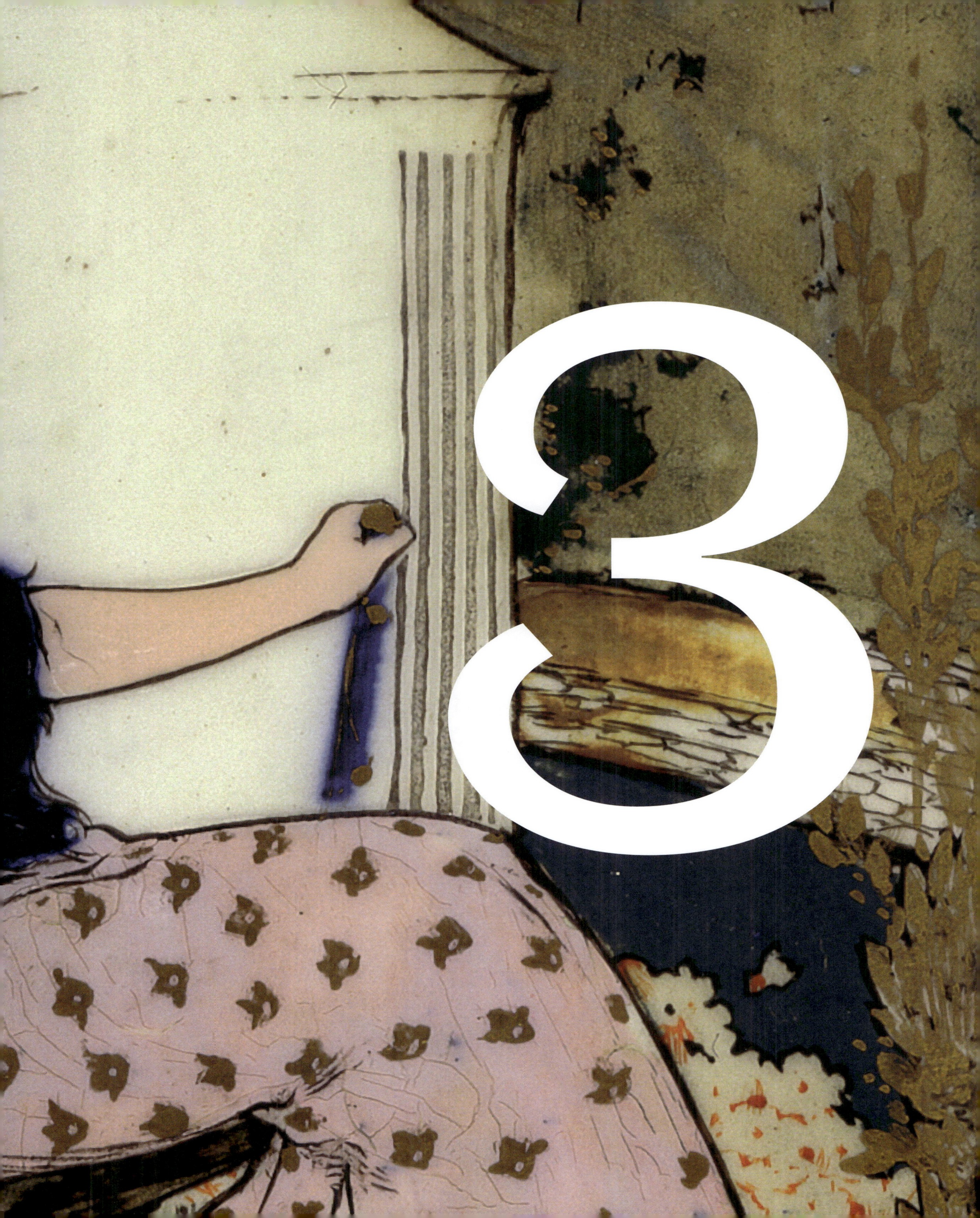
3

# ~Beauty's Awakening~

# Paris, the performing arts and the formation of Art Nouveau

~Barbara Bessac~

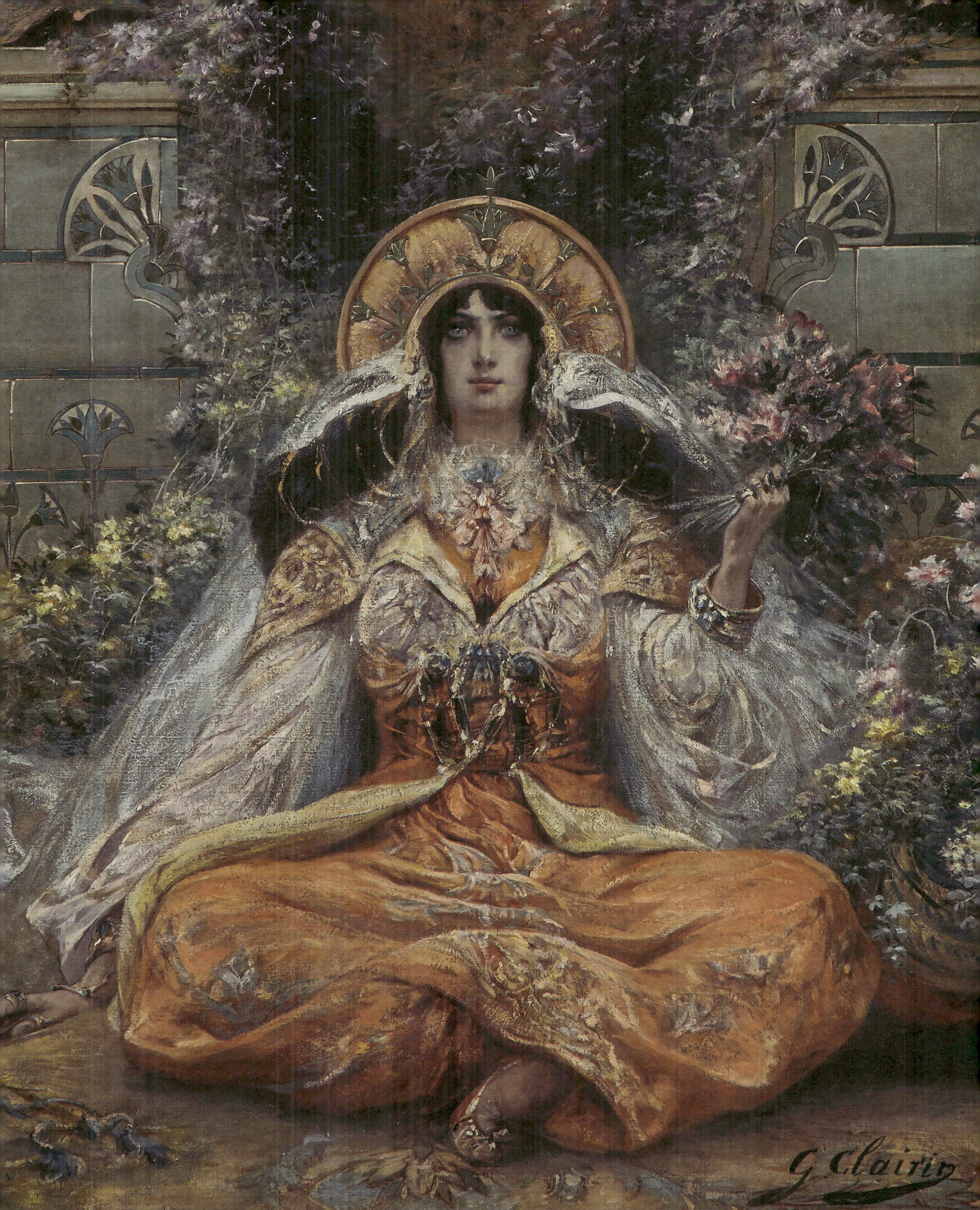
G. Clairin

T he growth pattern of the Art Nouveau style across Europe and beyond has frequently been explained with narratives about seminal artists who imported its forms and ideas into their respective cities. The case of Paris in this regard is particularly conspicuous: starting in 1894, the collaboration between the celebrated actress Sarah Bernhardt and Czech artist Alphonse Mucha became symbolic of the birth of the new style in the city. The subsequent opening of Siegfried Bing's gallery in 1895, *La Maison de l'Art Nouveau*, sealed the affiliation of Paris with the modern style. But these two major events, as crucial as they were, have tended to hide the complexity of the context, the rich and disparate network of lesser known craftspeople, art critics, playwrights, actors and actresses who contributed to the rise of Art Nouveau in Paris. In reality, the style was generated more through myriad incremental contributions, than through a few seminal occurrences.

The theatre and the decorative arts generated a dense, multifaceted artistic nebula from which Art Nouveau derived. At the crossroads of different crafts, the stage became the meeting place of artists, and a fertile ground for the new aesthetics. In the context of continual international interaction, the coming together of performance and the applied arts, exemplified by Bernhardt and Mucha's collaboration, reveals the role of theatre in the blossoming of Parisian Art Nouveau.

If Sarah Bernhardt's influence helped to spread the new style in Paris, it was, more than anything else, symptomatic of the connections and circulations between the applied arts and performance in the 1890s. The stage, deeply nested in the artistic spheres of that era, concentrated the delicate blend of tradition and modernity that was so characteristic of the new style. The exchange was constant and, partly because of it, ideas and aesthetics kept circulating between Paris and London: one was always keeping an eye on the other across the Channel.

In both capital cities, epicentres of cultural activity at the fin de siècle, theatre – at all levels – was the regular rendezvous of a broad and influential audience. Cinema was just beginning to emerge, but theatre was the central visual spectacle, and the audience expected veracity and attention to detail, crafted by numerous decorative artists: scene-painters, costume designers, jewellers and cabinetmakers. Design and its new forms were omnipresent in these productions: stages were filled with furniture, textile, decorative panels, graphic design and costumes, creating scenes from far-away ideal worlds or the interiors typical of those lived-in by the bourgeois audience. From fantastical ancient sets to re-created modern households, the stage was an excellent playground for theatre designers. Artists and stage directors exploited it as a showcase for the new aesthetics. Street posters, press illustration and photography contributed to spread theatrical designs outside the theatre world. Working both on- and off-stage, some of these artists belonged to the newest artistic circles. Furniture, jewellery, dresses – as seen on-stage – could be purchased by the audience in the newly established department stores. This very particular dynamic and urban environment stimulated creativity and promoted it, embodying the new decorative forms. The aesthetic world of Art Nouveau was highly eclectic and related both to pre-modern worlds – the Middle Ages, Byzantium, Classical Antiquity – and to contemporary interiors, and these were brought together onstage.

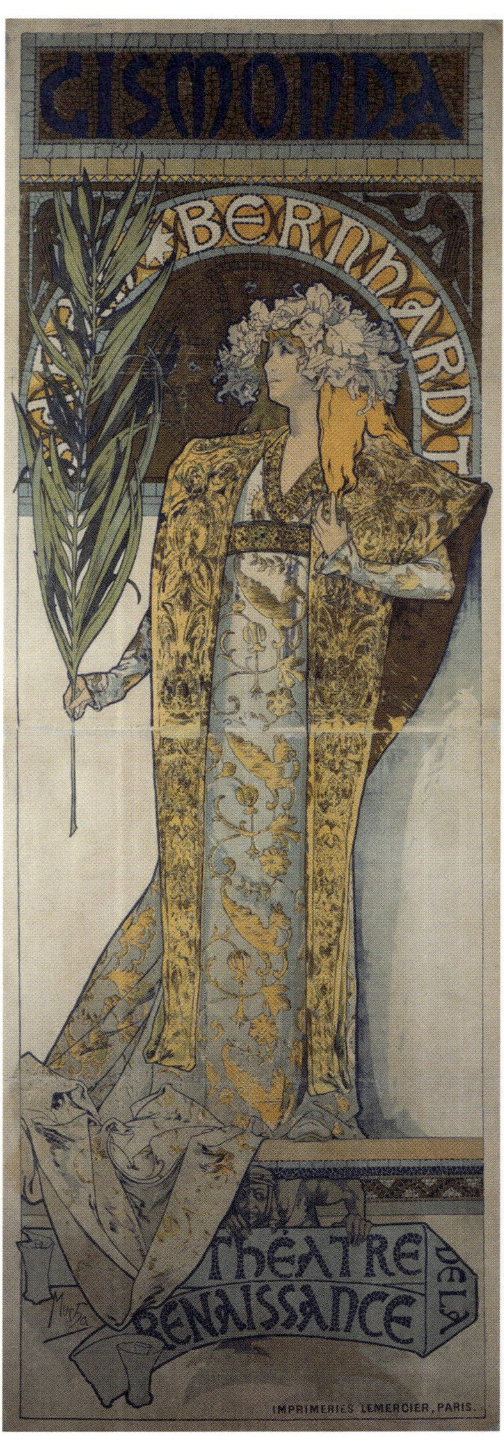

*Above and opposite:* Alphonse Mucha, poster for *Gismonda*, 1894, colour lithograph. Victoria and Albert Museum.

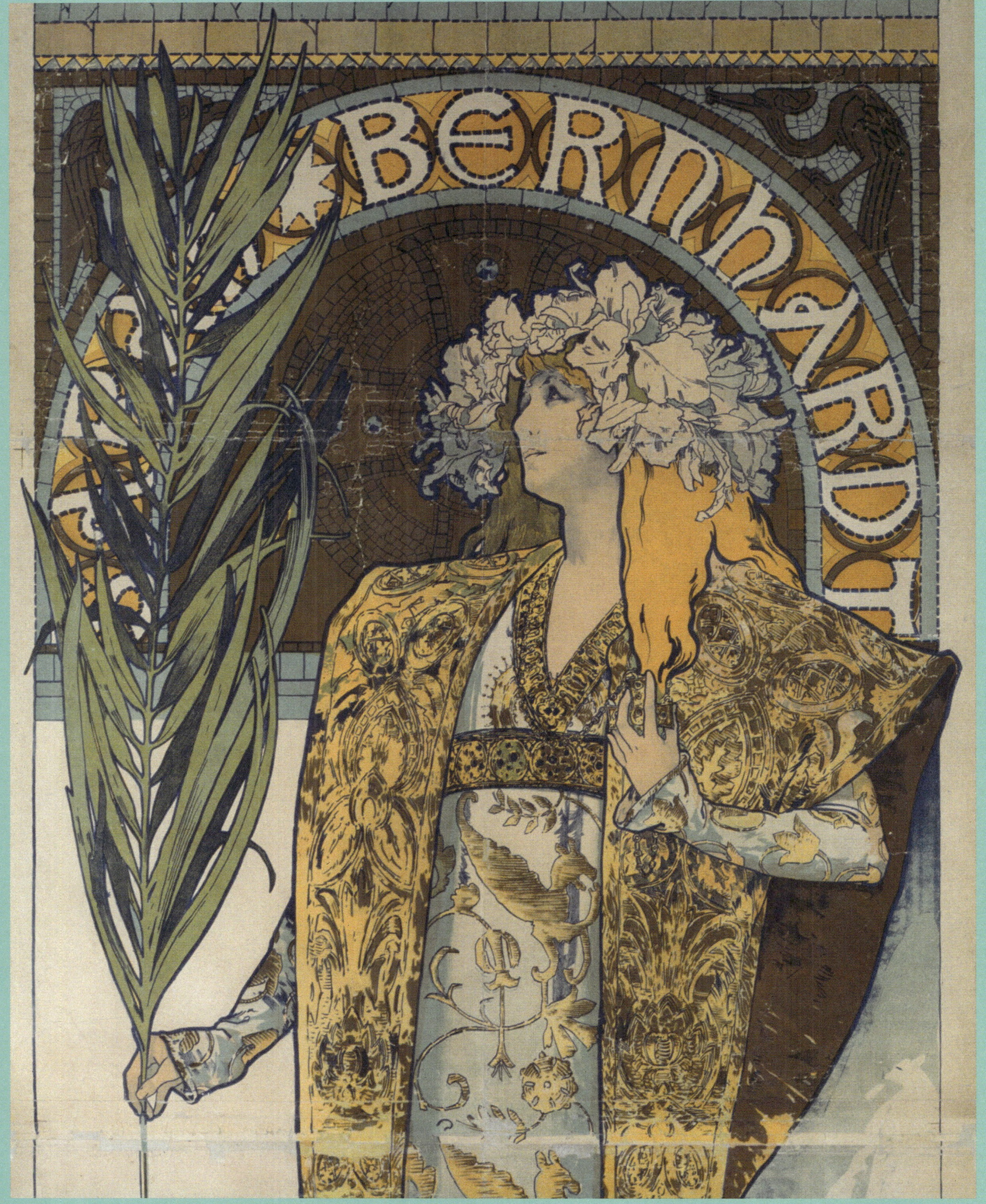
BERNHARDT

So in Paris it was very significantly through the theatre that Art Nouveau was launched and became visible, in no small part thanks to Sarah Bernhardt's direct intervention, her taste and her stage direction. Beyond the performance itself, she lent her network, her influence, her theatre and her image to upcoming artists: she carried the new art with her on her tours around the world. Following in her idol's footsteps, the American dancer Loie Fuller used performance as a vehicle for the promotion of the new art, fusing dance with design and the decorative arts. Her performances became a site of interdisciplinary activity, which was a characteristic of the new art in a number of spheres. By 1900 Fuller herself became a symbol of Art Nouveau and the subject matter of numerous designers. In fact a number of them started their careers working for the stage, since it was an excellent way to show their work, gain notoriety and attract new clients. Theatre was fully immersed in the ideological debates circulating around art, and was in many ways the physical and public realisation of the aesthetic reformation in Paris and London. If the development of an Art Nouveau movement was problematic in England, a number of late-Victorian productions nevertheless had a shared taste for the new decorative forms. A performance such as the enchanting masque *Beauty's Awakening* in 1899, written, crafted and played by members of the Art Workers' Guild, resonated in France, where art critics reported it as *'un théâtre d'artistes'*.[1] For them it embodied, both visually and theoretically, the characteristics of *gesamtkunstwerk*, a modern total work of art, which was the same intellectual ideal Art Nouveau designers across the Channel pursued. The performing arts contributed to intensify the production as a decorative revolution.

Sarah Bernhardt had been triumphant in Paris since the beginning of the 1870s. Her success became international in 1879 with her first tour in London with her troupe, the Comédie-Française. In 1893 – the year Victor Horta completed the first fully realised Art Nouveau building in Brussels – she started to direct the Théâtre de la Renaissance, allowing her to schedule and produce the plays of her choice. At the end of 1894 she was preparing the production of a new drama by Victorien Sardou, entitled *Gismonda*. When organising the production of the graphic materials for the play – the programme and poster – the very demanding actress was disappointed by the submissions, and eventually decided to commission the artist Alphonse Mucha, via the Imprimeries Lemercier for which he had previously worked. The director of Imprimeries Lemercier, André Marty, was no stranger either to the theatre or to the decorative arts. In 1893 he had produced posters for Loie Fuller, and in 1894 he opened L'Artisan Moderne, a gallery specialising in domestic accessories, *objets d'art* and costume jewellery.[2]

Alphonse Mucha was no stranger to the stage: he had already drawn Bernhardt when he worked for the magazine *Le Costume au Théâtre*, notably for *Cléopâtre* in 1890.[3] He knew how to capture the essence of a play, and how to summarise it in the poster medium. The *Gismonda* poster was an immediate success, and started a six year collaboration between the Czech artist and the Parisian actress. The designs were widely disseminated through 1895, a few months before Siegfried Bing opened his Maison de l'Art Nouveau. The *'style Mucha'* quickly became synonymous with Art Nouveau. The decorative aspect, using friezes and rosettes with floral outlines, was predominant, melting the feminine figures in a whirlwind of dynamic curves and stems. On *Gismonda*'s poster, the costume and the mosaic evoked the

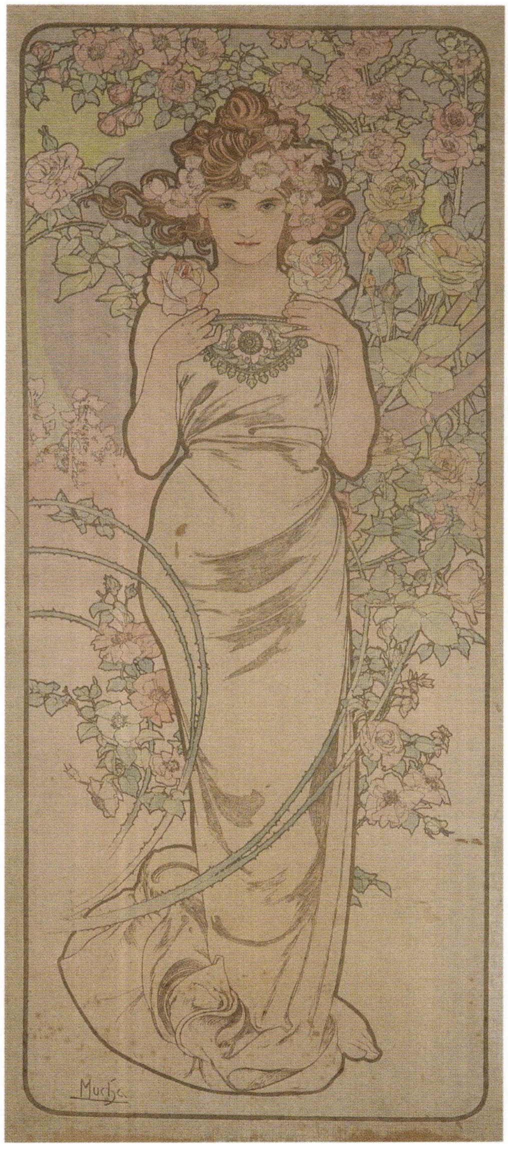

*Above:* Alphonse Mucha, *La Rose*, 1898, colour lithograph on silk. Sainsbury Centre.

historical context of fifteenth-century Greece in which the play takes place, contrasting with a resolutely original style, illustrating the balance between modernity and tradition in Art Nouveau productions. The famous poster very much overshadowed the other artists and craftspeople who worked on the performance, and played a decisive role in the unique appearance of *Gismonda*. The stage direction was an intense reflection of Sarah Bernhardt's style: she chose every costume, set design and accessory, oscillating between historicist references, modern creation and exoticism. The Gothic Revival and Aesthetic Movement across the Channel drew her attention.

Being friendly with her British counterpart Ellen Terry, Bernhardt absorbed Terry's taste, especially with regard to Terry's enthusiasm for Japanese culture, which had dramatically arrived in the English capital after 1862, when it was first shown at the *London Universal Exhibition* of that year. Bernhardt adopted Terry's tea-gown, inspired by the Japanese kimono.[4] And in turn Bernhardt was influential on British fashion. As early as her first appearance in front of a London audience in 1879, the art critic Matthew Arnold celebrated the influence of Sarah Bernhardt and her taste on the English cultural scene.[5] The two actresses weren't simply friends: they were also very similar in the way they managed their images through the visual arts. Both were widely depicted in contemporary paintings, and sold massively in postcard form. Ellen Terry's most famous costume for Lady Macbeth in 1888 was created by Alice Comyns Carr, her loyal costume designer, who was inspired by French couture and design, especially by Viollet-le-Duc's decoration dictionaries.[6] After being designed in London, the costume was sent to Paris to be made up. This sumptuous dress, covered with 1,000 beetle wings – which took 700 hours of work when it was recently restored – was directly comparable with the opulence of Sarah Bernhardt's costumes, which required the labour of at least twenty craftspeople, embroidering the dresses with gemstones and gilding.

The London shop Liberty & Co. supplied silk and cashmere fabrics for Ellen Terry's costumes, in typical Aestheticist colours: pale green, peacock blue, ancient gold, silver grey and emerald green. Terry's stages had to be harmonised, from the scene cloth to the costumes – a coherence that Bernhardt was also very committed to. And as with Terry, who had been compared to Rossetti's paintings onstage,[7] the French actress was often described through references to contemporary painters. The journalist Ernest Prosnier, in his report on *Izeyl*, wrote that she was the 'delicious and uncanny synthesis of all mysterious painters such as Gustave Moreau or Edward Burne-Jones'.[8] With both stage stars there was no frontier between theatrical and civilian life – they wore costumes on and off stage. The theatrical costumier Ada Nettleship made daily outfits for Ellen Terry, following the principles of Artistic Dress, the movement that promoted dress reform; and Sarah Bernhardt wore some of her outfits as exuberant instruments of expression, both on stage and in daily life.

While Bernhardt controlled sets and costumes, she would also work closely with the playwright, who would conduct studies to guarantee the historical correctness of the appearance of the play.[9] For *Gismonda*, Théophile Thomas was commissioned. The costume designer had already worked repeatedly with Victorien Sardou and Bernhardt, his most striking item probably being *Theodora*'s coat, an exact replica of the dress of the Byzantine Empress, and famous for its exorbitant price.[10] Thomas's plates for *Gismonda*

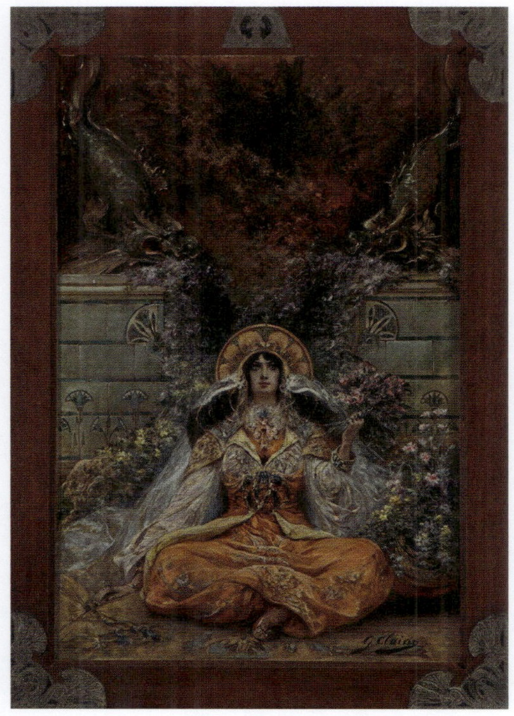

*Below:* Georges Clairin, *Sarah Bernhardt in the Role of Izeyl, c.*1894, oil on canvas. Jack Kilgore Gallery.

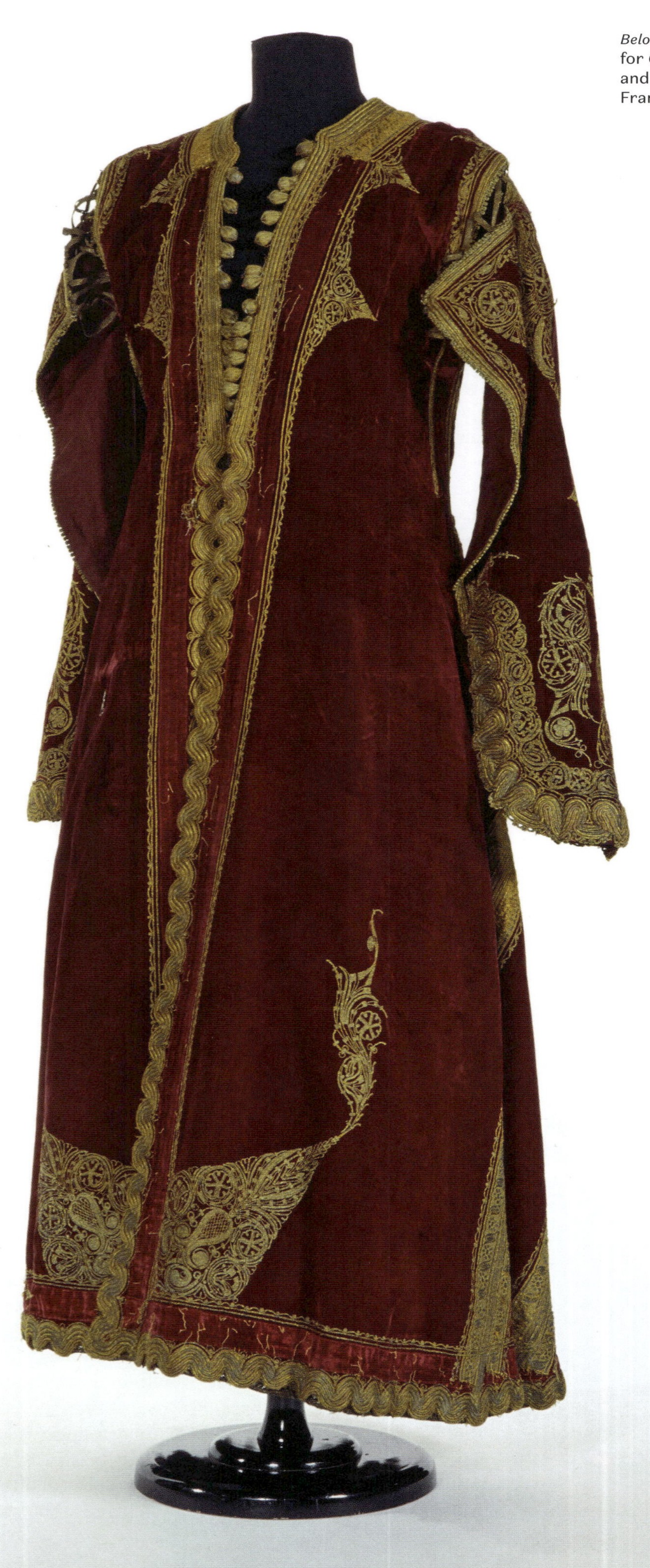

*Below:* Théophile Thomas, costume for *Gismonda*, 1894/1902, velvet and silk. Bibliothèque Nationale de France.

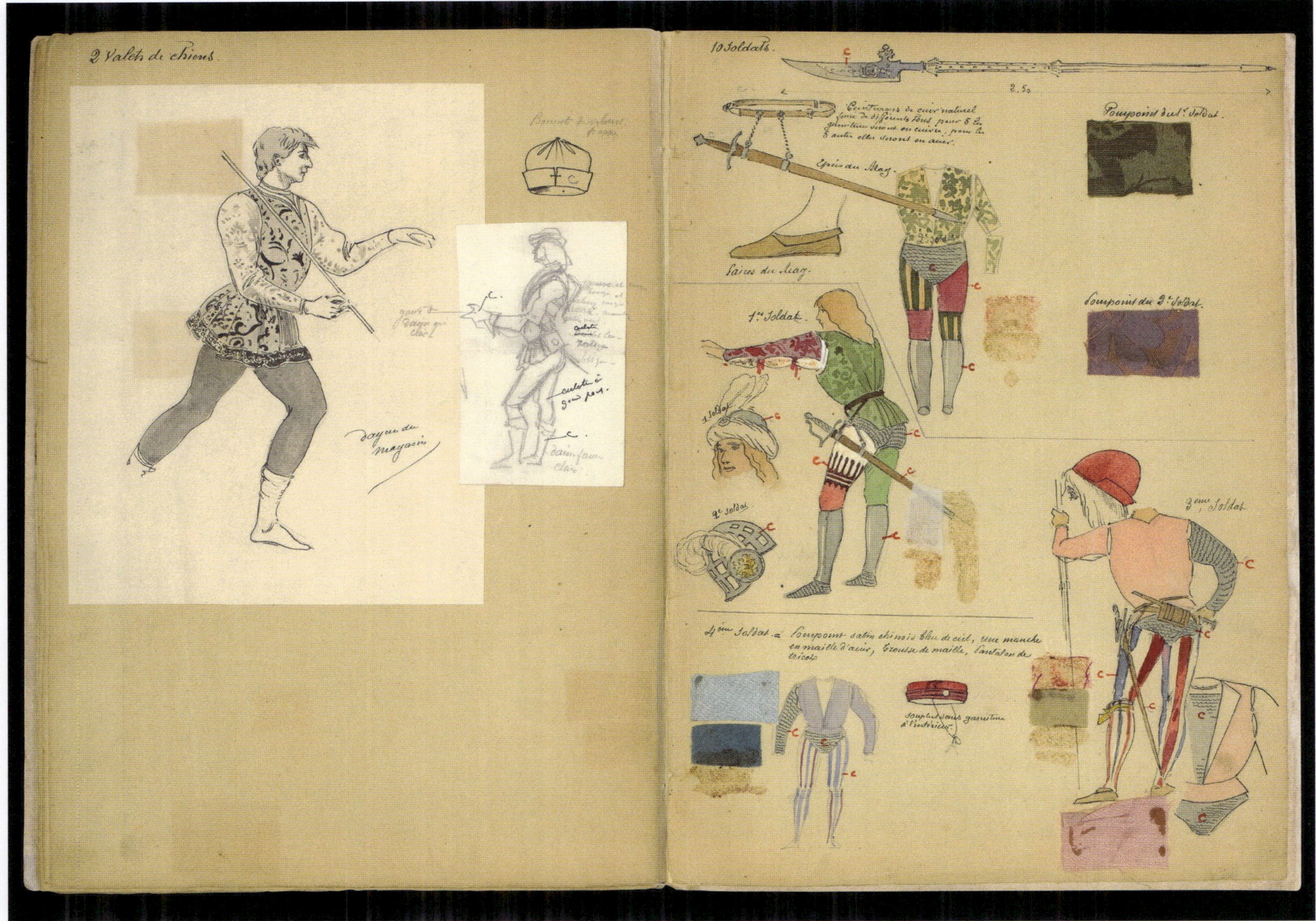



 Théophile Thomas, album of costume designs for *Gismonda*, *c.*1894. Victoria and Albert Museum.

– now in the Victoria and Albert Museum – relate closely to costumes in the Bibliothèque Nationale de France, and show the intense and meticulous work carried out by the costumiers: up to eighteen embroiderers worked day and night on a single item.[11] Bernhardt's dresses were so heavy that she struggled to move around the stage. On most of them, arabesque patterns were ubiquitous: brocades were covered with vegetalised ornaments, punctuated by gemstones. In an interview to *Le Matin*, she estimated the number of costumes as amounting to up to 160 items.[12] Only five of them have survived, but they prove the unabashed attempt to mesmerise and dazzle the audience, while respecting a certain historical accuracy. They were an integral part of the living picture framed by the set designs, and contributed vitally to the character of the subjects of the epic.

Impressively, for the accessories Sarah Bernhardt brought into play the renowned jeweller René Lalique. Recognised as being at the heart of the Art Nouveau style, he met the actress in 1893 via Victorien Sardou.[13] He designed various jewels for *Gismonda*, providing mutually important publicity for both.[14] All the crafts made for the play came to be seen by a massive international audience, as the play embarked on tour abroad from May 1895, first to London at Daly's Theatre, and then to the United States. In each venue, all the costumes and sets were brought from Paris, as was advertised in the programmes.[15]

*Gismonda*'s role in the development of French Art Nouveau was decisive, and it was not limited to the promotion of luminaries like Mucha and Lalique. The play positioned theatre generally at the heart of Art Nouveau, and

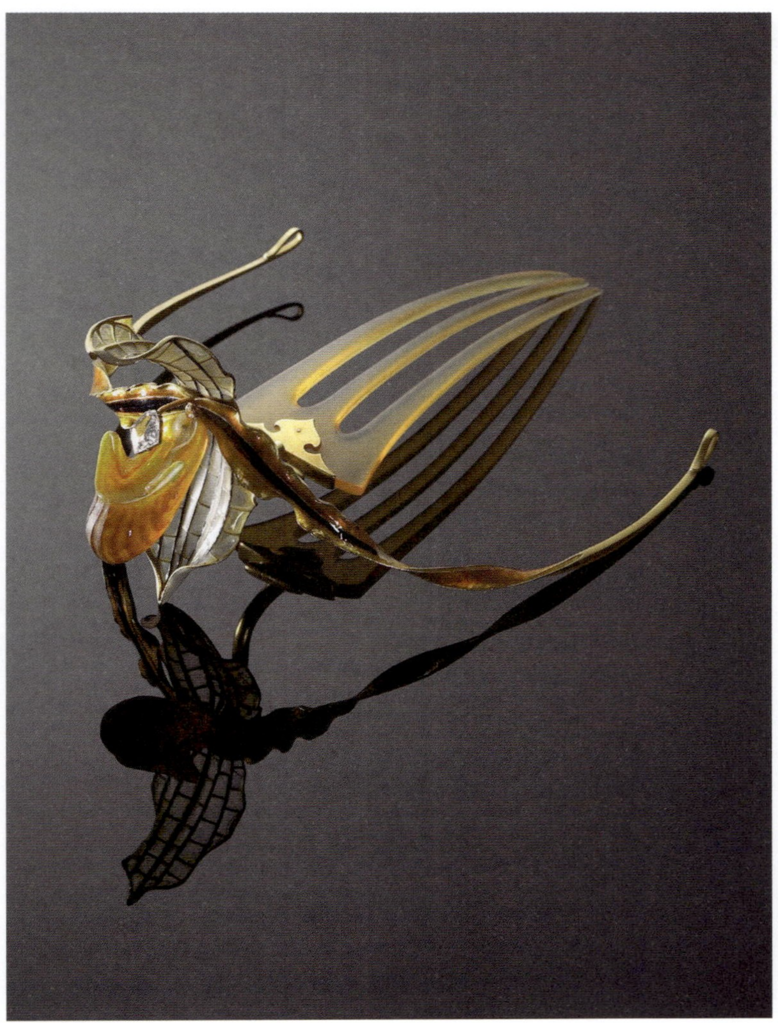

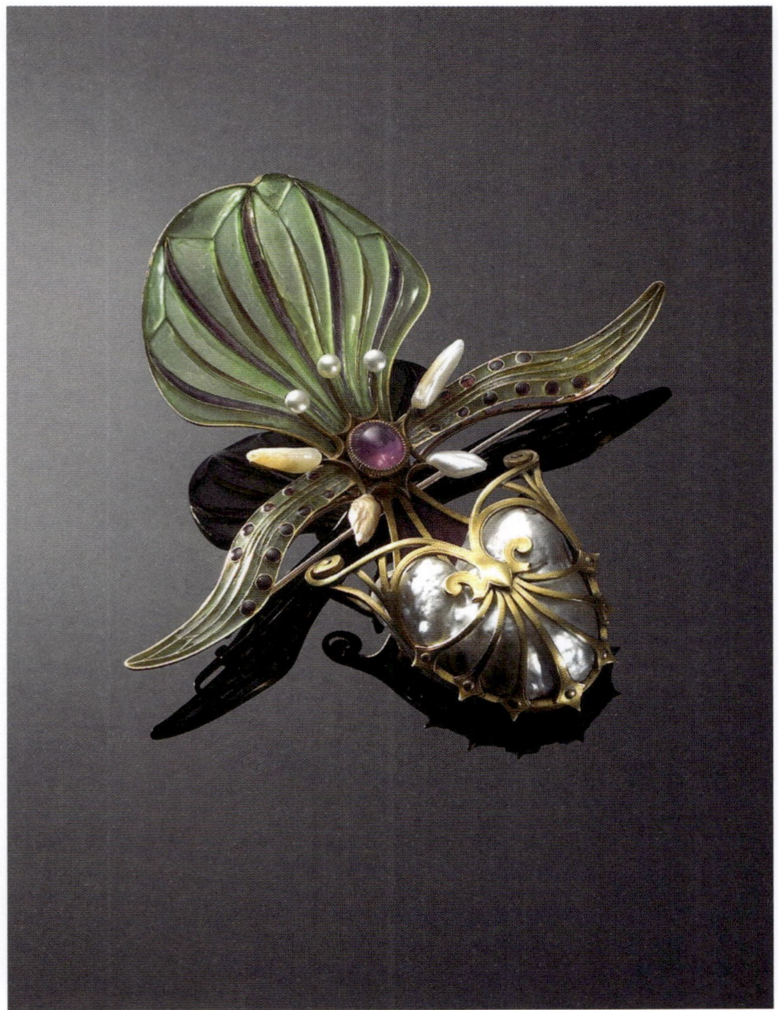

resulted in collaborations among designers beyond theatre itself. In 1899, still under contract with the Czech artist, Sarah Bernhardt commissioned the jeweller Georges Fouquet to make the bracelet that Mucha drew in *Médée*'s poster (1898). The result of this first collaboration between the two artists was one of the most important ensembles of French Art Nouveau: Fouquet's shop on rue Royale, designed entirely by Mucha.[16] While it would be inaccurate, and somewhat anachronistic, to see *Gismonda* as an 'Art Nouveau play' *per se* – it was as much an eclectic and historicist work as an expression of modernity – the general aesthetic was broadly reflective of the ethos, and it was the first play to incorporate Art Nouveau accessories onstage.

Art Nouveau quickly became recognisable by its contemporaries, above all by its distinctive profiles, which were pejoratively described by the English designer Walter Crane in 1902 as:

> long drawn-out, irregular spiral stem, often multiplied, and varied
> with "kinks" and elbows, and terminating in formal rows of disks and
> floral forms.[17]

Referred to at the time and later as *coup de fouet*, or negatively as style *nouille* (noodle style) this use of line became the visual identity of the new art.[18] Whatever harmony the new art had, however, this barely masked what were strong differences in opinion with regard to substance: artists were often uncomfortable with Art Nouveau, characterizing it as 'foreign'. This wasn't unconnected to the context of competitive nationalism. Walter Crane, a leading light in the Arts and Crafts Movement, for example, reveals this prejudice when discussing the work at the *First International Exposition of Modern Decorative Arts* in Turin in 1902. He was positive in admitting that:

*Left:* René Lalique, hair ornament, *c.*1902, gold, diamond, glass, horn and enamel. Sainsbury Centre.
*Above:* Georges Fouquet, brooch, *c.*1898, gold, ruby, pearl and enamel. Sainsbury Centre.

*Opposite:* Alphonse Mucha, interior design for the Boutique Fouquet, pencil on paper, 1900. Musée Carnavalet, Histoire de Paris.

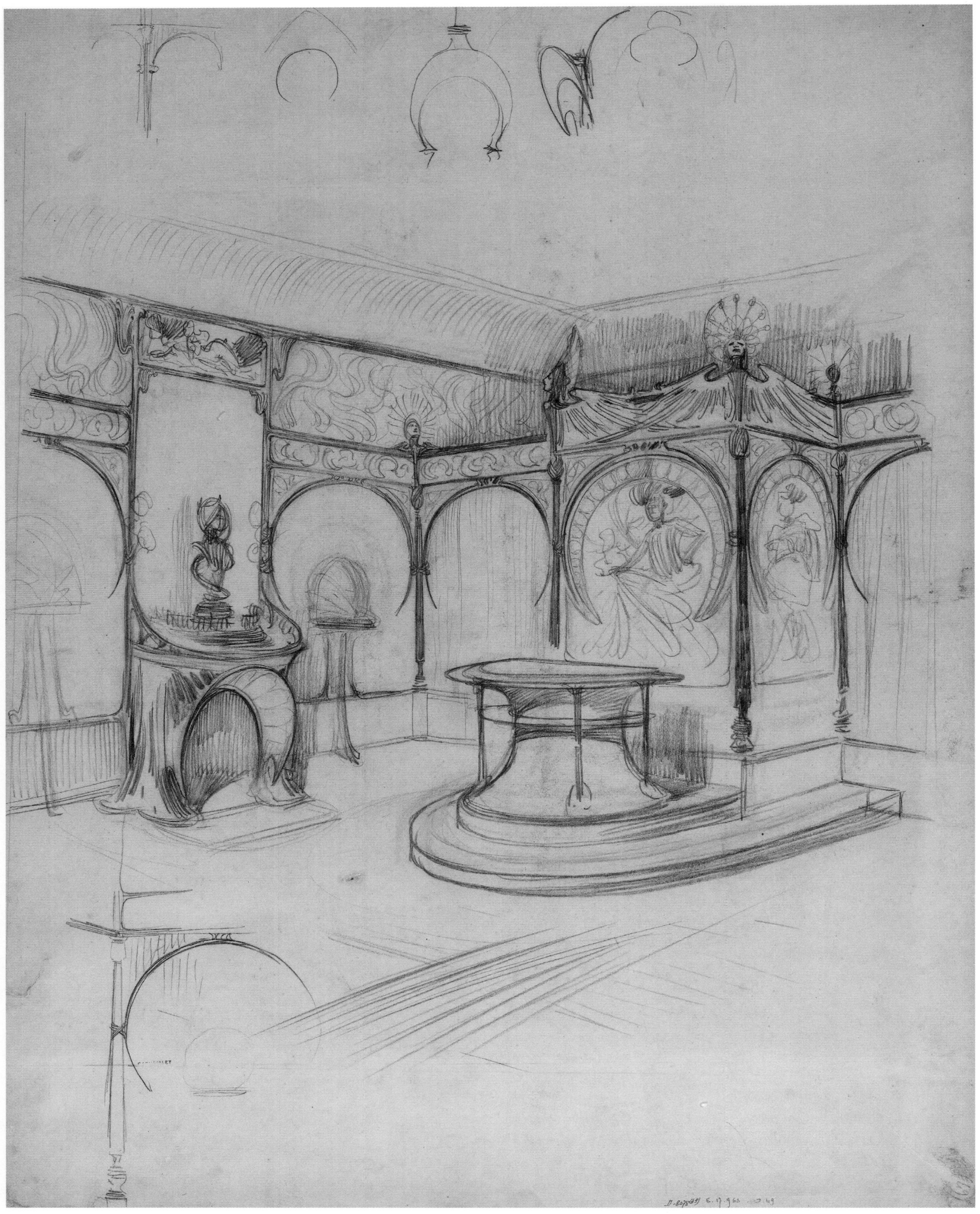

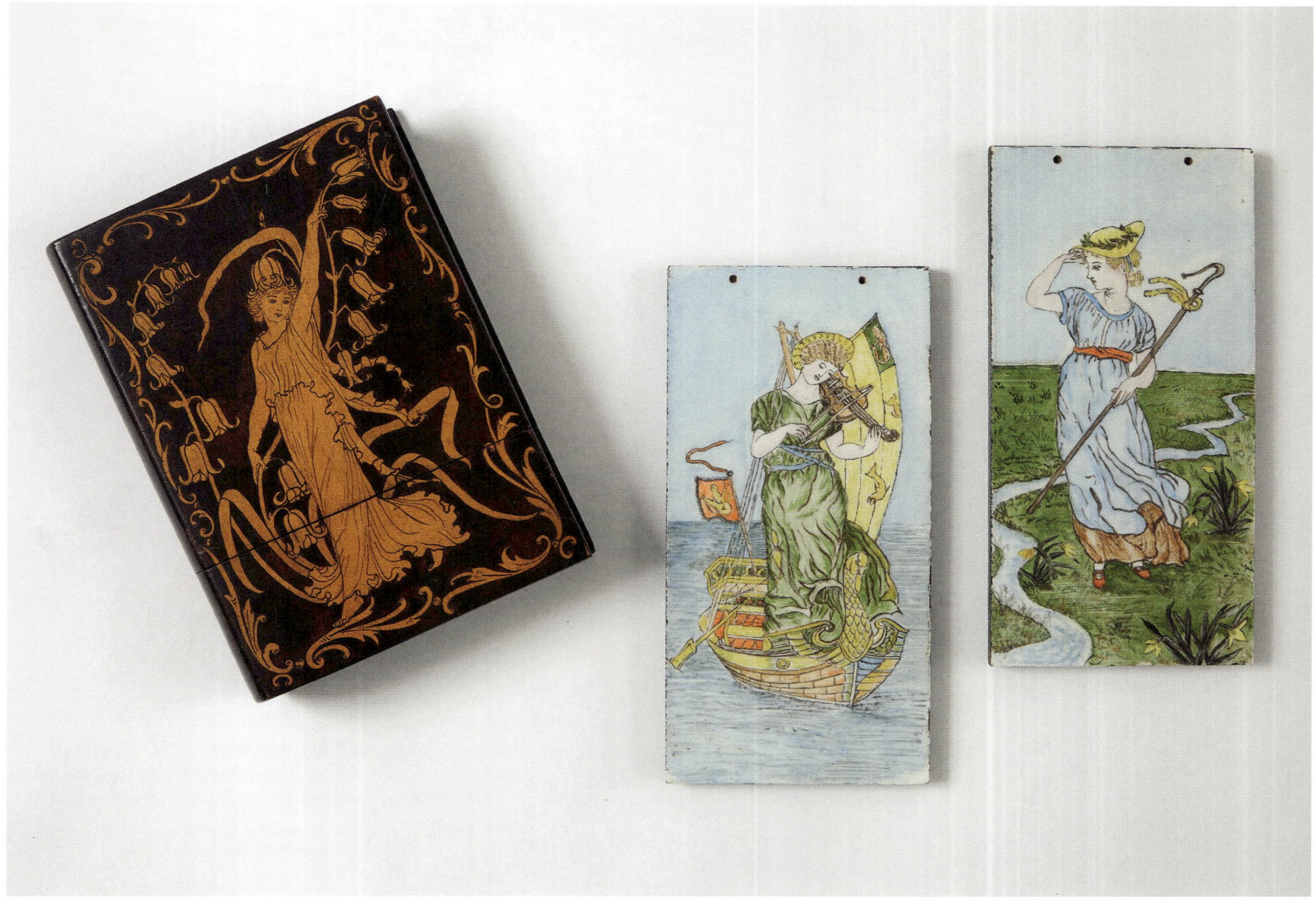



in the latter phases of modern decorative art we have the results of
modern intercommunication of ideas, of the constant intermingling,
through modern commerce, of travel, colonisation, scientific
discovery and historic research fused together.[19]

He was critical however of foreign attempts to 'modernise' decorative art.
French marquetry and cabinet-making, in his opinion, obeyed a 'principle of
decomposition and decay', a thoughtless and irrational use of material and
pattern, opposed to the 'principle of health, of life and growth' that he saw in
British works exhibited in Turin.[20] As a leading light in the Arts and Crafts
Movement he understood the crafts to be the physical embodiment of
socialist idealism.

In contrast to Crane's dismissal of French artworks, French art critics
mainly praised him, starting with novelist Joris-Karl Huysmans in 1881,
who considered Crane's illustrations to be the only works of art worthy
of that name, together with Japanese prints.[21] Admiration for Crane continued
through to the end of the century, and his essays were published in socialist
magazines such as *La Révolte* from 1893.[22] Parisian artists and art critics
rose against the decision to exclude him from the *Salon du Champ-de-Mars*
in 1896.[23]

This Anglophilia in French artistic and intellectual spheres in the 1890s
cannot be detached from the development of the decorative revolution in
Paris. Art Nouveau rose in the same years that literary men were importing
the British Arts and Crafts Movement. In 1892, three years before Siegfried
Bing's gallery opening, the writer and art critic Jean Lahor advocated the

establishment of 'artistic shops' mimicking the English prototype of Liberty & Co., to 'call, bring closer, unite the main representatives and reformers of decorative art, gathering and exhibiting their works, helping this movement to begin'.[24] Lahor considered England to offer a role model for the renewal of art, not least because its artistic production had formerly been so belittled and disdained by continental taste. According to him, the English had found a way to come alive again as an artistic culture.[25] His conference speech in Geneva in 1897 sounded like an appeal to the new generations of French designers to follow the example of William Morris.[26]

Like Lahor, the journalist, poet and translator Gabriel Mourey played a key role in the transfer of Art and Crafts ideals into the artistic spheres of Paris. He met William Morris while traveling to London. In 1895 in his *Chroniques de Londres* he defined Morris as the 'first worker and the first master [of the] resurgence of the decorative arts'.[27] A correspondent at *The Magazine of Art*, he also ran the French edition of *The Studio*, which was very much a vehicle for the promotion of British Arts and Crafts. Mourey was also a major figure in the theatre, creating controversial and political plays; he closely followed the drama productions of his contemporaries. Mostly unknown today, Mourey exemplified the link between theatre and the decorative arts as well as the powerful connection between London and Paris. He wrote the preface of Alphonse Mucha's *Documents décoratifs* of 1902, in which he explained the rise of a new decorative art around a common vision: 'only one thing left: our modern vision of nature'.

Some art critics were also designers themselves, like the extraordinary character Bojidar Karageorgévitch, a Serbian prince who lived for most of his life in Paris. Regularly writing for *The Magazine of Art*, he participated in the translation and propagation of the British Arts and Crafts into the Parisian cultural environment. He was close to both Sarah Bernhardt and Loie Fuller. Moreover, the prince was a silversmith and designed a range of wares, such as cutlery in the Art Nouveau style, which was advertised in 1901 in the same *Magazine of Art* that he wrote for.[28]

A number of French art critics were particularly envious of what they perceived to be the corporate instinct of English craftspeople; they lamented a lack of unity and direction in the French decorative revival, which they felt prevented a 'common overall plan'.[29] A fascinating demonstration of this English coordination, of Arts and Crafts ideals, and their fusion into theatre, took place in 1899 in London. Looked on by the French with an admiring eye, *Beauty's Awakening* was created and performed by the Art Workers' Guild. Founded in 1884 by five architects and designers – W. R. Lethaby, Edward Prior, Ernest Newton, Mervyn Macartney and Gerald C. Horsley – the Guild aimed to create a meeting space between artists and craftspeople, so generating a total equality between the major and minor arts. In their regular meetings the members debated and entertained themselves, but perhaps more important, they learned from each other, and expanded their areas of artistic and technical expertise. In 1888 members of the Guild, including Walter Crane, founded the Arts and Crafts Exhibition Society. The Guild, which was defined by one of its famous members, Charles Robert Ashbee, as 'the last citadel of traditionalism',[30] applied the principles of William Morris and John Ruskin and also acted them out. The members proclaimed a commitment to collaboration and collective activities, and condemned all forms of individualism. The Guild generated numerous participative projects

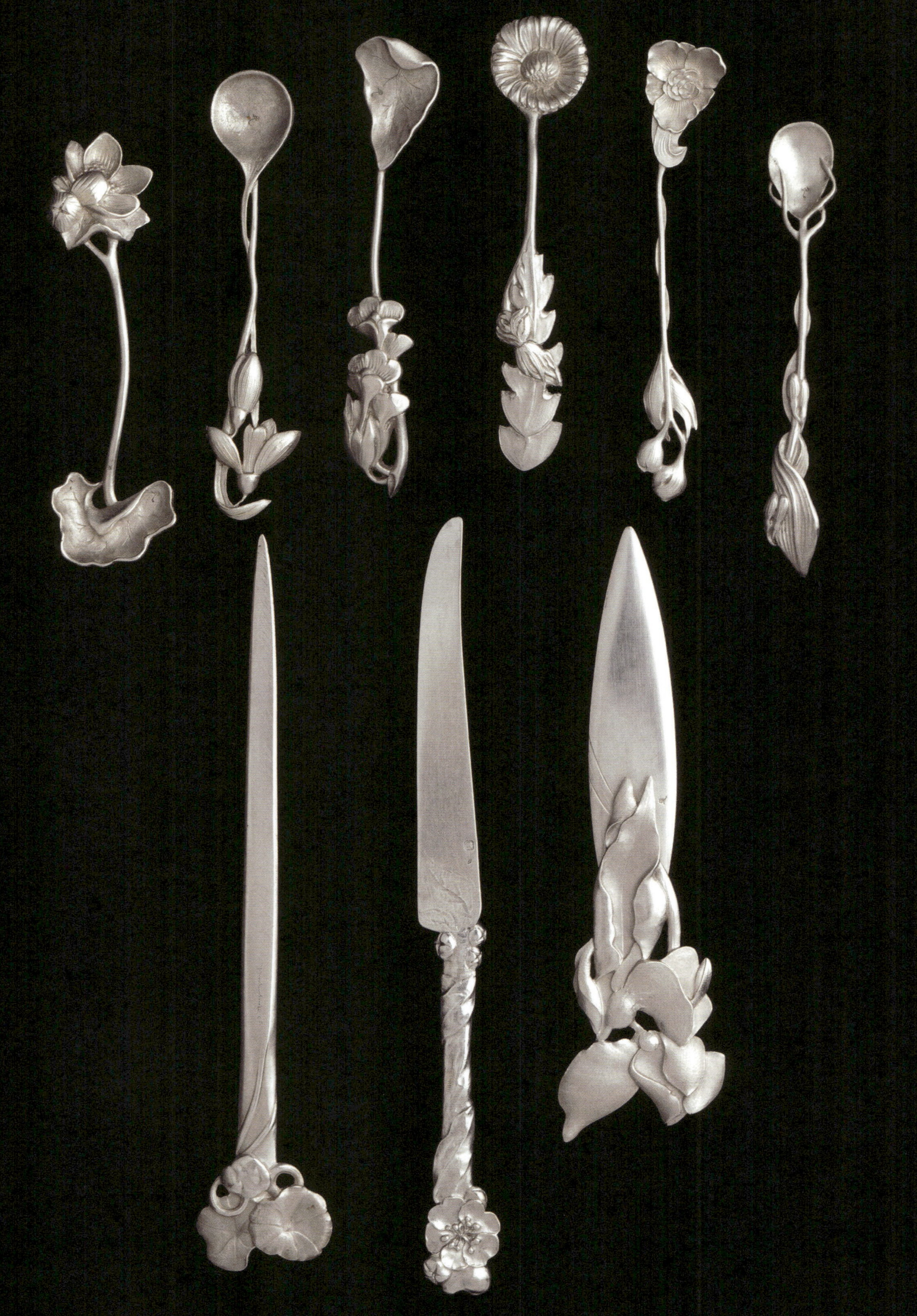

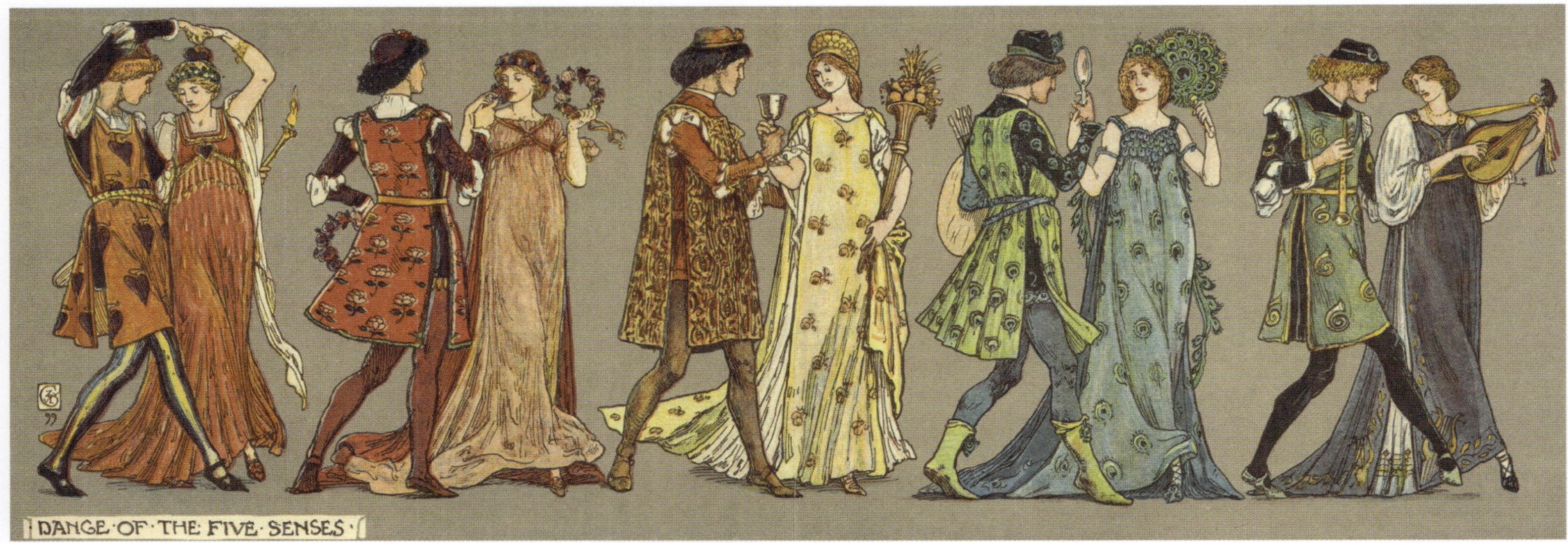


*Above:* Walter Crane, *Dance of the
Five Senses*, 1899, printed paper.
British Museum.

and events, a number of which were related to theatrical performance, taking place at the Guild's headquarters in Queen Square. Various meetings were theatricalised, as shown as in the 'entertainment' organised on March 2nd 1897.[31] Starting with a musical introduction, Walter Crane and Leonard Raven-Hill then performed a speech giving a short history of modern art.[32] Staying in the limelight, Crane then presented his artworks, before the members were invited to attend a living picture, the main attraction of the event. The tableau depicted Queen Victoria's Diamond Jubilee, with special lighting effects and hand-stitched historical costumes. The creation of *Beauty's Awakening* two years later appeared as a culmination of this practice to embody and perform their artistic ideology.

Premiered at the Guildhall of London on 28 June 1899, the performance – inspired by Ben Jonson's *The Masque of Beauty* (1608) – brought a contemporary vision to an Elizabethan genre, becoming emblematic of the Arts and Crafts Movement determined syncretism of modernity and tradition. This was a major component of Victorian crafts and theatre.[33] The masque intended to disrupt the very concept of performance, defining it as a symbiosis of all arts, past and present, minor and major, oral and written, aural and visual. The plural roles of the Guild members, functioning simultaneously backstage and onstage, broke down barriers between the arts, placing craftspeople in the spotlight. The cooperation of multiple personalities in the creation of a unified scenic space emphasised the idea of collaborative work as the ideal art form, claiming that:

> there is something still possible to do when Artists who are Designers, but who do not confuse their aim therein with too much attempt at realism and illusion, try to produce an allegory of the Beautiful which is their particular sphere and concern.[34]

The plot itself embodied Arts and Crafts ideology: alongside allegorical characters and natural elements (four winds, forest leaves, the five senses), the main protagonists were nine 'Fair Cities' each symbolized by an artist: Thebes, Athens, Rome, Byzantium, Florence, Venice, Nuremberg, Paris and Oxford. London was the main character, but was not considered a Fair City.

The main plot-line of the story was for London to achieve this status, thanks
to the allegorical characters of Art, Invention and the Seven Lamps of
Architecture – a direct reference to the eponymous essay by John Ruskin
in 1849.[35] If broaching the theme of architecture and crafts onstage was not
common, creating allegorical characters based on an essay about the renewal
of art was even more unprecedented and innovative. Near the end of the
performance, London reappeared onstage as a Fair City, richly dressed and
ornamented, guided by Freedom and Commerce, and receiving from Labour
and Invention the crystal sphere and the sceptre, then taking her place
among the other Fair Cities while the song of triumph resonated.[36] With
more than eighty actors and actresses onstage, the show offered a visually
astonishing experience, together with a strong ideological message about art.

Through the 1890s Sarah Bernhardt and Alphonse Mucha continued
working closely together, involving other Art Nouveau craftspeople, and
in this way the links between the new style and the performing arts kept
growing. French painters living in London linked up directly and abidingly
with the Arts and Crafts Movement. Among them was Lucien Pissarro, who
met William Morris and Walter Crane in 1891 and was also very close to the
designer and sculptor Alexandre Carpentier, one of the founding members
of the group *Les Cinq* in 1896, later called *Les Six* and finally *L'Art dans Tout*.[37]
This was the first in France to fully apply Arts and Crafts ideals, in advance
of the École de Nancy. When the group swelled in 1898, it welcomed several
artists working in the performing arts, including the architect Henri Sauvage.
His training in Brussels made him familiar with the Art Nouveau style,
which had fully formed there first, and shaped his sensibility as an architect.
At the Paris *Exposition Universelle* of 1900 he worked on several theatrical
commissions which became part of Parisian Art Nouveau: the Théâtre de
Guignol Parisien and the Théâtre Loie Fuller, collaborating with designer
Francis Jourdain. The highly expressive theatre Sauvage, created for the
American dancer Loie Fuller, was inspired by her famous serpentine dance:
the building itself replicated her choreography in white stucco.[38] Above
the door, her statue, sculpted by Pierre Roche, dominated the edifice.
The ceramist Alexandre Bigot also worked on the building, which contained
works by a range of other craftspeople. Sauvage continued to work closely
with Fuller in the following years, notably with his project for the construction
of an Art Nouveau dressing room for an actress, created for the first *Salon des
Arts Décoratifs* in Paris in 1904.

Loie Fuller became an icon of Art Nouveau. She had been performing in
Paris since 1892, and was concomitantly connected with poets and visual
artists, most of whom were inspired by her serpentine dance. She often
travelled to London, to engage with the culture of the music hall, which for
her was a bigger inspiration than ballet.[39] She was probably influenced by
the 'skirt dance' developed by the London burlesque artist Kate Vaughan.[40]
This alter ego was adored by John Ruskin and Edward Burne-Jones, who
called her 'Miriam Ariadne Salome Vaughan'.[41] Fuller was also attracted
and influenced by the biblical myth: in 1895 she created a new performance,
*Salomé*, written by Armand Silvestre.[42] While the show was not a great
success, it gave rise to two dances used in 1900 at the *Exposition Universelle*,
the *Dance of the Lily* and the *Fire Dance*.

Fuller was ferociously ambitious and independent. Instead of performing
at the Palais de la Danse, a structure tailor-made for the purpose at the

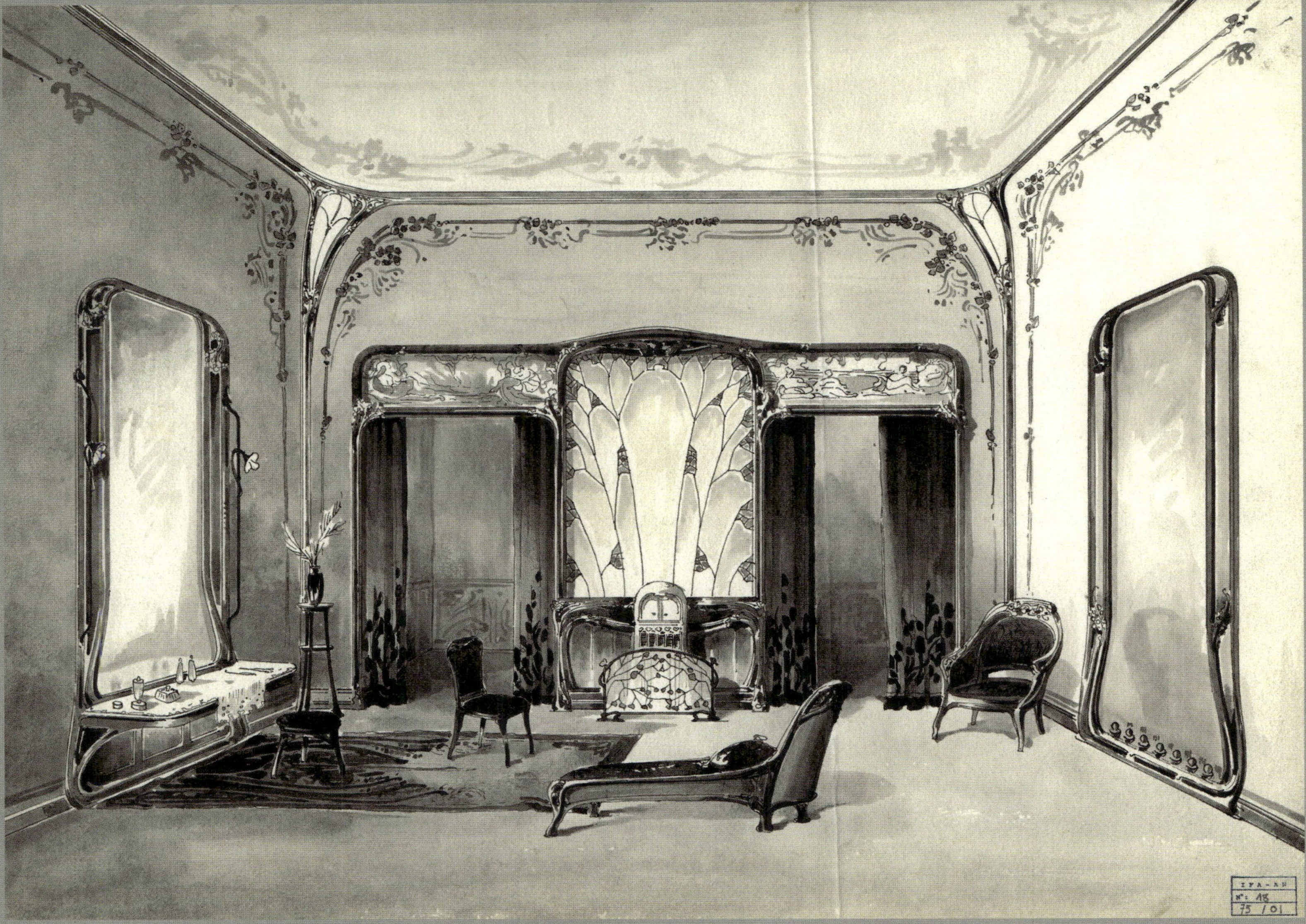

*Above:* Henri Sauvage, dressing room for an actress, 1904, ink on paper. Centre d'archives d'architecture du XXe siècle, Paris.

*Right:* Henri Sauvage, Théâtre de la Loie Fuller, 1900, ink on paper. Centre d'archives d'architecture du XXe siècle, Paris.

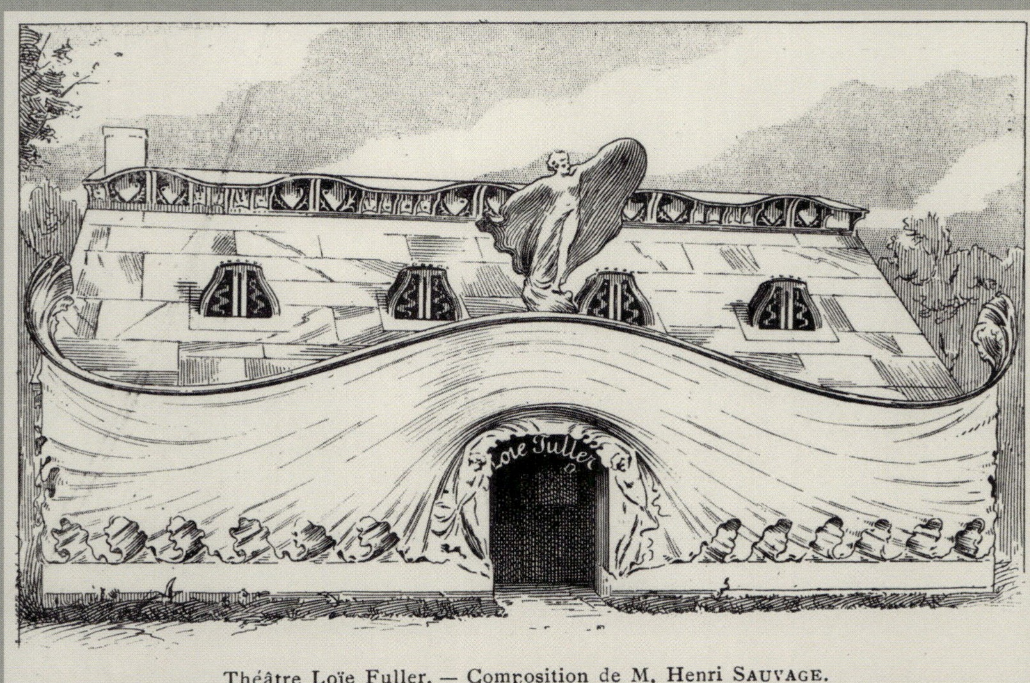


Théâtre Loïe Fuller. — Composition de M. Henri SAUVAGE.

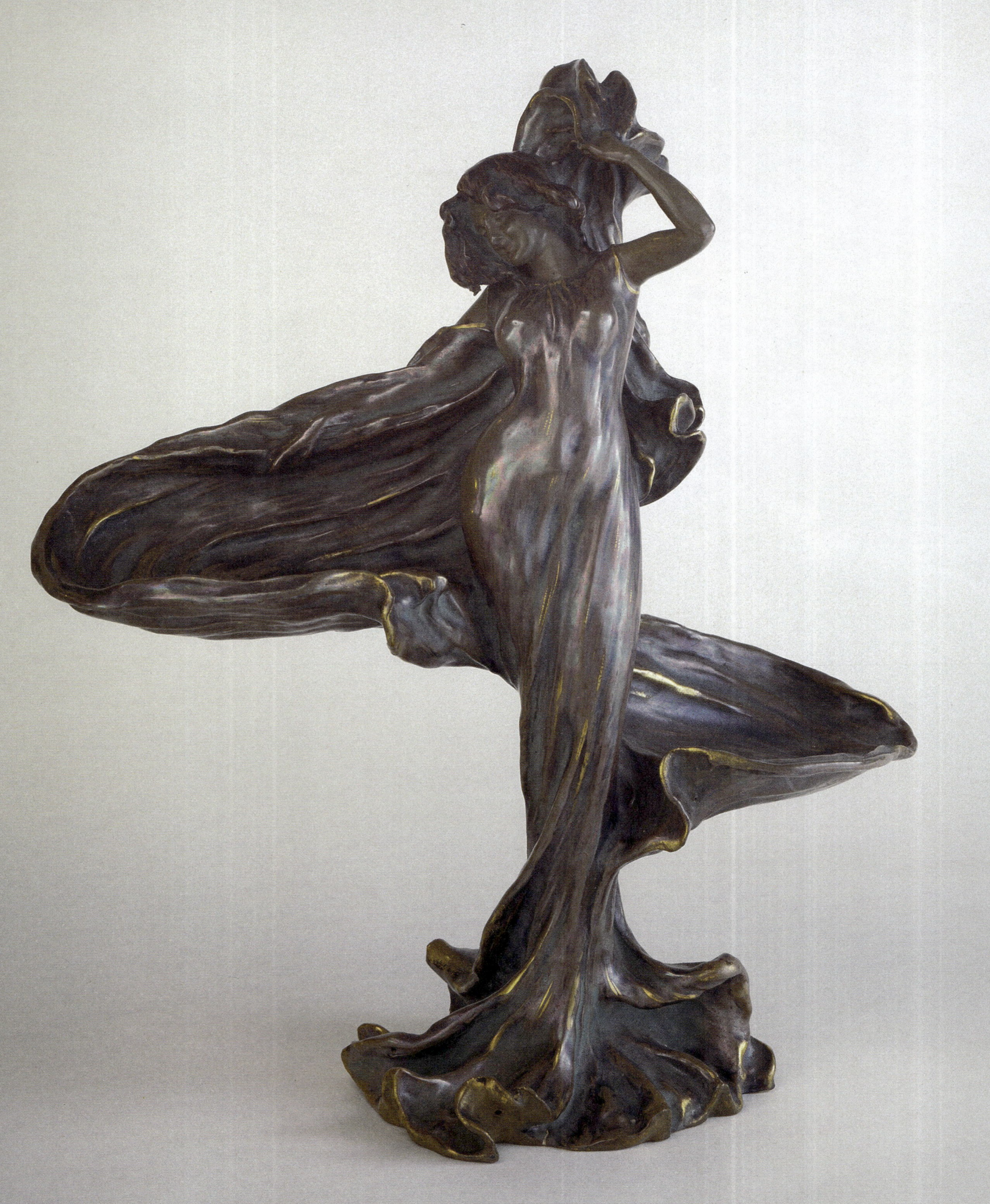

*Opposite:* Riessner, Stellmacher and Kessel, figure of Loie Fuller, *c.*1900, earthenware. Sainsbury Centre.

*Exposition,* She created her own *Théâtre-Musée* on the Rue de Paris.[43] Besides the performance space, the building contained an exhibition room that housed over one hundred works in various media representing her.[44] The art critic Arsène Alexandre referred to this room as: 'the preliminary poem of statuettes, statues, pastels, paintings, celebrate the frail and agile dancer with large wings'.[45] After discovering these paintings, statues, lamps and other objects, the audience could attend the dancer's famous performances, involving electricity and optical illusions, very much in the taste of the *Exposition* as a whole.[46] With this double function of harmonising objects and performance, the *Théâtre-musée* simultaneously animated the crafts, and froze the dance into a permanent work of art. It celebrated the symbiosis between decorative and the performing arts.

While the *Exposition Universelle* was still open, on 29 September 1900 the comedy *Les Demi-Vierges* premiered at the Théâtre de l'Athénée. This play showed once again how interwoven Art Nouveau and the theatre were. Unlike *Gismonda, Beauty's Awakening* or Fuller's *Théâtre-musée,* this play did not aspire to mesmerise the audience with ancient worlds or fairy-tale universes, but simply intended to represent a bourgeois interior in the style of the day. Five years after its first scenic adaptation from Marcel Prévost's novel, *Les Demi-Vierges* had a stage designed entirely in the Art Nouveau style. The decorator, M. Roncin-Rubé, was well known and admired for his realistic and detailed stage designs in the world of theatrical reviews. To ensure that the interiors would be plausible, furniture and decorative objects were rented from the Maison Soubrier, a shop selling furniture while also renting it to theatres for performances. This practice spread throughout the century, enabling shops to promote their products on-stage. In England, popular comedies also advertised the department stores from which the stage furniture originated. The theatre indicated the name and location of the shop on the programme, such as Oetzmann & Co., a department store often showcased at the highly successful Daly's Theatre.[47] From costumes to the detailed drawing-room decoration, all the designs in *Les Demi-Vierges* were in the latest fashionable style, with glass roofs and foliage-motif ironwork, chairs and sofas decorated with *coup de fouet* curves, and walls ornamented with stucco flowers. The care given over the sets was so fastidious that it delayed the premiere of the show for several days. Despite this, the decor was unanimously approved of by the critics, in contrast with the play itself, which was deemed to be poor.[48] *Les Demi-Vierges* was a performance anchored in its time, and illustrates how theatre is capable of crystalising collective representations of a society.[49]

The fin de siècle theatre was effectively an alternative exhibition space. Spectacular and visual, it was a unique site, and engaged fully with the concept of *gesamtkunstwerk,* the total work of art. The fusion of literary and visual art induced the spectator to believe that the world being represented was a continuation of their own. As shown in *Les Demi-Vierges,* the bourgeois audience was probably expecting to see the same furniture onstage as they had at home. The methodology met the audience's desire to have an omniscient and detailed perspective on what they were seeing.[50] The profusion of images in the press, the thriving city and quick-growing architecture played a part in stimulating the Victorian eye. Producing a play also meant producing these 'concrete images of historical and contemporary reality craved by the public'.[51]

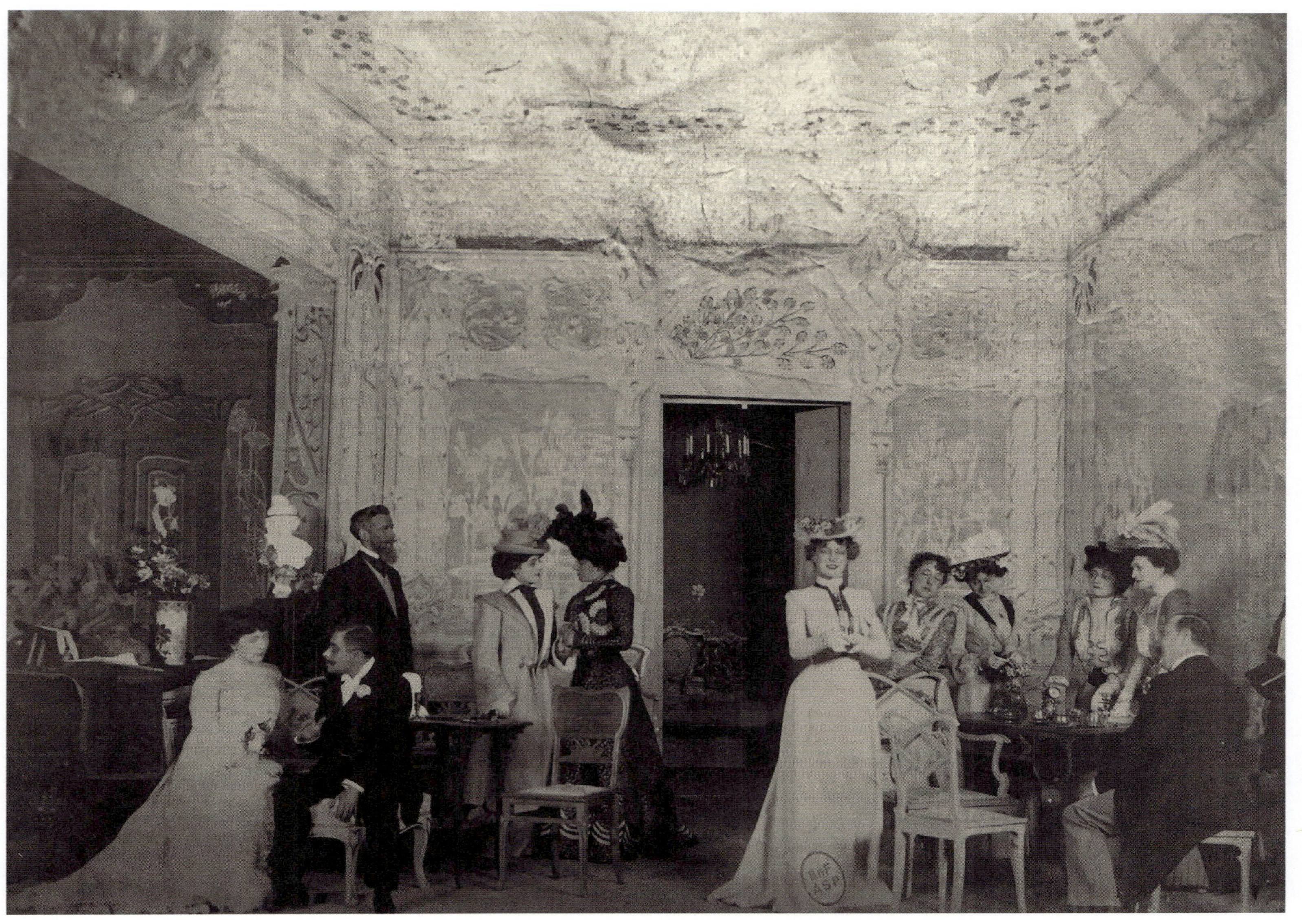

Above: *Les Demi-Vierges*, 1900.
Bibliothèque Nationale de France.

The spectator also perceived the theatre as an extension of their own domestic space. Loie Fuller's exhibition room, ahead of the performance hall, organised the visitors' route through a foyer designed like a 'mediating space between the home environment and the world of the stage'.[52] It also transformed the primary function of the foyer as an exhibition space for the graphic and decorative arts.

The theatrical site was both the anchorage point of decorative creation and the crossroads of the artists' professional trajectories. The personalities whose careers were highlighted there were not isolated or special cases; rather, they represent a wider international and interdisciplinary system, a network of fin de siècle artistic communities.

The decorative arts play a major role in giving tangible form to imaginary places, using the public language of patterns and shapes. Fin de siècle theatre production was an attempt to create a collective work – to make the stage a total experience by fusing all the modern decorative arts. This was epitomised by performances that were completely created by craftspeople, such as the unique and extraordinary case of *Beauty's Awakening*. The stage was a showcase for the decorative arts. The double function of fashionable shops in Paris and London – of creating costumes and selling dresses, or renting furniture that could also be purchased – shows that theatre influenced new trends and patterns of consumption. As summarised by the contemporary art critic Arsène Alexandre, 'Theatre starts fashion and fashion can largely provide from theatre.'[53]

§

## ENDNOTES


1   Octave Uzanne, 'Visions de notre heure, Choses et gens qui passent', *L'écho de Paris*, 7 July 1899.

2   Rossella Froissart-Pezone, *L'Art dans Tout: Les arts décoratifs en France et l'utopie d'un Art nouveau* (Paris: CNRS Éditions, 2005), p.68.

3   Alphonse Mucha, 'Illustrations pour Cléopâtre', *Le Costume au Théâtre*, 1890, BnF LJ W-142.

4   Mariella Rizzi, 'Sarah Bernhardt: le théâtre et l'art de la mode', in *Arts et usages du costume de scène*, Collection 'Le Studio-Lo Essais' (Paris: Editions Lampsaque, 2007), pp.105–17.

5   Matthew Arnold, 'The French Play in London', *Nineteenth Century*, 6 August 1879, p.229.

6   Lady Macbeth's dress was copied from Viollet-le-Duc's *Dictionnaire du Mobilier Français*; see Alice Comyns-Carr, *Mrs J. Comyns Carr's Reminiscences* (London: Hutchinson, 1926). The design she used can be found in the third volume of the dictionary entitled *Vêtements, Bijoux de corps, objets de toilette* (Paris: Librairie centrale d'architecture, 1873), pp.187–9.

7   E. R. Russell, *Liverpool Daily Post*, 31 December 1888.

8   'Sarah Bernhardt s'est montrée une artiste prodigieusement complexe et raffinée. Elle est, dans son art si magnifiquement corporel, un Gustave Moreau, un Burne-Jones. Elle est à elle seule une synthèse délicieuse et troublante de tous ces peintres mystérieux', quoted in Claudette Joannis, 'Sarah Bernhardt et le costume de théâtre ou le corps sublimé', in *Arts et Usages du costume de scène*, pp.398–9.

9   See Victorien Sardou, 'Notes sur *Gismonda*, 1894–1895', BnF Arts du spectacle RF 47 806.

10  A later version of the costume made in 1902 by Théophile Thomas is kept in the Bibliothèque nationale de France collection.

11  Especially for the dress of the fifth act, which involved day- and night-labour for an entire week; see Joannis, 'Sarah Bernhardt et le costume de théâtre'.

12  'La Duchesse d'Athènes: conversation avec Sarah Bernhardt', *Le Matin*, 8 September 1894, no. 3844.

13  According to René Lalique and Lucien Lévy-Dhrumer correspondence, quoted in Anne Jamault, *Sarah Bernhardt et le monde de l'art*, doctoral thesis (Paris: Presses Universitaire Paris Sorbonne, 2000) p.283.

14  See his contemporary's essay: Henri Vever, *La bijouterie française au XIXe siècle (1800–1900)*, (Paris : H.Floury, 1906–8), Vol. 3, pp.714–16. 'De 1891 à 1894, Lalique composa deux importantes séries de bijoux pour les rôles de Sarah Bernhardt dans Iseyl et Gismonda. Il déplore ne pas avoir été mis au courant du scénario de Gismonda, parce que ses créations auraient été plus appropriées au caractère de l'œuvre, tandis que se souvenant des recommandations qui lui avaient été faites pour Iseyl, d'être très sobre dans l'ornementation et d'éviter le clinquant, il fut amené à composer des bijoux du même genre qui étaient trop fins, trop atténués pour un rôle tel que celui de Gismonda.' If his collaboration for *Izeyl* could not be proved to this day, his works for *Gismonda* were attested in Emile Moreau's correspondence (Correspondance d'Emile Moreau, BnF Archives et Manuscrits, Collection Rondel, RMn 1050).

15  See Daly's Theatre programmes, season 1894–5, D'Oyly Carte Archive, V&A, Blythe House, THM/73.

16  See the reconstitution at Musée Carnavalet, Paris.

17  Walter Crane, 'Modern decorative art at Turin: General Impressions', *The Magazine of Art*, 1902, p.449.

18  Phrase by Paul Morand in his essay *1900* (Paris: Les éditions de France, 1930).

19  Crane, 'Modern decorative art at Turin', p.448.

20  Ibid.

21  'On peut hardiment, entre gens ayant la lassitude et le dégoût des pauvretés de peinture qui nous encombrent, convenir que ces albums sont aujourd'hui avec ceux des Japonais, les seules oeuvres d'art vraiment dignes de ce nom qu'il nous reste à contempler, à Paris, quand l'Exposition des Indépendants se ferme.' *Revue Littéraire et Artistique*, 15 August 1881.

22  *La Révolte*, created in 1887 by Jean Grave, who met William Morris and Walter Crane and was the first to translate Crane into French in 1893; see Catherine Meneux, *L'art social de la Révolution à la Grande Guerre* (Paris: Institut national d'histoire de l'art, 2014).

23  Camille Mauclair, 'Les Salons de 1896', *La Nouvelle Revue*, 1896, No. 5, p.349.

24  'magasins qui devraient appeler, rapprocher, grouper les principaux représentants et rénovateurs de l'art décoratif, réunir, exposer leurs oeuvres, aider à ce que ce mouvement qui commence, mais qui chez nous, tarde à se manifester, par manque d'une action d'ensemble, par faute d'unité et de direction.' Jean Lahor, *William Morris et le mouvement nouveau de l'art décoratif, Conférence à Genève le 13 janvier 1897* (Geneva: Ch. Eggimann & Cie, 1897), pp.25–6.

25  'L'Angleterre, à la stupéfaction de ceux qui l'ont connue jadis et qui la revoient en ce moment, est devenue un pays singulièrement artiste, singulièrement curieux des arts de la décoration, de la beauté, du charme ou de l'élégance, dans la maison, la rue, la cité, dans la vie privée ou publique.' Ibid., p.30.

26  'Il ne lui aura pas été donné de faire une réalité décisive: ce sera la tâche des artistes qui procèdent ou procèderont de lui.' Ibid., p.10.

27  Gabriel Mourey, *Passer le détroit. La vie et l'art à Londres* (Paris: P. Ollendorf, 1895), p.241.

28  M. H. S., 'Prince Bojidar Karageorgévitch as a silversmith', *The Magazine of Art*, 1901, pp.185–6.

29  Lahor, *William Morris et le mouvement nouveau de l'art décoratif*, pp.25–6.

30  C. R. Ashbee, quoted in Gavin Stamp,'A Hundred Years of the Art Workers' Guild,' in *Beauty's Awakening, the Centenary Exhibition of the Art Workers' Guild 1884–1984* (Brighton Royal Pavilion, 1984)

31  'Souvenirs of some AWG revels with 4 playbills', Art Workers' Guild archives, AWG 5/3/1.

32  'A Short History of Modern Art: from the earliest period to the present day, with original and striking illustrations by eminent artists. Never before seen – and once seen not likely to be forgotten!', London, 2 March 1897.

33  To the Guild, this Elizabethan masque is the symbol of the *contrepoids* of Shakespeare at that time, who paid too little attention to the visual aspect of his performances. The masque format brings a new dimension to the performance: 'There are certain things more necessary to Masque than they are to Drama, such as Poetic and Ethic Aim, Beauty of Design and Ornament.' Bound volume of the script and illustrations for the AWG Masque of 1899 *Beauty's Awakening, a Masque of Winter and of Spring*, p.5.

34  Ibid.

35  The first scene showed all seven lamps switched off and covered with forest leaves. In the following scene, a group of characters, led by the Trueheart knight, sang praises to their glory: *'Each lamp uplifted let us raise / Our paean of triumphal praise'*. Ibid., p.24.

36  Ibid., p.36.

37  Rossella Froissart-Pezone, *L'Art dans Tout: Les arts décoratifs en France et l'utopie d'un Art nouveau* (Paris: CNRS Éditions, 2005), p.84.

38  Frantz Jourdain, 'L'Art du décor à l'exposition universelle de 1900', *L'Architecture*, 1901, pp.27–30.

39  Guy Ducrey, 'Le mythe Loie Fuller', in *Corps et graphies. Poétique de la danse et de la danseuse à la fin du XIXe siècle* (Paris: H. Champion, 1996), pp.433–530.

40  Sylvia Ellis, *The Plays of W. B. Yeats: Yeats and the Dancer* (London: Palgrave Macmillan, 1999), p.160.

41  Ibid.

42  The 1907 version of *Salomé* was performed in a melodramatic libretto by Robert d'Humières, an Anglophile theatre manager and playwright who worked with Edward Burne-Jones for his play *La Belle au bois dormant* (*Sleeping Beauty*) in 1894.

43  Claudia Palazzolo, *Mise en scène de la danse aux Expositions de Paris, 1889–1937. Une fabrique du regard* (Paris: L'œil d'or, 2017), pp.53–83.

44  Jean-Baptiste Minnaert, 'Henri Sauvage et le théâtre de Loie Fuller à l'Exposition universelle de 1900', Musée de l'École de Nancy; Valérie Thomas; Jérôme Perrin (dir.). *Loie Fuller: danseuse de l'art nouveau. Catalogue d'exposition*, Réunion des musées nationaux, 2002, pp.53–62.

45  Arsène Alexandre, 'Le théâtre de la Loie Fuller', *Le Théâtre*, No. 40, August 1900, pp.23–4.

46  Rhonda K. Garelick, *Electric Salome: Loie Fuller's Performance of Modernism* (Princeton, NJ: Princeton University Press, 2007).

47  See, for instance, *Facciamo Divorzio*, an adaptation of Victorien Sardou's *Divorçons*, performed at Daly's Theatre in 1894. D'Oyly Carte Archive, V&A, Blythe House, THM/73.

48  See the reviews in *Le Pays*, 26 September 1900, and *La Lanterne*, 25 September 1900.

49  Jean de Guardia, *Théâtre et imaginaire. Images scéniques et représentations mentales (XVIe–XVIIIe siècle)* (Dijon: Editions Universitaires de Dijon, 2012), p.283.

50  Mark Seltzer, *Henry James and the Art of Power* (Ithaca, NY: Cornell University Press, 1984), p.50.

51  Michael R. Booth, *Victorian Spectacular Theatre 1850–1910*, Theatre Production Series (London: Routledge and Kegan Paul, 1981), p.14.

52  Hugh Maguire, 'The Victorian Theatre as a Home from Home', *Journal of Design History*, 2000, Vol. 13, No. 2, p.107.

53  'le Théâtre lançant la Mode et la Mode pouvant largement s'alimenter du Théâtre', Arsène Alexandre, *Les reines de l'aiguille, modistes et couturiers* (Paris: Théophile Belin, 1902), p.154.

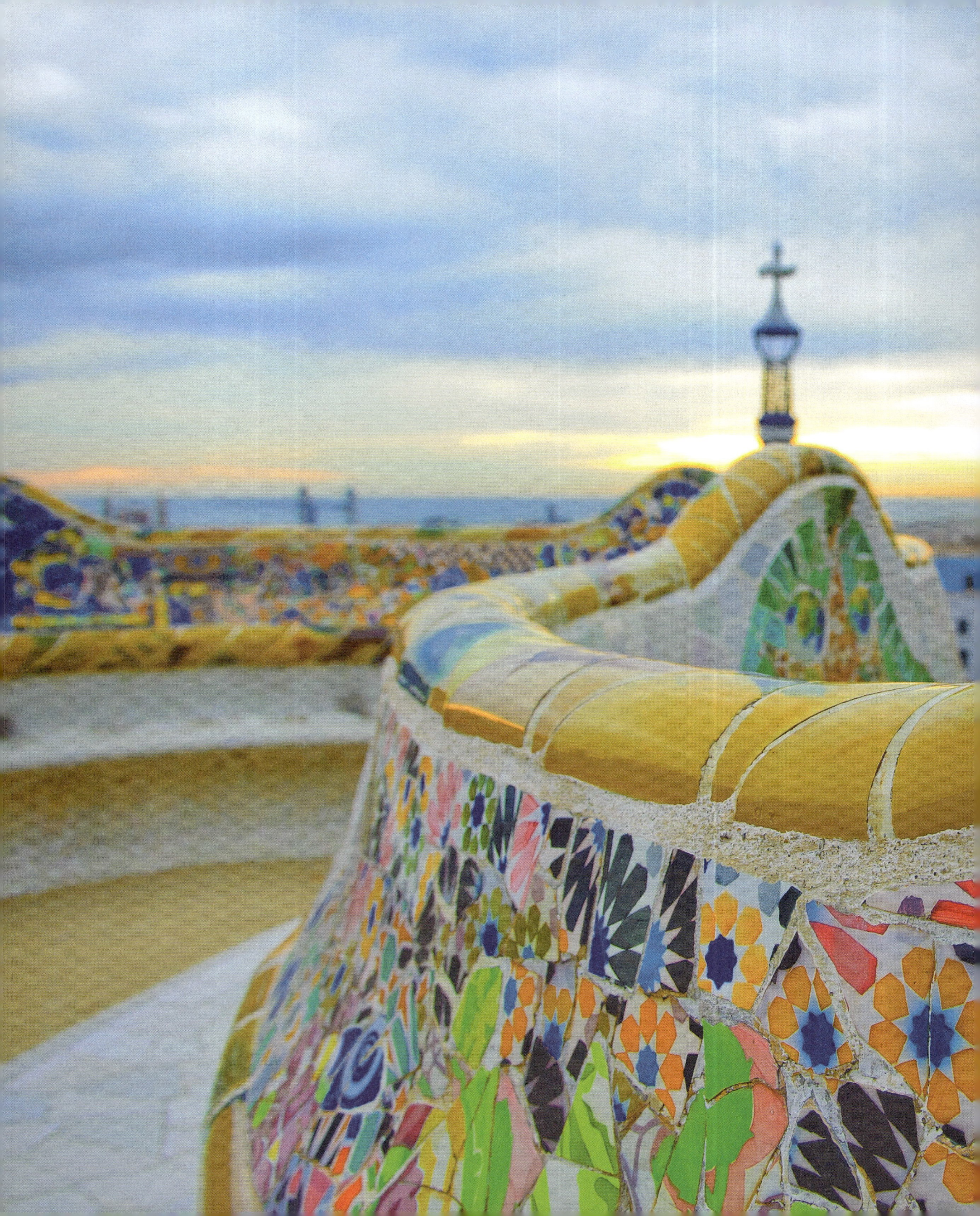

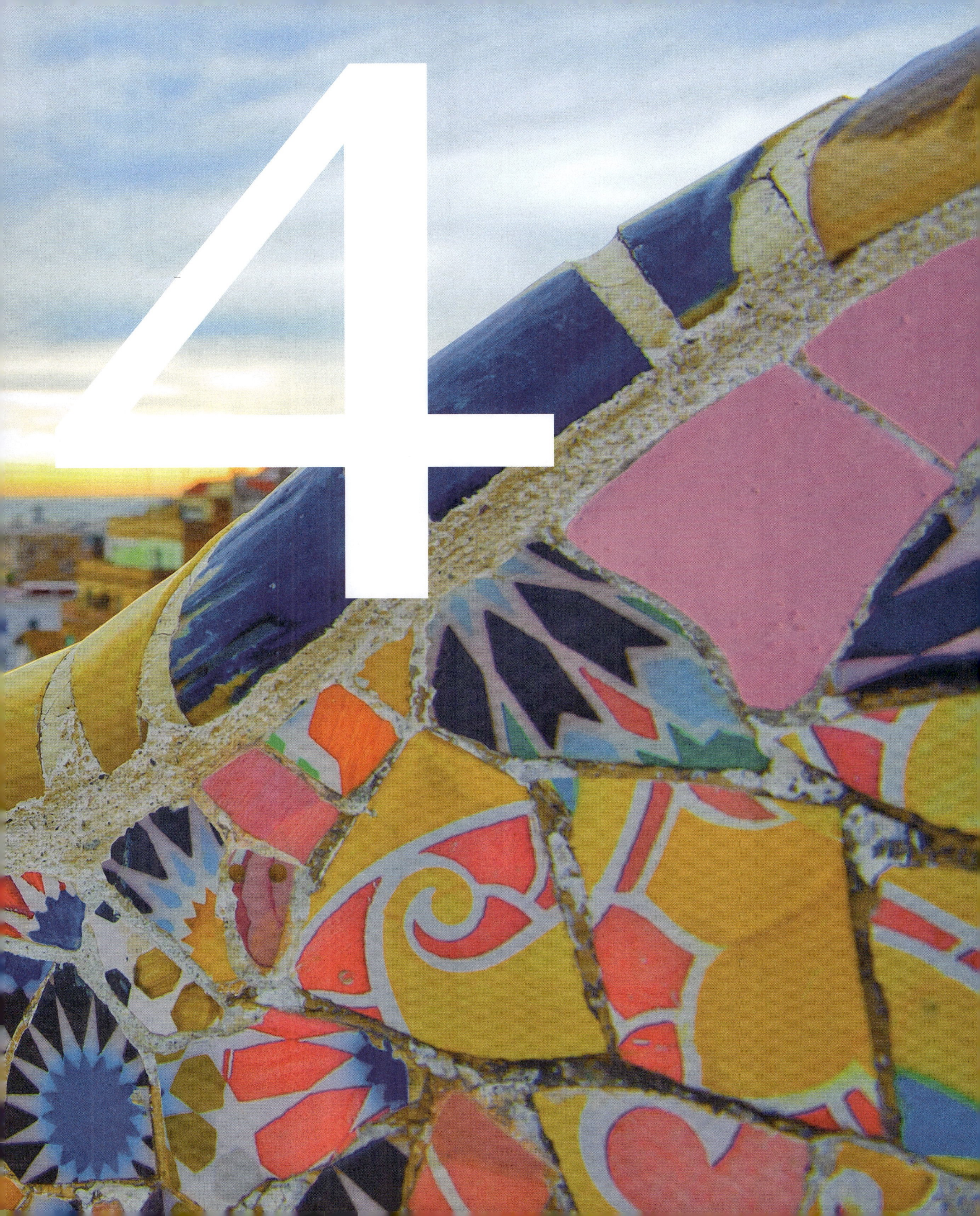
4

# ~Art Nouveau in Catalonia~

## The English connection

~Lluís Bosch~

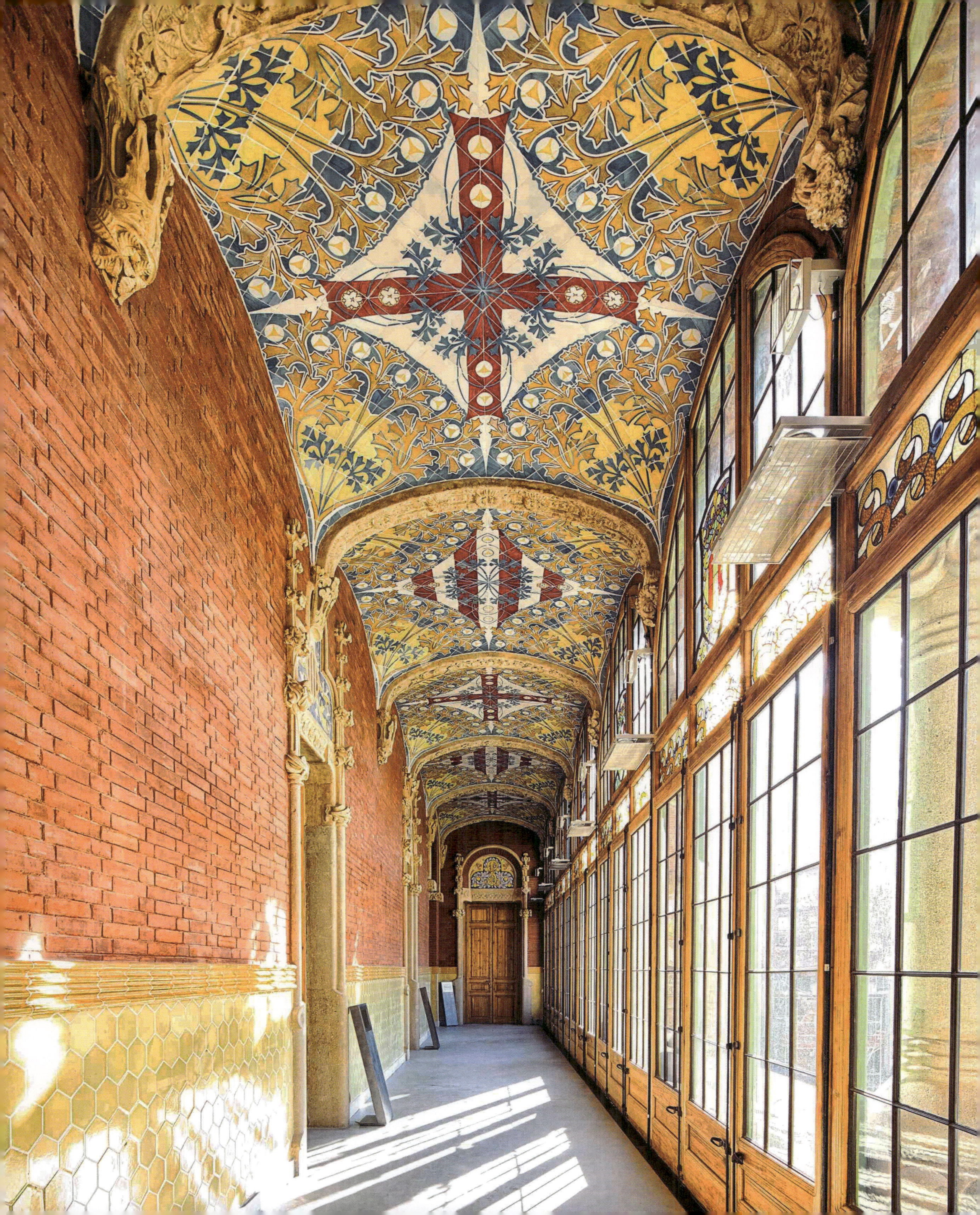

n recent decades, Art Nouveau has become increasingly popular worldwide. From Glasgow to Ljubljana, from Brussels to Budapest, Art Nouveau heritage attracts visitors by the hundreds of thousands every year. But nowhere has this phenomenon been stronger than in the city of Barcelona, and the name and the works of Antoni Gaudí in particular have become as well known as those of Picasso or Van Gogh. And although it could rightly be said that the millions of tourists who flock to the capital of Catalonia every year are attracted by the warm weather, the beaches, the food and cheap drink, the fact that they endure long queues under a scorching sun to see Gaudí's buildings is undeniable. And such interest is consistently confirmed by surveys: more than 80 per cent of visitors claim that their main reason to travel to Barcelona is to see its architecture and, when prompted, most of them name Gaudí.[1]

Why this should be so is not altogether clear. After all, *Modernisme*, as it was known in Catalonia,[*] shares the main attributes and contradictions of many other movements that arose throughout Europe at the fin de siècle and are today generically known as Art Nouveau. There was an acute ambition for novelty and modernity – as the names 'Modern Style', or 'Modernisme' itself, announced – but also a desire to revisit old styles and revive ancient crafts. The embracing of an urban lifestyle and an enthusiasm for technological advances and new materials came coupled with a romantic yearning for rural life and a passion for introducing nature into the city, and natural forms and symbols in the artworks. And the development of a cosmopolitan way of life gave rise to a thirst to know and learn from what was being done in other cities in Europe and beyond, but in many cases this did not dampen a strong will to create an art that reflected or embodied a particular culture, and a national spirit in search of recognition. This last aspect can be found in Hungarian, Finnish, Latvian or Slovenian Art Nouveau, and it was just as strong in Catalonia. On one hand, the Catalan movement was a magpie of sorts: throughout its short life it would seek inspiration from, and follow, the artistic trends of England, France, Belgium, Germany and Austria–Hungary in rapid succession. On the other hand, Modernisme would from its very beginning be a manifestation of 'Catalan-ness', and many works would unashamedly proclaim the uniqueness of Catalan culture and promote an ideal of national autonomy.

In this essay I will be looking into this apparent contradiction by highlighting the specifically Catalan aspects of Modernisme and how it was linked to the cultural, economic, social and political situation of Catalonia at the end of the 19th century, while seeking to explore how the Modernista movement looked to Britain (or, to be more precise, England) for artistic inspiration and cues of modernity and cosmopolitanism.

Modernisme is seen today as having evolved through three successive periods.[2] In the first one, running from the 1880s to the end of the century, several artists explored eclectic pathways to find a new artistic expression that could embody the aforementioned contradictory will to combine tradition with modernity and Catalan identity with cosmopolitanism. This period was marked by the opening in 1871 of the Architecture School in Barcelona, whose first director was Elies Rogent (1821–1897). A passionate follower of Viollet-le-Duc's postulates, Rogent would mentor the great Modernista architects, among them Antoni Gaudí (1852–1926) and Lluís Domènech i Montaner (1850–1923). In 1878 Domènech would publish the



---

* The word 'Modernisme' is widely used as the Catalan equivalent of 'Art Nouveau'. This can be a source of confusion when used in English, due to its similarity with the word 'Modernist', which of course refers to the Modern Movement, a different and in many ways opposing artistic movement. In this essay I shall use the noun 'Modernisme' and the adjective 'Modernista', without italics or further specifications, to identify Catalan Art Nouveau.

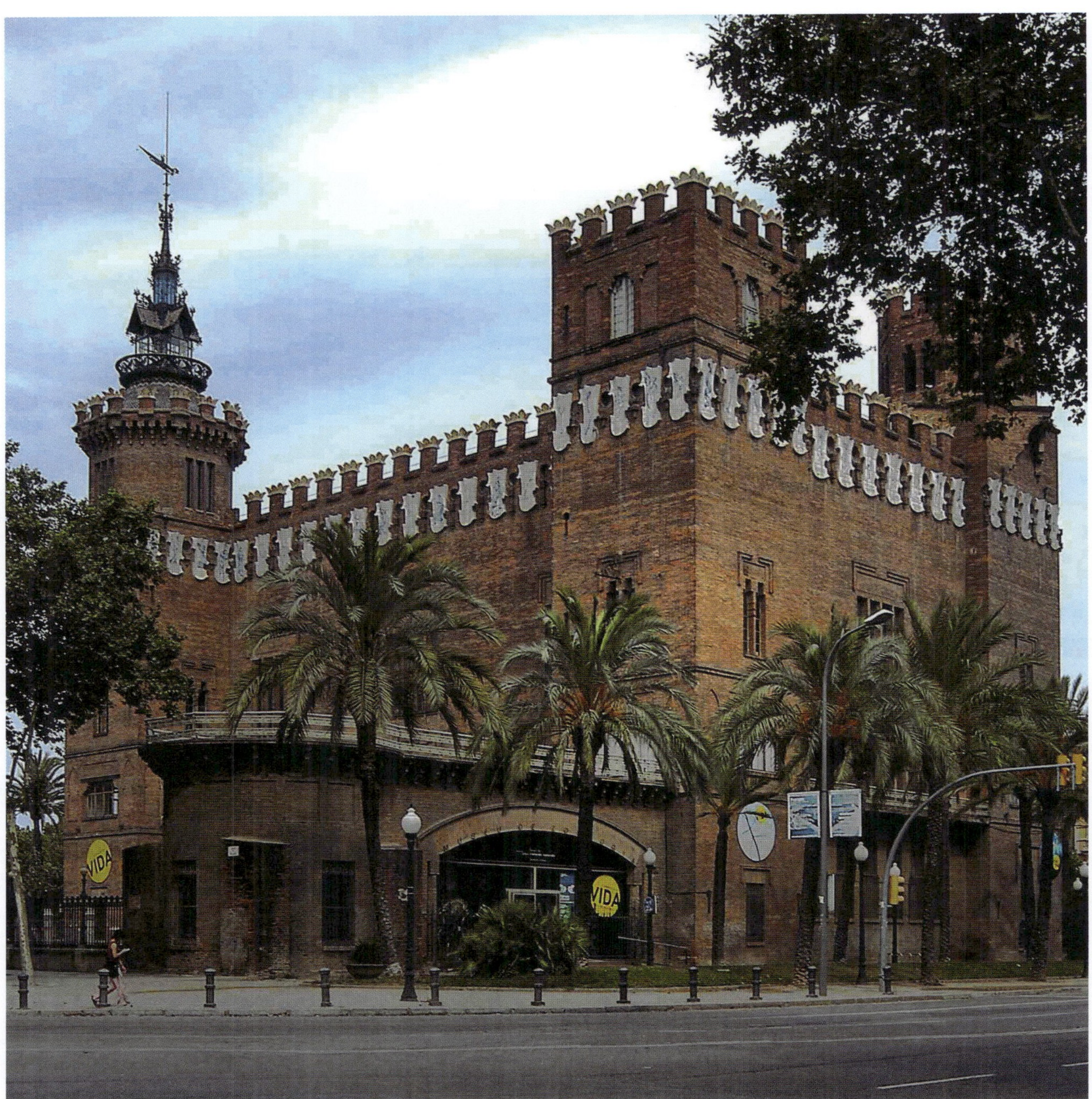

*Above:* Lluís Domènech i Montaner, *Universal Exposition* Café-Restaurant, 1888.

influential essay 'En busca de una arquitectura nacional' (The Quest for a National Architecture). In it, he espoused eclecticism and the return to Mediaeval art – in particular the Islamic Mudéjar style – as the path to find this new artistic expression. Examples of the first period of Modernisme are Domènech's building for the Editorial Montaner i Simon and the Café-Restaurant for the 1888 *Universal Exposition* in Barcelona (popularly dubbed the 'Castle of the Three Dragons' by Barcelonans, because of its fairy-tale appearance), and Gaudí's Casa Vicens and the gate and stables of the Güell estate (today known as Güell Pavilions). In these years Gaudí would also experiment with Neo-Gothic, most notably in Palau Güell, and with symbolism, as in the Theresian Convent and the Sagrada Família.

The second period of Modernisme came in the wake of the Paris 1900 *Exposition Universelle* and the diffusion of Art Nouveau throughout Europe. Modernisme incorporated the *coup de fouet* or whiplash form, a profusion of plant and flower decoration and an aesthetic expression following Alphonse Mucha's work. The new style would reach all forms of art and architectural types and would spread from Barcelona to other towns in Catalonia, Majorca and Valencia. And, through Catalan artists and architects, to some cities in

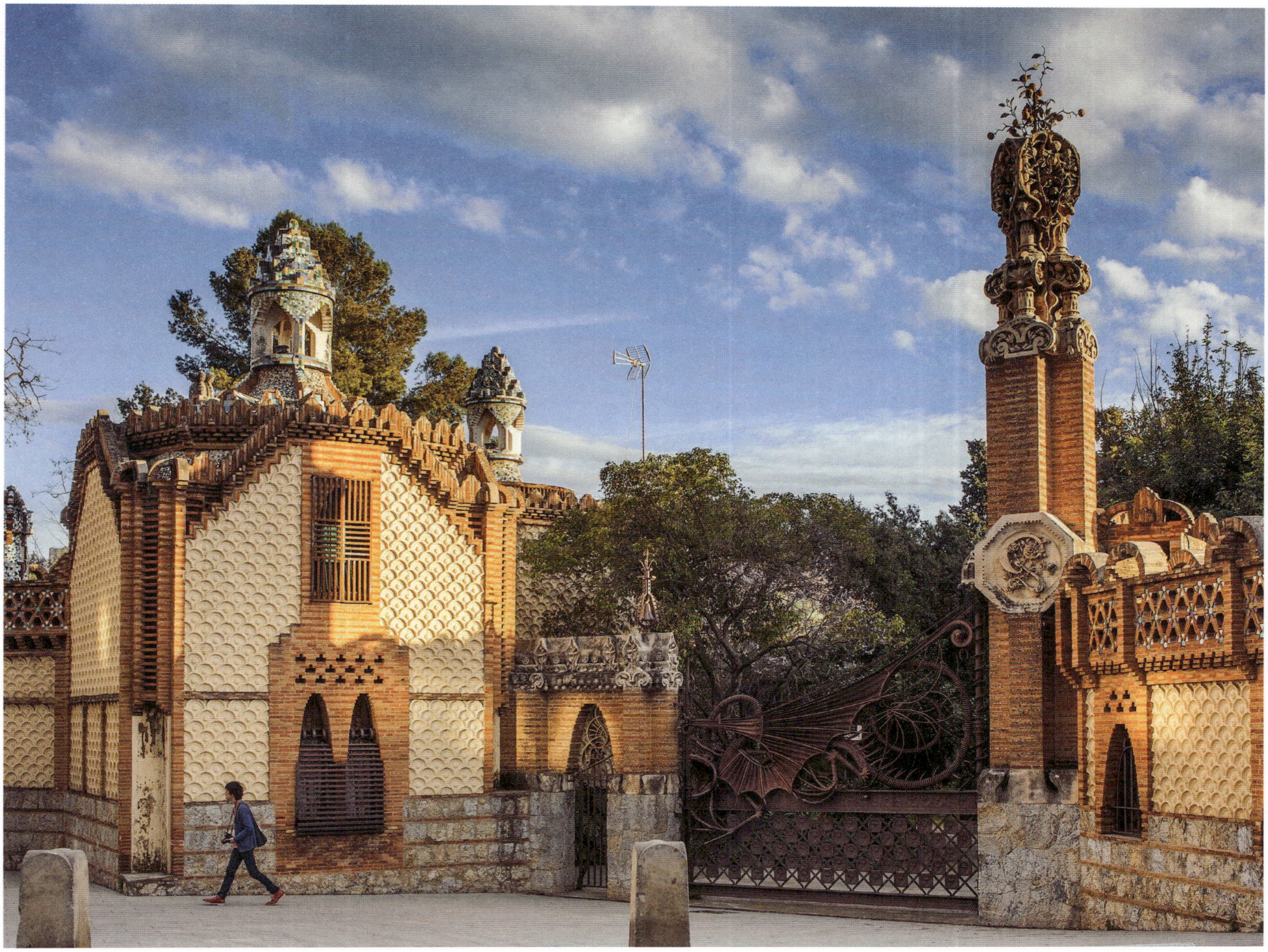

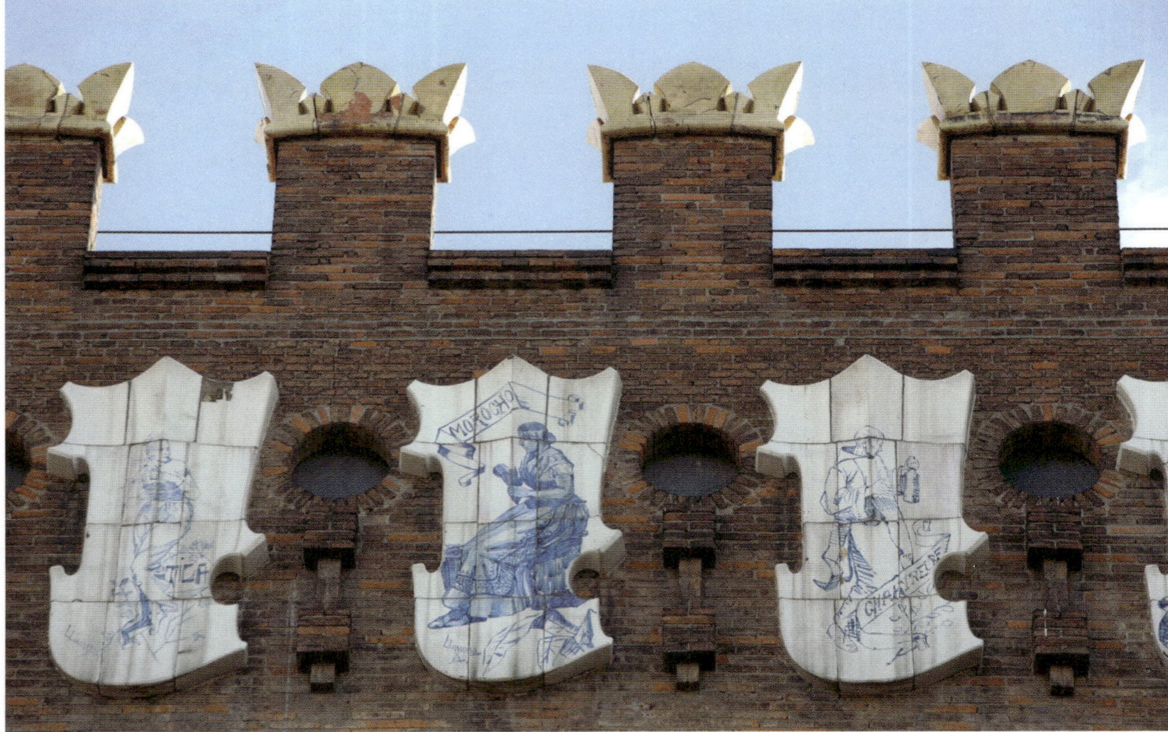

*Above:* Antoni Gaudí, Güell estate entrance gates and stables, 1884–1887.
*Left:* Alexandre de Riquer, ceramic placards for Domènech i Montaner's *Universal Exposition* Café-Restaurant, 1888.

the rest of Spain, for example Teruel, Zamora and Melilla, as well as other countries of Spanish culture, such as Cuba, Argentina and Mexico.

In the third period, from 1910 onwards, Modernisme began to go out of fashion, countered by a new impulse, the neo-classic *Noucentisme* movement. It would still continue well into the 1920s, but from 1907 interest would turn to German *Jugendstil* and especially the Viennese Secession. Architecture would be rather more geometric and sober, searching for effect with a strong play of volumes rather than organic forms or colourful decoration.

It was during the first phase, roughly from 1880 to 1900, that Catalan artists would receive strong influences from English art, particularly the Pre-Raphaelite and the Arts and Crafts schools, as well as the Aesthetic Movement. As we shall see, this connection would originate not only in a purely artistic interest, but also through the interest of businessmen and industrialists, who were looking to England as the model for the development and modernisation of the country – and, needless to say, their personal enrichment. To explain these dynamics, and the essence of the Modernista movement itself, some historical, cultural and political context is required.

The expansion of liberalism and modern nationalism throughout Europe that came from the echoes of the French Revolution and spread in step with Napoleon's conquering armies also reached Catalonia, and especially Barcelona. This would combine in the central decades of the 19th century with the wave of Romanticism to produce a specific cultural and, later, political movement known as the *Renaixença*, or Rebirth. Writers and poets would look to Catalan Mediaeval literature and rural culture and begin to produce works in Catalan, which had been largely abandoned as a literary language for more than a century. In 1859 they would re-create the *Jocs Florals*, a Mediaeval troubadour joust in verse, which in its modern version of poetry awards came to be revered by the erudite middle classes as an Eisteddfod-like celebration of Catalan culture (they are still held today, albeit

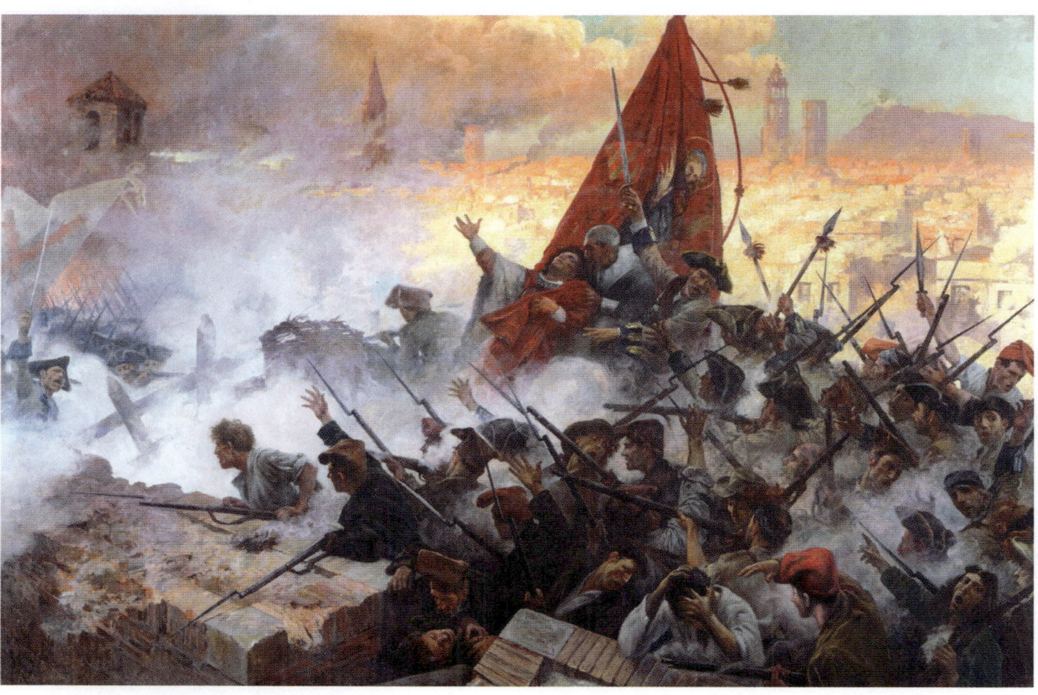

*Right:* Antoni Estruch i Bros, *L'Onze de Setembre de 1714*, 1909, oil on canvas. Espai Cultura Fundació Caixa Sabadel 1859.

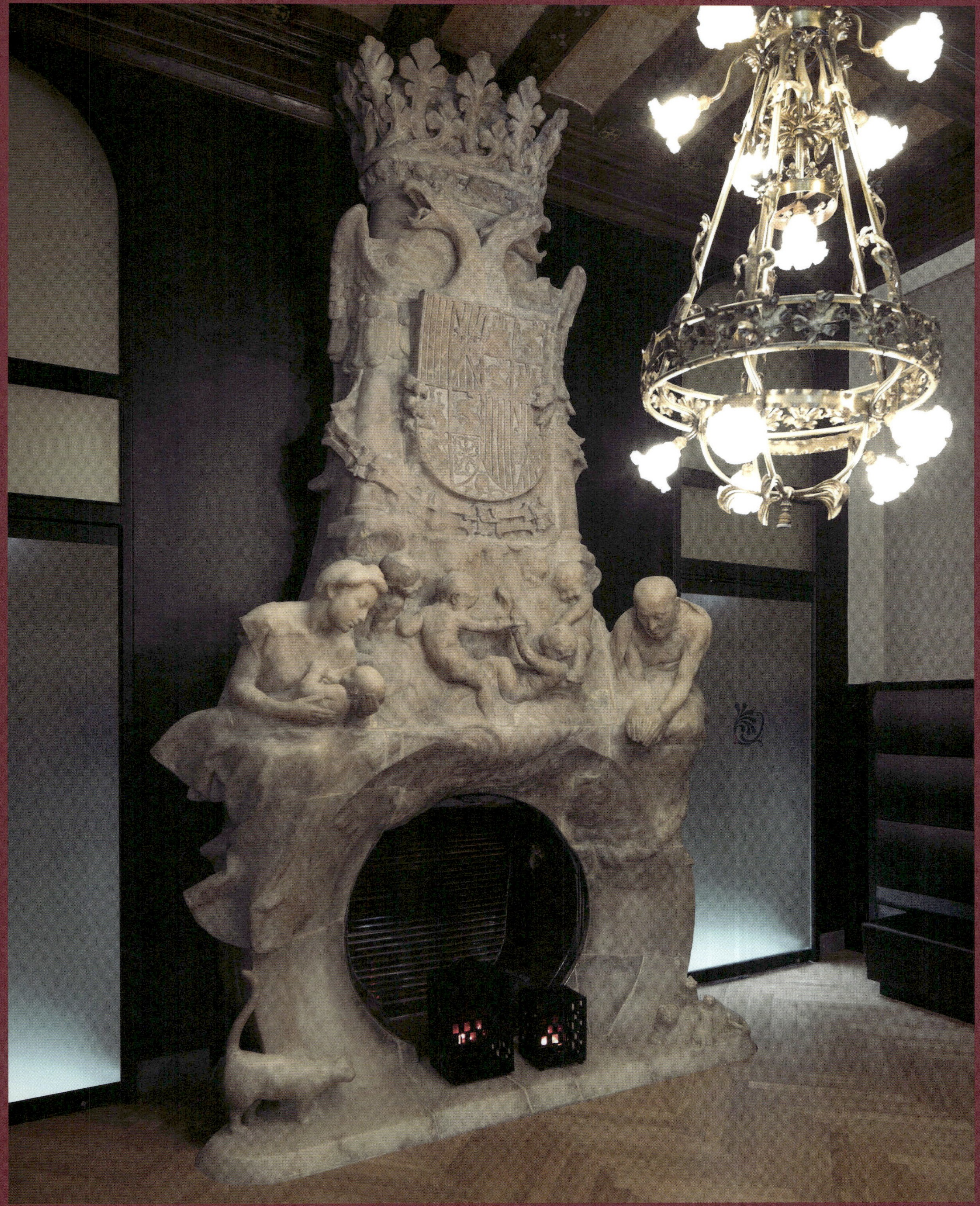

with less fervour). Likewise, historians would look to Mediaeval history in search of national origins and epic stories of past glories. To them, the gradual union of Catalonia with Castile to form the kingdom of Spain had been incrementally negative for the Catalan economy and identity, culminating in the War of Spanish Succession in which Catalans fought in support of the Hapsburg pretender and lost.

This was not altogether a romantic exaggeration, for after the fall of Barcelona in 1714 – famously depicted in Antoni Estruch's 1909 oil on canvas – the victorious Bourbon pretender, now King Philip V, had unleashed draconian repressive measures. These included the abolition of the traditional parliamentary institutions and laws, and the imposition of war reparations with a new tax system that would cripple the war-torn country's economy for decades. To keep the rebellious city of Barcelona under control, new walls were built enclosing it, the castle on Montjuïc hill was enlarged and a huge new citadel-prison was erected. The repression was also cultural: Catalan universities were shut down, and from then on the Catalan language was banned in all education, commerce, religious rituals, justice procedures and, in effect, any official or public matter, which had to be carried out in the foreign Castilian (Spanish) language. This state of affairs continued well into the 19th century, so to the Renaixença historians and literates – and, indeed, to Catalan nationalists today – 1714 and the Bourbon kings were the embodiment of all evils.

However, things did improve economically after 1778, when the restrictions on trade with the American colonies were lifted and Catalan merchants began to import raw materials such as sugar, cocoa and cotton, while exporting manufactured goods, above all brandy and calico textiles. During the 19th century commerce with America would reap huge profits, and a new elite of shippers and manufacturers would rise to the top, sometimes in a single generation. On their trips to America they would often detour to the United States or England, where they became acquainted with the Industrial Revolution and the comforts of the modern bourgeois home. They developed a strong will to modernise their own country: They were soon importing Crompton spinning mules and coal from England, and by the 1840s Catalonia had begun a full-blown textile industrial revolution of its own. And while thousands of peasants migrated from the countryside to Barcelona to engross an incipient proletariat, the city's nouveau-riche developed new ambitions. They vied for aristocratic titles, built handsome mansions for themselves and sought refinement in all walks of life. They began to appreciate the social and cultural value of art and to buy, commission and collect art, partly out of true interest, but also as a way to exhibit their newly acquired wealth and power.

It was in this context that the Catalan 'rebirth' or Renaixença appeared. The main protagonist of the literary Renaixença movement was the poet and priest Jacint Verdaguer, who exercised a huge influence on Catalan culture, to the point that some of his poems and songs are still well known today by the 'Catalan-in-the-street'. His work was well loved by most Modernista artists, and his epic poem *L'Atlàntida* was the motif that Gaudí used in the décor of the aforementioned Güell Pavilions. Strictly speaking, Verdaguer was not a symbolist, nor is there evidence that he knew the work of the Pre-Raphaelites in any depth –although he probably did know something about them, as he was a great friend of Alexandre de Riquer, the introducer of the Pre-Raphaelites to

Catalonia. And as Jordi Castellanos points out, like the Pre-Raphaelites he was an admirer of the Roman Nazarenes, and his use of images, myths and symbols was very much in line with that of the symbolists.[3] In a way, it could be said that the immense popularity of the poetry of Verdaguer and other members of the Renaixença movement made Catalonia fertile ground to receive English influences at the end of the 19th century.

The Renaixença would also foster the growth of cultural groups and hiking clubs, which, as in other countries in Europe, would become a preferred collective activity of the middle class and would go well beyond literature and hiking. Cultural associations such as the Ateneu Barcelonès would be centres for the rediscovery of Catalan history and for the diffusion of scientific, cultural and political novelties from abroad. Hiking clubs like the Centre Excursionista de Catalunya would provide a means to see not only the Catalan countryside, but also Catalan Mediaeval art and architecture, as well as a means to advance in sciences such as botany, zoology or geology. These clubs would be the breeding ground of Catalan nationalism and republican federalism, and many of the Modernista artists would be involved – most notably Lluís Domènech i Montaner and Josep Puig i Cadafalch (1867–1956), who both had long political careers.

*Below:* Plan of the *Eixample* (Enlargement) development project, designed by Ildefons Cerdà, 1859

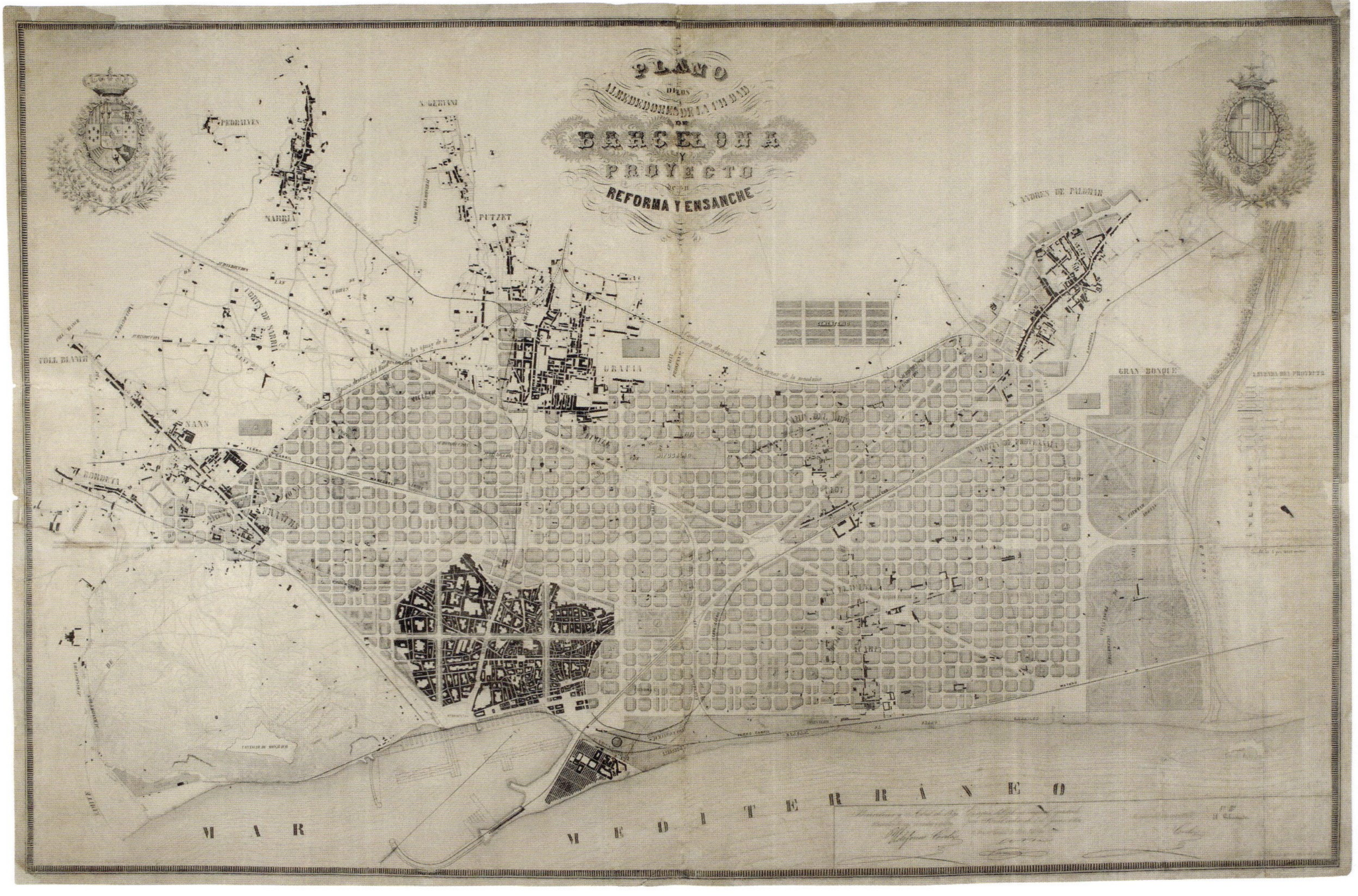

The European revolutionary wave of 1848 did not spread to an underdeveloped and profoundly Catholic Spain (the Spanish Inquisition had not been abolished until 1836). But the events of 1848 did shock the Spanish elites profoundly and stirred them to do something to quell revolutionary appetites in the country. Conscious of the large proletariat in the city and the ease with which they would rebel every so often – and influenced by the liberal, free-trade ideas of part of the British upper classes, as for example Prince Albert – most of the Catalan elites believed that economic development and modernisation were a good way to improve the lives of the dispossessed and prevent revolution. And the first task at hand was to achieve their old ambition of getting rid of the post-1714 walls and citadel that choked the city and did not allow it to spread out. Armed with detailed reports of the deplorable squalor in the old city, they lobbied intensely in Madrid, until in 1854 the government allowed the walls to be torn down. Despite the enthusiasm of the people, who turned up by the thousands on the ramparts, wielding tools to demolish the walls themselves, it would take a whole decade to finish the task, and permission for the demolition of the huge and hated citadel-prison would not come until 1969. But now Barcelona could grow and occupy the whole plain between the old city and the surrounding villages, in what would be the largest urban-planning project of 19th-century Spain.[4]

The plan for the *Eixample* (Enlargement) of Barcelona fell to Ildefons Cerdà, an engineer who devised the grid layout of square blocks with wide, perpendicular streets that is the centre of modern-day Barcelona. Cerdà was a utopian of socialist ideas who, inspired by Étienne Cabet's *Icaria*, envisaged an ideal new city in which strict regulations ensured that all houses were equal – the same for factory workers as for factory owners – while the interior of the blocks were public, open-access gardens. But the Barcelona bourgeoisie would have none of that nonsense. Once the plans were approved by the Madrid government in 1860, the City Council and the developers proceeded to ignore the attached regulations. The basic grid plan with chamfered corners was respected, but business is business, and the public gardens became commercial real estate, while the regulations regarding houses were watered down. Seen from an idealistic point of view, this may have been a pity, but on the other hand a few decades later it would allow the Modernista architects to unleash their creativity and build marvels such as Gaudí's Casa Milà, *La Pedrera*, or Domènech i Montaner's Hospital de Sant Pau – both UNESCO World Heritage sites today – not to mention the wonderful contrast of Gaudí's Casa Batlló right next to Puig i Cadafalch's Casa Amatller, near Domènech i Montaner's Casa Lleó i Morera and Enric Sagnier's Casa Mulleras, in what Barcelonans fondly call *La Mansana de la Discòrdia*, or Block of Discord.*

Meanwhile, the intense commercial connection of Catalan industrialists with England would heighten their interest in the application of art to industrial products. In 1870 they lobbied the Provincial Government of Barcelona to send an envoy to London to report on the work being done in the industrial sector and the new decorative museums, particularly the South Kensington Museum (later the Victoria and Albert Museum), and to visit the *Workmen's International Exhibition*. They chose Salvador Sanpere, an ideal candidate: politician, poet and historian of Mediaeval art, he was a typical Romantic who would become a staunch supporter and promoter of

*The name refers to the striking aesthetic diversity of the houses, but it is also an erudite pun: *Mansana* in old Catalan also meant 'apple' and can therefore be related to the 'apple of discord' in the classical Greek myth of the Judgement of Paris.

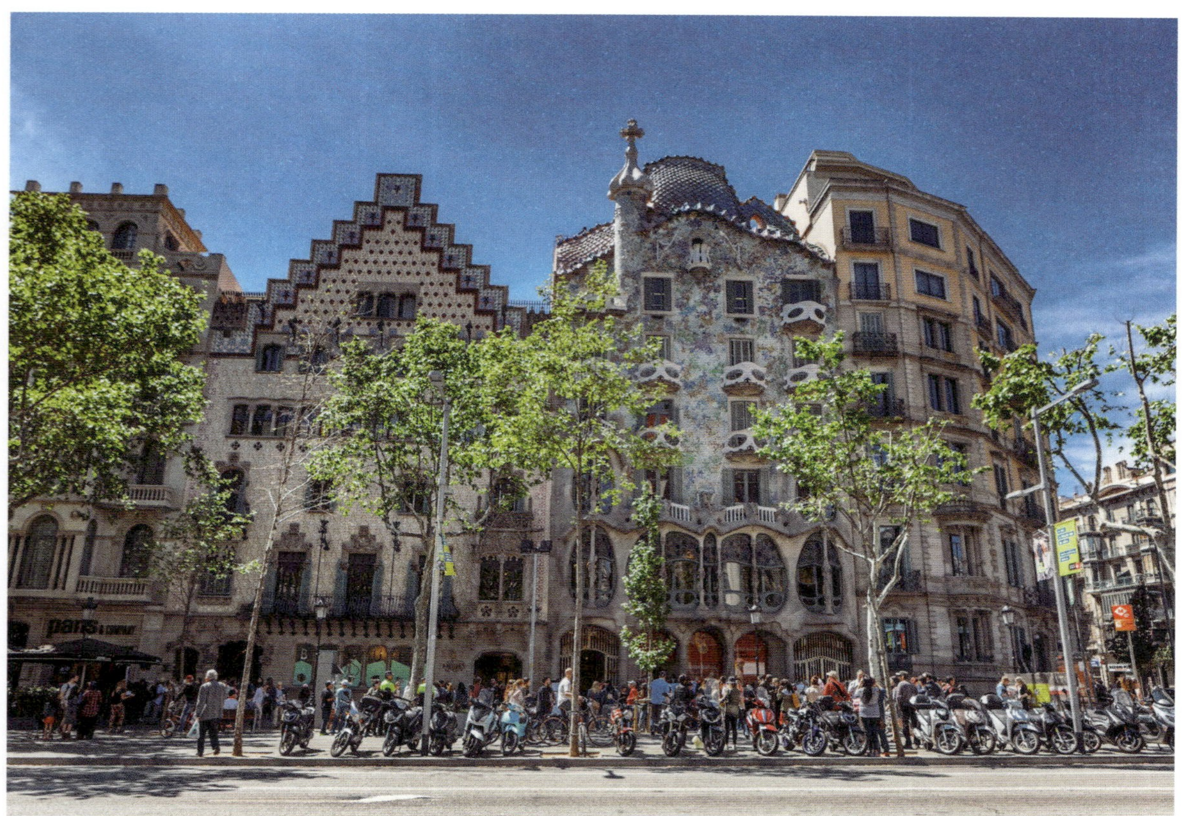

*Left:* Mansana de la Discòrdia, with buildings by Josep Puig i Cadafalch, 1900, and Antoni Gaudí, 1904.
*Below left:* Antoni Gaudí, Casa Batlló, 1904.
*Below:* Antoni Gaudí, Casa Batlló (roof detail), 1904.

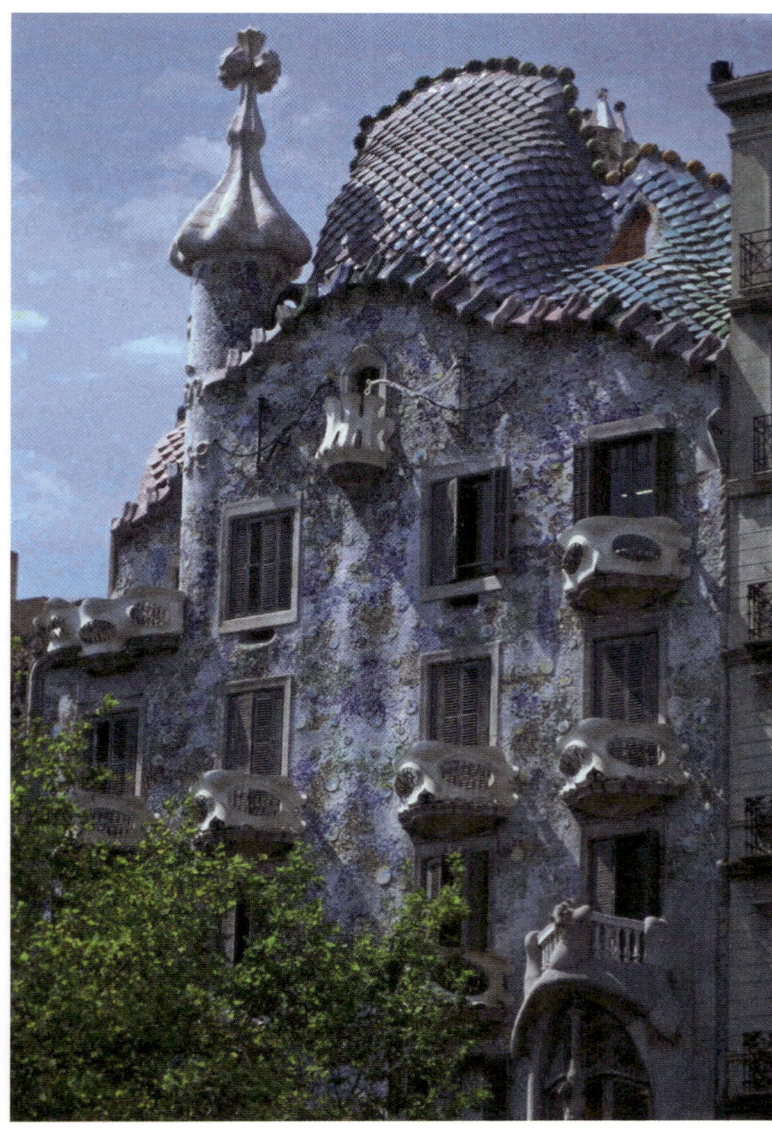

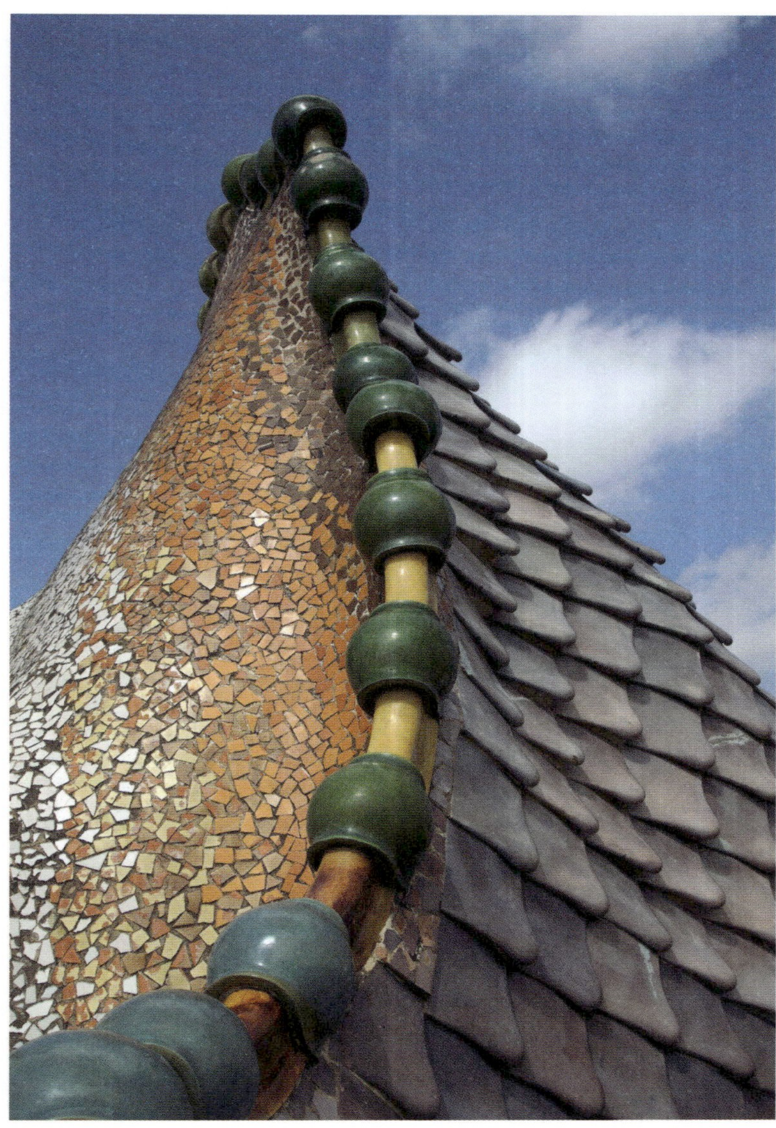

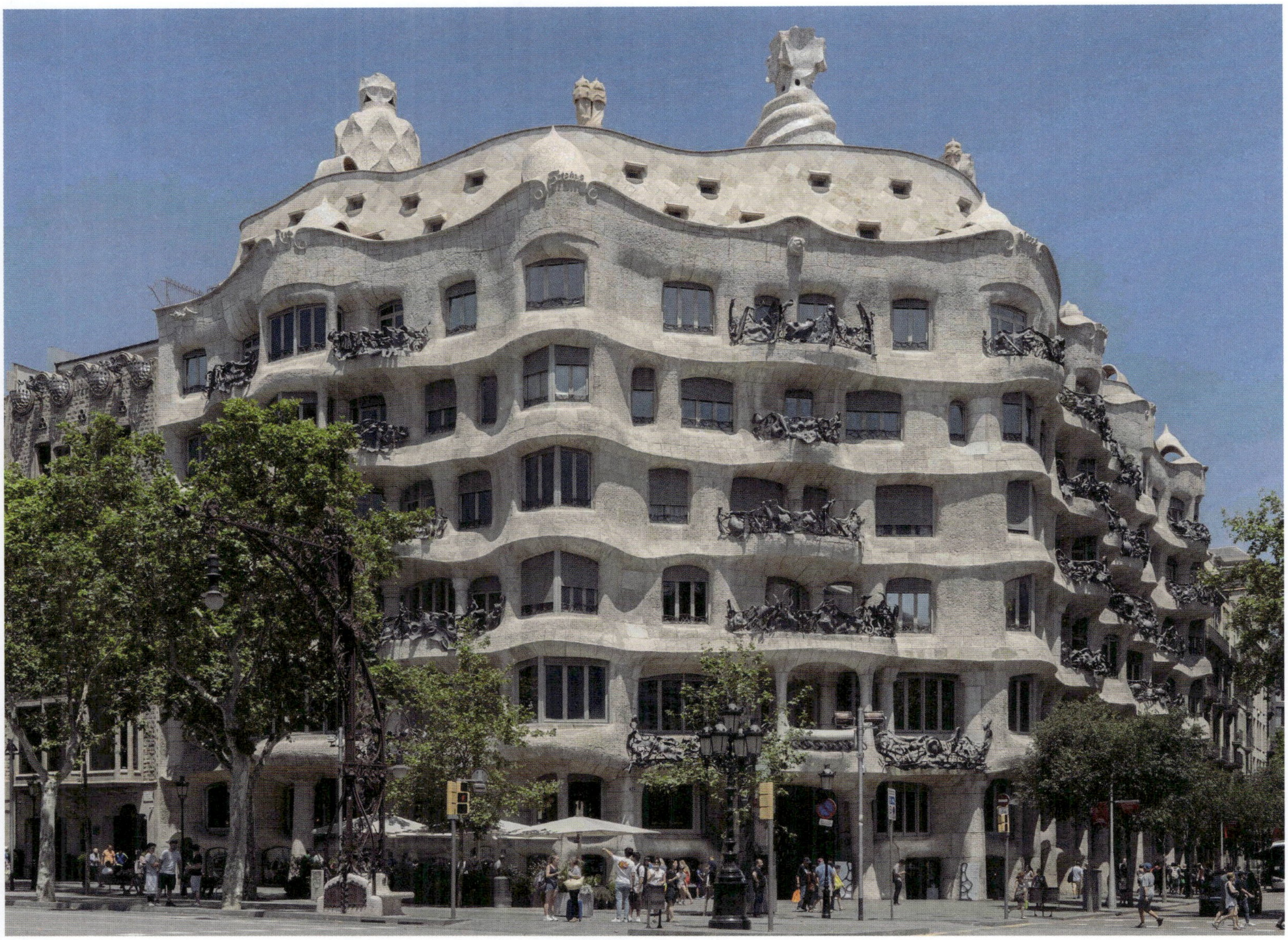

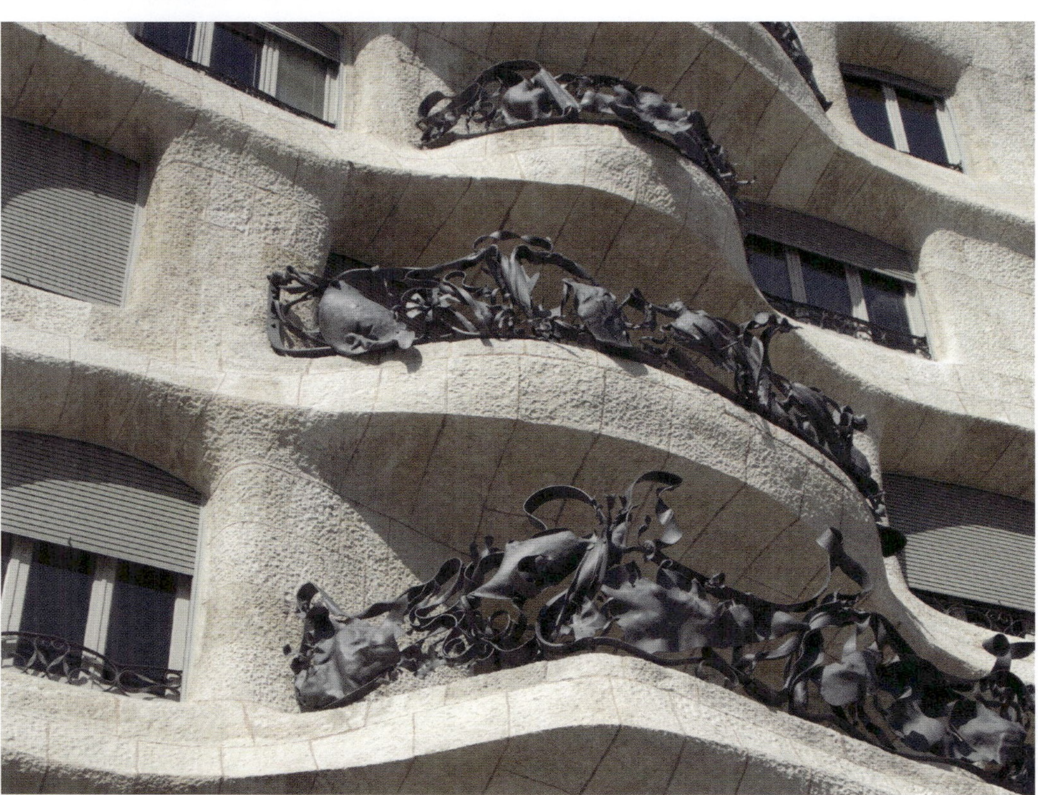

*Above and right:* Antoni Gaudí,
Casa Milà (*La Pedrera*), 1906–1912.

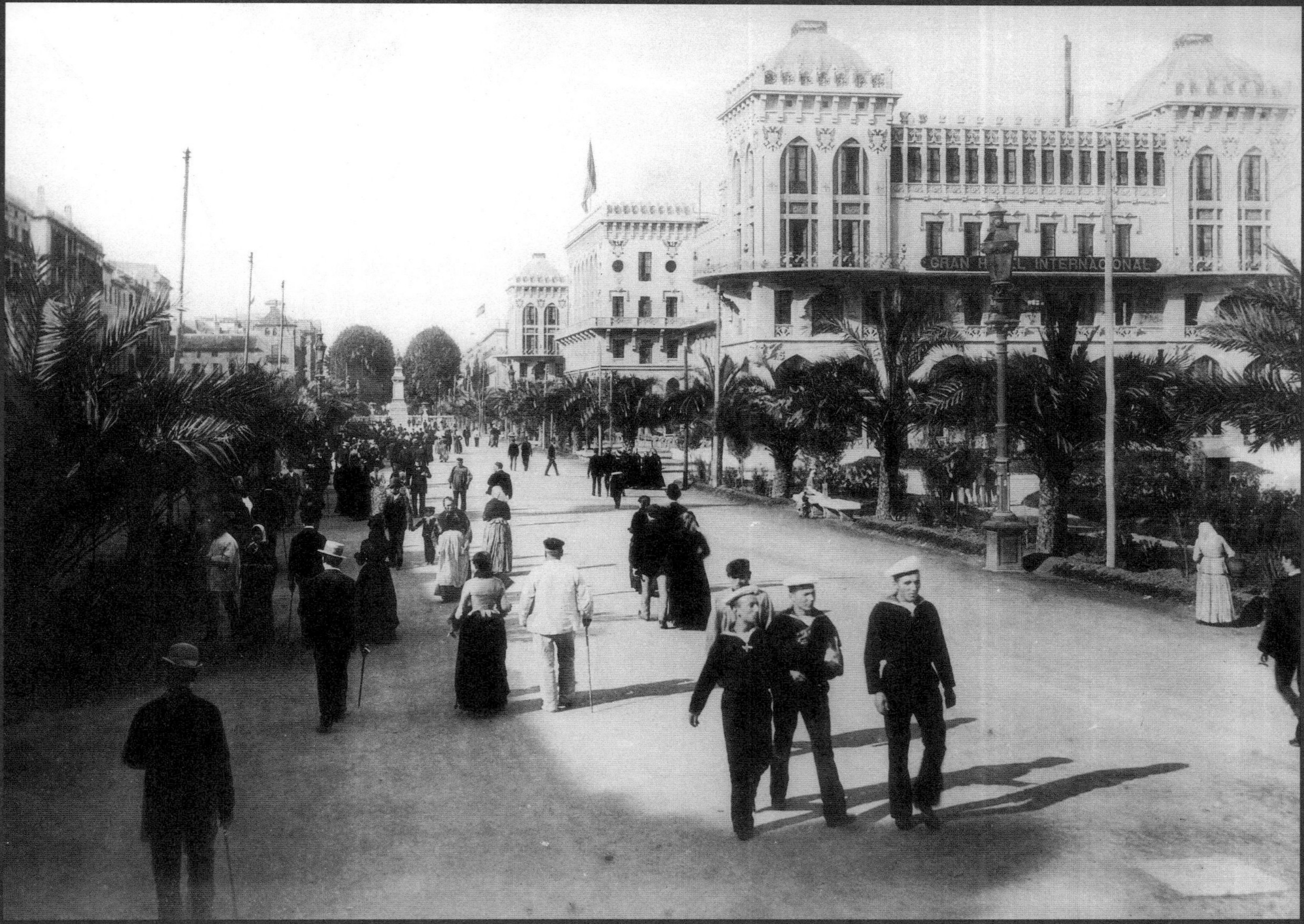

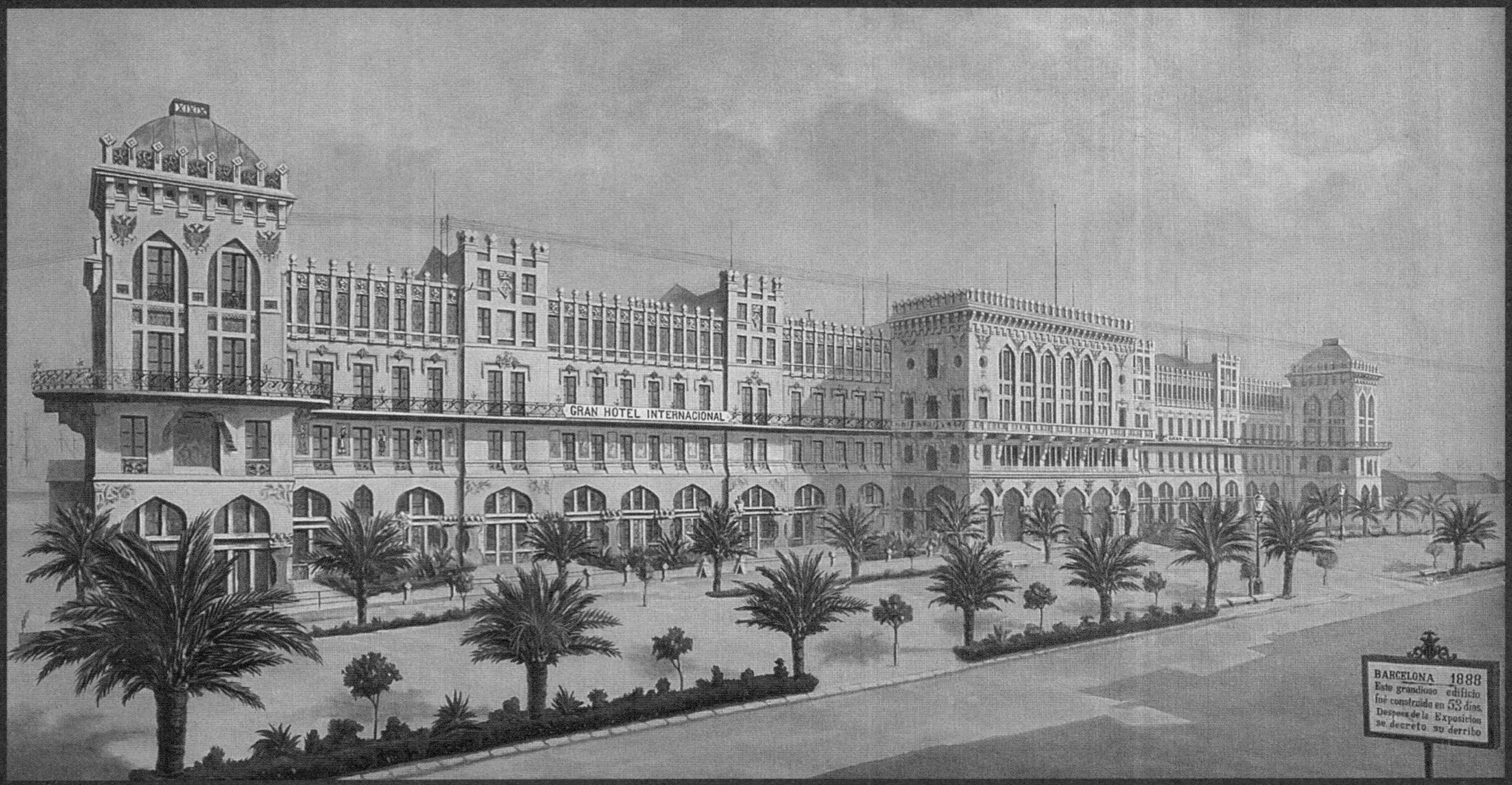

GRAN HOTEL INTERNACIONAL
BARCELONA 1888
Este grandioso edificio
fué construido en 53 dias.
Después de la Exposición
se decretó su derribo

applying the arts to industry – he became, in the words of art historian Mireia Freixa, 'the Catalan Henry Cole'.[5] His report called for the creation of museums of applied art and the promotion of exhibitions modelled on the London Exhibition of 1851. His words were heeded: in 1888 Barcelona would hold its first *Universal Exposition*. The Expo itself would be a commercial flop, even if it was seen as a moral victory by Catalans, as it was held in the grounds of the demolished citadel. More importantly, it would firmly install the desire for modernity in the minds of the Catalans and would signal the beginning of the Modernista movement.

The architectural flagship of the *Exposition* was the Hotel Internacional by Lluís Domènech i Montaner. Designed and built in less than four months, this work was conceived with a truly modern mind and would certify the architect's genius in managing construction teams; he would hitherto be known as 'the orchestra conductor'. In order to finish the hotel in time for the inauguration, Domènech would organise teams in round-the-clock construction shifts under electric lights – the first ever electric-light installation in the city streets. And to simplify things he used standard railway iron rails for the structure frame and a single type of standard brick, calculating all the dimensions of the huge building as multiples of these two units.

The local authorities also followed Sanpere's advice on the matter of museums, and in the years following the 1888 *Exposition* the Museum of Fine Arts, the Museum of Art Reproductions and the Barcelona History Museum would open. Further exhibitions were to come in the next decades too, most of them devoted to the relation of industry with art, and this would culminate in the creation in 1903 of Foment de les Arts Decoratives (FAD), an institution that still exists today and has been central in the evolution of contemporary design in Catalonia.

The many decades of industrial relationship with England would create a significant number of Anglophiles among the Catalan bourgeoisie. Gaudí's main patron Eusebi Güell (1846–1918), for example, was a staunch Anglophile and was always on the watch for any novelty in Britain. And not only regarding industrial advances or machinery: his flopped urban development, Park Güell, was a bourgeois version of Ebenezer Howard's Garden City concept (which is why its proper name is spelt 'Park', in English, rather than the Catalan *Parc* or Spanish *Parque*). Howard's ideas were introduced to Catalonia by the Majorcan aristocrat Cebrià de Montoliu (1873–1923), another enthusiast of English culture who would translate works by Ruskin, William Morris and Shakespeare into Catalan. The Güells were also Shakespeare fans. Their mansion in Barcelona, Palau Güell, still preserves four stained-glass windows which portray four Shakespearian characters: Hamlet, Macbeth, King Lear and Bertram from *All's Well That Ends Well* (Bertram is the 'Count of Rousillon' and therefore a Catalan character; the Roussillon was not annexed by France until 1659). The panels are in fact English-made: they were commissioned from the Smethwick stained-glass artist T.W. Camm in the late 1880s, as glass experts Núria Gil and Jordi Bonet have recently confirmed.[6] Güell's son, also called Eusebi, wrote a version of *Romeo and Juliet* in 1903. Many Modernista artists were Shakespearians, but perhaps none as passionate as Lluís Domènech i Montaner: his love for the Bard's work was so intense that he refused to recite it in public, for according to art critic Robert Hughes, 'he would lose control in the more emotional passages, break down, and weep'.[7]



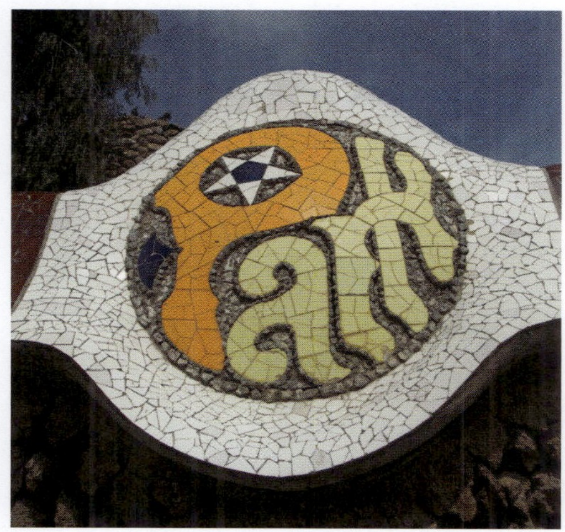

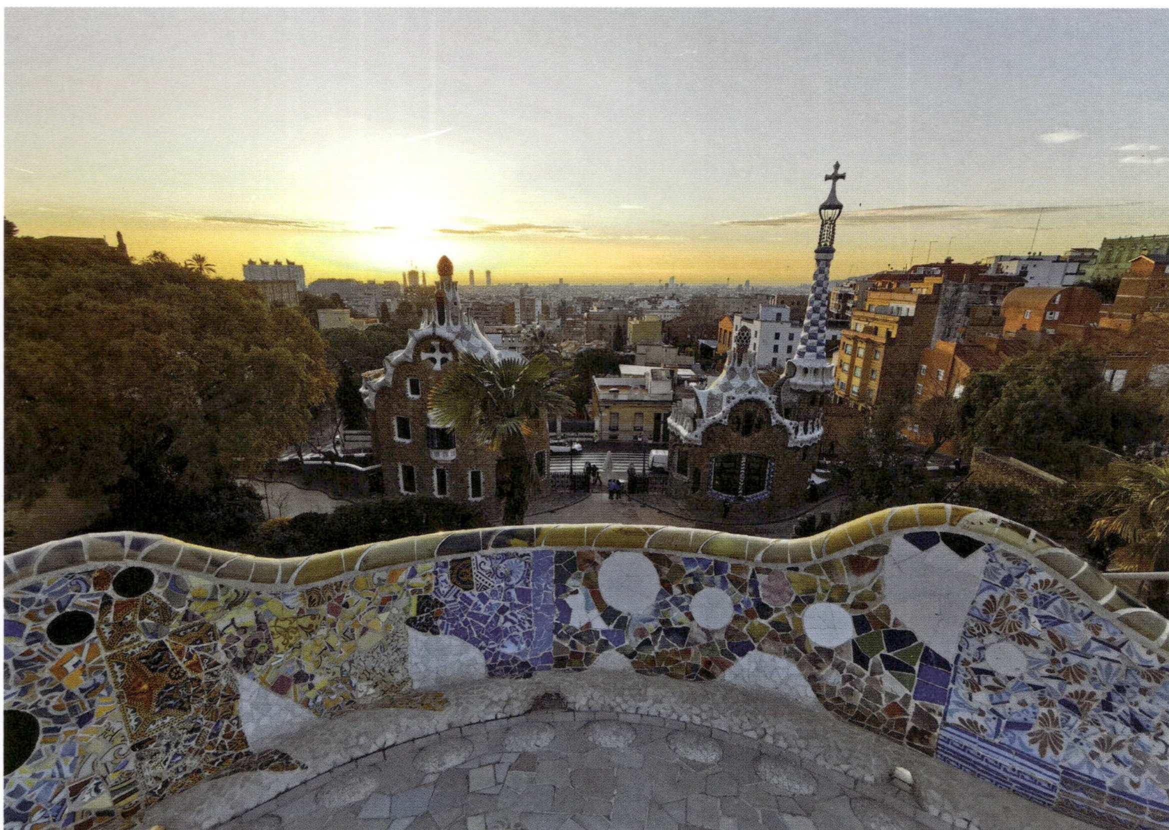

*Left and below:* Antoni Gaudí, Park Güell, 1900–1914.
*Opposite:* Antoni Gaudí, Park Güell, 1900–1914.

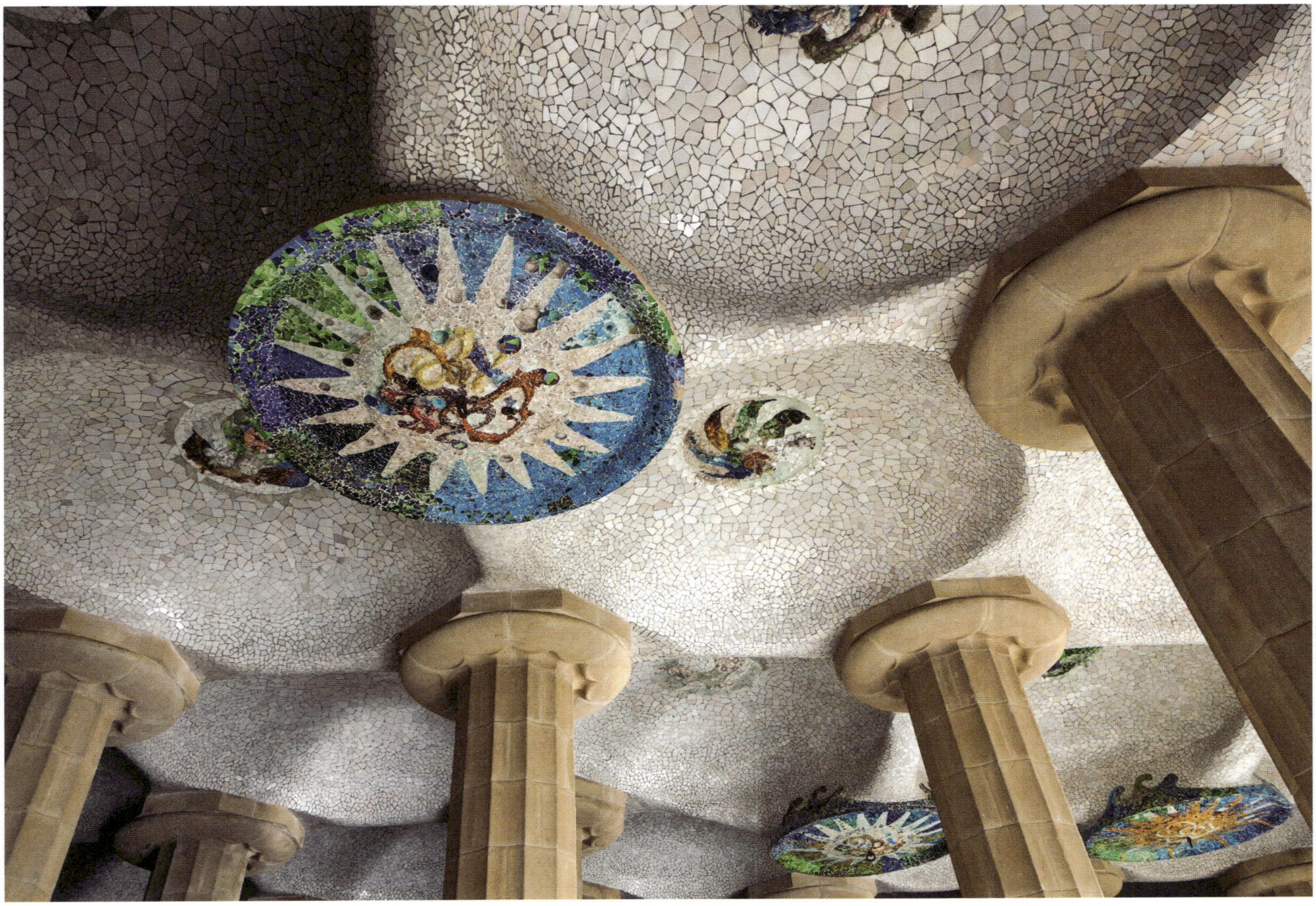

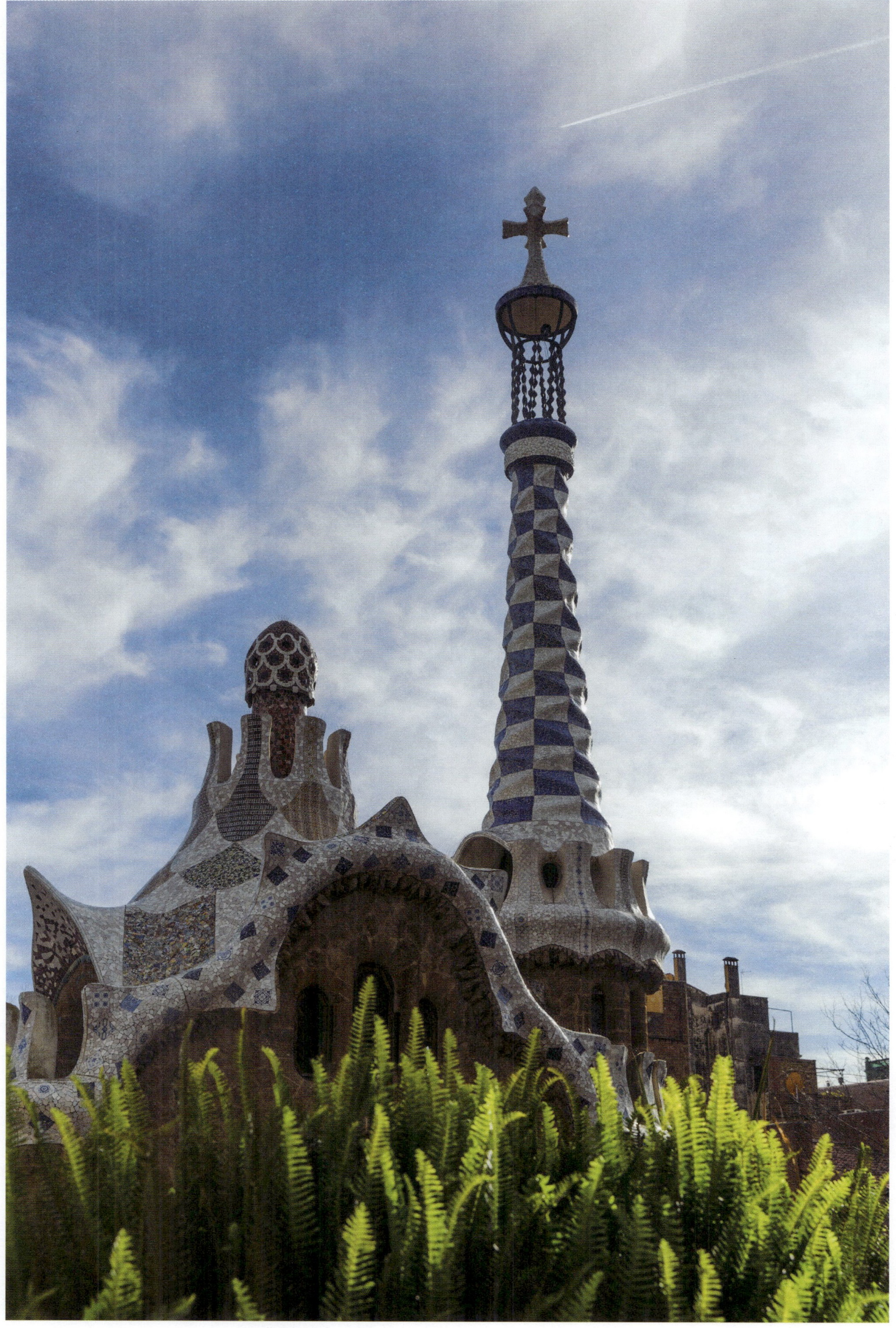

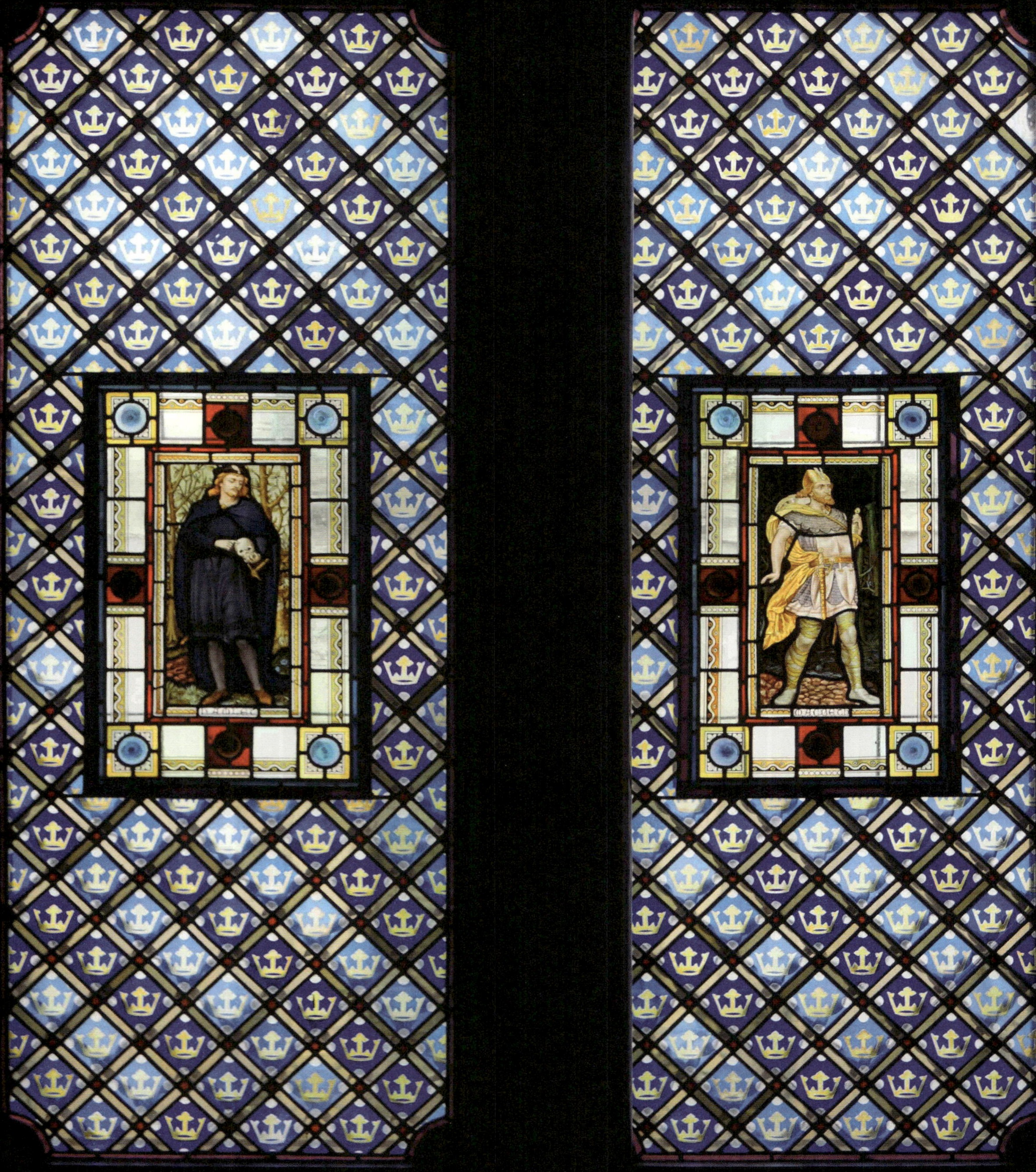

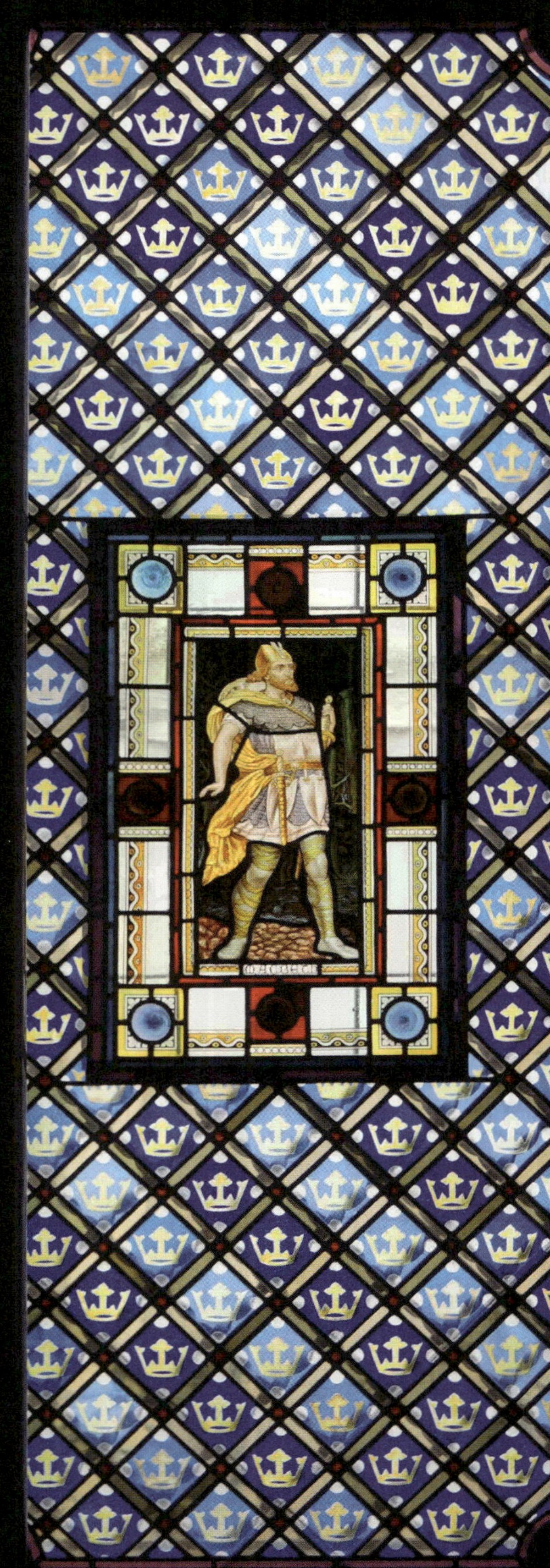

*Oppsite:* T.W. Camm, Hamlet and
Macbeth stained-glass windows
for Palau Güell, *c.*1890.

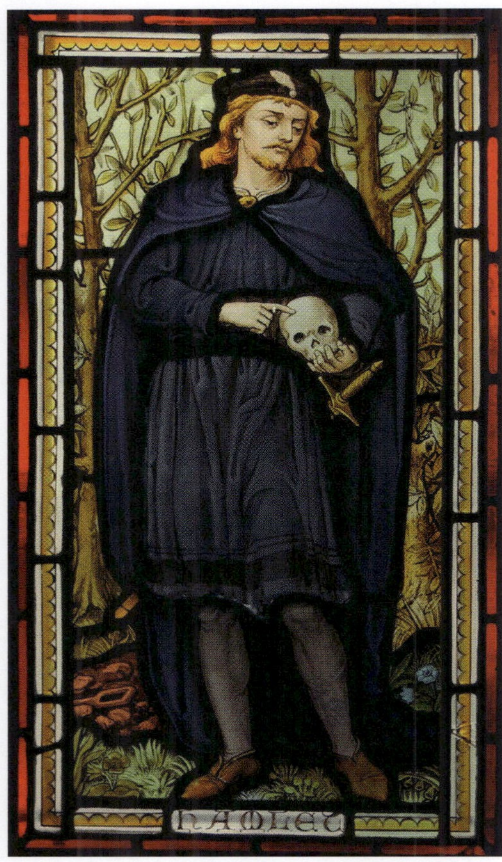

*Above:* T.W. Camm, Hamlet
stained-glass window for Palau
Güell, *c.*1890.

In the 1880s magazines such as *L'Avenç* and *La Ilustración Ibérica* would begin to make the work of the Pre-Raphaelites known to Catalans. This last journal was directed by Alfred Opisso (1847–1924), who translated two of Dante Gabriel Rossetti's poems, 'The Blessed Damozel' and 'St Luke the Painter', which were very well received by locals. Art critic Ramon Casellas (1855–1910) was especially fond of the Pre-Raphaelites, and his work *La damisela santa* (The Saintly Damsel), directly inspired by Rossetti's poem, received an award at the Literary Contest of the 1894 Sitges Modernista Festival. These festivals, organised by painter Santiago Rusiñol (1861–1931), were a celebration of all artistic disciplines modelled on the Pre-Raphaelite Brotherhood that brought together the more bohemian Modernista artists. However, it was Alexandre de Riquer (1856–1920) who best embodied the poet-artist ideal of the Pre-Raphaelites and worked hardest to make their art known in Catalonia. This was highlighted in his obituary by the rabid anti-Modernista writer Eugeni d'Ors: 'Riquer had received the influence and teachings of the English Pre-Raphaelites ( ... ) and he did his best to spread them throughout Catalonia, the country in the world in which such influences and teachings could perhaps do most harm.'[8]

Alexandre de Riquer was a multifaceted creator: painter, illustrator, engraver, designer and poet, he excelled in each of these disciplines. Today his work is hardly known outside academic circles, which is somewhat unfair, for it could be said with no exaggeration that the Modernista movement may not have gone very far – or, indeed, ever existed – without him. And certainly English art would not have been so influential in Catalonia had it not been for him. In his younger years he was a follower of Viollet-le-Duc, and most of his work was Neo-Gothic and of a bucolic nature. Extant examples from this early period are the ceramic placards at the top of the walls of Domènech's Café-Restaurant for the 1888 *Exposition*, some designs he did for the Masriera jewellers and the decoration of a fireplace at Palau Güell. According to Eliseu Trenc, he became interested in Japonisme before it was popular in Barcelona, and this would quite naturally lead him to Pre-Raphaelitism and to the Arts and Crafts Movement.[9]

In 1889, like many other Catalan artists, Alexandre de Riquer would visit the Paris *Exposition*. His main intention was to use the trip to visit the Cluny Museum and see French Mediaeval art, following Viollet-le-Duc. But at the *Exposition* he was smitten by the Pre-Raphaelite paintings shown at the English section, and his passions shifted. His work would soon show this, with paintings such as *Among Lilies* or *Saintly Shepherd*, both of which were presented at the 1893 Chicago *Columbian Exposition*, where he won the only gold medal in the Spanish section for a chest described as 'a superior piece of cabinet work'.[10] In 1894 Riquer would make a two-month trip to England to see British art at first hand. There, he would befriend Edward Burne-Jones and William Morris and discover the stylistic Art Nouveau model propagated by the journal *The Studio*. According to an article published by F. Arteaga in this same magazine in 1900, Riquer had told him that what he had encountered in England was a catalysing inspiration, and that he would make it his mission 'to proclaim these hitherto unknown glories in Catalonia'.[11]

He would certainly carry out this mission. Particularly by means of the Cercle Artístic de Sant Lluc (St Luke Artistic Circle), which he had founded in 1893 together with the sculptor Josep Llimona (1864–1934). This association was profoundly Catholic – it was in fact a break-off from the Cercle Artístic de Barcelona, which, in their opinion, had become dominated by rather frivolous and bohemian types, such as the painters Casas and Rusiñol – to the point that it banned nude female models in its sketching sessions. Yet despite their piety, the *Lukes* looked to the Pre-Raphaelite Brotherhood as their model. They also admired the artistic philosophy of the Arts and Crafts Movement, and Aubrey Beardsley's work. Their library contained all the relevant English art magazines and publications of the time. Other members, among many in this group, were the painter Joan Llimona (1860–1926), the draughtsman Antoni Utrillo (1867–1944) and Antoni Gaudí himself. Ironically, from 1903 on, the group's venue was the ground floor of Puig i Cadafalch's Casa Martí, which had previously been the tavern Els Quatre Gats, where the more bohemian artists of Modernisme met and held literary soirées and exhibited their most radical work.

Alexandre de Riquer would also be the editor of the magazine *Joventut*, the main publication of the Modernista movement, and would contribute to several others, with English modern art as his constant theme. Further on, he would excel in etchings, mainly book-plates, which he produced with a press that he had brought over from London. And he introduced poster art, which he had discovered in England, to Catalonia. This did not prove easy, though: during the first years businessmen would reject the idea of modern posters, even when he offered to design them free of charge.[12] But eventually his stubbornness would pay off and Catalans would develop a taste for posters. Alexandre de Riquer is now considered the father of Catalan poster artwork, which would continue in an unbroken evolution up to the great posters of the Spanish Civil War. His work was recognised in England, too: in 1900 Volume X of *The Studio* devoted an entire article to him.[13]

The Arts and Crafts Movement provided Catalan artists with the model they were searching for – one that could reconcile their ambition for cosmopolitan modernity with the recovery and veneration of Catalan history and tradition. And they could place emphasis on individual craftsmanship while raising the status of industrial objects by adding aesthetic value to large-scale productions. Cabinet-maker Francesc Vidal (1848–1914) had set up his workshop Les Industries Artístiques (The Artistic Industries) in 1879 in Barcelona to produce furniture and a vast array of other applied-art objects to decorate home interiors, from ironwork to glassmaking and tapestries. Although his production was initially inscribed in the historicist style, thanks to a long collaboration with Alexandre de Riquer he would become very interested in the new artistic expressions that were dawning across Europe, particularly the Arts and Crafts Movement. He visited England several times and in 1889 even tried to promote his workshop's productions in London, Birmingham and Manchester, without much success.[14]

Vidal's workshop was equipped with an Alexander steam engine and mechanical saws, which gave it a productive advantage over its competitors. It would fully decorate the interiors of several Modernista mansions, and would train or employ many of the artists and artisans of the movement. For example, the Majorcan Gaspar Homar (1870–1955), foremost among all Modernista cabinet-makers, who apprenticed at Vidal's manufacturing firm and drew much inspiration from the Arts and Crafts masters, particularly Philip Webb of Morris and Company.[15] In 1898, Vidal sent his son Frederic (1882–1950) to England to apprentice at the Barthels and Pfister and the

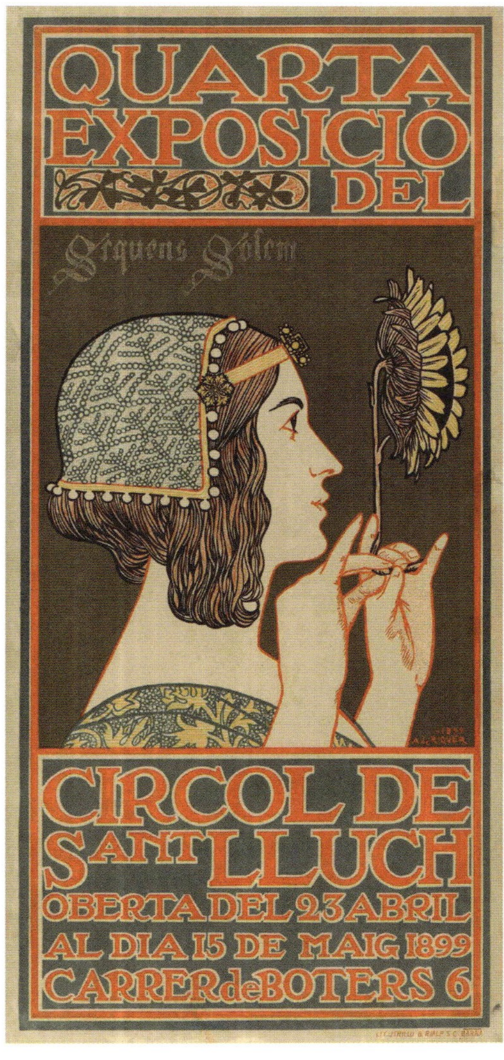


*Above:* Alexandre de Riquer, poster for a St Luke Artistic Circle exhibition, 1899, colour lithograph.

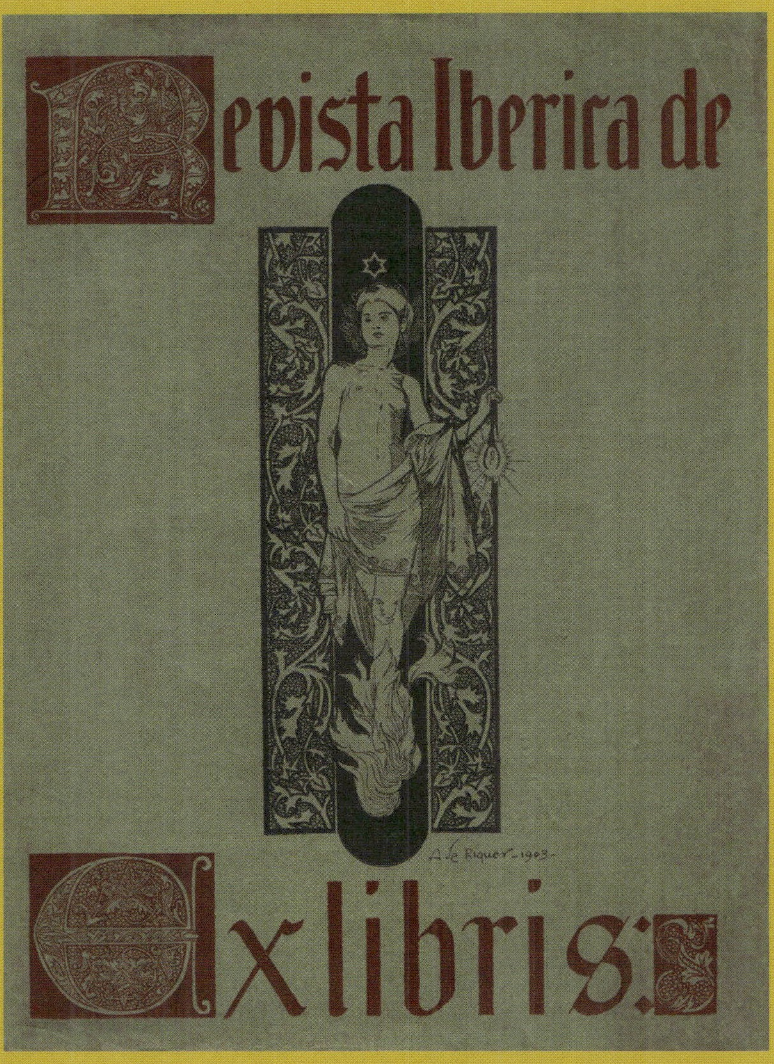



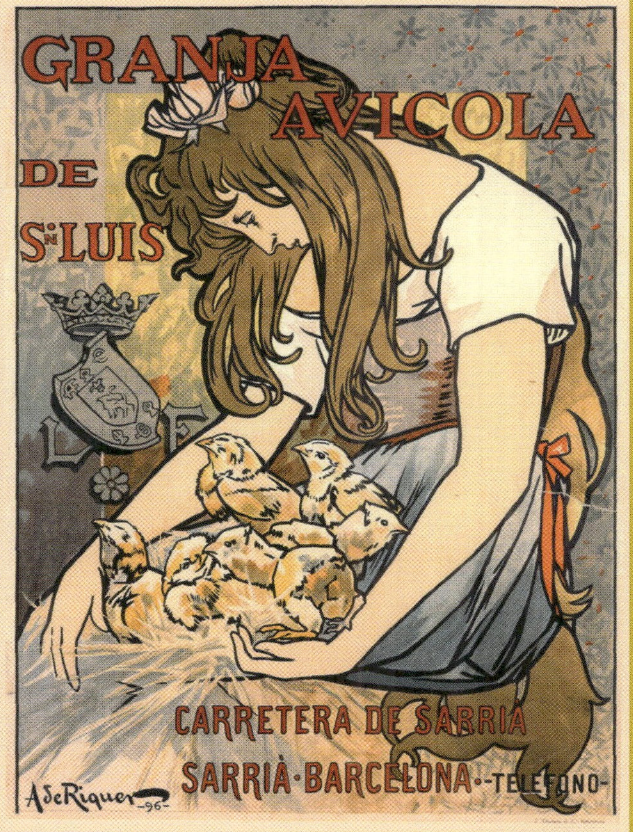

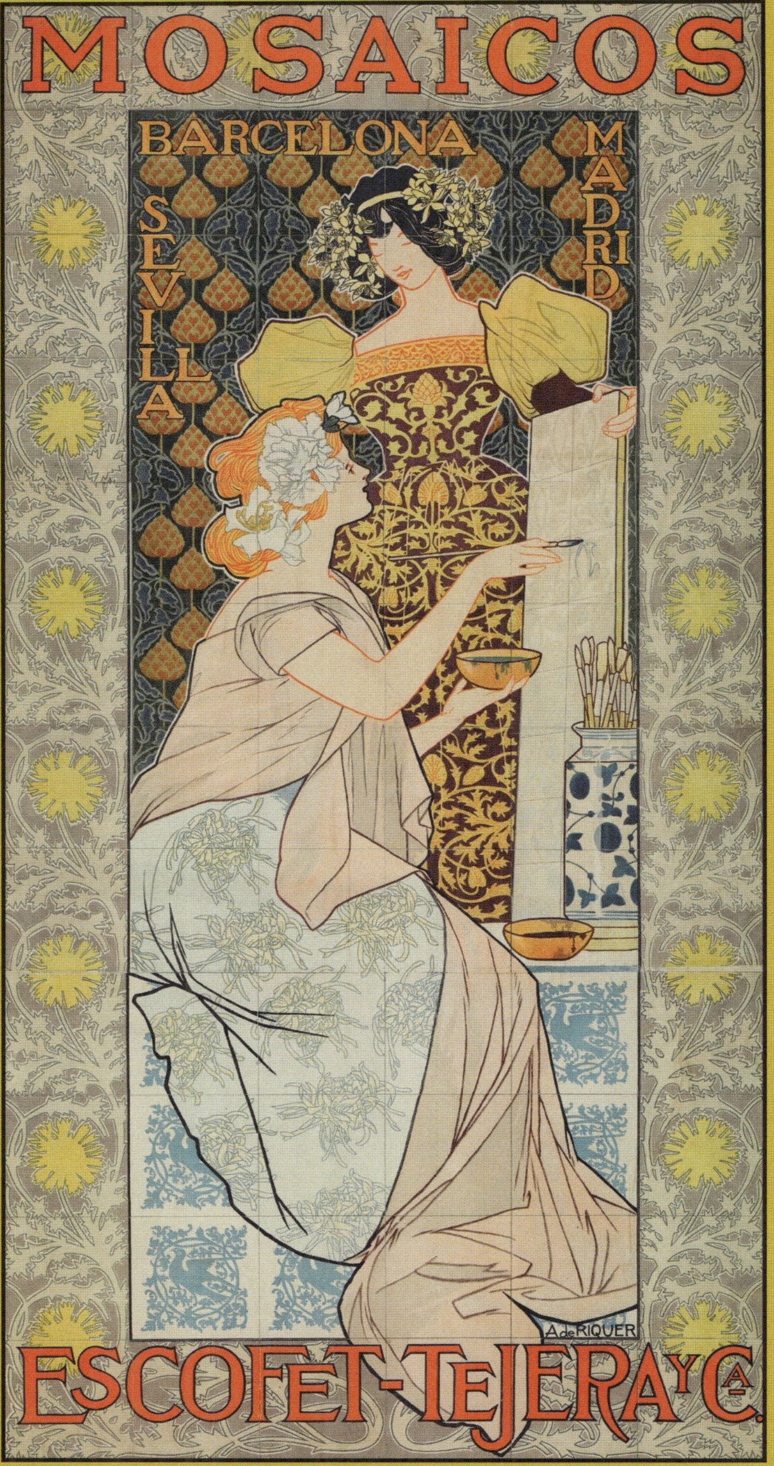




*Left:* Alexandre de Riquer, cover for the *Iberian Magazine of Bookplates*, 1900.
*Below:* Alexandre de Riquer, poster for Escofet-Tejera & CA Tiles, 1900. Jordi Carulla Collection.

*Left:* Alexandre de Riquer, poster for a poultry farm, 1896.

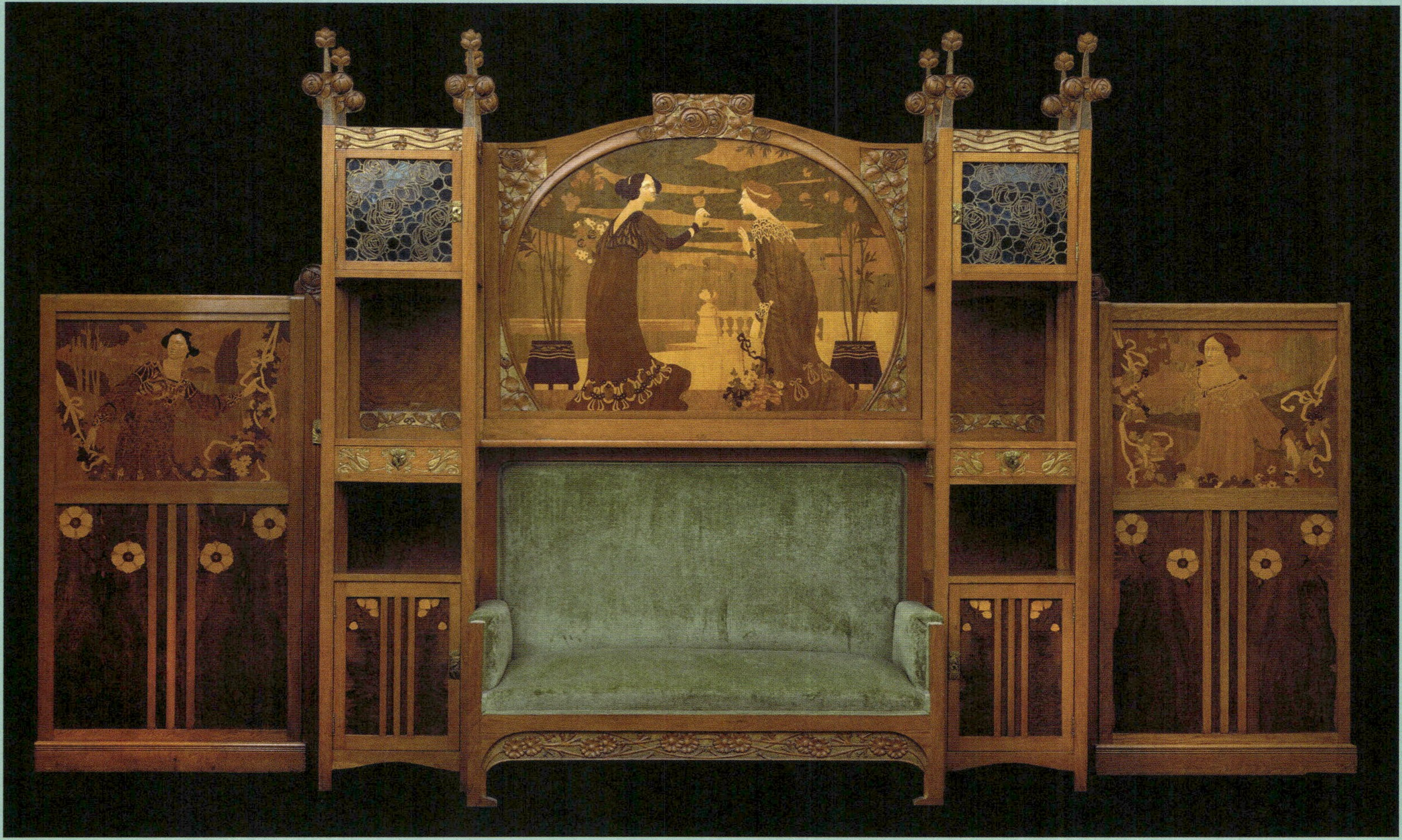

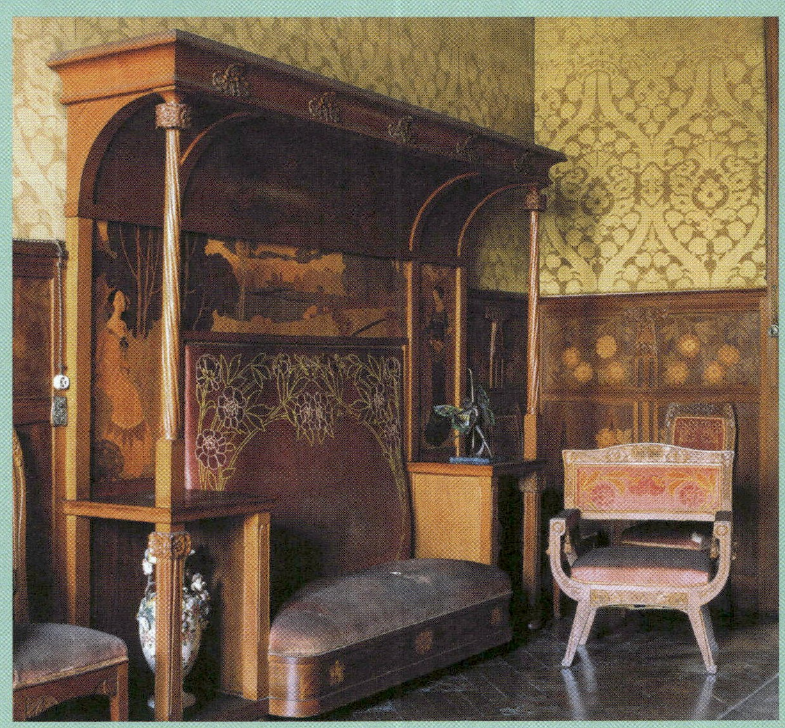

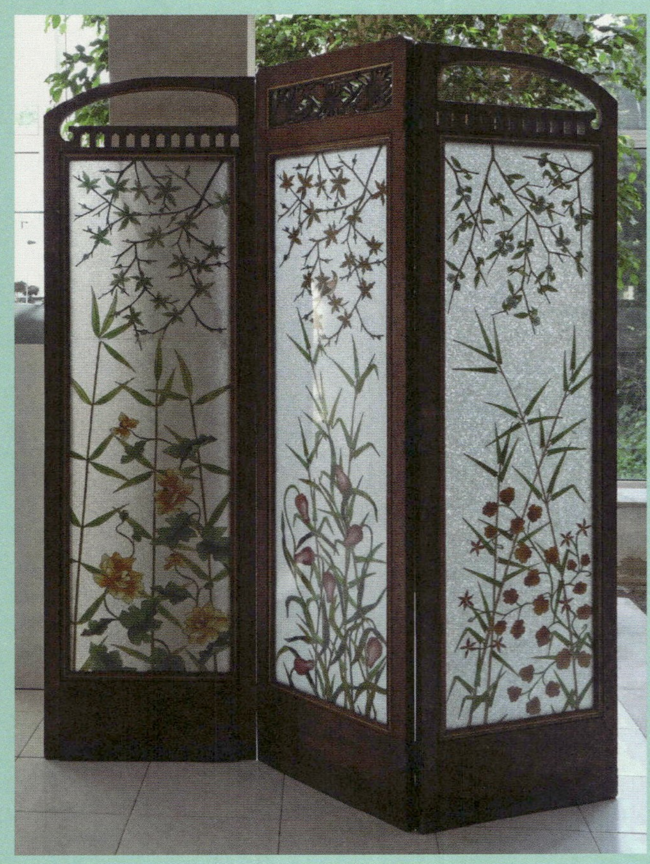

*Left:* Frederic Vidal, folding screen, date unknown, cloisonné glass. Private Collection.

*Top:* Gaspar Homar, dining-room furniture for Casa Lleó i Morera, 1905. Museu Nacional d'Art de Catalunya.
*Above:* Gaspar Homar, living-room furniture for Casa Navàs, Reus, 1905–1906.

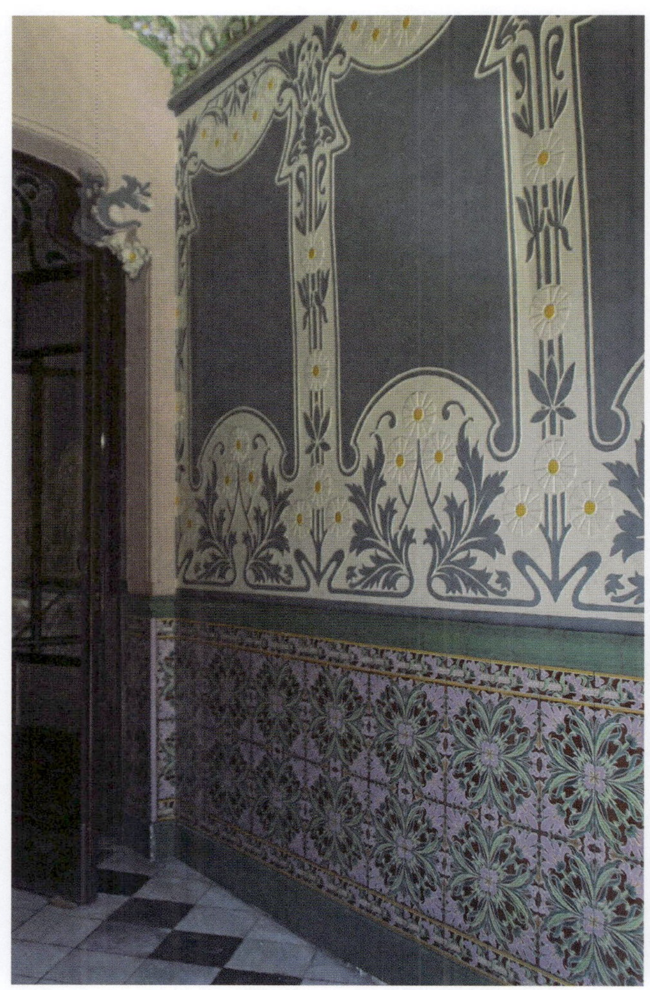

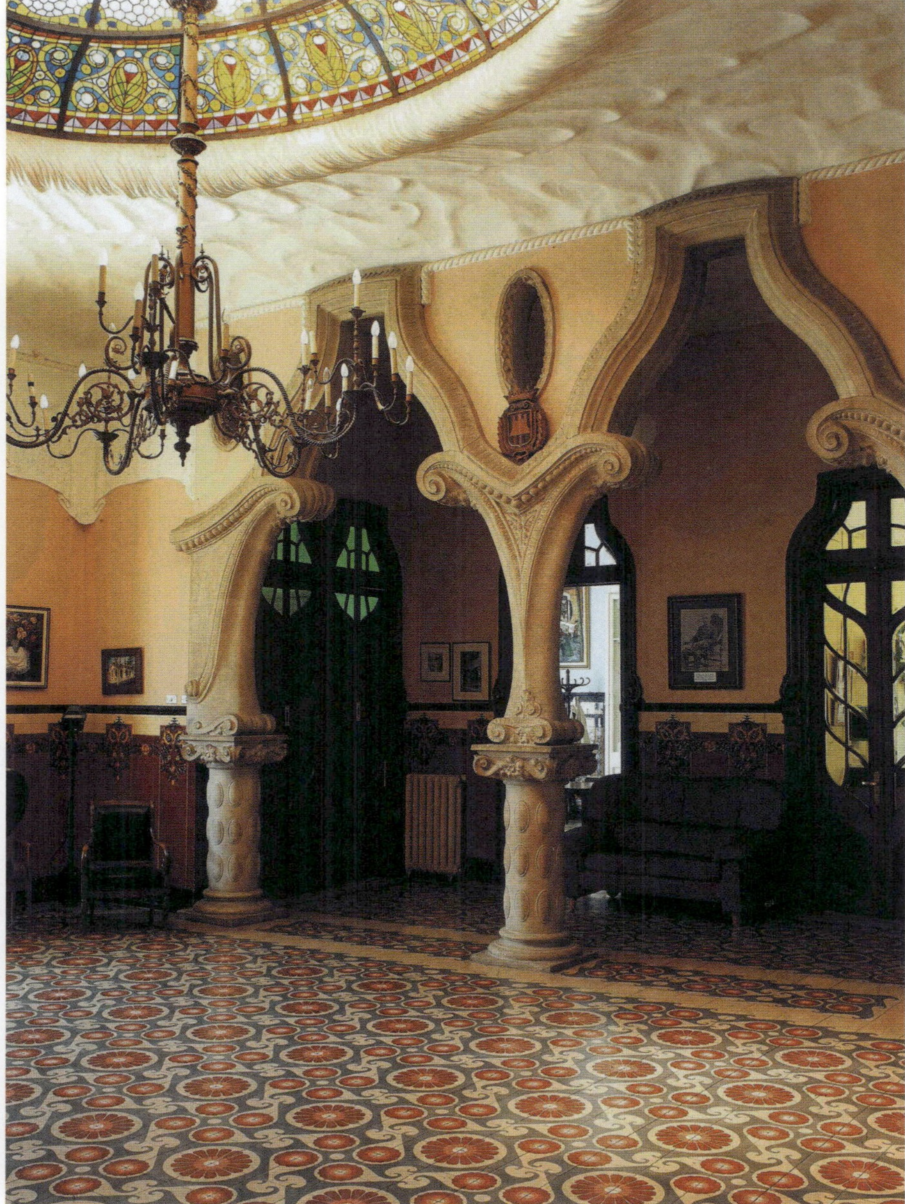

*Above:* Josep Graner i Prat, hallway decoration for Casa Joan Lladó, 1906–1908.
*Right:* Josep M. Miró, hydraulic cement tile floor for Can Pahissa, Vilanova, 1921.

Cloisonné Glass companies. On his return to Barcelona in 1899, Frederic introduced the cloisonné glass technique in Catalonia using materials imported from England, and the interior decoration of many Art Nouveau houses carried out by the Vidal firm would include cloisonné glass objects. There is also some evidence that he introduced the technique in Argentina. Today, Vidal's cloisonné pieces held in museums and private collections throughout the world form what could be the largest surviving representation of this technique.[16]

The work of William Morris and his colleagues was extremely important for Catalan textile design, a field explored by many artists and even architects. Such influence may be traced in designs by Gaspar Homar, Gaudí, Josep Maria Jujol, Antoni Gallissà, Domènech i Montaner and Puig i Cadafalch, and of course the inevitable Alexandre de Riquer. The Modernista designs by the lace-maker Aurora Gutiérrez also drew from Arts and Crafts models. But the greatest Catalan textile designer was Mariano Fortuny (1871–1949). Son of the Orientalist painter Marià Fortuny, he would live most of his life in Venice, though he never lost contact with Catalonia. He was considered by many to be as good as William Morris, and in his time he was so well known throughout Europe that he was mentioned in Marcel Proust's *A la recherche du temps perdu*.[17] Much of his work can be seen today in the Museo Fortuny in Venice, which is in Palazzo Pesaro degli Orfei, where he

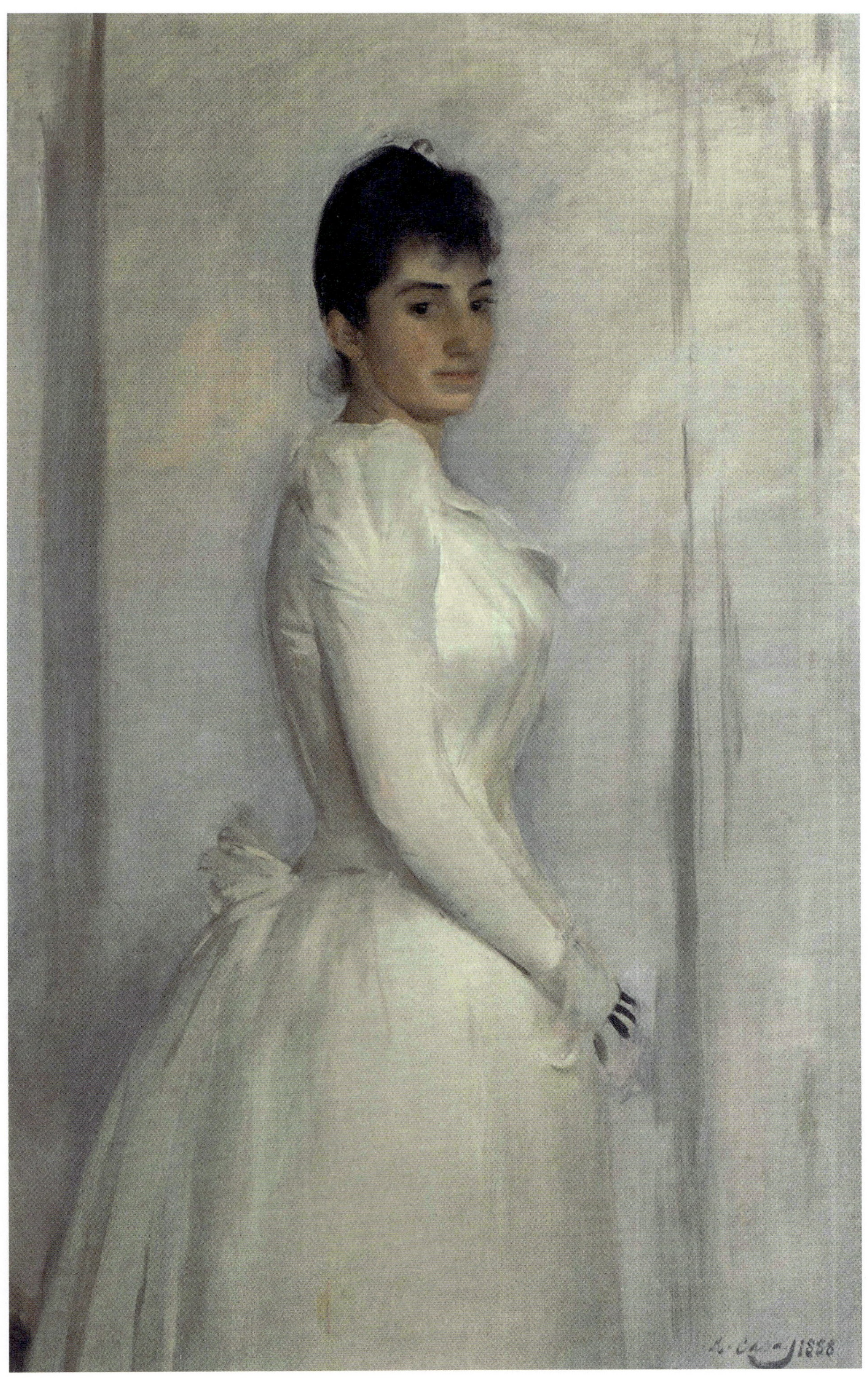

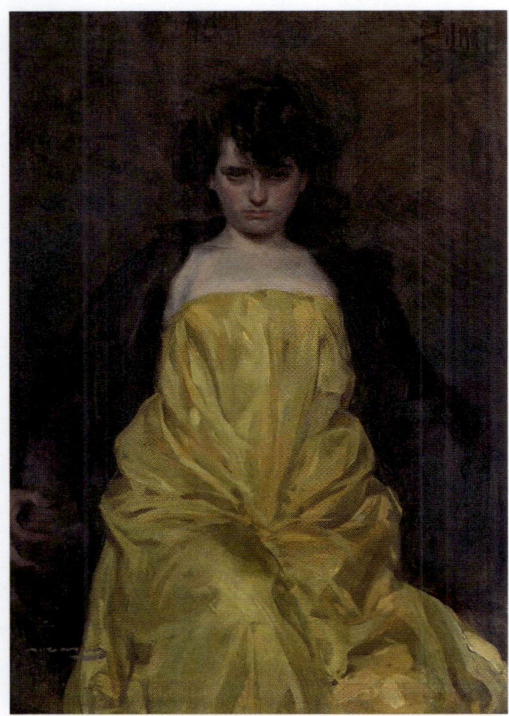

*Opposite:* Ramon Casas, *Portrait of Montserrat Carbó*, 1888, oil on canvas. Museu Nacional d'Art de Catalunya.

*Above:* Ramon Casas, *La Sargantaine (Portrait of Júlia Peraire)*, 1907, oil on canvas.

set up his workshop. The influence of William Morris and the Arts and Crafts Movement can also be found in the sgraffitos of the Modernista buildings' facades and interiors. Sgraffito art would first arrive in Catalonia from Italy in the 16th century, and would evolve through baroque and eclecticism to the impressive and colourful artworks of the Art Nouveau period.[18] Inspiration drawn from English designers contributed to the craft of Modernista glazed ceramic tiles, too, in which the Mudéjar origins and the Manises tradition blended with modern design to produce original creations. Likewise, the new industry of hydraulic cement tiles often dipped into Arts and Crafts design models to produce modern, carpet-like floors for the interiors of Art Nouveau houses. This type of flooring became so habitual and cheap that it would even be installed in working-class tenement flats.

The Aesthetic Movement was important; several Modernista journals, such as *Joventut* or *La Ilustración Ibérica*, would include and celebrate drawings by Aubrey Beardsley. Yet the influence of James McNeill Whistler on Catalan Art Nouveau deserves special mention. Many painters were drawn to him, in part through contemporary Spanish painters such as Zuloaga or Regoyos, but especially thanks to the writings of the most renowned art critic of the time, Raimon Casellas, who first saw Whistler's works on trips to Paris in 1889 and 1893 and described him as 'perhaps the painter who is exercising the strongest influence in French and English art'.[19] Ramon Casas (1866–1932), who in 1881 had moved to Paris to study under Carolus-Duran, soon showed 'Whistlerian' techniques in his work, particularly white-on-white exercises, following Whistler's 'Symphonies in White'. Casas would continue to develop such monochromatic themes and eventually excel in the technique. And, according to Robert Hughes, he would introduce a young Tom Roberts to Whistler's style while the Australian painter was visiting Spain. On returning to his country, Roberts would apply the style to his work, thus initiating the Australian Impressionist movement.[20]

Another great Modernista painter, Santiago Rusiñol, also made frequent stays in Paris and applied Whistler's lessons to his works, particularly in portraits – for example, his 1894 *Female Figure*, which incorporates traits both of Whistler's *Mother* and *Symphony in White No. 2*. It has been said, too, that his depictions of the typical blue courtyards of the seaside town of Sitges are reminiscent of the American painter's style. And some art historians go on to see an influence of Whistler through Rusiñol's blue courtyards in Picasso's 'Blue Period'. For her part, Lluïsa Vidal (1876–1918), daughter of the cabinet-maker Francesc Vidal and one of the best painters of the Modernista movement, was strongly influenced by the English art of the time, despite having studied in Paris at the Julian and Humbert academies. She is known to have declared her fondness for Turner and Constable, and her oil on canvas *Francesca Vidal, Sister of the Artist* (1909) has evident links with Whistler's 1871 portrait of his mother.[21]

The Spanish-American War of 1898, by which Spain lost her last colonies of Cuba and Puerto Rico, as well as the Philippines and Guam, shook Spain to the core. It became known as *'el Desastre de Cuba'* (it still is, today), and the prestige of the Spanish army suffered a severe blow. Spanish nationalists resolved not to lose another inch of territory and sought compensation by expanding their possessions in Africa and by stifling regional aspirations in the Peninsula. In Catalonia, however, people saw things differently.

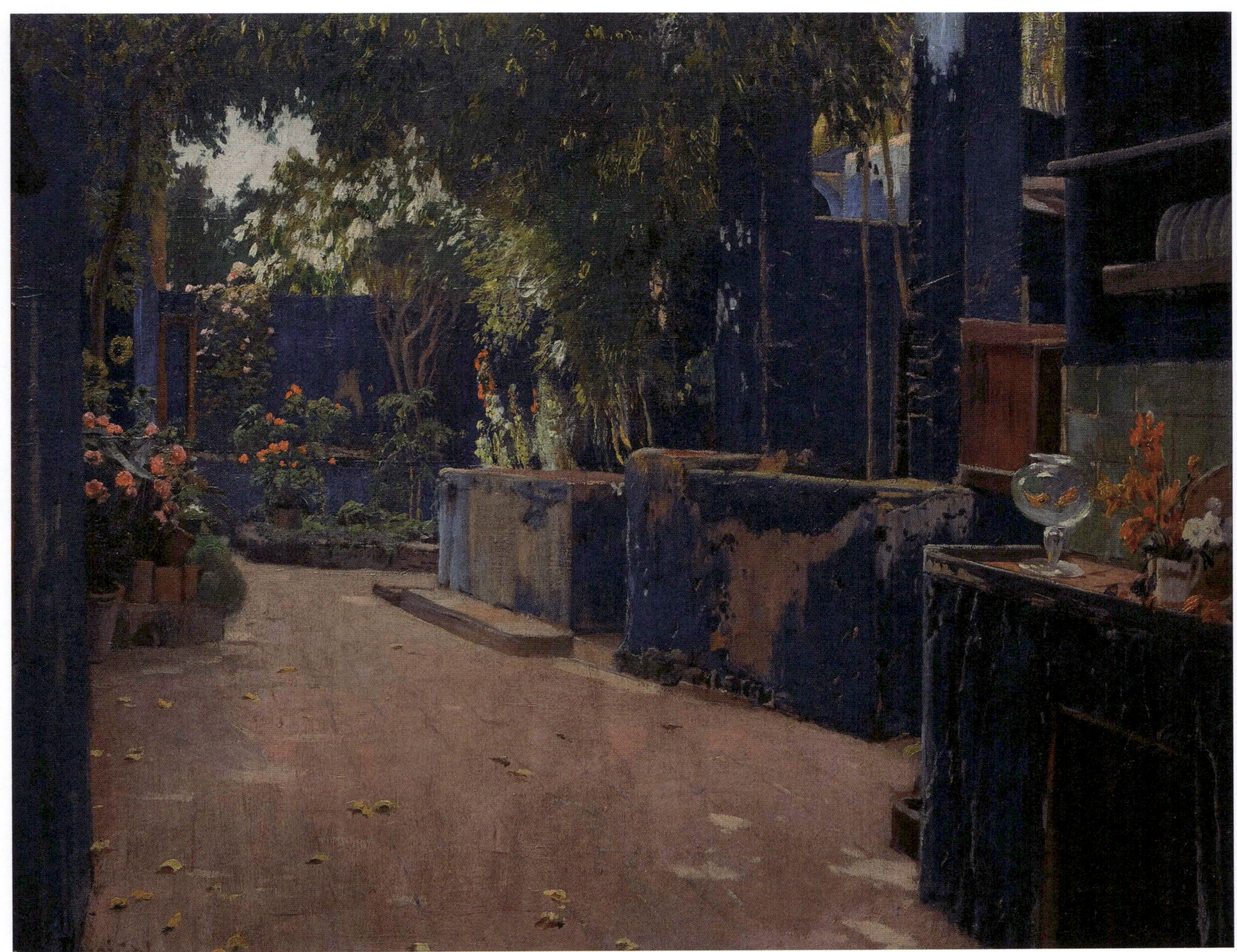



There was sympathy for Cuban independence, which had had the support of many Catalan expatriates on the island,* and some of the most irreverent Modernista writers and editorial cartoonists enjoyed lampooning the wounded Spanish pride. In retaliation, in 1905 a group of rogue army officers raided the satirical weekly *Cu-Cut!* (to which caricaturists such as Opisso, Junceda and Feliu Elies contributed) and the newspaper *La Veu de Catalunya* (The Voice of Catalonia, a conservative Catalanist newspaper with cover and layout designed by Lluís Domènech i Montaner). The affair unleashed a crisis to which Spanish conservatives responded with the approval of a new law, the *Ley de Jurisdicciones*, by which any 'offence' by civilians to the army or to Spanish pride in general was to be tried by military courts.**

Catalan society, on the other hand, reacted by stitching a broad coalition of political parties left and right, *Solidaritat Catalana* (Catalan Solidarity), which took forty-one of the forty-four parliamentary seats in play in the 1907 elections (among the elected was Josep Puig i Cadafalch). This was the first landslide victory of political Catalanism in history, and it had a tremendous impact in all walks of life, including art and architecture. The exaltation of Catalan symbols, such as the four-red-stripe flag and the image of St George, patron saint of Catalonia, would become even more ubiquitous than they had been until then. A good example of this is Domènech i Montaner's Hospital de Sant Pau, with hundreds of representations of the flag depicted

*The first Catalan pro-independence movement is said to have been born in 1906 in Santiago; the present-day pro-independence Catalan flag follows the design of the Cuban flag.
**The cartoonist Feliu Elies (aka *Apa*) would have to flee to Paris in 1911 to avoid trial and certain imprisonment under this law, for a series of cartoons that he published in the satirical weekly *Papitu*.

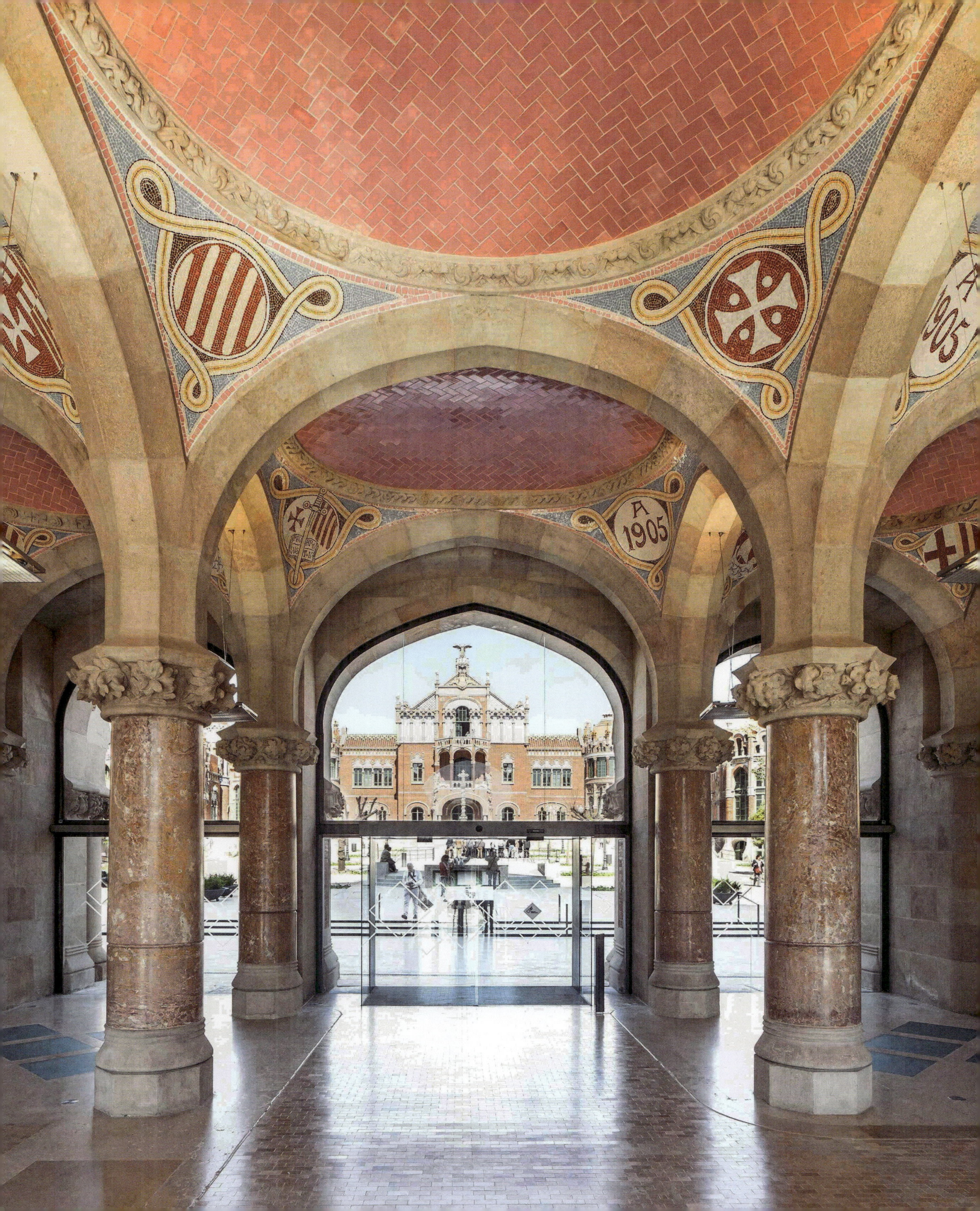

*Opposite:* Antoni Gaudí (1852–1926), chair for Casa Battló, *c.*1906, oak. Museu del Modernisme Català, Barcelona.

in ceramic tile coatings throughout its pavilions. Another example is Casa Batlló, the dreamlike house that Antoni Gaudí refurbished in 1907 with the help of a young Josep Maria Jujol (1879–1949). Its whole facade is a symbolist reference to the legend of St George and the Dragon. The ceramic tile-clad roof is the scaled body of the dragon, pierced by the cross-bearing sword of the warrior saint. The sculpted window openings and iron balconies are the bones and ribs of the beast's victims, while the multicoloured ceramic coating of the facade and the stained-glass windows with colourful circles represent the gems of its treasure hoard. The huge window of the main floor and the main staircase are entrances to the dragon's cavern, an organic interior of wavy walls with no right angles.

Although some of Ruskin's ideas had naturally arrived in Catalonia through the Pre-Raphaelites and the Arts and Crafts, and in Robert de la Sizeranne's book *Ruskin et la réligion de la beauté*, ironically it was not until his death in 1900 that his writings received full attention. Leading Modernista authors like Joan Maragall (1860–1911) and Pompeu Gener (1848–1920) wrote extensive obituaries, and soon the English writer's work became available in Catalan, much of it translated by the Montoliu brothers. In 1901, the magazine *L'Avenç* published a collection of writings translated by Cebrià de Montoliu, and in 1903 his brother Manuel (1877–1961) would publish *Modern Painters* (with the title *Natura*) and *Sesame and Lillies* (as *Els lliris del jardí de la reina*). In 1903, the painter and designer Sebastià Junyent (1865–1908) would write an article in the journal *Joventut* in which he would claim that Ruskin 'contributed to make England the birthplace of what here we have come to call Modernisme'.[22] The architect Jeroni Martorell (1876–1951) would also write extensively about Ruskin, whom he claimed 'strove after beauty only as a by-product of his pursuit of perfection'.[23]

Furthermore, Ruskin's model for the education of women was incorporated into the founding philosophy of Catalan feminism. More in line with French Social Catholicism than the British suffragettes, the early Catalan women's movement conceived an education that would enable women to earn professional respect and dignity without forfeiting their traditional role as mothers and housewives. This would be reflected in the women's magazine *Feminal*, founded in 1907 by the writer and composer Carme Karr (1865–1943). It received contributions from Modernista writers such as Dolors Monserdà (1845–1919) and Caterina Albert (aka Víctor Català, 1869–1966), and painters like Lluïsa Vidal, as well as Pepita Teixidor (who participated socially in the Catalan Art Nouveau movement, although her paintings were not considered Modernista).

The years from 1895 to 1910 were the most intense and fruitful of Catalan Modernisme, especially after 1900 when it incorporated Francophone Art Nouveau into its artistic melting pot. In this golden period the greatest works of Catalan Art Nouveau would be designed. Among them, the Palau de la Música Catalana (Palace of Catalan Music), created by Lluís Domènech i Montaner between 1905 and 1908, is perhaps the best example of *Gesamkunstwerk* in Catalan Art Nouveau. In this formidable building, which still serves its function as a concert hall, the renowned architectural 'orchestra conductor' directed a team of first-class artists and artisans to create a dreamlike symbolist ensemble featuring superb sculpture, wrought ironwork, ceramics, stained glass and woodwork in a fabulous decorative display that even contemporaries saw as rather excessive.

*Below:* Antoni Gaudí, chair, *c.*1890, ash wood. Museu del Modernisme Català, Barcelona.

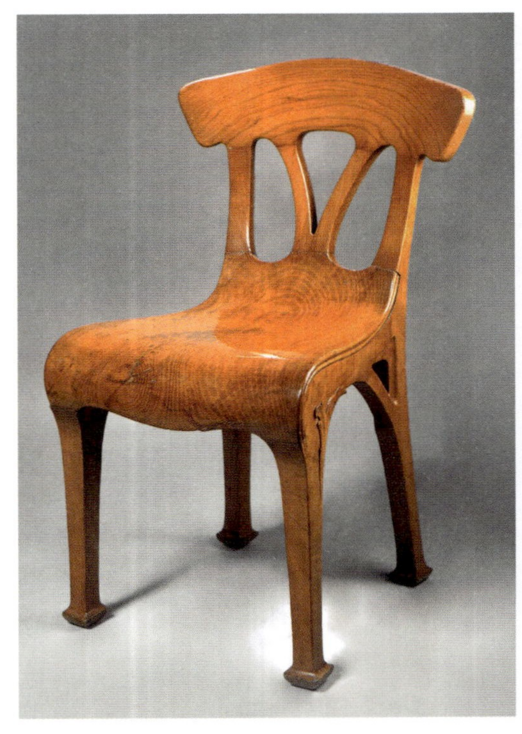

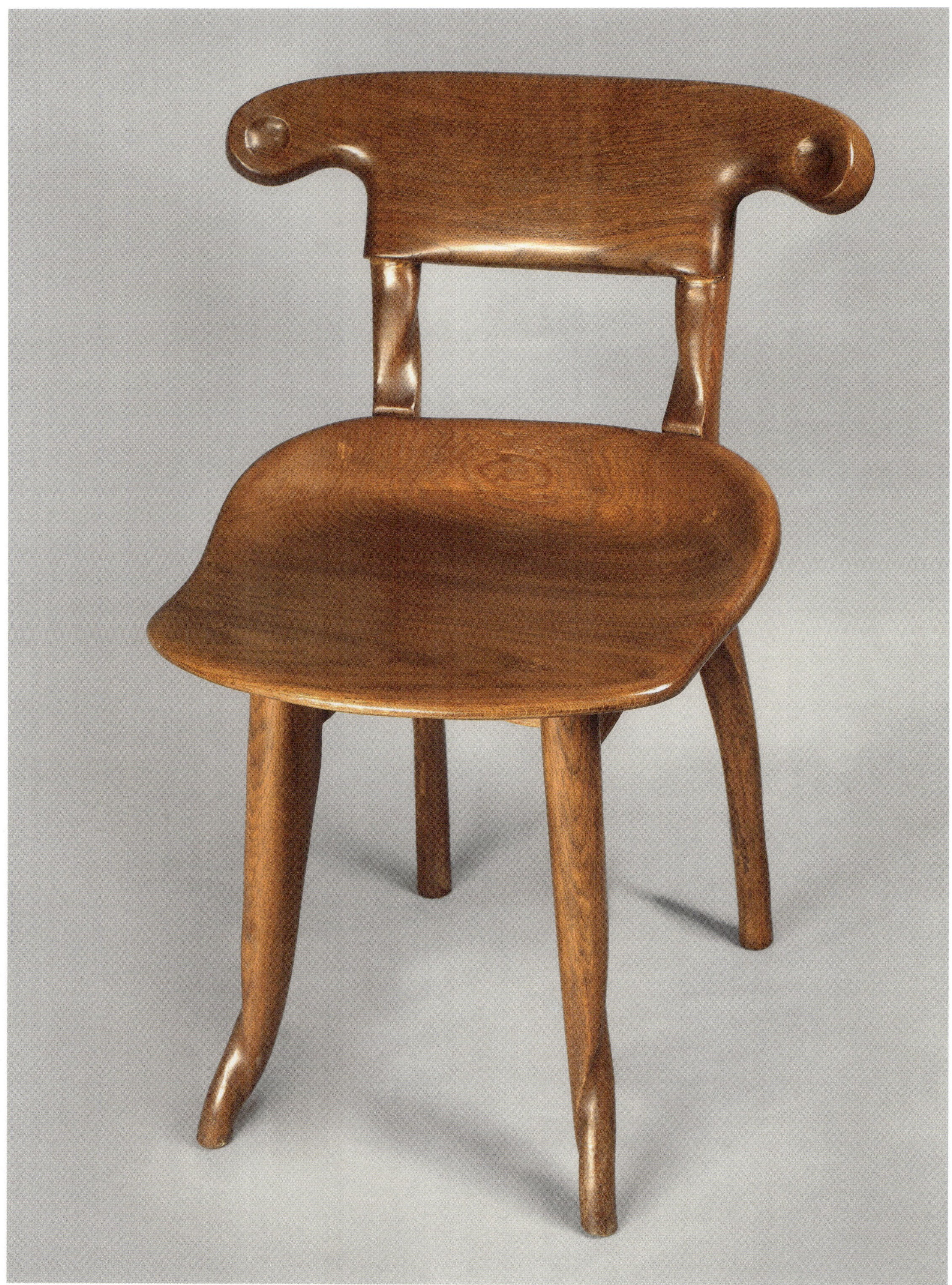

Yet if Domènech's Palau was the utmost of Catalan Art Nouveau décor, the paradigm of modernity would be Antoni Gaudí's Casa Milà. Its famous massive undulating stone facade – which earned it its popular nickname *La Pedrera* (the Quarry) – is deceptive, for it is in fact a curtain wall. The huge apartment building is supported by a steel and concrete armature, the first of its kind in Barcelona. A daring experiment at the time, which required enormous efforts of calculation from Gaudí and his engineer Josep Bayó. The building also included an underground parking space, again the first in the city at the special request of the promoter Pere Milà, who was one of the earliest motor-car owners in Spain. Raised in 1906–1912 on a ground plan with three interior courtyards to bring natural light and ventilation to all the rooms, Casa Milà incorporated everything that today is still considered essential for quality of life: from spacious kitchens and bathrooms with water closets (both with tiled walls for improved hygiene), to water, electricity and gas supply, central heating, sewerage systems and even several lifts, all planned in from the first design. This was to be the last house built by Gaudí – from then on, he would devote himself exclusively to the Sagrada Família church – but he did indeed impart a last and lasting lesson on modernity to 20th-century architects!

*Below:* Lluís Domènech i Montaner, Palau de la Música Catalana, 1909–1912.

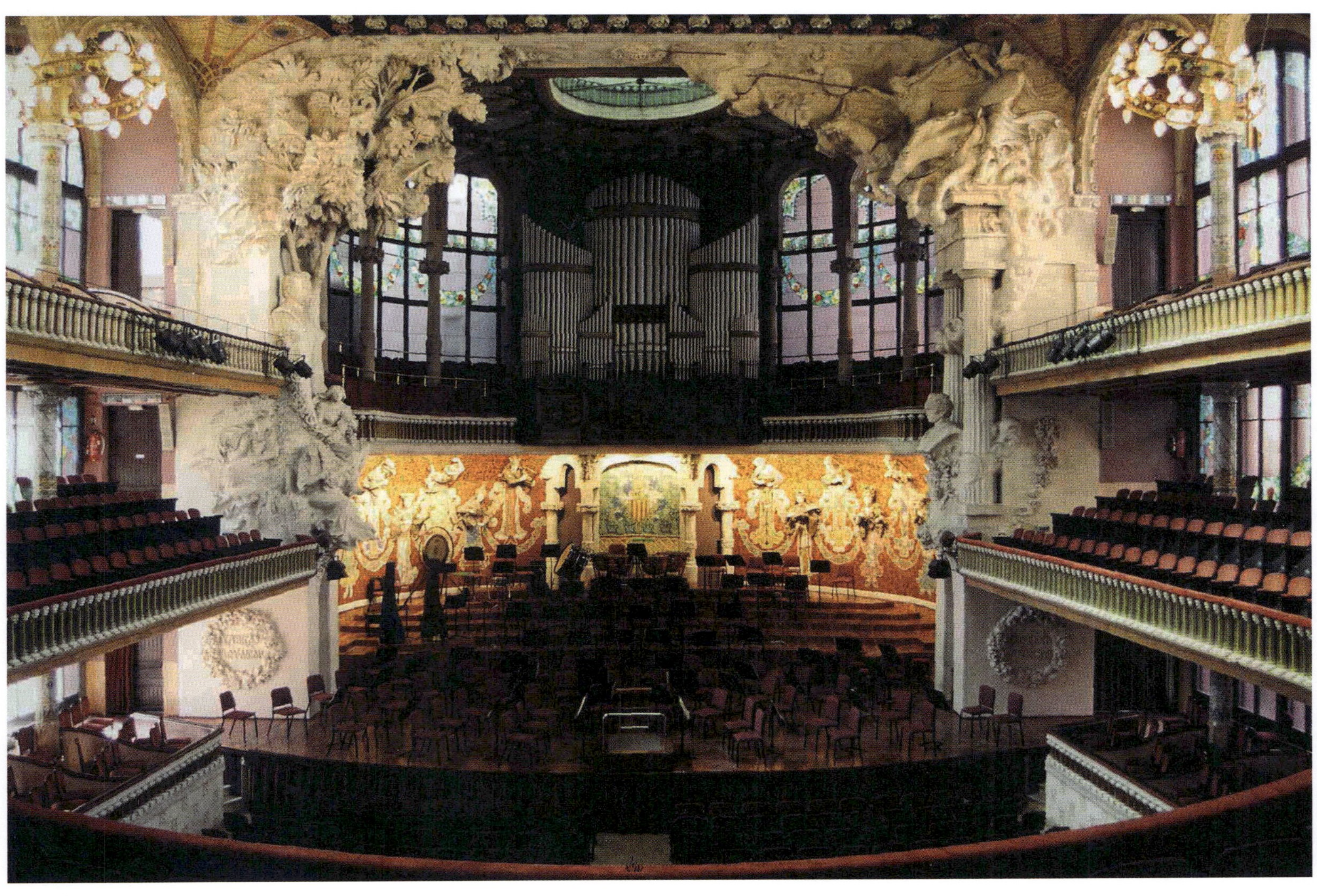

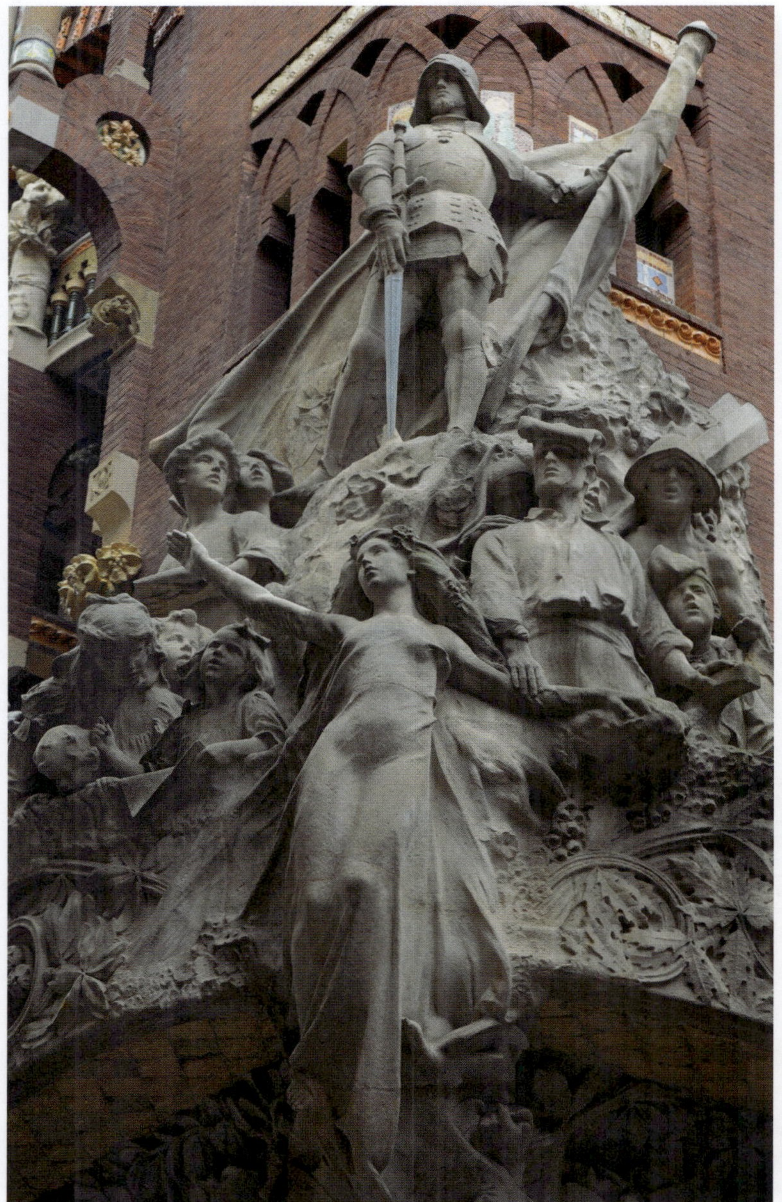

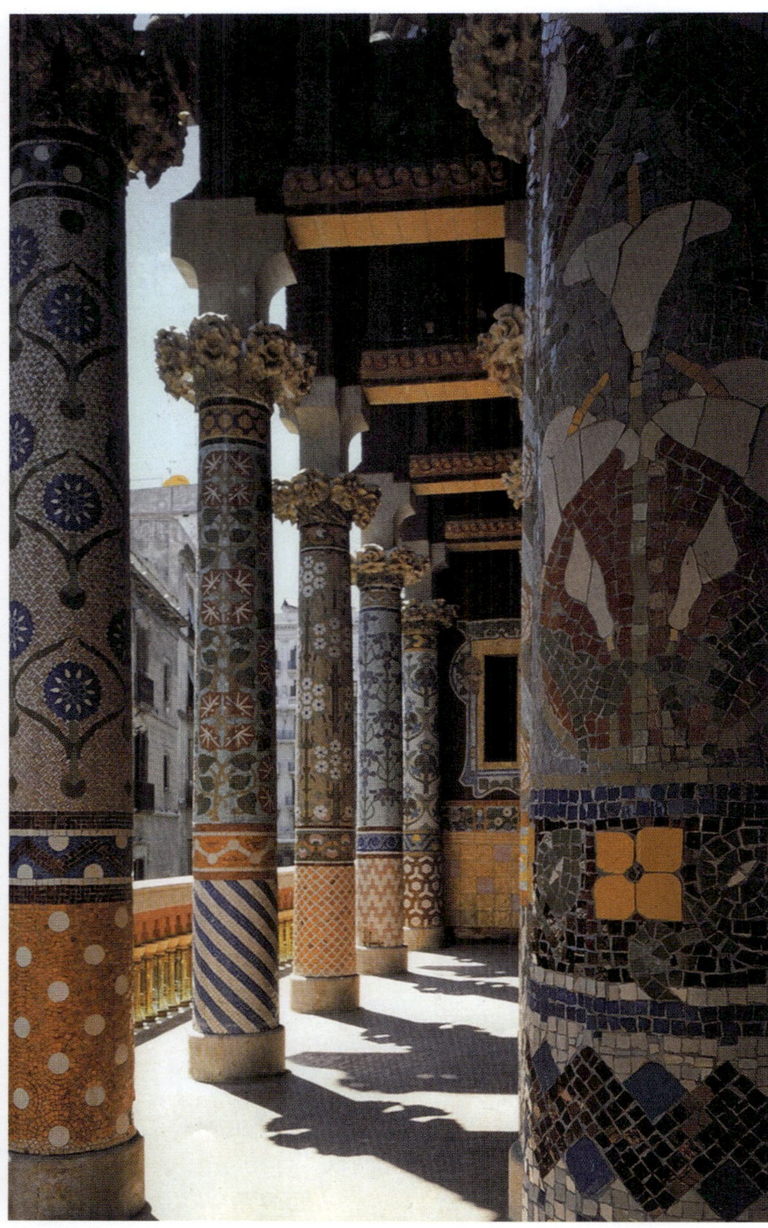

*Above and right:* Lluís Domènech i Montaner, Palau de la Música Catalana, 1909–1912.

English art, too, would have its *grand finale* in this 1895–1910 phase. In 1906 Alexandre de Riquer was appointed curator of the English section of the *Fifth Exhibition of Beaux Arts and Industrial Arts* of 1907 in Barcelona. This gave him the chance for another long trip to England, where he met Walter Crane and Arthur Rackham and contacted William Morris's Kelmscott Press. He would manage to bring back, on loan or acquired, 231 works by an impressive roster of names, including Rackham, Whistler, Edward Burne-Jones, Alice Woodward, Marc-Louis Solon and Alexander Fisher, among others.[24] They were all shown in a salon decorated by Riquer himself, following a design by Frank Brangwyn. The section, which defined England as 'master and protector of the arts', was a great success.[25]

But new winds were blowing in Catalonia. Many artists had turned their interest towards Germanic Art Nouveau, especially the Viennese Secession. And Catalan art would soon be convulsed by an anti-Modernista reaction, the Noucentista neo-classic movement. This was spurred on in 1909 by two events: the discovery of new artistic treasures at the Roman and Greek ruins in Empúries, on the Costa Brava, and by what came to be known as the *Setmana Tràgica*. This 'Tragic Week' began with a workers' strike against forced drafting of men to fight in Morocco, evolved into chaos with the sacking and burning of convents and churches, and ended in a bloodbath when the army was sent in to quell the revolt. Horrified by such violence, the

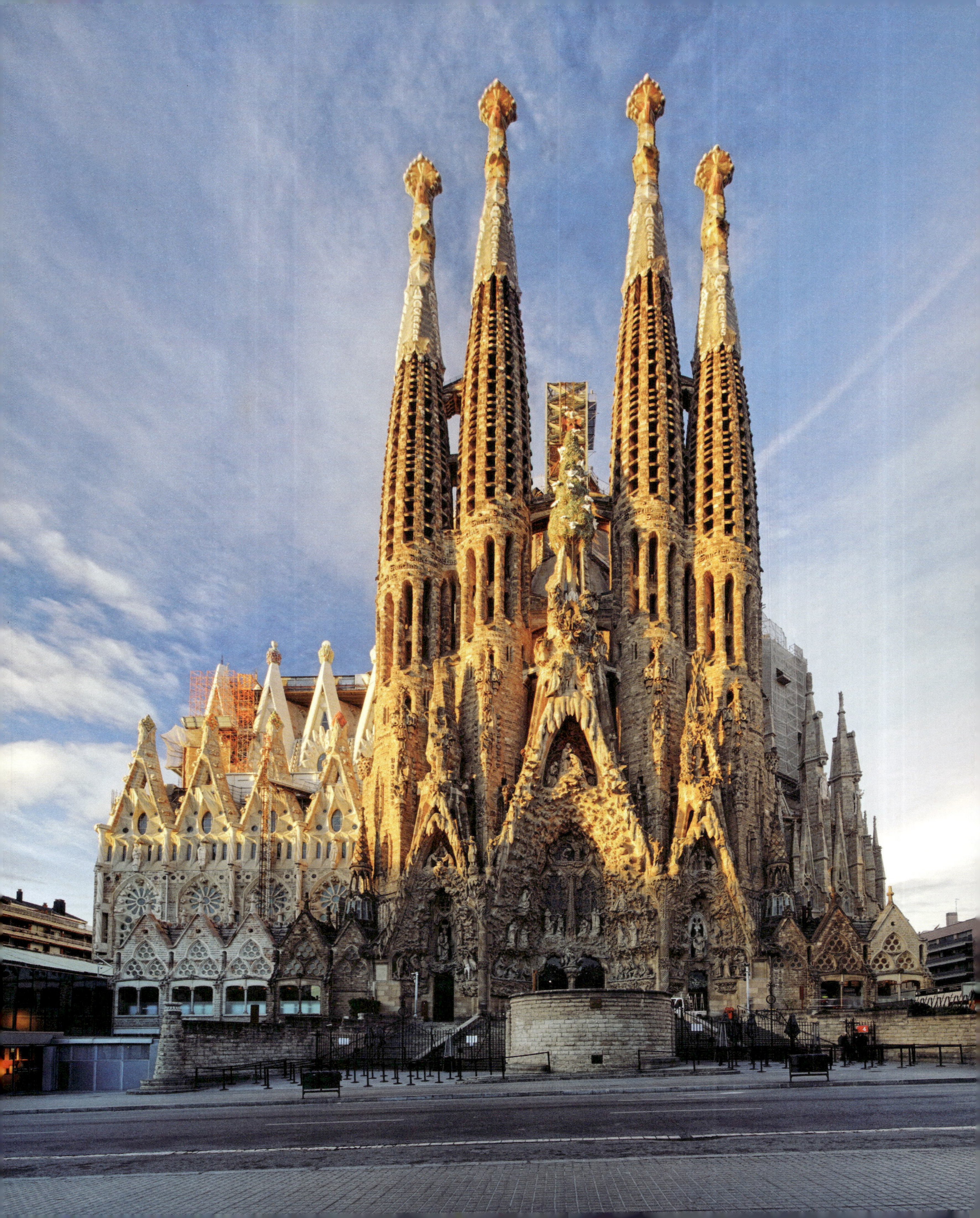

*Opposite:* Antoni Gaudí, Sagrada Família, 1883 (present day).

well-to-do decided to abandon the 'excesses' of Modernisme and embraced the new sobriety of Noucentisme, which espoused an idealised Greco-Roman sense of virtue and chastity, the simplicity of rural Mediterranean life and a concept of modernity more akin to scientific rigour and technical education than to adventurous innovation.*

Several artists, such as the architect Josep Puig i Cadafalch, would join the new movement, but others would stay loyal to Modernisme until it petered out in the 1920s. In other words, the decline of Art Nouveau in Catalonia followed a different pattern and lasted longer than in most other European cities. It could be argued, also, that the immediate heritage of Modernisme inspired a number of contemporary artists.[26] Undoubtedly Pablo Picasso, whose brief Modernista phase in Barcelona was a key stepping stone in his professional career. The symbolist spirit of his Blue and Rose Periods testifies to this: He had moved to Paris in 1900, in fact, on the advice of his Catalan friends who were enamoured of French Art Nouveau. Also Joan Miró, who as a young man had been a member of the St Luke Circle, met many of the Modernista artists and participated in their passion for English art. Miró's organic and biomorphic forms clearly owe a debt to Gaudí. His use of the broken ceramic *trencadís* technique overtly recognises his great forebear, and his 1979 series of twenty-one watercolours and collages named *Gaudí* would attest to that.[27] And, of course, Salvador Dalí, who relished shocking the 20th-century art establishment by declaring his love for Modernisme and Art Nouveau and famously contributed an article to the Parisian magazine *Minotaure* in 1933 entitled 'On the Terrifying and Edible Beauty of Modern Style Architecture'.

§

*The *Setmana Tràgica* had another, more anecdotal effect on Gaudí's plan for Casa Milà, *La Pedrera*. The first designs included a huge statue of the Virgin Mary flanked by archangels, crowning the central facade of the building. But after the revolt – what with all the church and convent-burning – the promoter, Pere Milà, decided it would be safer to forgo the sculpture.

ENDNOTES

1   https//ajuntament.barcelona.cat/turisme.
2   Joan Molet, 'Catalan Modernisme, Between two World Fairs', *coupDefouet* magazine, 2013, No. 21, pp.38–45. Online version available at www. artnouveau.eu.
3   Castellanos, 'Verdaguer i el prerafaelisme. Algunes notes per a un estudi', in VVAA, *Verdaguer, un geni poetic*, 2002.
4   Robert Hughes, *Barcelona* (London: The Harvill Press, 2001 / 1992), p.321.
5   Mireia Freixa, 'Arts and Crafts in Catalonia and Great Britain in the 19th and 20th Centuries: Parallels and Contrasts', paper pending publication, 2020.
6   Jordi Bonet and Núria Gil, 'The English Stained Glass in Palau Güell', *coupDefouet*, 2019, No. 32, pp.16–23. Online version available at www. artnouveau.eu.
7   Hughes, *Barcelona*, p.459.
8   Mariàngela Cerdà, 'Els prerafaeilites anglo-catalans', in *Enciclopèdia de Catalunya*, 2014; www.enciclopedia.cat.
9   Eliseu Trenc, 'Alexandre de Riquer i les arts decoratives', in *EMBLECAT, Revista de l'Associació Catalana d'Estudis d'Emblemàtica, Art i Societat*, 2017, No. 6.
10  Eliseu Trenc and Alan Yates, *Alexandre de Riquer (1856–1920): The British Connection in Catalan Modernisme* (Sheffield: The Anglo-Catalan Society Occasional Publications & Sheffield Academic Press Ltd, 1988), p.26.
11  Ibid., p.28.
12  Francesc Quílez Corella, 'La incidencia del moviment Arts and Crafts en l'art gràfic català', in Manuel Fontán Del Junco and María Zozaya (eds), *William Morris i Companyia: el moviment Arts & Crafts a Gran Bretanya* (Madrid: Museu Nacional d'Art de Catalunya & Fundación Juan March, 2018), p.200.
13  Freixa, 'Arts and Crafts in Catalonia and Great Britain'.
14  Mariàngels Fondevila, 'Anglaterra, "mestra i protectora de les arts"', 2018, in Fontán Del Junco and Zozaya (eds), *William Morris i Companyia*, p.191.
15  Mariàngels Fondevila, 'The ensemblier Gaspar Homar: A pioneer in the revival of marquetry worj', 2013, Paper presented at the 4th Historical Lab of the Réseau Art Nouveau Network, Aveiro, in VVAA, *Art Nouveau and Ecology. Miscellany*, 2015.
16  Núria Gil and Jordi Bonet, 'Cloisonné Glass, an Art Nouveau Phenomenon', *coupDefouet*, 2015, No. 26, pp.27–37. Online version available at www. artnouveau.eu.
17  Fondevila, 'Anglaterra, "mestra i protectora de les arts"', p.196.
18  Daniel Pifarré, 'The Success of Art Nouveau Sgraffito in Catalan Architecture', *coupDefouet*, 2020, No. 33, pp.24–37. Online version available at www.artnouveau.eu.
19  Juan C. Bejarano, 'L'esteticisme de Whistler i la seva recepció a la Catalunya modernista'', in Irene Gras, Cristina Rodríguez-Samaniego and Núria Aragonés (eds), *Catalunya-Amèrica: L'art entre el viatge i l'exili (s. XIX i XX)*, (Barcelona: Edicions de la Universitat de Barcelona, 2018); e-pub at www. publicacions.ub.edu.
20  Hughes, *Barcelona*, p.493.
21  Bejarano, 'L'esteticisme de Whistler'.
22  Fondevila, 'Anglaterra, "mestra i protectora de les arts"', p.194.
23  Ibid.
24  Francesc Quílez Corella, 'La incidencia del moviment Arts and Crafts en l'art gràfic català', in Fontán Del . and Zozaya (eds), *William Morris i Companyia*, p.199.
25  Fondevila, 'Anglaterra, "mestra i protectora de les arts"', p.185.
26  Paul Greenhalgh, 'Art Nouveau, the First International Modern Style', Conference delivered in Barcelona, 2014, available in video format at www. artnouveau.eu.
27  Marta Palau, 'Miró: penso en Gaudí', in the newspaper *Avui*, 18 June 2019. In the summer of 2019, the Fundació Miró in Barcelona organised the exhibition *Miró-Gaudí-Gomis*, devoted to Miró's relationship with Gaudí, as seen through the lens of the photographer Joaquim Gomis.

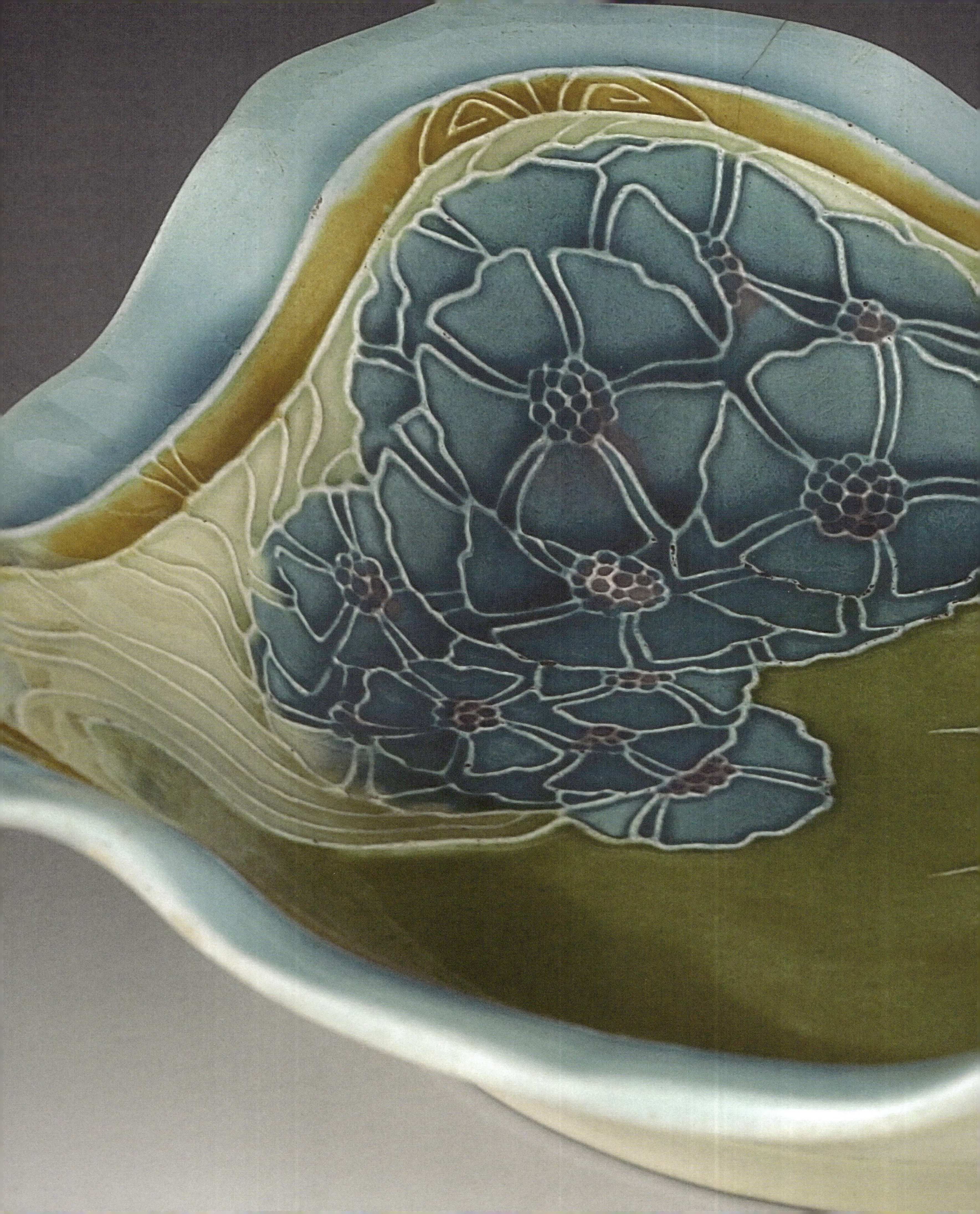

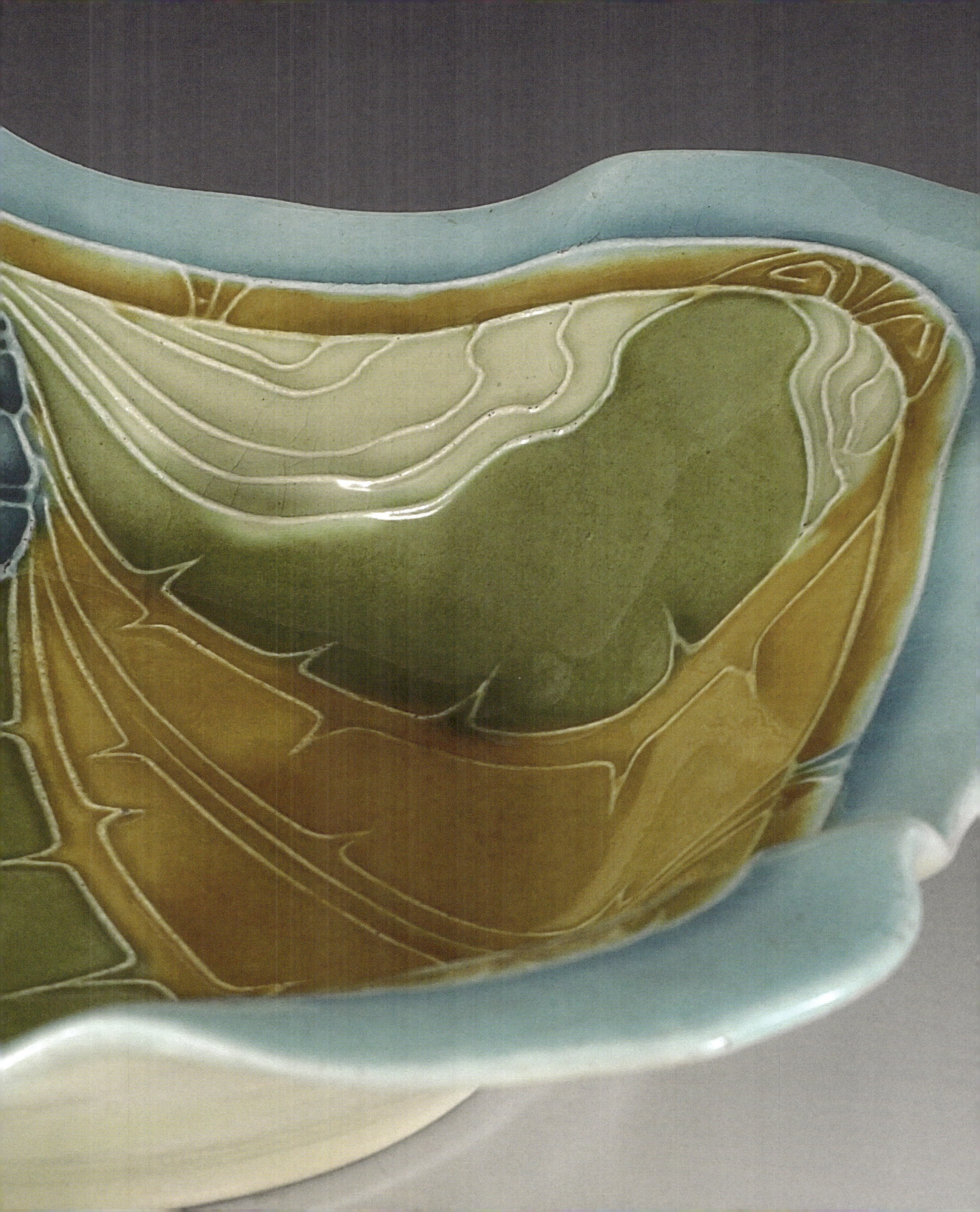

# ~Bibliography~


## PRIMARY SOURCES
### JOURNALS
*Architectural Record* (New York, from 1891)
*L'Architecture* (Paris, 1888–1939)
*L'Art Décoratif* (Paris, 1898–1914)
*Art et Décoration* (Paris, 1897)
*The Art Journal* (London, 1839–1912)
*L'Art Moderne* (Brussels, 1881–1914)
*Le Costume au Théâtre* (Paris, 1886–1890s)
*The Craftsman* (New York, 1901–1916)
*La Lanterne* (Paris, 1877–1938)
*The Magazine of Art* (London and New York, 1878–1904)
*La Nouvelle Revue* (Paris, 1879–1940)
*Le Pays* (Paris, 1899–1909)
*La Plume* (Paris, 1889–1914)
*Revue des Arts Décoratifs* (Paris, 1879–1902)
*Revue Littéraire et Artistique* (Paris, 1879–1882)
*The Studio* (London, 1893–1964)
*Le Théâtre* (Paris, 1898–1914)

### BOOKS
Alexandre, Arsène, *Les Reines de L'Aiguille, Modistes et Couturiers* (Paris: Théophile Belin, 1902)
Batchelder, Ernest, *The Principles of Design* (Chicago: Inland Printer Company, 1911)
Bayard, Émile, *Le Style Moderne* (Paris: Garnier Frères, 1919)
*La bijouterie française au XIXe siècle (1800–1900)*, (Paris: H. Fleury, 1906–1908), Vol. 3
Comte, Jules, *L'Art à L'Exposition Universelle de 1900* (Paris: Librairie de l'art ancien et moderne, 1900)
Crane, Walter, *The Claims of Decorative Art* (Boston; New York: Houghton, Mifflin and Co., 1892)
Dresser, Christopher, *The Art of Decorative Design* (London: Day and Son, 1862)
Gonse, Louis, and Lostalet, Alfred de, *Exposition Universelle de 1889, Les Beaux Arts et les Arts Décoratifs* (Paris: Le Temps, 1900)
Guérin, Daniel (ed.), *Paul Gauguin: Writings of a savage* (New York: De Capo, 1978)
Hulme, F.E., *Art Studies from Nature, as applied to design, for the use of architects, designers, and manufacturers* (London: Chapman and Hall, 1872, 1902)
Lahor, Jean, *William Morris et le mouvement nouveau de l'art décoratif, Conférence à Genève le 13 janvier 1897* (Geneva: Ch. Eggimann & Co., 1897)
Le Corbusier, *The Decorative Art of Today* (Paris: 1925)
Lilley, A.E. and Midgley, W., *A Book of Studies in Plant Form* (London: Richard Clay and Sons, 1902)
Mourey, Gabriel, *Passer le détroit: La vie et l'art à Londres* (Paris: P. Ollendorf, 1895)
Prisse d'Avennes, Émile, *The Decorative Art of Arabia* (Paris: Morel et Cie, 1877)
Racinet, Albert, *The Encyclopedia of Ornament* (London: Henry Sotheran, 1873)
Symons, Arthur, *Aubrey Beardsley* (London: John Baker, 1898, reprinted 1966)
Wilde, Oscar, *L'Envoi* (Philadelphia: J.M. Stoddart and Co., 1882)

## SECONDARY SOURCES
### GENERAL TEXTS
Belanger Grafton, Carol, *Art Nouveau: The Essential Reference* (New York: Dover Publications Inc., 2015)
*coupDefouet*, the magazine of the Art Nouveau European Route (2003–2019)
Dorra, Henri, *Symbolist Art Theories: A critical anthology* (Berkeley, CA: University of California Press, 1994)
Duncan, Alastair, *Art Nouveau* (London: Thames & Hudson, 1994)
Garelick, Rhonda K., *Electric Salome: Loie Fuller's Performance of Modernism* (Princeton, NJ: Princeton University Press, 2007)
Geitner, Amanda and Hazell, Emma (eds), *The Anderson Collection of Art Nouveau* (Norwich: Sainsbury Centre for Visual Arts, 2003)
Greenhalgh, Paul (ed.), *Art Nouveau 1890–1914* (London and New York: V&A Publications and Harry N. Abrams, 2000)
Greenhalgh, Paul, *The Essential Art Nouveau* (London: V&A Publications, 2000)
Greenhalgh, Paul, *Modernism in Design* (London: Reaktion Books, 1990)
*Journal of Design History* (Oxford, from 1988)
Masini, Lara Vinca, *Art Nouveau* (London: Thames & Hudson, 1984)
Papadakis, Andreas (ed.), *Art Nouveau: An architectural indulgence* (London: New Architecture, 2000)
Russell, Frank, *Art Nouveau Architecture* (London: Academy, 1983)
Sembach, Klaus-Jurgen, *Art Nouveau: Utopia, reconciling the irreconcilable* (Cologne: Taschen, 2016)
Van de Velde, Henry, *Récit de ma vie: Anvers-Bruxelles-Paris-Berlin. I. 1863–1900*, with a commentary by Anne Van Loo (Brussels: Flammarion / Versa, 1992)
Wood, Ghislaine, *Art Nouveau and the Erotic* (London: V&A Publications, 2000)

### BELGIUM
Adriaenssens, Werner and Aubry, Françoise, *Philippe Wolfers: Civilisation et Barbarie* (Brussels: Fondation Roi Baudouin, 2002)
Adriaenssens, Werner and Steel, Raf, *La dynastie Wolfers: De l'Art Nouveau à l'Art déco* (Antwerp: Pandora, 2006)
Aubry, Françoise, Vandenbreeden, Jos and Lautwein, Reiner, *Horta: Art Nouveau to Modernism* (Ghent: Ludion Press, 1996)
Cauchie, Paul, *Architecte, peintre, décorateur* (Brussels: Edition Maison Cauchie, 1994)
Delhaye, Jean and Dierkens-Aubry, Françoise, *La Maison du Peuple de Victor Horta* (Brussels: Atelier Vokaer, 1987)
Dernie, David and Carew-Cox, Alastair, *Victor Horta: The architect of Art Nouveau* (London: Thames & Hudson, 2018)
Duliere, Cécile (ed.), *Victor Horta: Mémoires* (Brussels: Ministry of the French Community of Belgium, 1985)
Goslar, Michèle, *Victor Horta 1861–1947* (Brussels: Fondation Pierre Lahaut et Fonds Mercator, 2012)
Kuenzli, Katherine M., *Henry van de Velde: Designing Modernism* (New Haven, CT, and London: Yale University Press, 2019)
Loyer, François, *Paul Hankar: La naissance de l'Art Nouveau* (Brussels: Archives d'Architecture Moderne, 1986)
Loyer, François and Delhaye, Jean, *Victor Horta: Hôtel Tassel 1893–1895* (Brussels: AAM, 1986)
Luwel, M. and Bruneel-Hye de Crom, M., *Tervueren 1897* (Tervueren: Musée Royal de l'Afrique Centrale, 1967)
Mesnil du Buisson, Etienne and Bigot, Françoise, *Serrurier-Bovy, un créateur précurseur 1858–1910* (Dijon: Editions Faton, 2008)
Réseau Art Nouveau Network, *Art Nouveau and Ecology. Miscellany* (Brussels: Réseau Art Nouveau Network & Bruxelles Développement urbain, Ministère de la Région de Bruxelles-Capitale, 2015)
Sembach, Klaus-Jurgen, *Henry Van De Velde* (London: Thames & Hudson, 1989)

BRITAIN
Booth, Michael R., *Victorian Spectacular Theatre 1850–1910*, Theatre Production Series (London: Routledge and Kegan Paul, 1981)
Briggs, Asa (ed.), *William Morris: Selected writings and designs* (London: Pelican, 1962)
Brown, Julia Prewitt, *Cosmopolitan Criticism: Oscar Wilde's Philosophy of Art* (Charlottesville, VA: University of Virginia Press, 1997)
Calloway, Stephen, *Aubrey Beardsley* (London: V&A Publications, 1998)
Cormack, Peter, *Arts and Crafts Stained Glass* (New Haven, CT, and London: Paul Mellon Centre for the Study of British Art and Yale University Press, 2015)
Crawford, Alan, *C.R. Ashbee, Architect, Designer, and Romantic Socialist* (London and New Haven, CT: Yale University Press, 1985)
Dormant, Richard, *Albert Gilbert* (London: Paul Mellon Centre, 1985)
Ellmann, Richard, *Oscar Wilde* (London: Penguin, 1989)
Evengelista, Stephan (ed.), *The Reception of Oscar Wilde in Europe* (London: Continuum, 2010)
Fontán del Junco, Manuel and Zozaya, María (eds), *William Morris i Companyia: el moviment Arts & Crafts a Gran Bretanya* (Madrid: Museu Nacional d'Art de Catalunya & Fundación Juan March, 2018)
Gould, Veronica Franklin, *Mary Seton Watts: Unsung heroine of Art Nouveau* (London: The Watts Gallery, 1998)
Halen, Widar, *Christopher Dresser* (London: Phaidon, 1990)
Hamerton, Ian, *W.A.S. Benson: Arts and Crafts luminary and pioneer of modern design* (Woodbridge: Antique Collectors' Club, 2005)
Harris, Alexandra, *Romantic Moderns* (London: Thames & Hudson 2010)
Harvey, Charles and Press, Jon, *William Morris: Design and enterprise in Victorian Britain* (Manchester: Manchester University Press, 1991)
Hyde, H. Montgomery (ed.), *The Trials of Oscar Wilde* (London: William Hodge, 1948)
McCarthy, Fiona, *The Last Pre-Raphaelite: Edward Burne-Jones and the Victorian Imagination* (London: Faber, 2012)
McCarthy, Fiona, *William Morris: A life for our times* (London: Faber, 1994)
Merrill, Linda, *A Pot of Paint: Aesthetics on trial in Whistler v. Ruskin* (London: Smithsonian, 1991)
Parry, Linda (ed.), *William Morris* (London: Philip Wilson, 1996)
Stamp, Gavin, *A Hundred Years of the Art Workers' Guild* (Brighton: Royal Pavilion, 1984)
Tilbrook, A.J., *The Designs of Archibald Knox for Liberty and Co.* (Somerset: Richard Dennis, 1995)
Wood, Christopher, *The Life and Works of Sir Edward Burne-Jones, 1833–1898* (London: Weidenfeld & Nicolson, 1998)

FRANCE
Arthur, Paul, *French Art Nouveau Ceramics: An illustrated dictionary* (Paris: Norma, 2015)
Borsi, Franco, *Paris 1900* (Brussels: Vokaar, 1976)
Brunhammer, Yvonne, *Art Nouveau: Belgium and France*, catalogue of the exhibition of that title, Institute of the Arts, Rice University (Houston, TX: Rice University, 1976)
Butterworth, Alex, *The World That Never Was* (London: Pantheon, 2010)
Dandova, Jessica, *Nature and the Nation in Fin-de-Siècle France: The Art of Émile Gallé and the École de Nancy* (London: Ashgate, 2017)
Ducrey, Guy, 'Le mythe Loie Fuller', in *Corps et graphies: Poétique de la danse et de la danseuse à la fin du XIXe siècle* (Paris: H. Champion, 1996)
Froissart-Pezone, Rossella, *L'Art dans Tout: Les arts décoratifs en France et l'utopie d'un Art nouveau* (Paris: CNRS Éditions, 2005)
Guardia, Jean de, *Théâtre et imaginaire: Images scéniques et représentations mentales (XVIe–XVIIIe siècle)*, (Dijon: Editions Universitaires de Dijon, 2012)
Julian, Philippe, *The Triumph of Art Nouveau: Paris Exhibition 1900* (New York: Larousse, 1974)
Meneux, Catherine, *L'art social de la Révolution à la Grande Guerre* (Paris: Institut national d'histoire de l'art, 2014)

Musée de l'école de Nancy, *Emile Gallé Au musée de l'école de Nancy* (Nancy: Musée de l'école de Nancy, 2014)
Pinacotheque de Paris, *La Revolution Decorative* (Paris: Skira, 2012)
Rheims, Maurice and Ferré, Felipe, *Hector Guimard* (New York: Abrams, 1985)
Rizzi, Mariella, 'Sarah Bernhardt: le théâtre et l'art de la mode', in *Arts et usages du costume de scène*, Collection 'Le Studio-Lo Essais' (Paris: Editions Lampsaque, 2007)
Sato, Tomoko, *Alphonse Mucha* (Paris: Réunion des musées nationaux, 2018)
Silverman, Deborah, *Art Nouveau in Fin de Siècle France* (Berkeley, CA: University of California Press, 1989)
Weisberg, Gabriel, *Art Nouveau Bing, Paris Style 1900* (New York and Washington: Abrams and SITES, 1986)

SPAIN AND CATALONIA
Bru, Ricard, *Els orígens del japonisme a Barcelona* (Barcelona: Institut d'Estudis Montjuïc, 2011)
Carbonell, Sílvia and Casamartina, Jordi, *Les fabriques i els somnis: modernisme textil a Catalunya* (Terrassa: Centre de Documentació i Museu Textil, 2001)
Castellanos, Jordi, 'Verdaguer i el prerafaelitisme. Algunes notes per a un estudi', in VVAA, *Verdaguer, un geni poetic* (Barcelona: Biblioteca de Catalunya, 2002)
Cerdà, Mariàngela, *Els pre-rafaelites a Catalunya* (Barcelona: Curial Edicions, 1981)
Gil, Núria (dir.), *Virtuosisme modernista, Tècniques del moble* (Barcelona: Associació per a l'Estudi del Moble & Museu del Disseny de Barcelona, Ajuntament de Barcelona, 2019)
Hughes, Robert, *Barcelona* (London: The Harvill Press, 1992 / 2001)
Permanyer, Lluís, *Enlightened Barcelona: The City in the 18th Century* (Barcelona: Institut Municipal del Paisatge Urbà i la Qualitat de Vida, Ajuntament de Barcelona, 2009)
Sala, Teresa-M. (ed.), *Barcelona 1900* (Amsterdam: Van Gogh Museum / Brussels: Mercatorfonds, 2007)
Solà-Morales, Ignasi de, *Antoni Gaudí* (Barcelona: Edicions Polígrafa, 1983 / 2003)

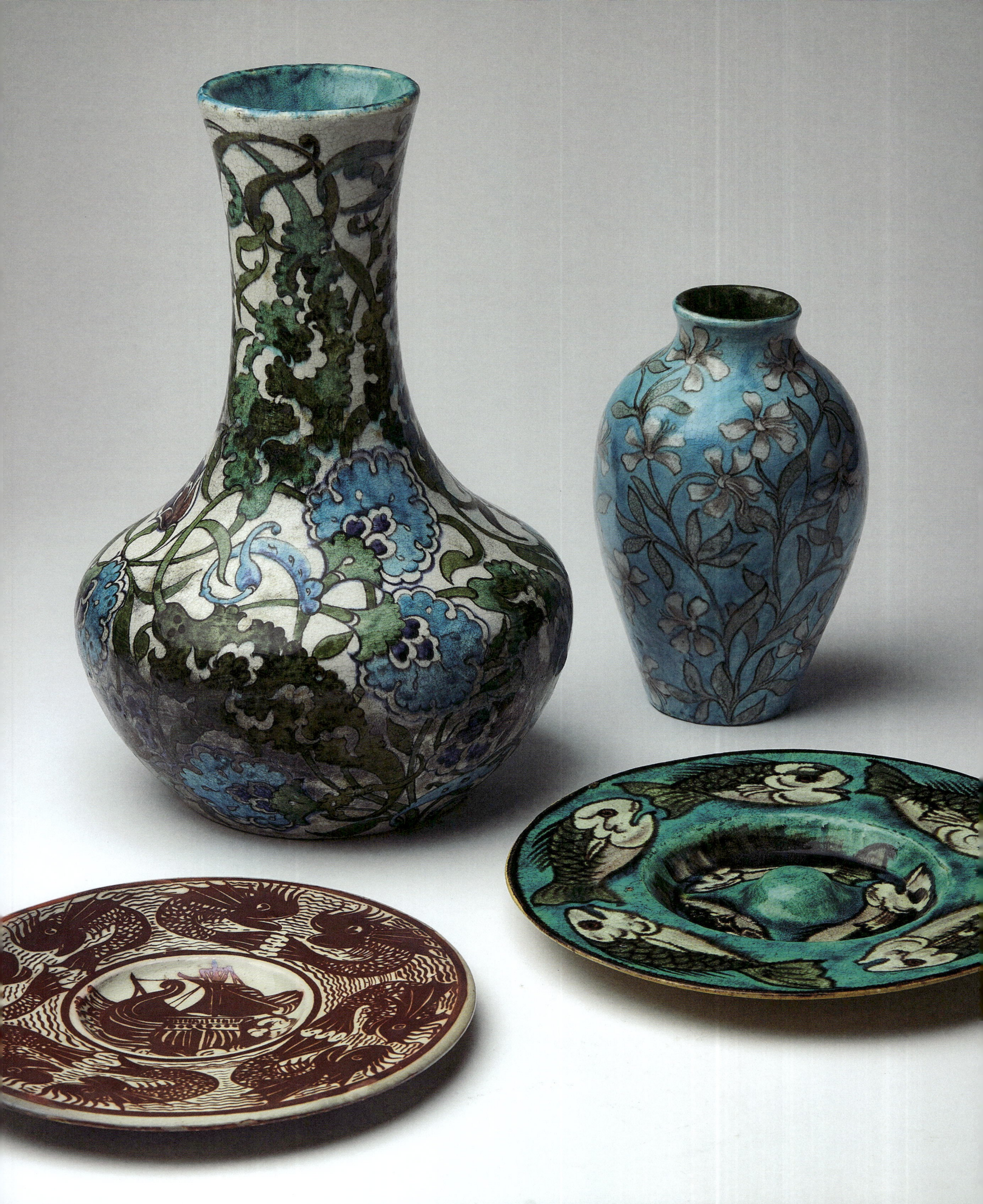

# ~Acknowledgements~

*Art Nouveau: The Nature of Dreams* exhibition and publication exist only because of the work and support of a large number of people.

We are very grateful to all the lenders to the exhibition. Our museum colleagues were hugely helpful: the Musée Horta, Brussels, the Museu del Modernisme, Barcelona, and the Fitzwilliam, Cambridge. Our private lenders gave the exhibition a beautiful and exclusive edge: deepest thanks go to Gretha Arwas, Brian Clarke, Sally and Simon Curtis, Pete Huggins and the lenders who wish to remain anonymous. And we are ever grateful to Anderson's heirs, the Carver family.

The curator and authors would like to thank our colleagues internationally who helped with the project, including Paul Arthur, Gretha Arwas, Jordi Bonet, Sally Curtis, Simon Curtis, Mireia Freixa, Núria Gil, Sarah Newman, Consol Oltra, Daniel Pifarré, Eric Turner and Benjamin Zurstrassen.

The Sainsbury Centre team is always a joy to work with. Nothing would look as it does, without them. Special thanks to Paul Kuzemczak and Andrew Johnson for their design work on the exhibition and book. Roger Bishop led our brilliant technical team that built the exhibition. George Sexton Associates did the lighting. Mandy Greenfield and Brenda Stones were part of the book production. Adriana Capadose translated François Aubry's chapter. The Centre's Joyce and Michael Morris Chief Curator of Art, Tania Moore, Project Curator Lisa Newby and Assistant Gallery Registrar Laura Reeves were vital to the entire process, and Maria Ledinskaya, our Conservator, completed complex work.

We couldn't function without our supporters. Our exhibitions wouldn't open and our books wouldn't get published. Deepest thanks go to Loveday & Partners for support of the exhibition. And, as always, the Gatsby Charitable Foundation underpins everything we do. *Paul Greenhalgh*



AUTHOR BIOGRAPHIES

### Editor

Paul Greenhalgh is Director of the Sainsbury Centre, University of East Anglia, and Professor of Art History and Museum Strategy. He has published widely on the visual arts and the history and theory of exhibition practice, particularly on the period 1850–1940. He is also interested in ceramic.

### Contributors

Françoise Aubry has been central to the conservation, restoration and presentation of Belgian Art Nouveau heritage for the last forty years. She was curator at the Musée Horta between 1981 and 2018, as well as the scientific advisor for the Horta Museum's refurbishment, alongside the architect Barbara Van der Wee. She has written extensively on Belgian Art Nouveau, particularly related to architecture and the decorative arts.

Barbara Bessac is a museum and university professional based in Paris. She is currently completing a doctoral thesis in the History of Art jointly at the University of Paris (Nanterre) and the University of Warwick, UK. Her focus is on the relationship of the decorative arts to British and French theatrical stages between 1851 and 1908. More broadly, her work is concerned with the connection between design reform, the performing arts and entertainment in the second half of the 19th century.

Lluís Gonç Bosch Pascual has for the last twenty years been dedicated to the conservation and promotion of the Art Nouveau heritage in his native city, Barcelona, and across Europe. He has degrees in History and Sociology. Since 1999 he has been with the Barcelona City Council, working on the promotion and diffusion of the Catalonian architectural heritage. He is editor of *Coup de Fouet*, the international magazine focused on Art Nouveau, and also leads the organising team of the regular *Coup de Fouet* International Congresses on Art Nouveau.

*Opposite:* William de Morgan, vase in the Iznik style, *c.*1885; turquoise vase, *c.*1880; plates, *c.*1883; earthenware. Private Collection.

# ~Photographic credits~

Every effort has been made to seek permission to reproduce the images in this book. We are grateful to the individuals and institutions who have assisted us in this task. Any omissions are unintentional.

© ADAGP, Paris and DACS: *back cover*, 98
© Aitor Quiney: 131 (top left)
© AML (Archives et Musée de la Littérature): 67
© Arxiu fotogràfic de Barcelona: 124 (top)
© Arxiu Històric de la Ciutat de Barcelona: 120
© Bastin & Evrard, Brussels: 74, 76, 77, 79
Bibliothèque des Arts Decoratifs, Paris: 55
© Bibliothèque nationale de France: 96, 108
Birmingham Museums Trust, licensed under CC0: 32
B.O'Kane / Alamy Stock Photo: 11
British Library: 69
Carlos Iglesias © IMPUiQV: 115
Centre d'archives d'architecture du XXe siècle: 41
© Christie's Images / Bridgeman Images: 17
CIVA, Brussels: 81, 82–3
© Collecció Jordi Carulla: 131 (bottom)
Coll. King Baudouin Foundation, entrusted to the Art & History Museum, Brussels, Belgium, © Studio Philippe de Formanoir: 86
© DACS 2019: 67
Fonds Henri Sauvage. SIAF / Cité de l'architecture et du patrimoine / Archives d'architecture du XXe siècle: 105
Heritage Image Partnership Ltd / Alamy Stock Photo: 62–3, 65, 80
imageBROKER / Alamy Stock Photo: 24
© IMPUiQV: 116, 140
INTERFOTO / Alamy Stock Photo: *inside covers*
© Jack Kilgore & Co.: 91, 95
James Jagger / Alamy Stock Photo: 47
© Jordi Bonet: 128, 129
© Jordi Bonet / Private Collection Fundació Arts i Artistes: 132 (left)
Lesley Pardoe / Alamy Stock Photo: 59
© Michele Curel: 118
© Musée Carnavalet, Histoire de Paris: 99
Musée Horta: 68, 72, 75
© Museu d'Història de Barcelona: 124 (bottom)
© Museu del Modernisme Català, Barcelona: 138, 139
© Museu Nacional d'Art de Catalunya: 132 top
Museu Nacional d'Art de Catalunya, public domain: 134, 136
© National Galleries of Scotland. Photography by Antonia Reeve: 22 (bottom)
© National Portrait Gallery, London: 30
© Pascual-Ramírez: 133 (right)
Pete Huggins: 6, 13 (right), 26–7, 29, 34, 35, 36, 37, 38, 42, 43, 46, 50, 52, 53, 55, 58 (left), 61, 148
PVDE / Bridgeman Images: 48
© Ramon Manent: 131 (bottom left), 132 (bottom right)
© Robert Ramos / Fundació Privada Sant Pau: 113, 137
© RMAH, Brussels: 84, 85

© Sainsbury Centre. Photography by Pete Huggins: *front cover*, *back cover*, 2, 13 (top), 13 (bottom left), 15, 25, 45, 58 (bottom), 60, 71, 87, 88–9, 98, 100, 106, 144–5, 151
© Sainsbury Centre: 21 (right), 23, 56, 57, 94
© Sant Lluc: 130
Shutterstock: 110–11, 122 (left), 122 (bottom left), 126 (bottom), 141 (left), 142
© Tate: 16
The Art Fund of the Fundació 1859 Caixa Sabadell: 117
The Art Institute of Chicago, licensed under CC0: 21 (bottom)
© The Fitzwilliam Museum, Cambridge: 44
The Metropolitan Museum of Art, licensed under CC0: 19, 22 (left)
The Paul J. Getty Museum, licensed under CC0: 20
© The Trustees of the British Museum: 103
Thomas Ledl, licensed under CC0: 123 (top)
© Universitätsbibliothek Heidelberg: 70
© Victoria and Albert Museum, London: 49, 92, 93, 97, 102

*Opposite:* Émile Gallé, sellette, *c.*1900, walnut, rosewood and oak. Sainsbury Centre.

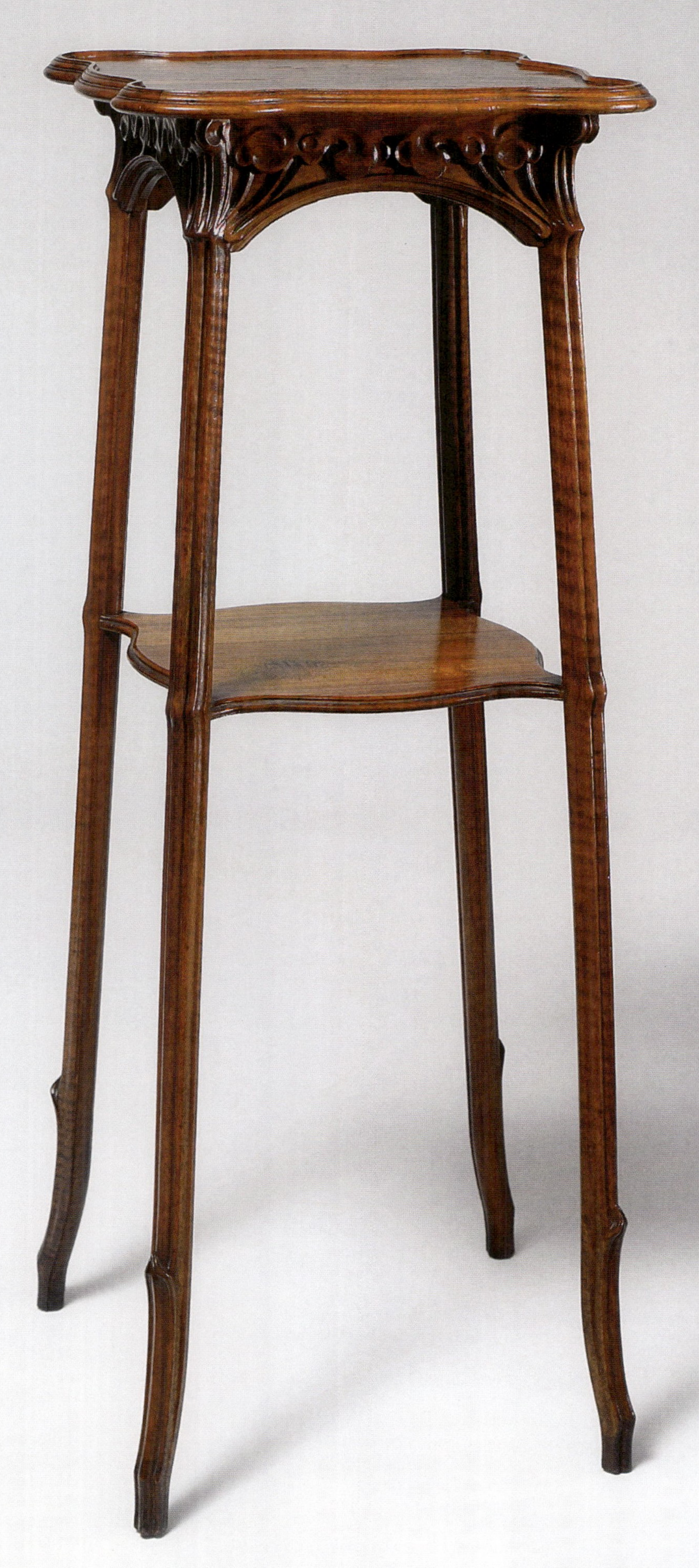

# ~Index~